CONTENTS

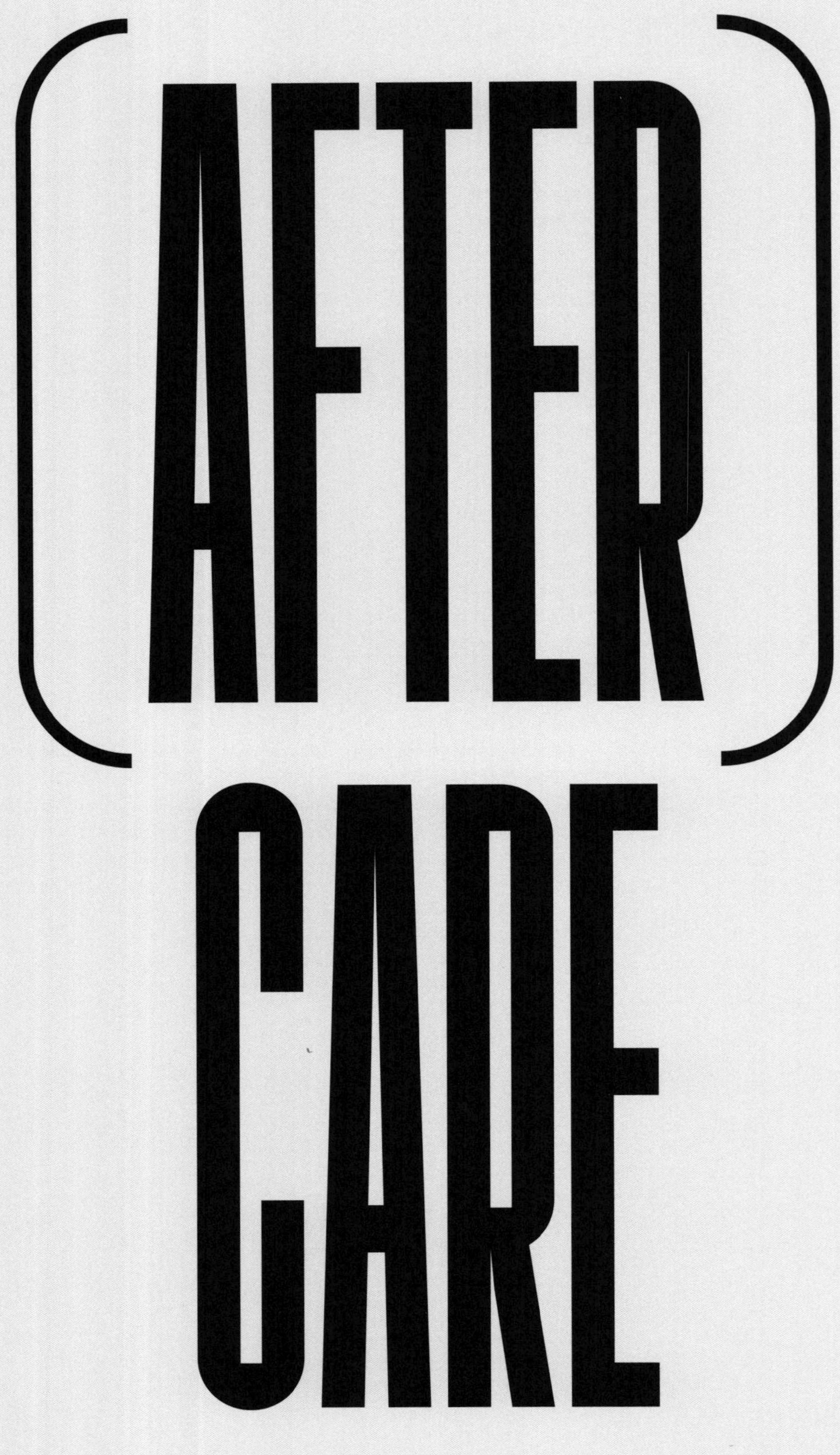
(AFTER)
CARE

Taous Dahmani

Dear readers,

For a few years now, in an attempt to respond to the rising number of crises – economic, social, political or environmental – and their various consequences – intensifying conflicts, spreading wars and, of course, the pandemic – the humanities and social sciences have turned to the concept of *care*. Fundamentally hard to characterize because of its elusive and evolving definition, the word as it is used by contemporary thinkers extends far beyond the medical notion of care.[1] Indeed, talking about care is using a single word to talk about several other things. It is, at one and the same time, attention, gentleness, conscience, diligence, consideration, duty, prudence, concern, vulnerability and responsibility – a list that could be longer or shorter, depending on people and perspectives. In attempts at theorization, as in the characterization of the term, it is individuals who do and undo the notion of care.

Historically, care is a burden entrusted to a particular group of individuals: women. Incidentally, the constellation of words to explain care is commonly given a "feminine" connotation.[2] Hyginus, the Latin author of the Augustan period, tells the allegory of Cura, a Roman goddess, personification of care and associated with the creation of humankind. Here, unlike in other theogonies and in an obvious relationship to reality, it is indeed woman who creates man – with concern and devotion. So, beyond the "feminine" burden, could care be considered a feminist power? Such is the perspective considered in this issue, at the intersection of vulnerability and engagement. The point is not to mobilize care as an empty shell but to observe its tangible manifestations: to call upon an active and operating sense of care.

Because care is above all a defence against collective and personal violence – let us point to capitalism, colonialism, racism and sexism, among others – it overthrows the relations of domination that shape our societies. Interpersonal by nature, this concern for the other invites us to imagine a "social contract of care". Hence in their essay entitled "The New Politics of Care", Gregg Gonsalves and Amy Kapczynski explain political care as "a new kind of politics ... organized around a commitment to universal provision for human needs; countervailing power for workers, people of colour, and the vulnerable; and a rejection of carceral approaches to social problems".[3] Thus, a policy, an ethic sometimes – dear to many generations of feminists, from Patricia Hill Collins to Deva R. Woodly[4] – care rhymes with commitment and duty, perhaps with obligation, and even sometimes with indebtedness, yet, on the contrary, it shouldn't be either moralizing or humiliating.

Such is the balance, oscillating between commitment and vulnerability, found in Laia Abril's photographic work. Born in Spain in 1986, Abril studied journalism, but promptly turned away from it to establish a practice rooted in research and driven by the politics and ethics of a humanist and feminist sense of care. It is the foundational philosophy of Laia Abril's projects when she tells stories of abortion and rape. Together, for this issue, we asked ourselves what was the place and role of care in photography. Thus, it was conceived with a desire to share the diversity of collaboration between care and the image; to imagine the possible bridges between vulnerability and photography.

From its beginnings, photography has been particularly marked by an absence of care. Over time, the medium, a creator of visual ideologies, established a variety of power relations between the photographed and the photographer. The introduction of care in the photographic context thus settled into a silence too often not properly thought about: the space between something (a subject) and an action (the shooting). In this context, care is as much an attitude as it is a methodology, a device at the service of the creation of photographic images. To make images. But why? And how? For this issue, we have thought of photographic care as a collection of principles and a constellation of practices. The photographers presented here are preoccupied with a responsibility to themselves, to their subjects and to the viewers – us! This consideration translates into an attention to detail; a full awareness of the stakes; respect for – even duty towards – what surrounds them; and finally a form of vulnerability that concedes the possibility of making an image. With this issue, we would like to try to understand the ways in which care can be embodied in photography. We decided to add the word *after* – "(After)care" – because this composite care is most often generated *after* an event, a moment or a circumstance that requires special attention.[5] It is, therefore, necessary to consider the temporality of care as well as its longevity and continuity. Thus, save a few exceptions, most of the projects presented in this issue do not show an image of care, but rather the published photographers have shown a sense of care in the process of making their images.

For "(After)care", we have turned to a large diversity of artists who embody, each in their own way, a practice of photographic care. For photographic care is not necessarily conceived in the same way, not always experienced in the same manner and not always seen from the same perspective. However, they all share the desire to develop ways of visualizing the aftermath of an episode of contemporary or historical violence or personal trauma. Several projects are stories of intimate experiences – photographers being both actors and narrators of facts that are close or familiar to them. The activating of care occurs in the strength necessary to share vulnerability. The subject is, directly or indirectly, the operator. For example, through the images of the intimate details of their lives, sometimes provocative but always delivered with tenderness, Robert Andy Coombs tells of the need for social relations and for care for others. Kitra Cahana documents her father's illness, locked in his paralyzed body, and his gradual recovery. Cahana tells the story of an attachment to life, of a family's hope. Another example, Gal (Cipreste Marinelli) and Hiroshima (Rodrigo Masina Pinheiro) use the symbolic power of images to ward off sexist and transphobic trauma. Shooting is an exercise in self-determination in Brazil, where violence against LGBTQIA+ people is wreaking havoc. Other projects are narratives that lie halfway between the private realm and the public sphere. The images attest to a moment in history but are woven into the authors' personal experiences. Consider, for example, the development of ethical considerations about the image in the face of the history of the medium, as with the work of Vietnamese American An-My Lê. Joana Choumali practises photography as therapy, a photography of resilience following a terrorist attack in Côte d'Ivoire. Mayumi Suzuki mobilizes photography as a trace of the 2011 tsunami in Japan that took away her family. Suzuki's book becomes a tool for mourning, an object for reconstruction. Finally, some photographers explore other ways of documenting events in our common history or news that are personally foreign to them. These photographers, such as Hoda Afshar and Max Pinckers, navigate delicately with intelligence and commitment, from the standpoint of an outsider filled with a sense of care. The choice of subject, the photographer's perspective, the method, the practices: all are subject to reflection and are elements that allow these photographers to encompass "(after)care".

Appropriating the literature on the concept of care to "think" the image is what this issue proposes. The American scholar Christina Sharpe writes in a note at the end of her book *In the Wake*: "Care as a way to feel and to feel for and with, a way to tend to the living and the dying."[6] Perhaps a consideration to keep in mind when we imagine photographic care: for and with the image, the author and the subject.

1 For recent references, consider Boris Groys *Philosophy of Care* (Verso Books, 2022) and Maggie Nelson *De la liberté – Quatre chants sur le soin et la contrainte* (Éditions du Sous-sol, 2022).
2 For historical references, check Carol Gilligan *In A Different Voice* (Harvard University Press, 1983) or Nel Noddings *Caring: A Feminine Approach to Ethics and Moral Education* (University of California Press, 1984).
3 Boston Review (ed.) *The Politics of Care* (Verso, 2021), 13 (e-book).
4 Patricia Hill Collins *Black Feminist Thought Knowledge, Consciousness, and the Politics of Empowerment* (Routledge, 1990), 765 and Deva R. Woodly *Reckoning: Black Lives Matter and the Democratic Necessity of Social Movements* (Oxford University Press, 2022).
5 In this issue, Daniela Vicherat Mattar discusses the importance of placing care at every stage of our human and social interactions.
6 Christina Sharpe *In the Wake: On Blackness and Being* (Duke University Press, 2016), 139.

Taous Dahmani is a London-based French, British and Algerian art historian, writer and curator specialising in photography. Her projects mainly involve the links between photography and politics – such as the visual culture of protests, migratory narratives and intersectional feminist discourses. Dahmani is a content editor for *The Eyes*, a trustee of the Photo Oxford Festival and on the editorial board of *MAI: Visual Culture and Feminism*. She was the 2022 curator of the Louis Roederer Discovery Award at the Rencontres d'Arles.

THE ORGANIC METHOD

LAIA ABRIL

"Care" is a concept that has been an intrinsic part of my practice since before I understood its meaning. I was caring for the subjects of my projects but also for the public that was going to have to face those complex stories and, unquestionably, I needed to care for myself. I often tell young (and not so young) artists a consideration that may be obvious at first glance, but that took me years to understand: how can we represent the pain of others if we do not know our own? In my case, this delicate balance of care was not always very balanced.

With my background as a journalist, I had been instilled with beliefs of neutrality and author–subject separation that not only did not make sense for the stories I wanted to tell – and how I wanted to tell them – but also made me disappear from the equation. And if I was not personally involved in the situation, why did I have to worry about whether I would be affected by documenting someone else's trauma? However, beyond the potential personal damage to the subject, the problem was compounded when that false objectivity also oriented me away from my subjects, and consequently, away from a reflection on how to care for them and their image.

What often alerted me to the fact that these stories were "getting to me" were the continuous indications from peers and audience members (e.g. grimaces of concern) after sitting through one of my talks or visiting my exhibitions. Being "lucky" enough to have developed bulimia from a very early age meant that I started therapy as early as 14. And I say luck because psychology not only helped me face my own demons, it also became a key tool for my artistic practice. On the one hand, I learned to no longer hurt myself – and above all, others. And on the other hand, this journey of self-discovery gave me the tools that became my compass in navigating how to represent grief.

Back in the day, in the photojournalistic framework, I remember peers referring to the concept of "catharsis" when talking about their subjects and especially right after they had told their painful stories. Years later, a psychiatrist friend warned me: "Be very careful with that, you can end up severely re-traumatizing the person sharing their story with you." Somehow, instinctively, it was something I had already sensed, but it was now confirmed. Another contradiction I was battling with: how to tell those stories I felt the tremendous urge to share, without adding more pain? I then realized that I still did not quite put myself into the equation. In all honesty, becoming a "fully present" artist in my work – even if I was telling the stories of others – scared me. I was afraid of exposing myself, I was afraid of the pain, but most of all I worried about the responsibility that came with it. But there is something incredible about the practice of art, in that there are parallel forces that push you along the way even when you are not fully aware of them.

It all came together a couple of years ago when I was photographing the testimonial series for my book *On Rape* (Dewi Lewis, 2022) – life-size images of the outfits representing the rape culture that let the attack happen, like a military uniform or a nun's habit. Indeed, it had taken me two years to access a case where the survivor was an infant abused by their teacher. I met with Melissa and she told me the story of her 4-year-old daughter and how absolutely no one believed her. She sent me her daughter's school uniform and another that belonged to a classmate who had been through the same abuse. When setting up the photo shoot, I opened the package that had been sitting in my studio for months, and when I saw how small the uniforms were I broke down. The idea of depicting rape survivors' stories through their outfits was intended as a change of focus, to avoid survivors having to go through the public eye to be heard, and instead to put pressure on the institution that had abandoned them. However, the moment I made that image, I became, in a way that is difficult to describe, a channel of her pain and experienced a kind of alchemy. That image undoubtedly came with a price for my body and mind. This realization was the culmination point: I decided that from now on I had to be much more appreciative and aware of the impact of working on these types of stories.

It was a couple of years later that I met Robert Andy Coombs at a round table entitled "Practices of Representation" organized by Magnum Photos and led by Australian artist and educator Anthony Luvera. It was my first encounter with Robert's work. A photographer and queer man, he had suffered an accident in 2009 that had left him semi-paralyzed. His projects explored, through self-portraiture, the intersections between disability and sexuality. His tone was unapologetic, raw and fun; a slap in the face to any historical representation of disability from the point of view of pity. Then he pulled out a photo in which a partner was taking care of him after sexual intercourse, when he said (I am paraphrasing here): "In my case, the concept of (after)care in sex [care needed after kink and BDSM practices] goes beyond the evident, because obviously I even need to be cleaned." It was the first time that I had heard of the concept of "(after)care." I had heard of "self-care", but I wasn't familiar with this practice, so I started researching. How could something as obvious as being taken care of after such an intimate moment not be the norm? How could the notion of (after)care not be the norm for any extremely draining situation?

At that time I drew a parallel with artistic practices. Why don't artists have protocols of care? For ourselves, for our subjects, for our audiences. I had always thought that the opposite of objectivity was subjectivity, but got to understand that I was wrong: it is vulnerability. The vulnerability of accepting, in front of the person you are portraying, that you are another person: with your own baggage, your own fears, your own prejudices, your own desires and ambitions. The vulnerability of accepting that you are not invisible nor made of stone, and that whatever the intensity of empathy you might have, the grief of others will affect you. That your own emotional state will affect the subjects too. It is about the responsibility of accepting that what you create has consequences.

As such, in this issue, you will find the work of contemporary artists who have made us reflect on the concept of "(after)care". Like Robert Andy Coombs, who introduced me to the concept itself, and whose visual essay depicts the intersection of disability and relationships. Or Kitra Cahana, who uses photography to narrate the journey of her father's recovery from a stroke while helping him dictate his religious sermons. Or Max Pinckers, whose new project involves a more collective concept of "(after)care" as social accountability, through the re-enacting of the pains of war on Kenyan veterans in order to tell their side of the story. Or in taking care of the intimacy of the subjects and their anonymity with fascinating new forms of 3D portraiture or collage, as with Hoda Afshar's whistle-blowers series and Aida Silvestri's work around female mutilation.

In the 1970s feminists had already opened the way for us. Carol Gilligan describes the ethics of care as "an ethic grounded in voice and relationships, in the importance of everyone having a voice, being listened to carefully (in their own right and on their own terms) and heard with respect. An ethics of care directs our attention to the need for responsiveness in relationships (paying attention, listening, responding) and to the costs of losing connection with oneself or with others. Its logic is inductive, contextual, psychological, rather than deductive or mathematical[1]".

With this "(after)care" issue, we have tried to ask ourselves a series of questions so we can all think about the relationality at play in the arts. Far from having firm answers, we let our thinking evolve organically, especially since the world is in constant – and lately, abrupt – change. We conclude that if artists and photographers want to see a change in audiences by confronting them with these complex issues and narratives, then we have to be open to changing ourselves, as well as to reframing our work and processes.

Laia Abril is a research-based artist working with photography, text and sound. After graduating in journalism and working as an editor at the magazine *Colors*, she focused on developing long-term projects on uneasy and hidden realities about women's rights, grief and bio-politics. She is the author of several books: *The Epilogue* (2014, Dewi Lewis); *Lobismuller* (2016, RM); *On Abortion* (2018, Dewi Lewis), which was nominated for the Deutsche Börse Photography Foundation Prize and was the winner of the Paris Photo – Aperture PhotoBook Awards; and *On Rape* (Dewi Lewis, 2022). Her installations have been exhibited in more than 15 countries and are part of collections such as the Centre Pompidou, FRAC, Musée de l'Elysée, Fotomuseum Winterthur, MoCP and MNAC. Her career has been recognized with the Prix de la Photo Madame Figaro – Arles, the Hood Medal in London and the Foam Paul Huf Award in Amsterdam, among others. She is based in Barcelona and is represented by the Parisian gallery Les Filles du Calvaire.

1 *Ethics of Care*, interview of Carole Gilligan (21 June 2011), https://ethicsofcare.org/carol-gilligan/

ANA VALLEJO

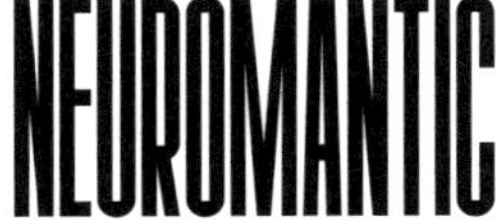

NEUROMANTIC

In the spring of 2020, during the COVID-19 pandemic, Colombian photographer Ana Vallejo found herself locked up at home, on her own to confront her all-consuming anxieties. Pushed towards introspection, she began an investigation into her addictive relationship with love. Dependent on the feeling of love, Ana Vallejo seeks through passion to dissociate herself from reality, to anaesthetise the emotional pain that has always been in her. She dissects her past traumas – stories of violence and addiction.

In the enclosed space of her home, Ana Vallejo turns self-care into a life-saving existential questioning, a collective reflection in which companions, intimate friends, family members and strangers are solicited to give meaning to her own emotional dysfunctions. By favouring the process of image alteration, *Neuromantic* explores neuroses. The artist brings together photographs, scientific documents, textual elements and objects to express the derealization of the first "fixes" of love.

The artist attends meetings for emotionally dependent people. Through extensive documentation, she identifies recurring motifs and manages to relate traumas, emotions and addictions. Popping colours, overexposures, cut-outs, collages and superimpositions tell the story of the grip of drugs and isolation as well as the vital need to fill the void, to sublimate the tears of our attachments. Turning self-care into an instrument of knowledge of self, the photographer encourages a greater relational reflexivity and examines our relationship to romantic love.

Neuromantic, 2020
© Ana Vallejo

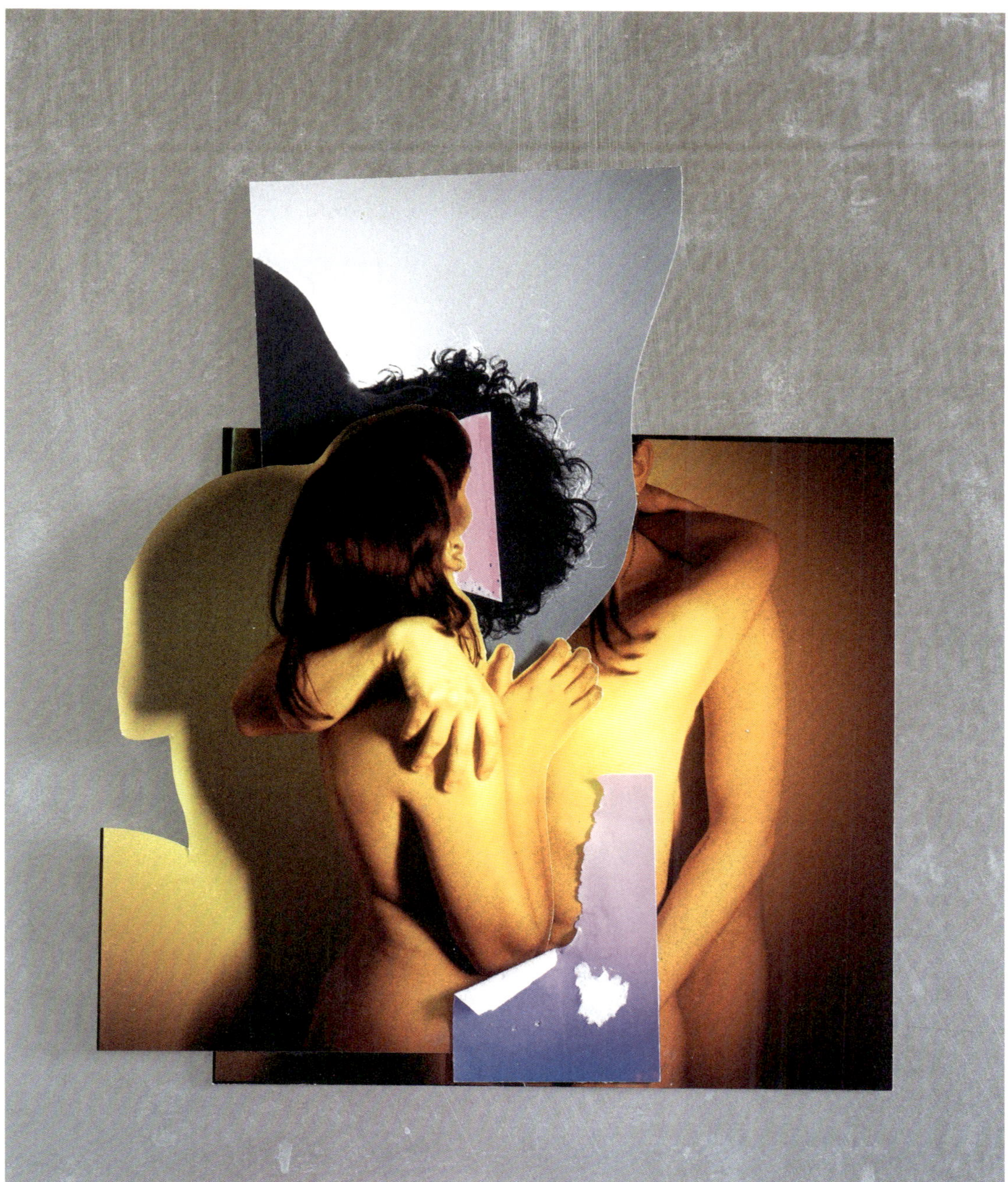

Co-Dependence
"Anxious individuals may be more willing than others to tolerate sustained abuse from intimate partners. Even when a partner's response is negative, preoccupied individuals may perceive this as evidence that their partner is engaged, and, in a perverse sense, more intimately involved. Thus, preoccupied individuals could be at an increased risk of tolerating abuse from a partner."*

* Henderson, Antonia J., et al. (2005) "When Loving Means Hurting: An Exploration of Attachment and Intimate Abuse in a Community Sample", *Journal of Family Violence*, 20(4). doi: 10.1007/s10896-005-5985-y.

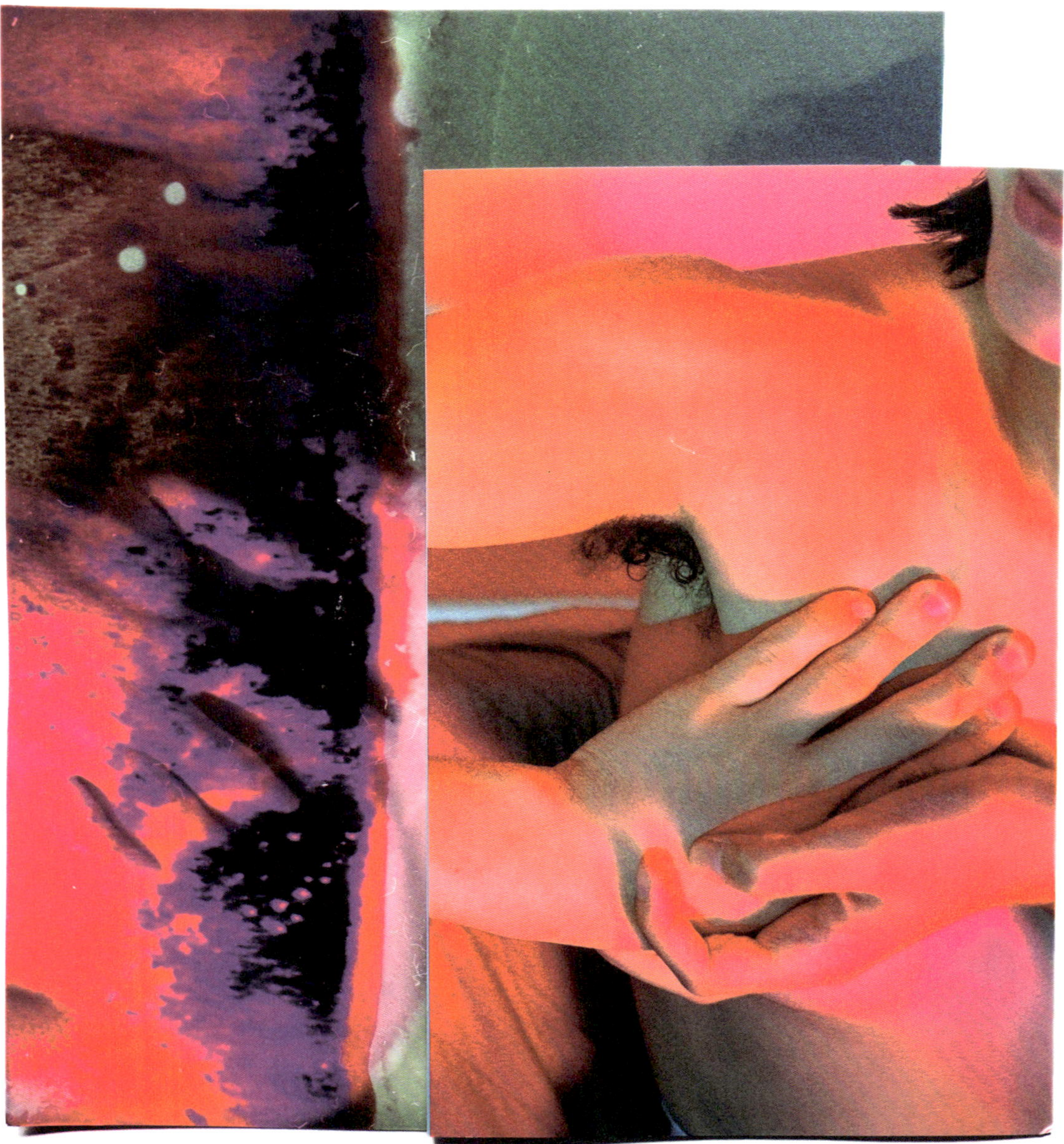

A Natural High

"Brain-scanning studies show that feelings of intense romantic love engage regions of the brain's 'reward system', specifically dopamine pathways associated with energy, focus, learning, motivation, ecstasy and craving, including primary regions associated with substance addiction."*

* Fisher, Helen E., et al. (2016) "Intense, Passionate, Romantic Love: A Natural Addiction? How the Fields that Investigate Romance and Substance Abuse Can Inform Each Other", *Frontiers in Psychology*, 7(687), 10 May. doi: 10.3389/fpsyg.2016.00687.

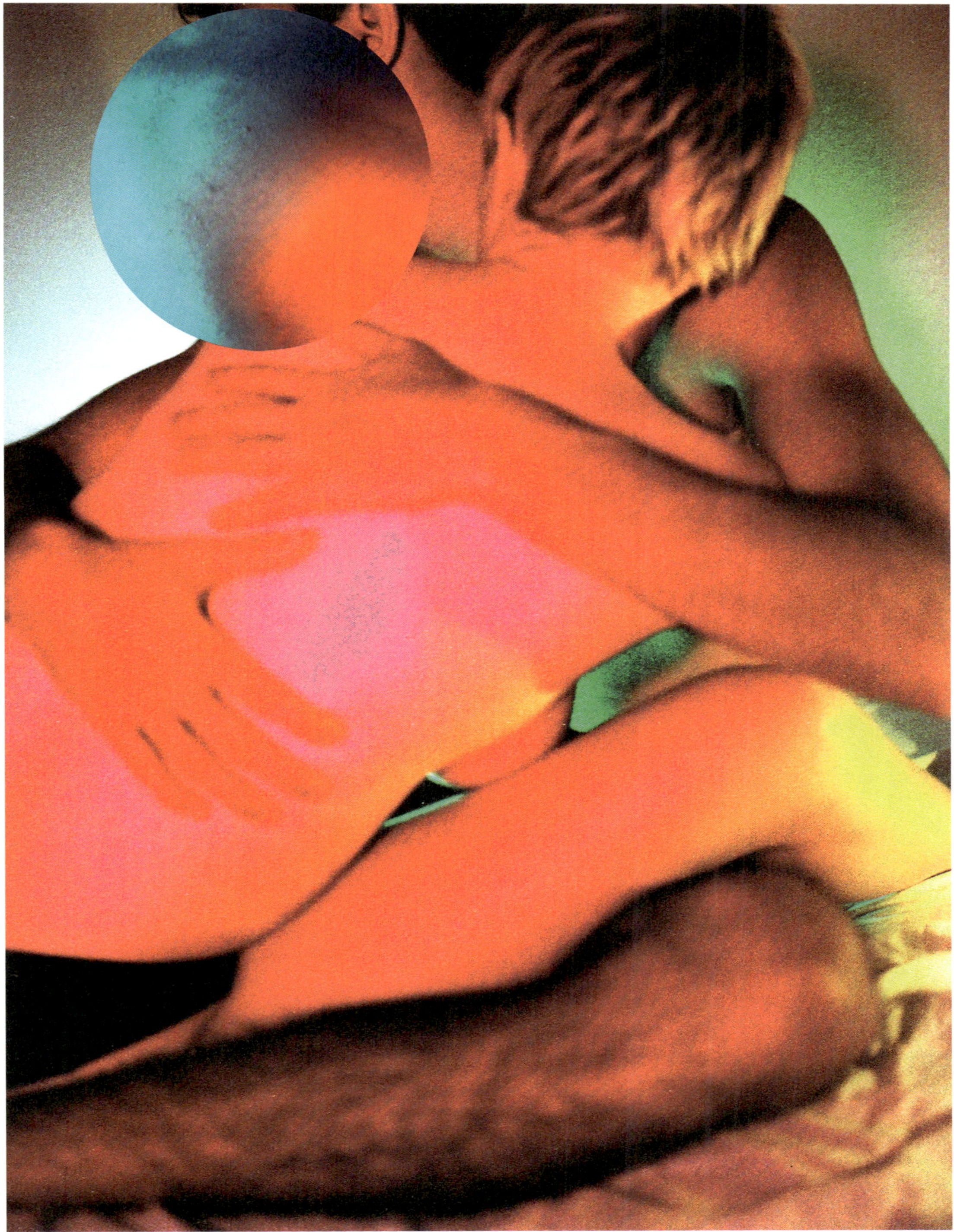

Love-Induced
"Romantic love activates pleasure in the reward system. Thus, love-induced analgesia reduces emotional and physical pain."*

* Aron, Arthur, et al. (2013) "The Self-Expansion Model of Motivation and Cognition in Close Relationships", Oxford Handbooks Online. doi: 10.1093/oxfordhb/9780195398694.013.0005.

Dopamine Rush
"Cognitive research suggests that a process of rapid self-expansion takes place when we fall in love and start to uncover the experience of the other. With time, we begin to include a partner's characteristics into our own self-concept, treating partners as an extension of ourselves."*

*Henderson, Antonia J., et al. (2005) "When Loving Means Hurting: An Exploration of Attachment and Intimate Abuse in a Community Sample", *Journal of Family Violence*, 20(4). doi: 10.1007/s10896-005-5985-y.

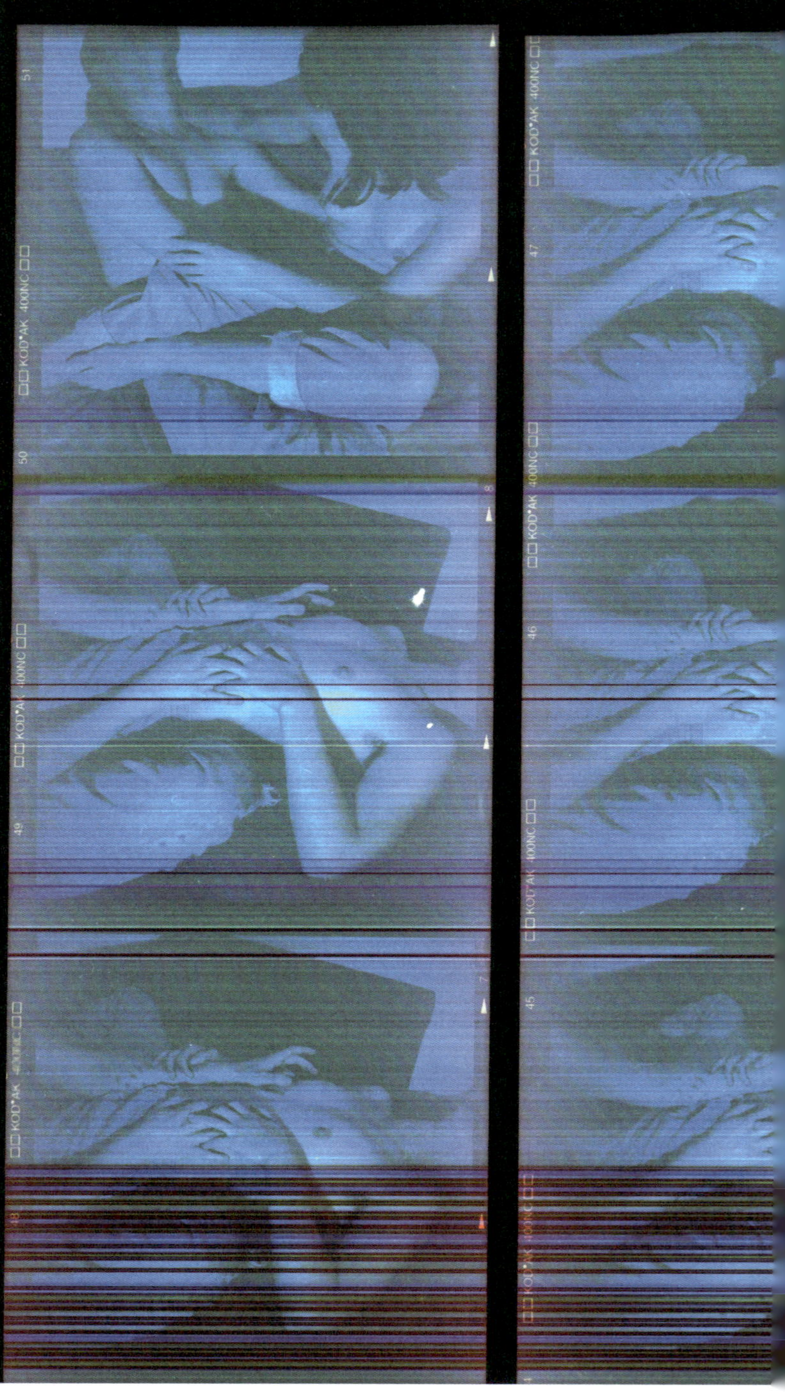

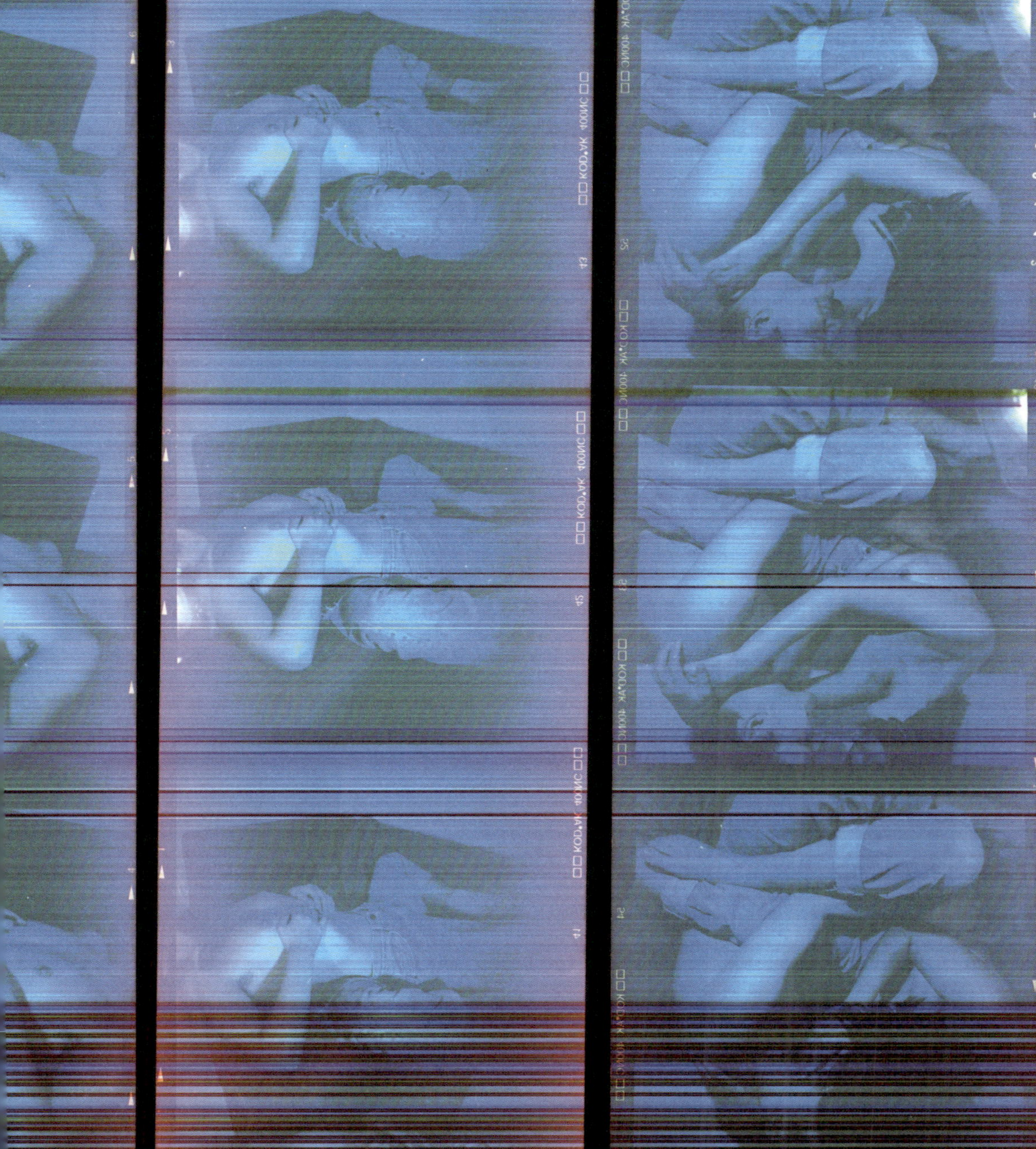

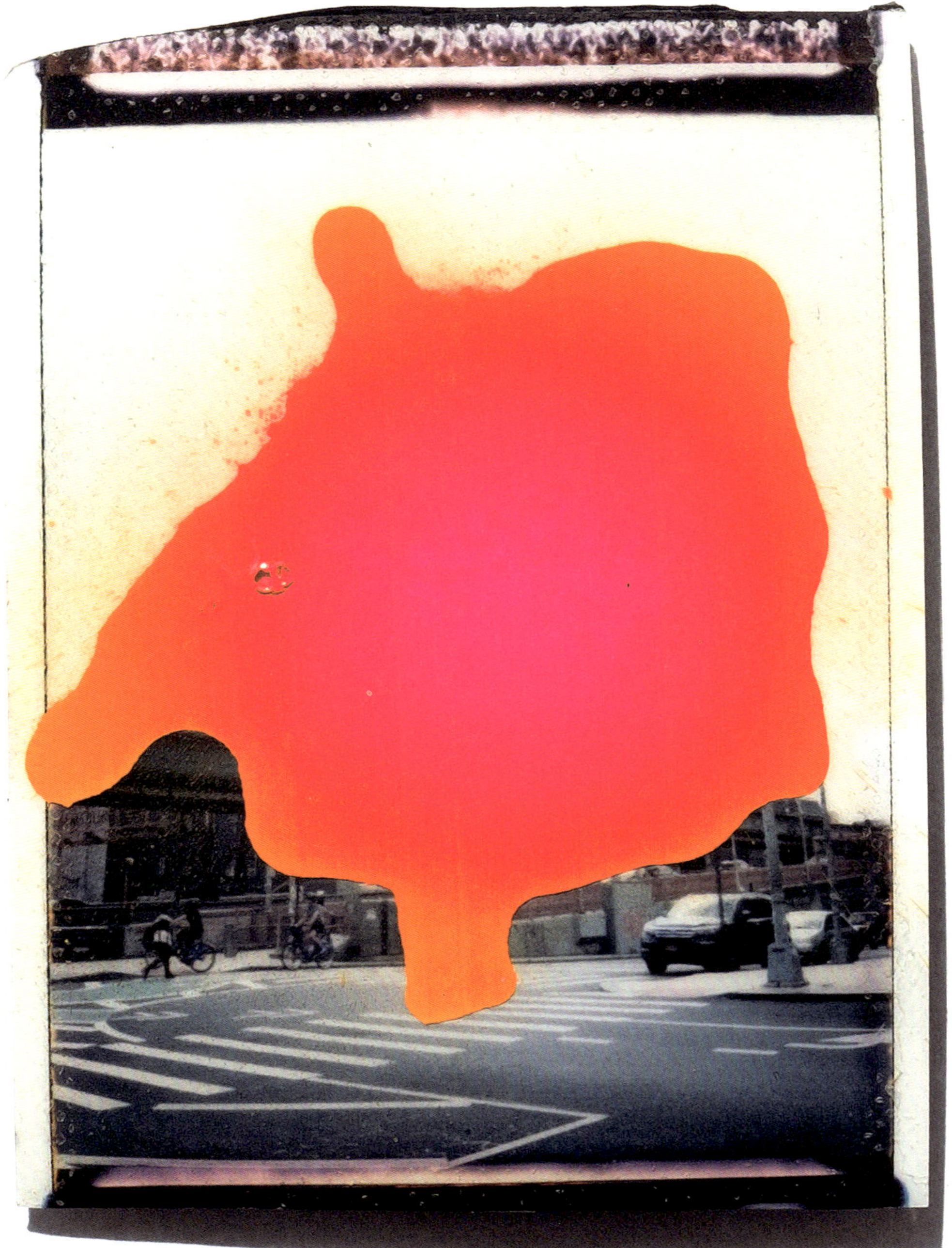

Repressed

"Many times we can't acknowledge the life-long shame and the pain of growing up with unmet needs. The repression of these emotions and anger leads to the chronic secretion of stress hormones, such as cortisol, that suppress the immune system. When anger turns against the self, as it does in people unable to express it, hormonal imbalances can induce the immune system to mutiny against the body."

* Lee, Stephanie (2017) "The Healing Force Within", *Dr. Gabor Maté*, 17 May. Available at: https://drgabormate.com/healing-force-within/

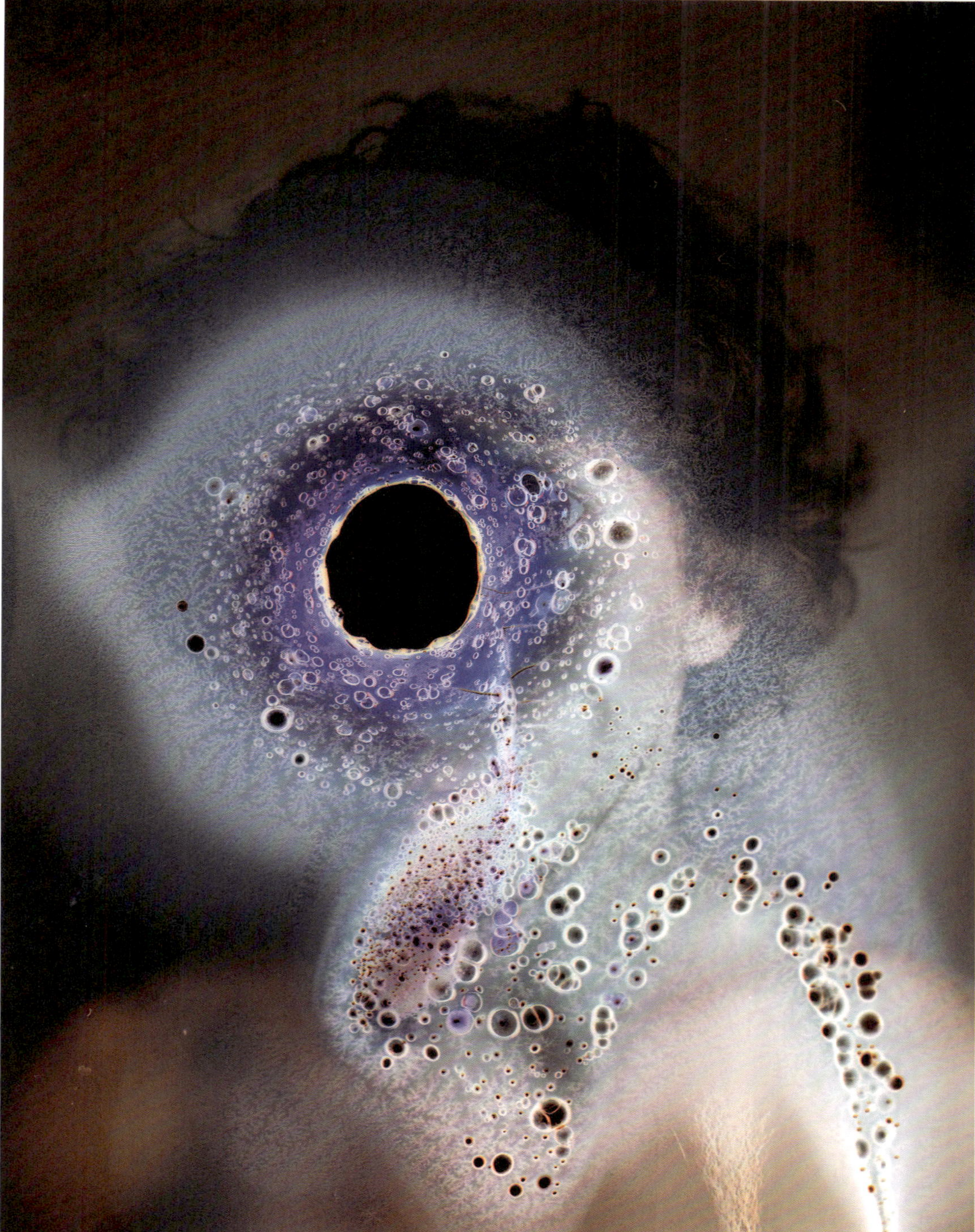

Insecure
"Human beings who do not experience a sufficiently secure base develop insecure patterns of attachment. Insecure individuals will face difficulties in forming relationships with others. Psychotropic substances then might become attractive as one way to 'self-medicate'."*

*Schindler, Andreas (2019) "Attachment and Substance Use Disorders – Theoretical Models, Empirical Evidence and Implications for Treatment", *Frontiers in Psychiatry*, 10(727). doi: 10.3389/fpsyt.2019.00727.

HODA AFSHAR

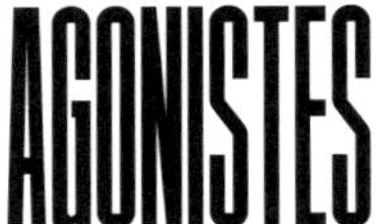

An agonist is one who is engaged in a struggle whose weight they must bear, one who assumes the price of having spoken, denounced or informed on behalf of the vulnerable reduced to silence by their state institutions. The agonist is a whistle-blower, prosecuted and gagged, who has to live with the consequences of their rebellious record.

It was while working with refugees detained on Manus Island, Papua New Guinea, that Australian-based Iranian photographer Hoda Afshar became interested in the fate of those who fought corruption; or violence – police, medical, sexual; or abuses – ill treatment, torture – of migrants, minors and elderly or disabled people. Thanks to 3D scanning technologies and the mobilization of 110 cameras, the artist reproduces a sense of surveillance and control and denounces the consequences of these seditious acts.

Through her chilling portraits, which draw as much on ancient statuary as on the death mask, she gives voice to those who are tried to silence and who fight for their cause. Paying scrupulous attention to the chains of "invisibilization" and silencing, Afshar presents almost ghostly faces without identity, true figures of suffering, self-denial, mistrust or combativeness. No heroic posturing here, but solemnity and reverence to embody their oppositionality.

Agonistes, 2020
© Courtesy the artist and Milani Gallery

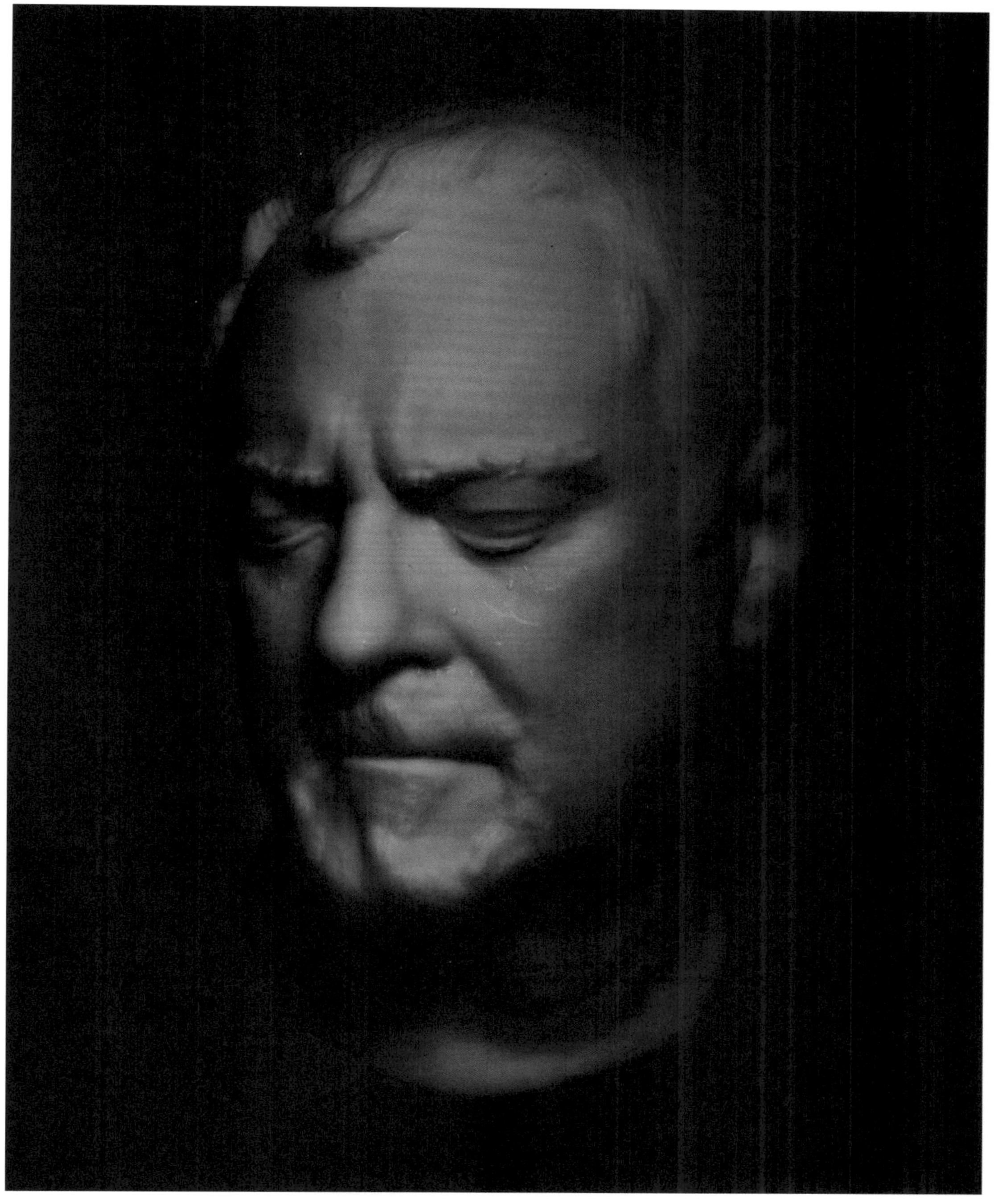

AN OCCUPATIONAL HEALTH AND SAFETY MANAGER WORKING FOR SECURITY FIRM G4S AT MANUS ISLAND IMMIGRATION DETENTION CENTRE

He raised his concerns with the Department of Immigration about the atrocious conditions he witnessed there. When instances of sexual abuse and torture were uncovered, he expressed his doubts to the department about its ability to protect asylum seekers and meet its duty-of-care obligations. He resigned after his concerns were ignored, and spoke to the media as a whistle-blower. He was threatened with a two-year prison sentence for speaking out and has been haunted by legal battles since.

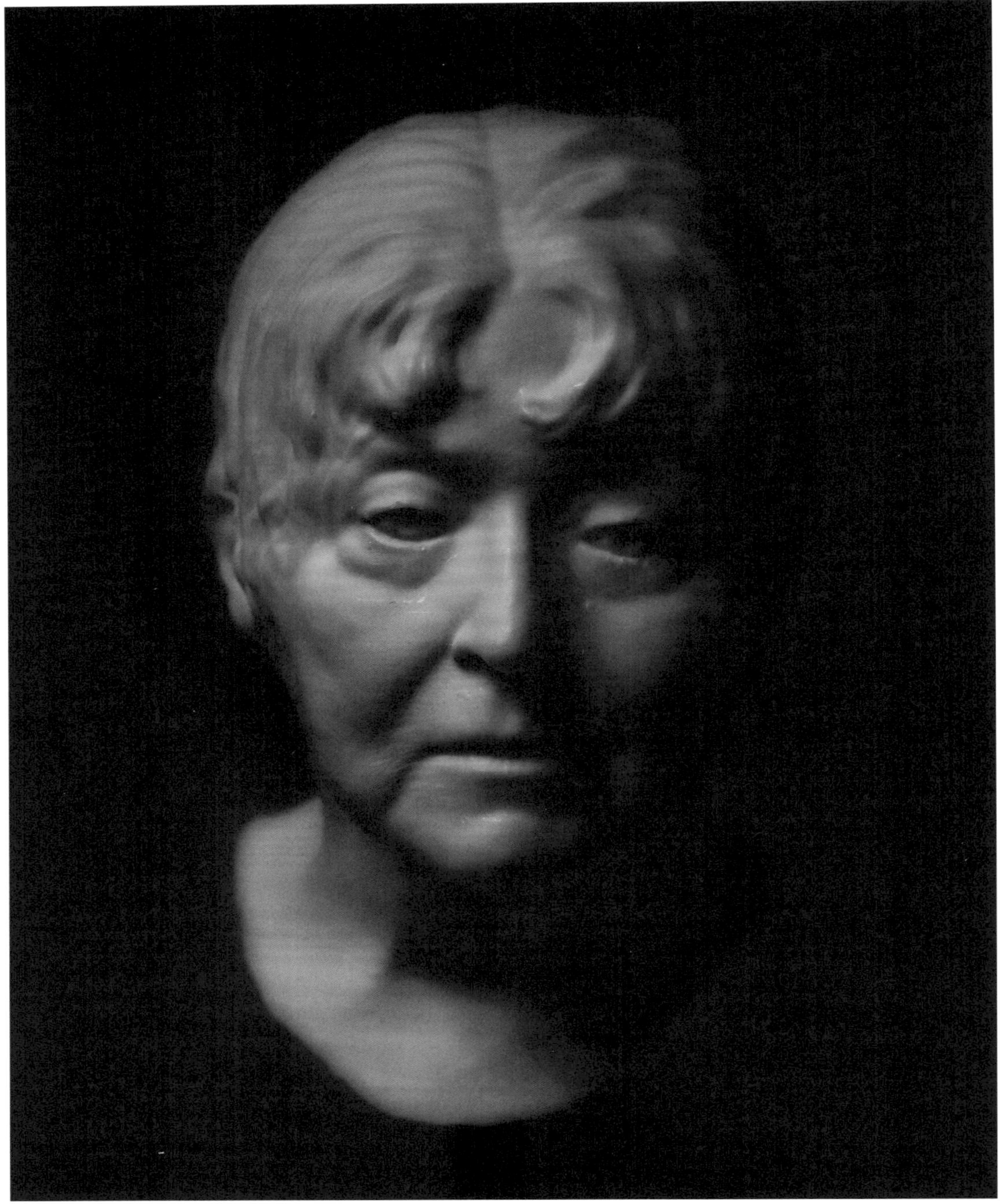

A DISABILITY CARE WORKER

Over several years, she reported the abuse of people with disabilities at a number of residential care homes in Victoria, Australia. Her concerns were repeatedly dismissed by management. She reported the abuse to the Department of Health and Human Services, the Office of the Public Advocate, and Victoria Police, but no action was taken and the abuse continued. She went to the media, but was not protected by the Whistle-blower Act. She was ostracized by the department, and faced institutional denial and cover-ups over 30 years. She lost her job and has ongoing trauma from her experiences.

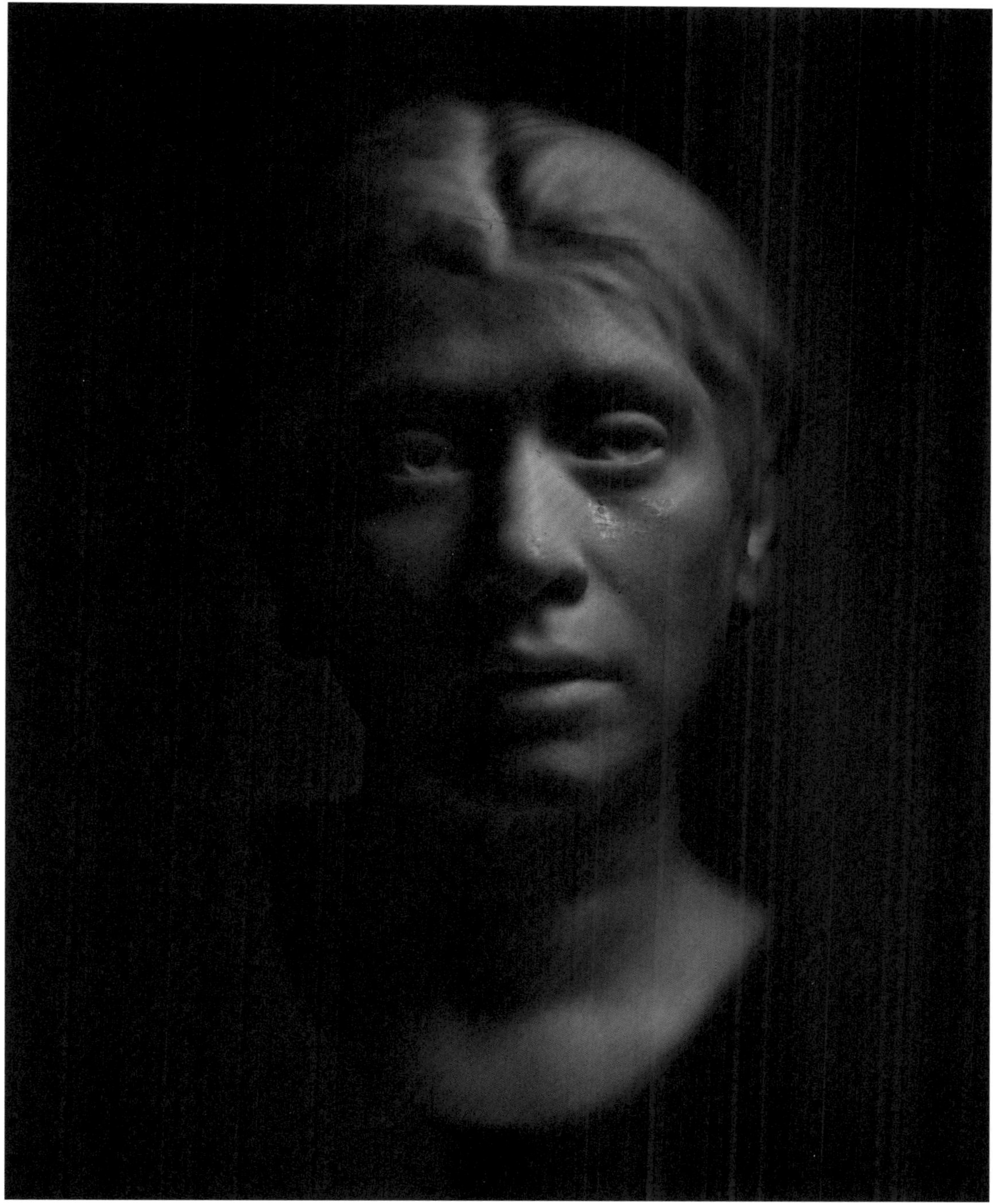

A GENERAL PRACTITIONER

She founded “Doctors for Refugees” to ensure that detained refugees can access medical care. In 2015 the Australian federal government imposed a “gag order” on anyone working in the immigration detention network, including doctors, with a penalty of a two-year prison sentence if they publicly challenge the government on their policies or speak out. In 2016 her organization challenged the “secrecy provisions” in the 2015 Border Force Act. She was investigated in private and public by the Australian federal police at the government’s insistence.

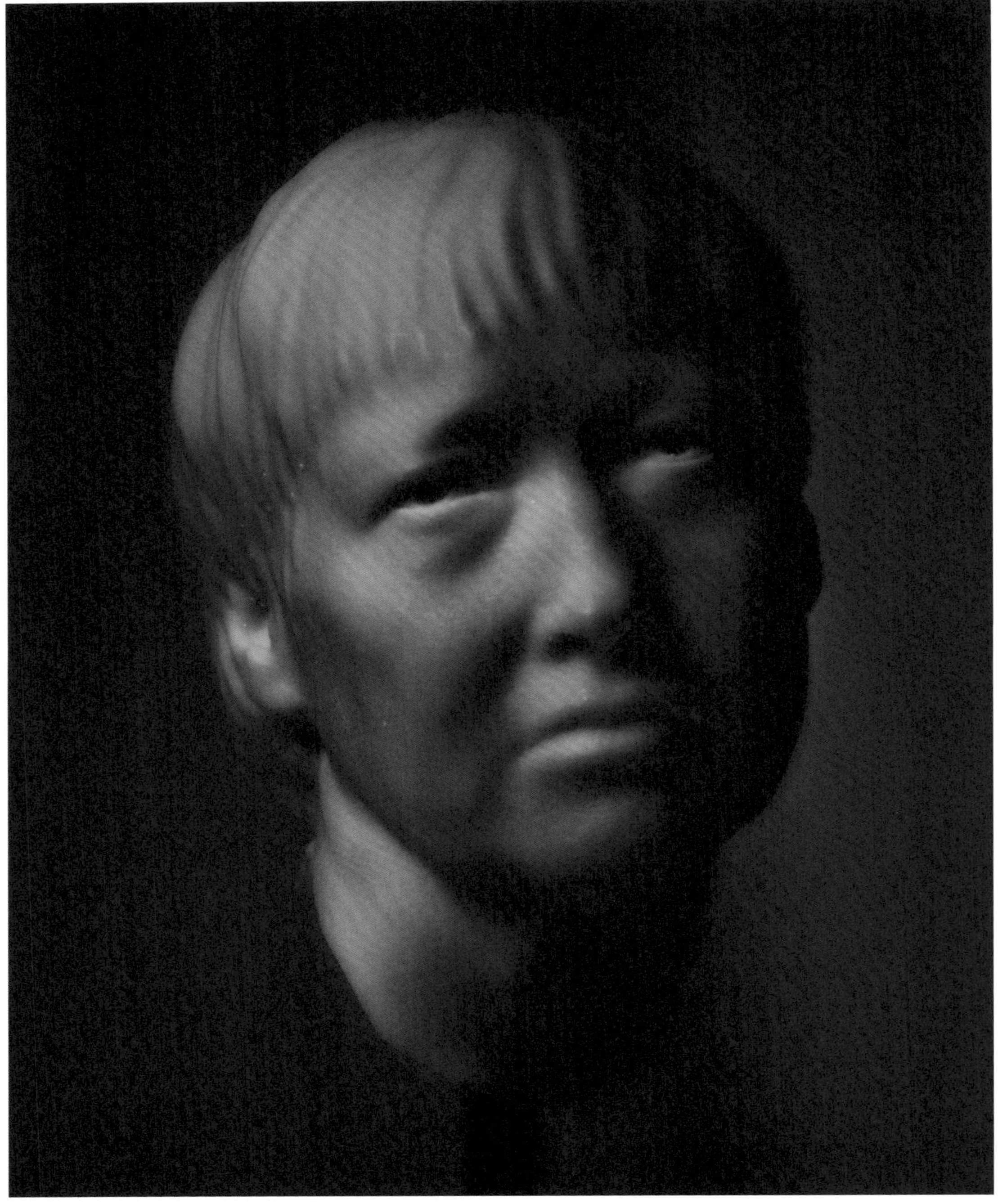

A WRITER WHO WAS BORN INTO A CLOSED CHRISTADELPHIAN COMMUNITY

She suffered sexual and other abuse, perpetrated by her "protectors" and family. After exposing stories of intergenerational sexual violence in the community, she became a human rights activist, advocating for asylum seekers held in Australian and offshore detention camps, especially for women subjected to sexual abuse in these camps. These experiences have exerted a significant physical, social and emotional toll on her. She continues to write about the suffering of others and to advocate for those subjected to sexual violence in detention.

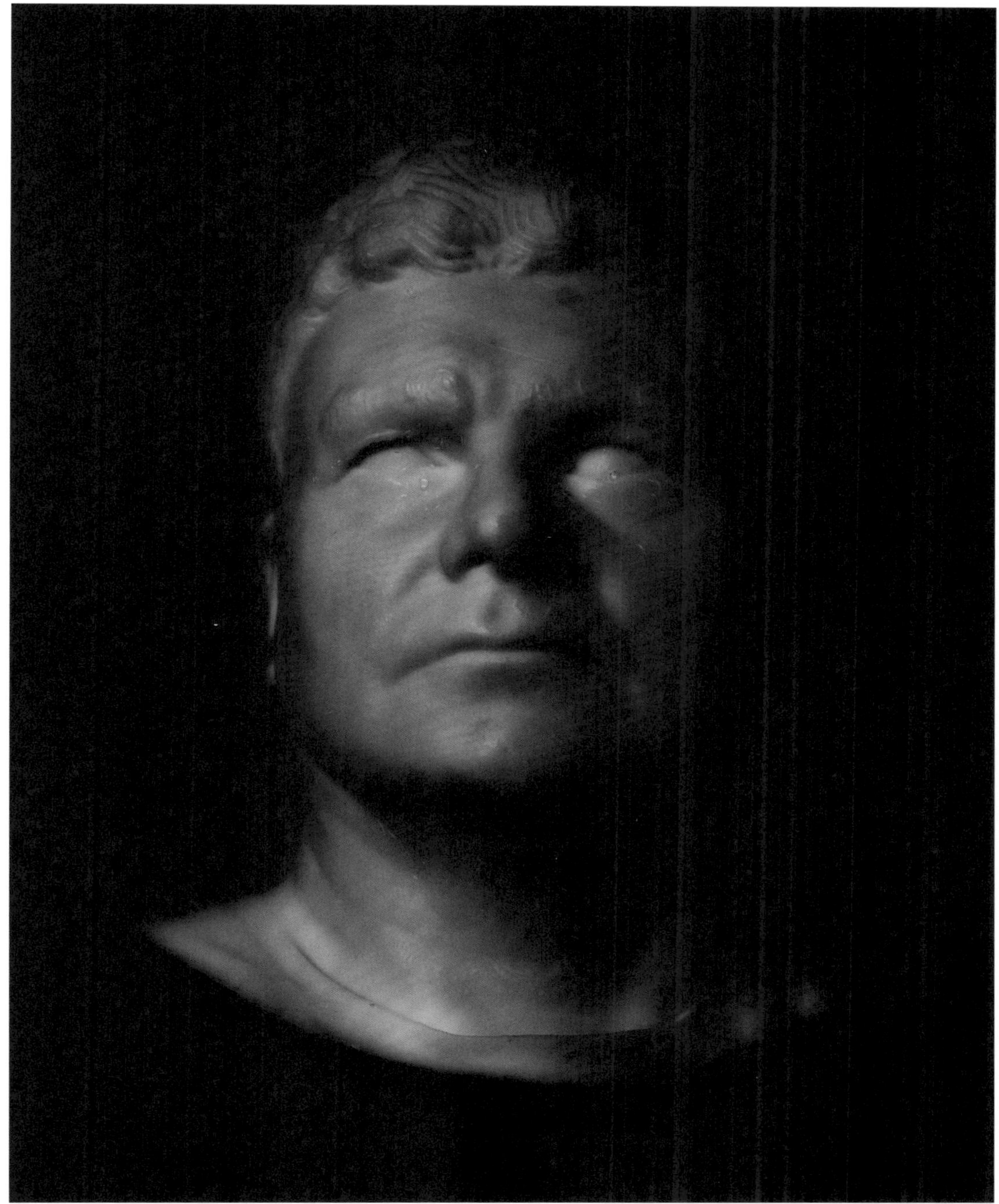

AN OFFICER AND LAWYER IN THE AUSTRALIAN SPECIAL FORCES

While serving in Afghanistan, he raised concerns that the Australian government was covering up the corruption of Australia's defence force for political gain, and sacrificing the lives of Australian soldiers. After his concerns were consistently ignored, he copied 100 secret documents and distributed them to several journalists and to the ABC. He faces trial on five charges relating to national security. If found guilty, he will face life imprisonment.

TITLE

LICKING WAR WOUNDS

COVER

LICKING
WAR
WOUNDS

ARTISTS	Andrii Dostliev & Lia Dostlieva
PUBLISHER	89books
MONOGRAPHY	- 248 pages - first published in 2022 - size: 22 x 24 cm
SUMMARY	At the end of 2016, the Ukrainian photographer duo Andrii Dostliev and Lia Dostlieva bought a tank-shaped salt lamp in Bakhmut, a city in eastern Ukraine known for its salt farming. The incongruous object appeared in Bakhmut's souvenir shops following the eviction by the Ukrainian army of Russian terrorists affiliated with the Donetsk Metropolitan Republic who had occupied the city since 2014. The ice-coloured lamp, with dim lighting, became one of the symbols of the trauma inflicted by the Donbass war. Committed to understanding how to describe and make visible such a "difficult past", the duo began to lick the salt tank in a performative gesture. By photographing, week after week, its slow disappearance, the artists document a painful process of repair and healing. For four years, the duo portrayed the subtle duration of their resilience. In 2021, as their project was coming to an end, they made one wish: that the war would end in their region. "But instead, on 24 February 2022, Russia invaded Ukraine. And art suddenly became futile in the face of the shelling of peaceful Ukrainian cities."
BIOGRAPHY	Born in 1984, Ukrainian photographers Andrii Dostliev and Lia Dostlieva are interested in representations of traumatic memory and question totalitarian views. Andrii was trained in computer science and Lia in ethnology and anthropology, and since 2019 they have been carrying out several joint projects combining documentary photography, video and performance.

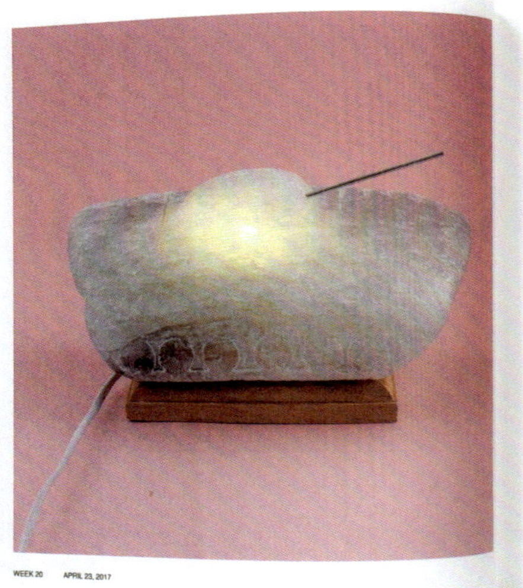

WEEK 20 APRIL 23, 2017

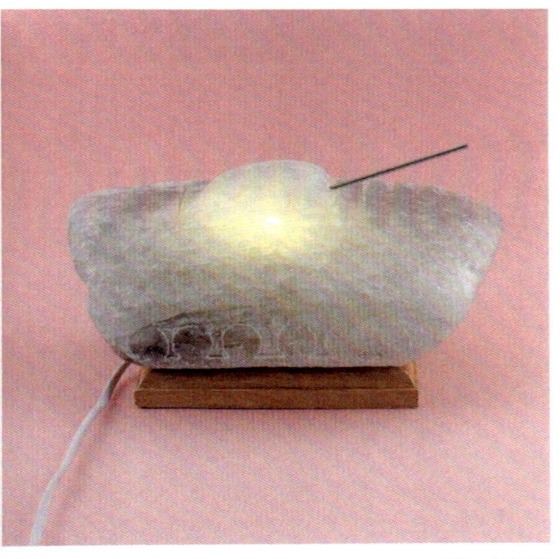

WEEK 21 APRIL 30, 2017

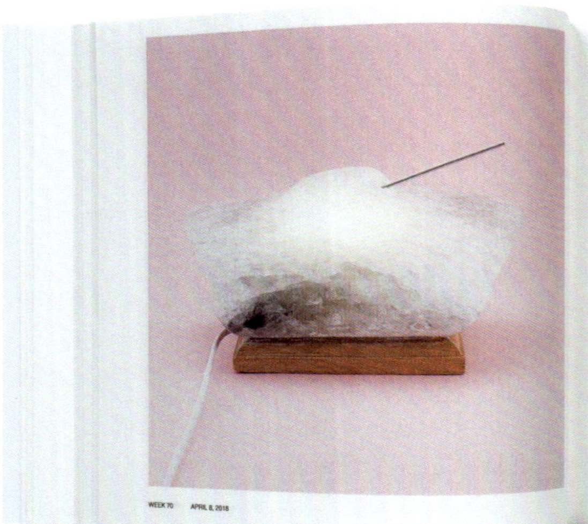

WEEK 70 APRIL 8, 2018

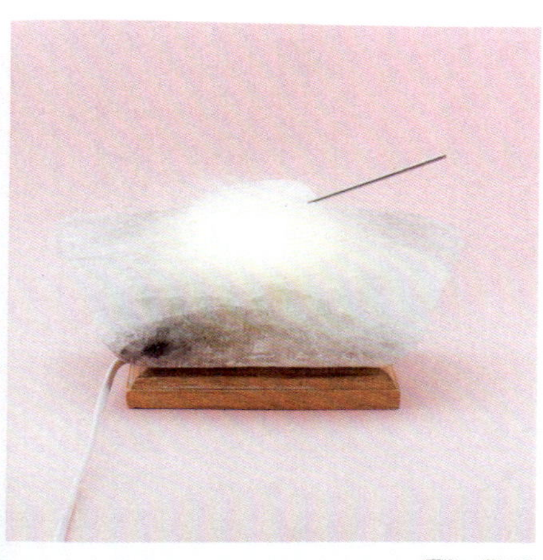

WEEK 71 APRIL 15, 2018

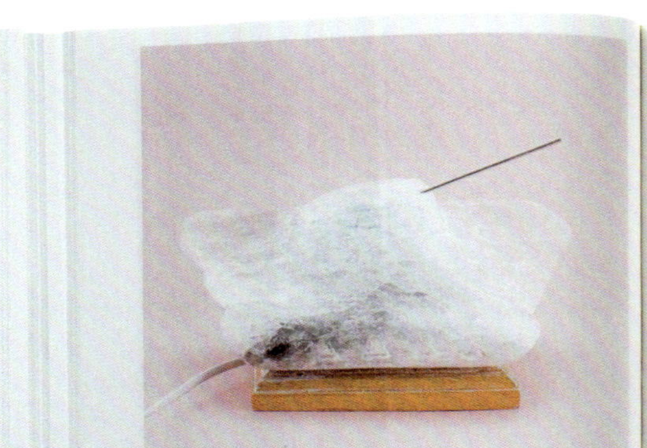

WEEK 102 NOVEMBER 18, 2018

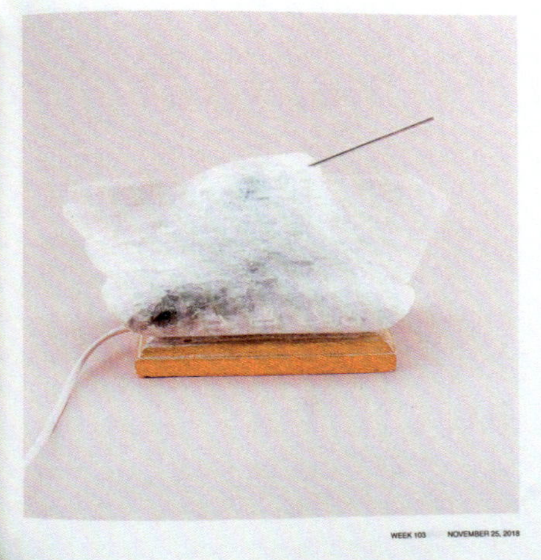

WEEK 103 NOVEMBER 25, 2018

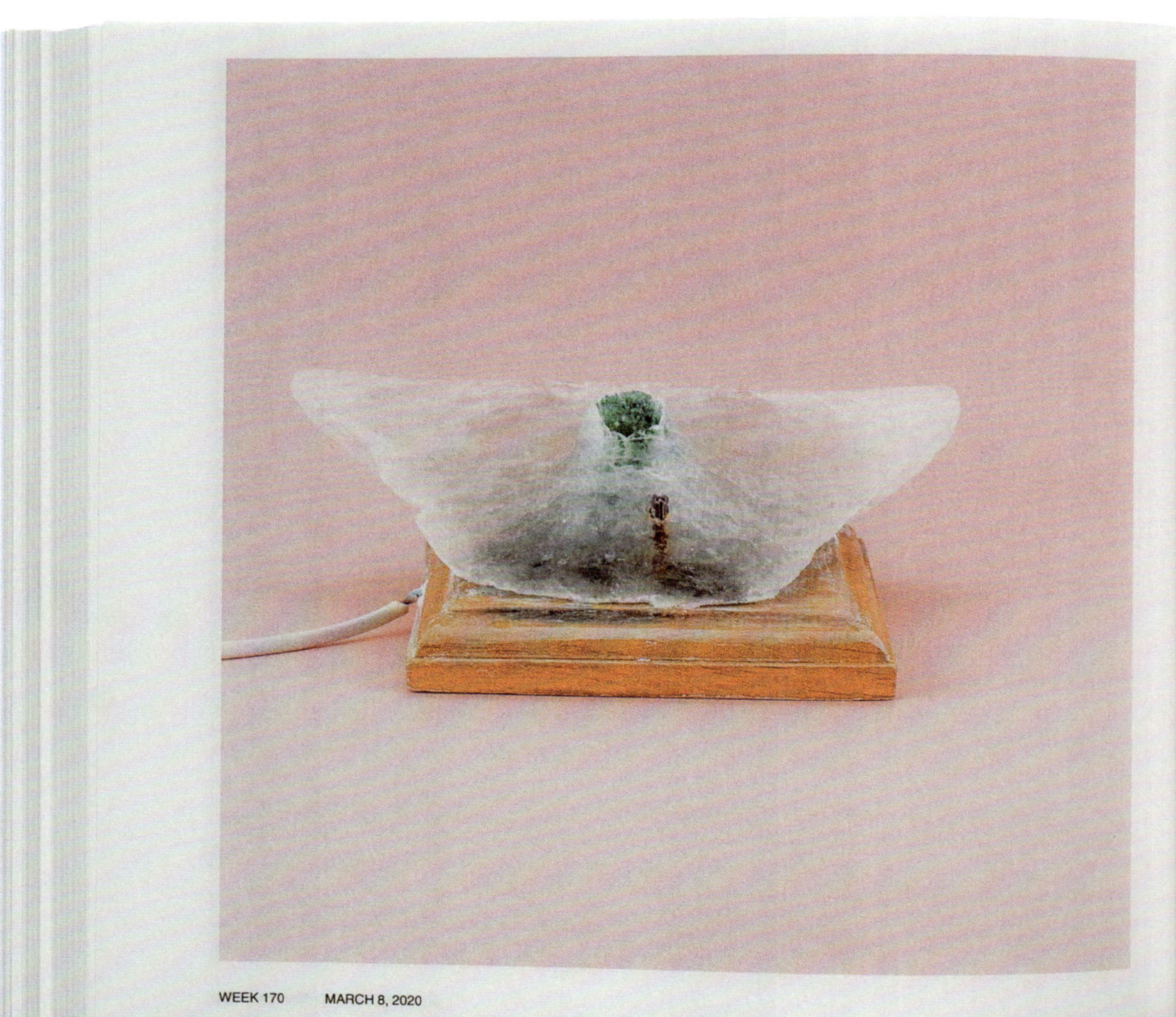

WEEK 170 MARCH 8, 2020

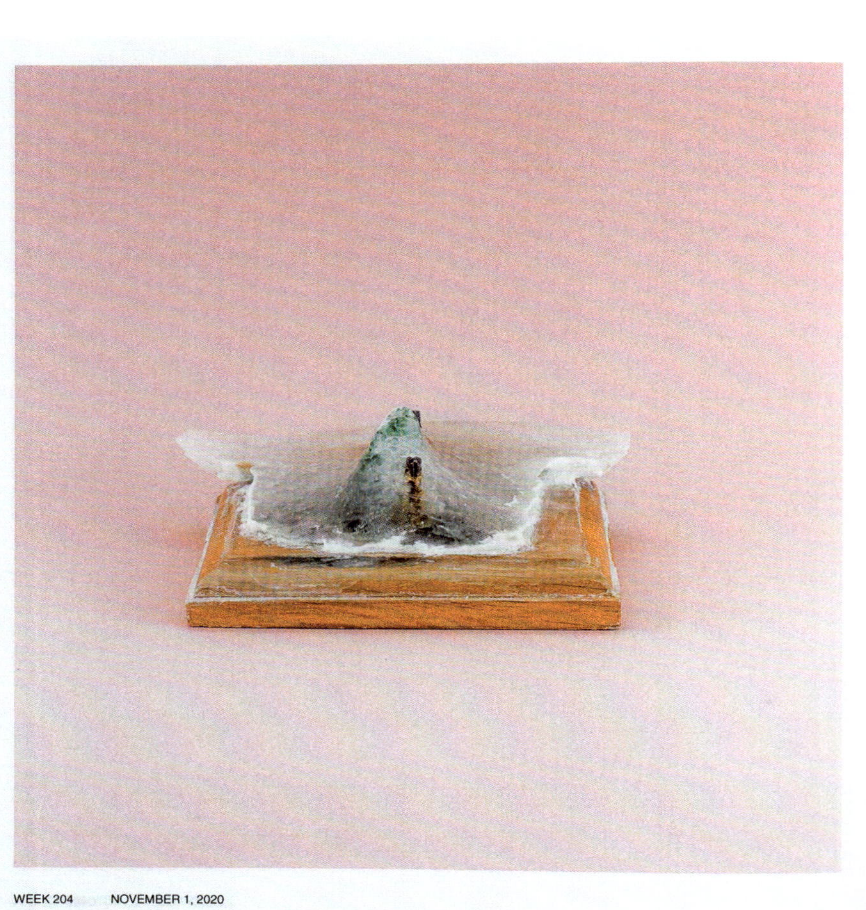

WEEK 204 NOVEMBER 1, 2020

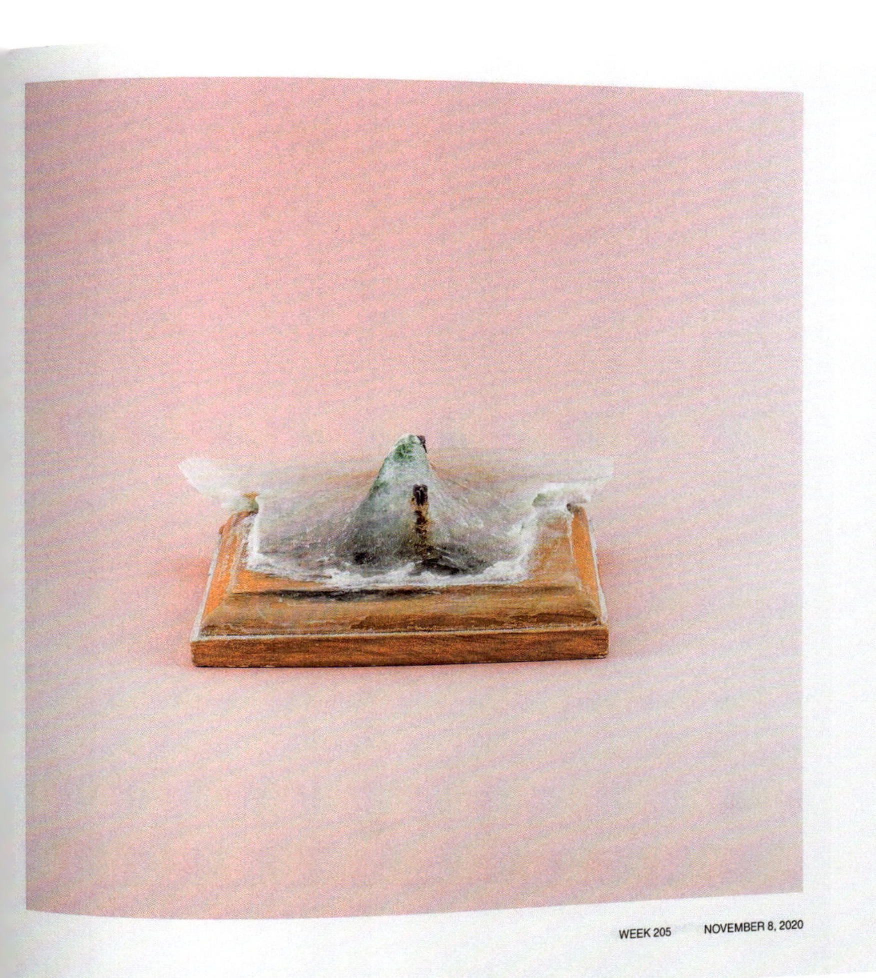

WEEK 205 NOVEMBER 8, 2020

AIDA SILVESTRI

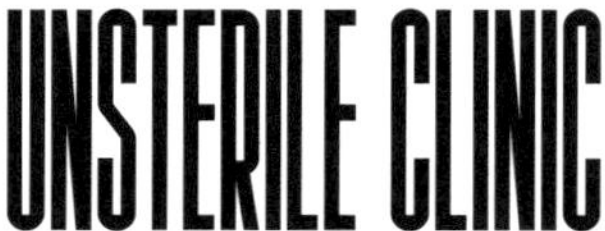

According to the World Health Organization, over 200 million girls and women worldwide have been victims of female genital mutilation, most often performed between childhood and the age of 15. Such violence, inflicted primarily on women, remains taboo and surrounded by shame and pain. In the shadows, women are screaming, their sex amputated on the edge of their lips.

Unsterile Clinic brings together silhouette portraits of East African women living in London. Each image is associated with a poem. Returning to the origins of figuration, the artist of Eritrean descent Aida Silvestri practises a form of restorative photography that embodies the invisibility of the phenomenon while exposing the wounds of the flesh. On indistinct mouths, the scars speak: leather vulvae lined with pearls and flowers represent the different types of mutilations. A dignified and grave chorus of women singing its rage and resentment.

I was 10 years old. The mutilated choir shouts the unspeakable pain that erases pleasure, the ablation that forbids orgasm. *I was 9 years old.* For some, feelings vanish when the razor slices. *I was 6 years old.* They say they have lost their humanity. *I was 11 years old.* They say they live in incompleteness. *They did it to me when I was 4 years old.* All of them experience painful sexual lives. *I was 6 years old.* Deliveries that replay the trauma. *I was 13 years old.* They refer to themselves as warriors rather than victims or survivors. *I was 10 years old.* Blindfolded warriors, with gagged mouths. *I was 6 or 7 years old.*

Unsterile Clinic, 2014–2016
New commission courtesy © Aida Silvestri/ Autograph ABP, 2016
TYPE III C
TYPE II G
TYPE II D
TYPE I B-Distance
TYPE I B

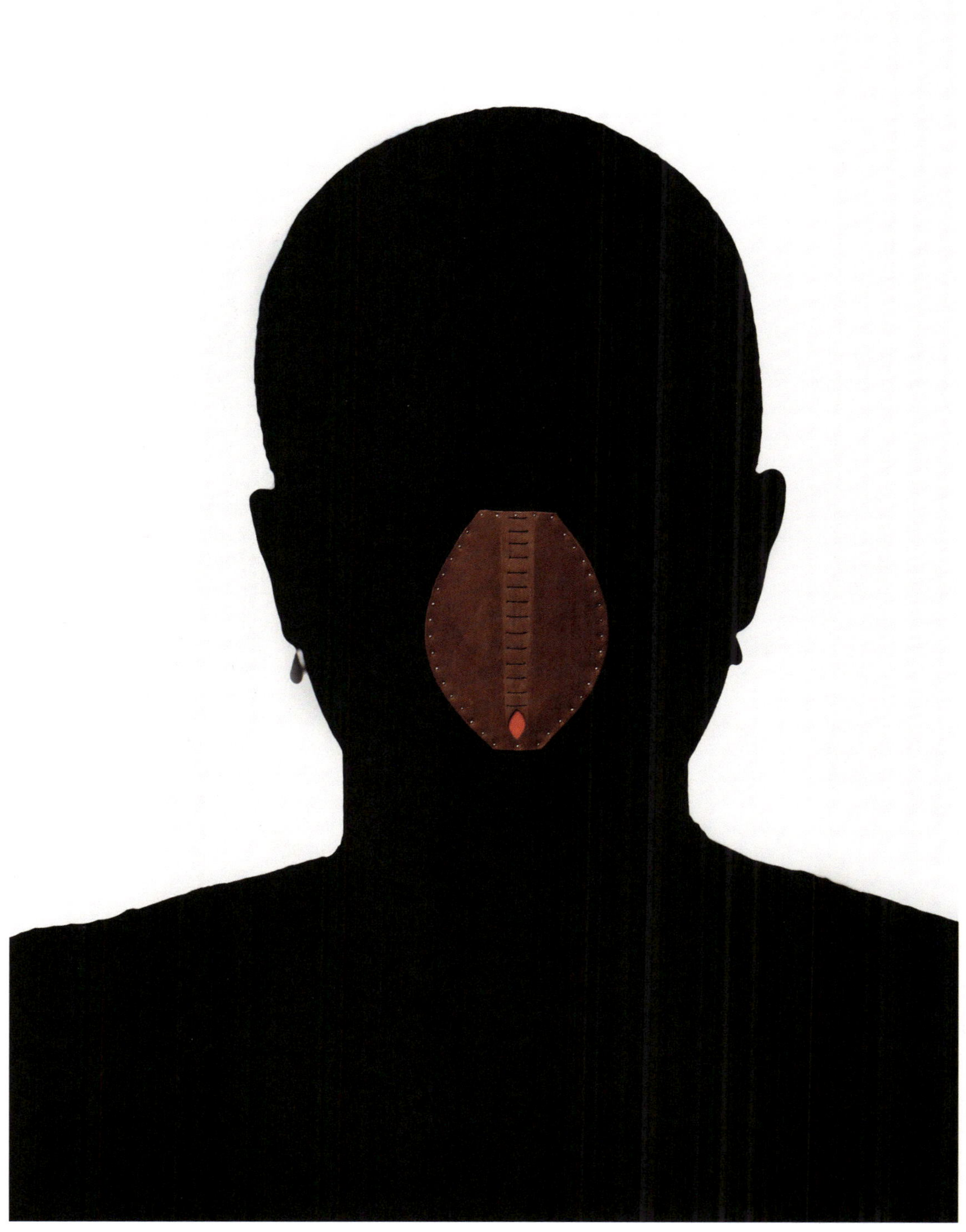

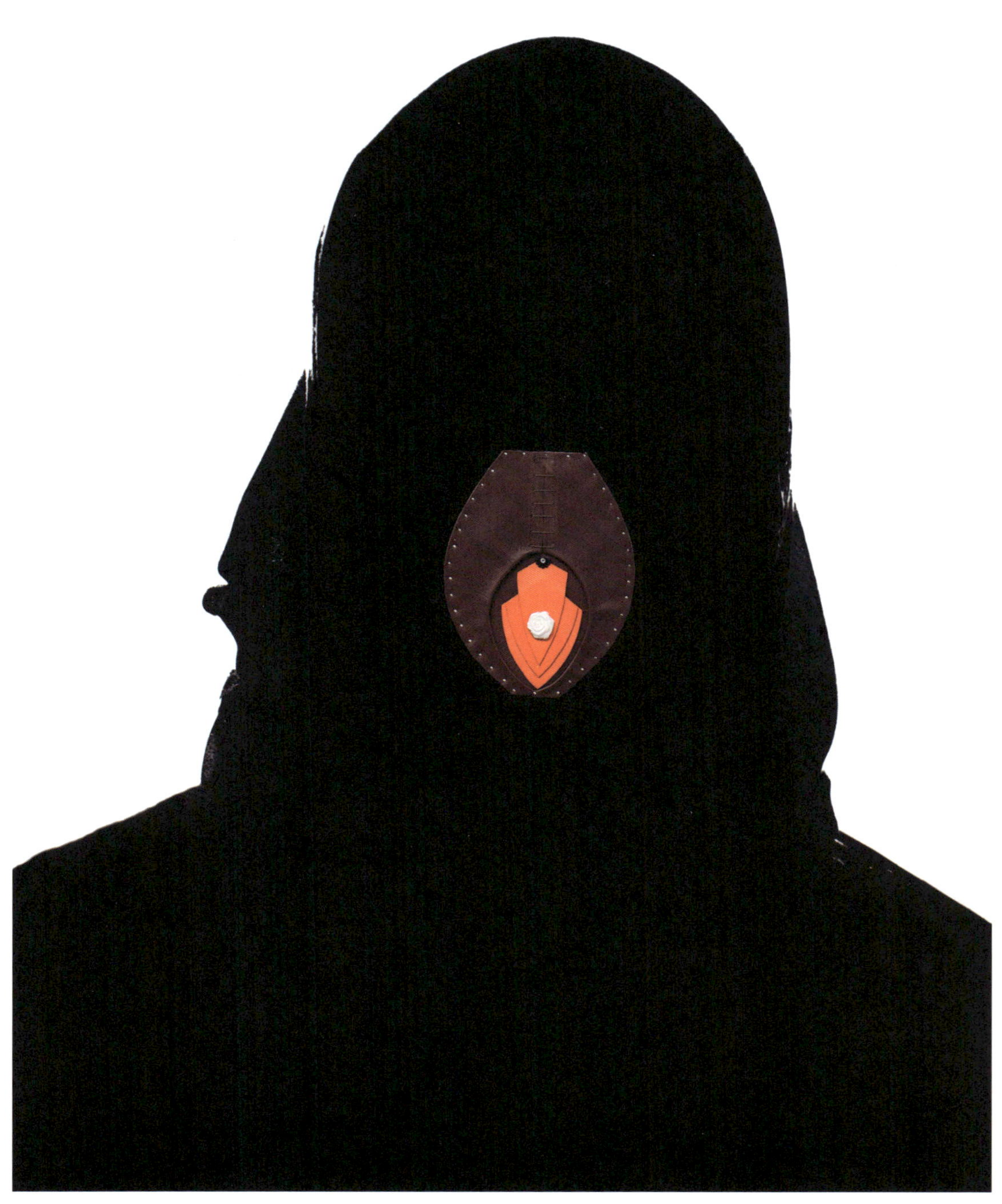

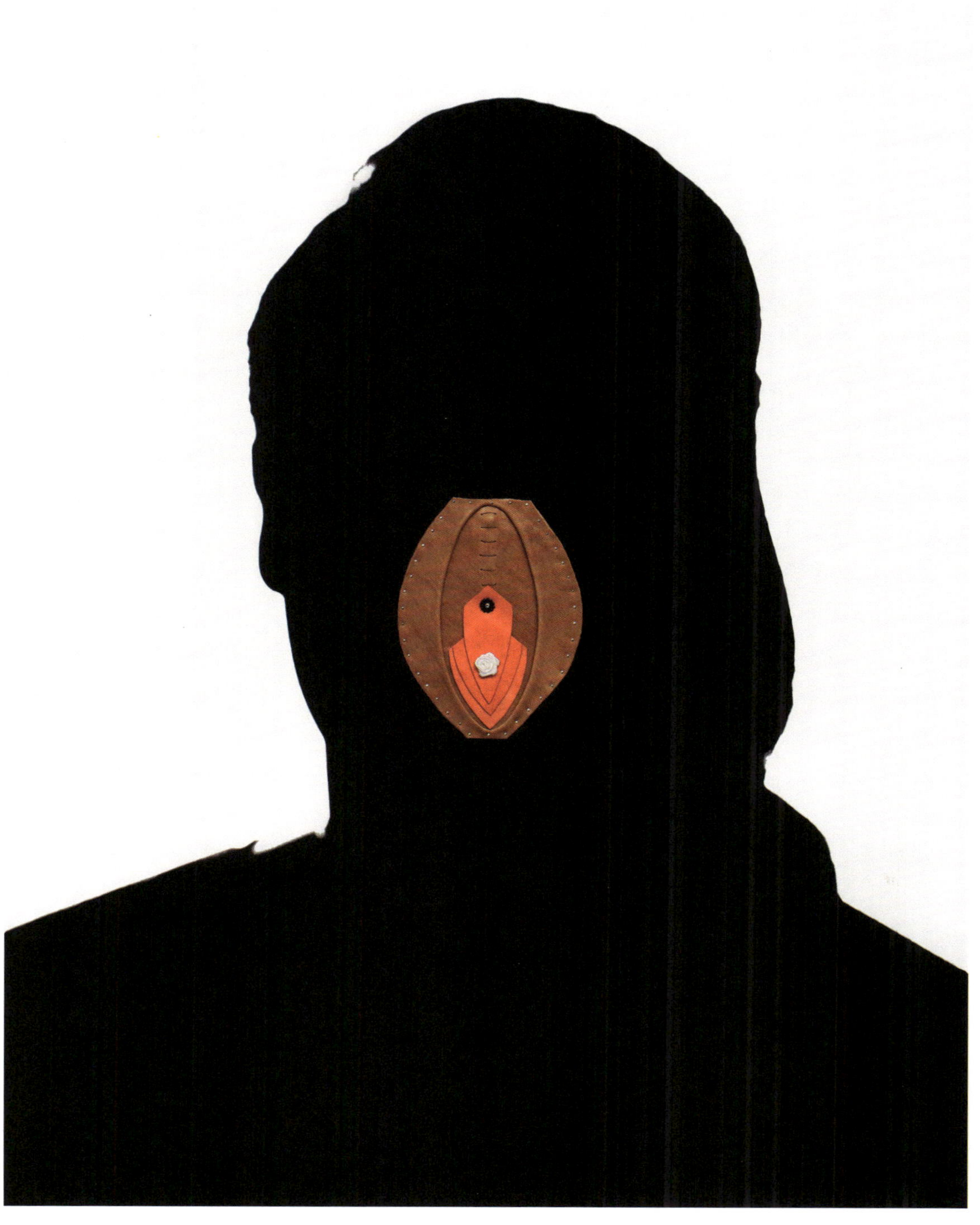

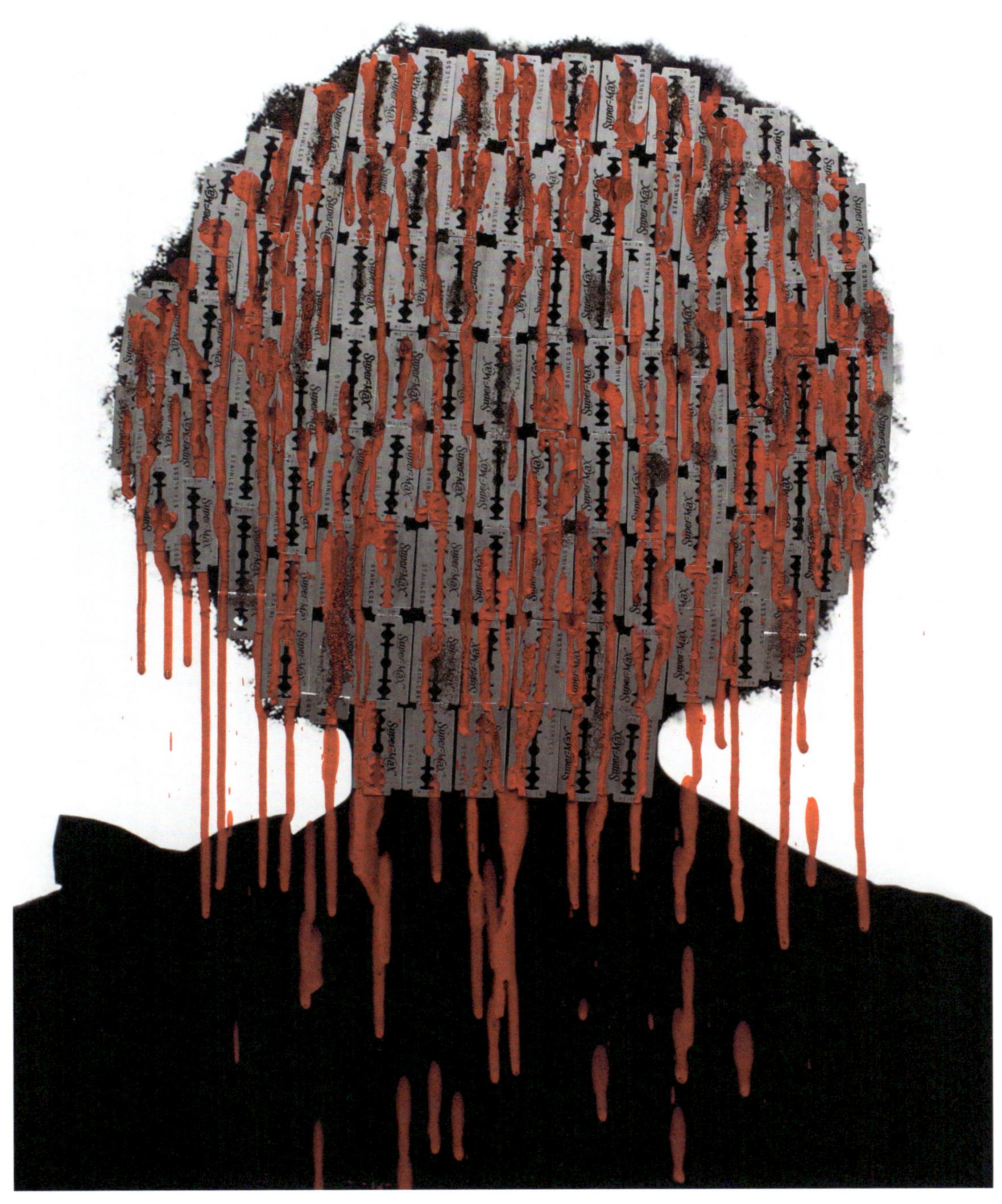
Super-Max
STAINLESS

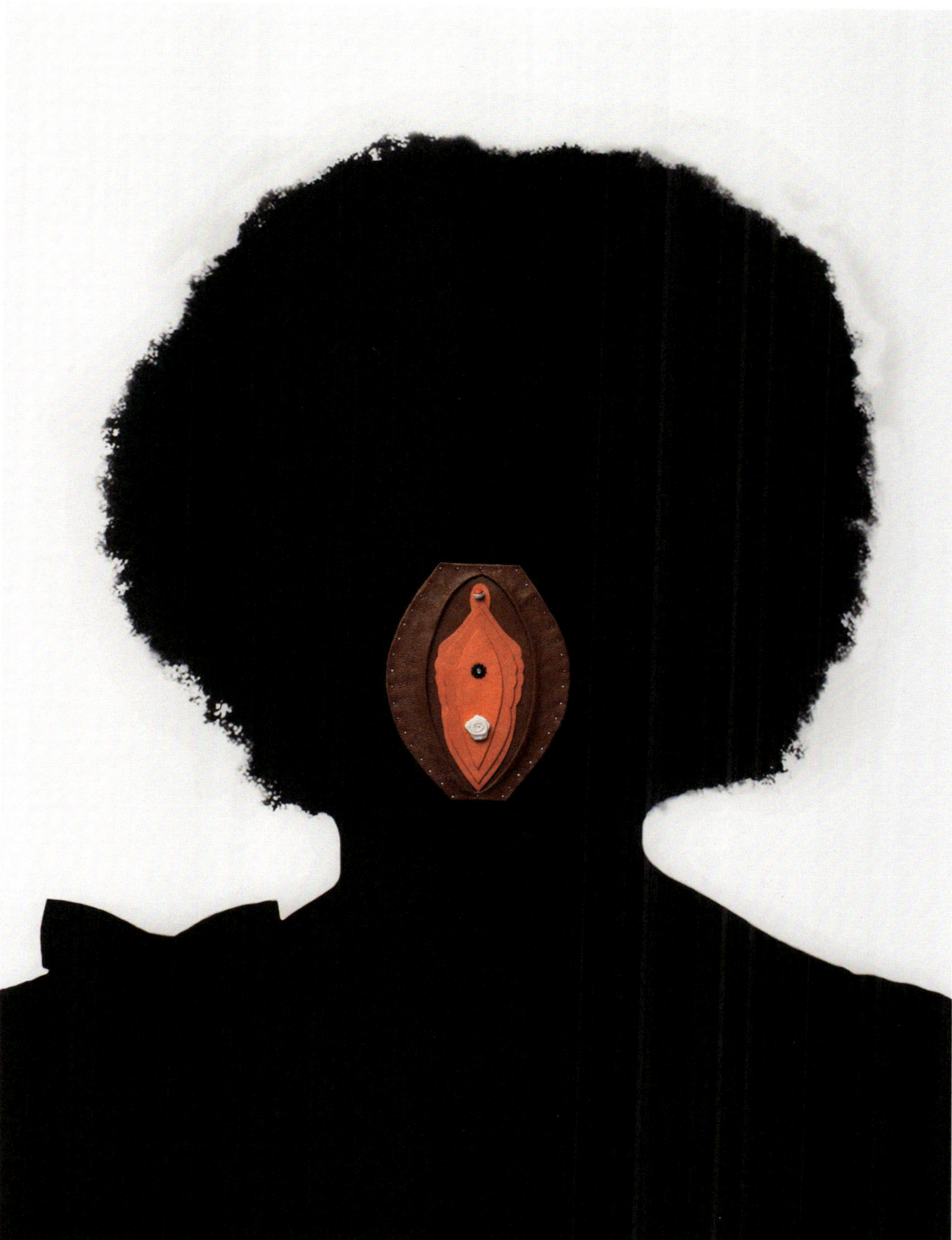

TITLE

FAIRE FACE: HISTOIRES DE VIOLENCES CONJUGALES

COVER

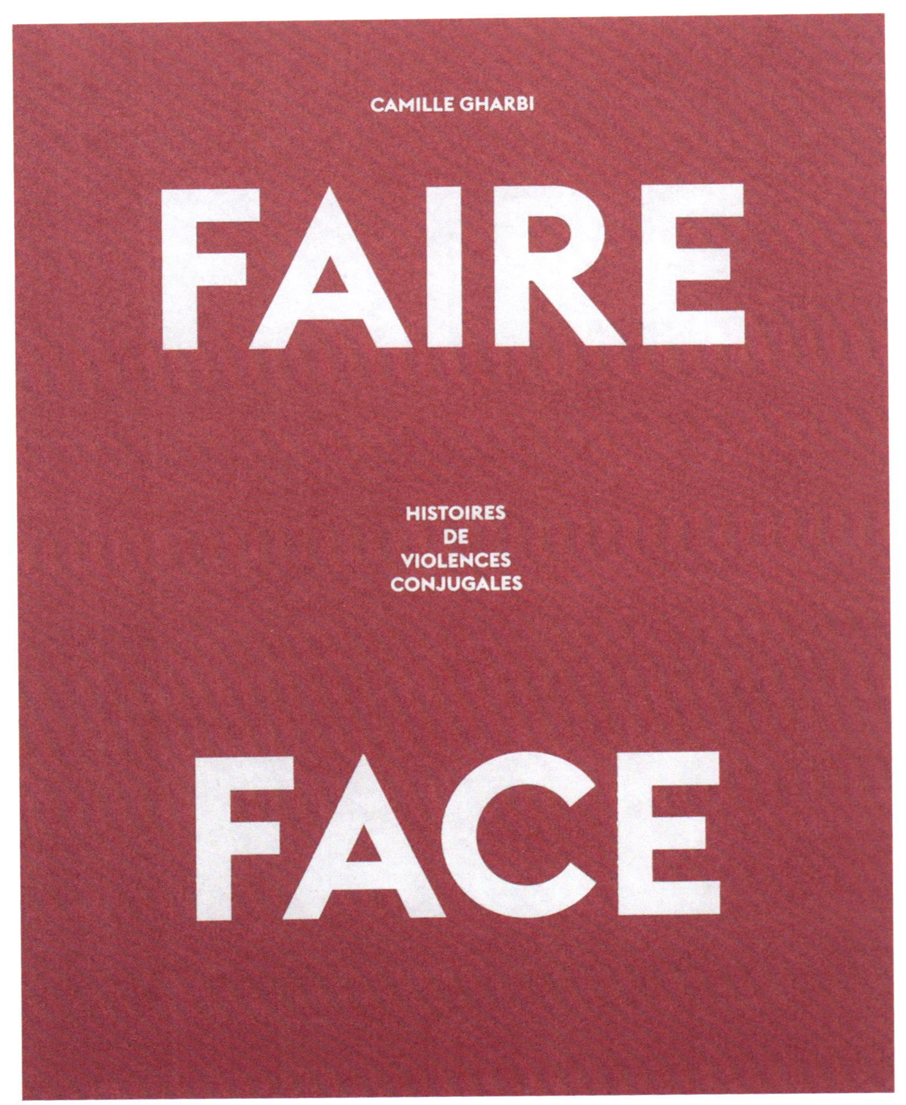

ARTIST	Camille Gharbi
PUBLISHER	The Eyes Publishing
MONOGRAPHY	- 196 pages - first published in 2022 - size: 21 x 27 cm
SUMMARY	With a documentary approach, *Faire Face* (Facing up: stories of domestic violence) combines portraits and testimonies from three photographic series on the issue of violence against women and domestic violence. "Preuves d'amour" (Proof of love) gathers a series of everyday objects transformed into weapons of crime: a white plastic bag, small sewing scissors, a tall wooden baffle, an ordinary pan, a blue cushion, a chrome tap, a bobbin. "Les Monstres n'existent pas" (Monsters do not exist) brings together the portraits, taken in prison, of those who engage in a process of deconstruction and accountability in relation to their deeds. Finally, "Une chambre à soi" (A room of one's own) shows the homes where young women who are victims of domestic or intra-family assault take refuge. An architect by training, Camille Gharbi's photographic approach is clinical and committed. With her three series, she reflects on gender-based violence – femicides in particular. Her work sheds some light over these stories that are made banal and invisible while unpacking the systemic and patriarchal logics that govern them. Combining image and voice, she gives a body and existence back to those who are irremediably reified by the acts, sometimes murderous, that they have committed. Through a symbolic dialogue between victims and perpetrators, she acts towards restoration.
BIOGRAPHY	Born in 1984, Camille Gharbi practises architectural photography and portraiture. She collaborates for the press in parallel with her personal projects for which she favours a documentary approach. Her series for *Le Monde*'s investigative piece "Féminicides: mécanique d'un crime annoncé" (Femicides: mechanics of an announced crime) received the 2020 Visa d'Or for Digital Information. She lives in Pantin (93).

CAMILLE GHARBI

« LA RÉCURRENCE DE CES CRIMES NE RELÈVE PAS DU HASARD. ELLE RÉVÈLE UNE PROFONDE VIOLENCE DE GENRE QU'IL EST TEMPS DE REMETTRE EN QUESTION. »

MARTHA

20 ans

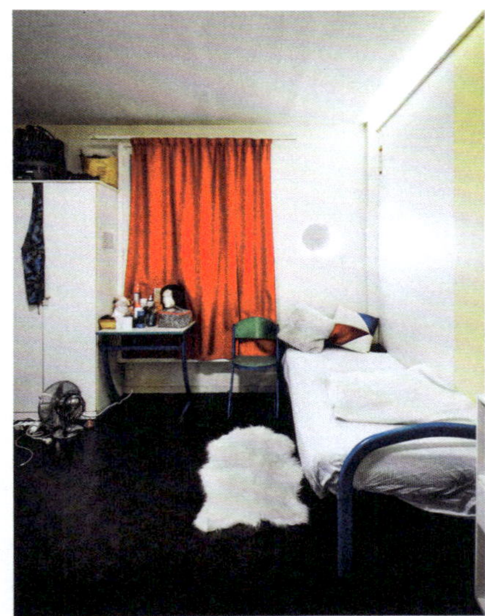

UNE CHAMBRE À SOI

Pour la série « Une chambre à soi », je suis allée à la rencontre de jeunes femmes hébergées par l'association FIT Une Femme Un Toit, qui accueille des femmes âgées de 18 à 25 ans en situation de violences sexuelles, intrafamiliales, et / ou conjugales. C'est le seul centre d'hébergement en France exclusivement dédié à ce public particulier.

À cet âge fragile, fait d'enthousiasme et de vulnérabilité, les résidentes du FIT ne se construisent pas, elles se re-construisent. Après des mois voire des années de violences et parfois d'errance, ces jeunes femmes trouvent entre les murs du foyer un espace de sécurité et de répit. Les chambres qui leur sont attribuées sont souvent le premier espace d'intimité qu'elles investissent depuis très longtemps. Ces chambres sont à leur image : touchantes, abîmées parfois, pleines d'espoir souvent.

J'ai proposé à ces jeunes femmes de me raconter, si elles le pouvaient, leur parcours, et surtout leurs rêves, leurs envies. Comment elles se projettent dans le futur, comment est-ce que, à cet âge auquel on est supposé se construire, ces jeunes victimes de violences conjugales font face à ce long chemin de re-construction.

« Il manquait à celles qui étaient douées pour affirmer leur génie de quoi vivre, du temps et une chambre à soi. »
Viriginia Woolf

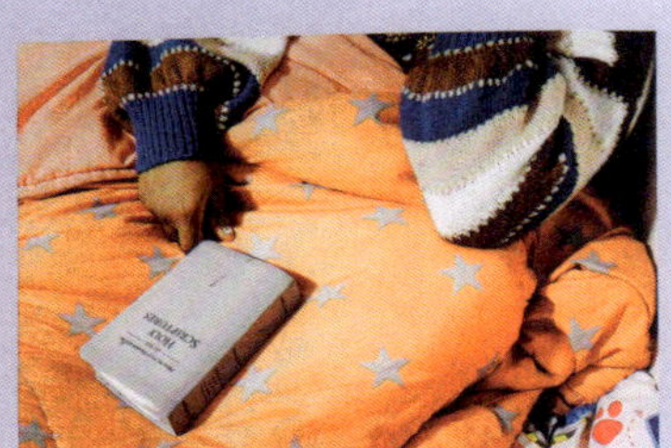

Entretien traduit de l'anglais.

Dans les moments difficiles, on a besoin de mots comme « culture », « encouragement », « concentration », « force ».

« Je suis née le 25 octobre 1997, j'ai 23 ans. Je viens du Nigéria, vers Lagos. Mais je suis en France maintenant. J'ai embrassé la France. Je suis là depuis presque 2 ans maintenant. J'ai changé. J'ai commencé des études pour devenir auxiliaire de vie scolaire. Je suis dans cette chambre depuis 9 mois. Avant je vivais aussi à Paris... Mais j'ai trouvé cet endroit. Je me sens chez moi ici, je me sens chez moi partout. Il faut accepter ce qui est et profiter.
Ça coûte beaucoup trop de ne pas accepter le moment qu'on traverse.

Je n'ai pas de famille en France, ma famille est au Nigéria. J'espère qu'un jour je pourrai leur rendre visite. Mes études vont me prendre un peu de temps, j'ai encore 1 an à faire.

J'espère devenir une meilleure personne, grandir, mûrir. J'espère que le futur sera bon.

Dans les moments difficiles, on a besoin de mots comme « culture », « encouragement », « concentration », « force ».

Il faut s'accrocher aux choses qui vous font aller de l'avant. Il faut accepter d'être en bas, avant de pouvoir remonter, pour prouver aux autres qu'on ne subit pas mais qu'on agit. Il faut se relever. La vie continue.

« Une reine. Tu restes une reine. »

C'est ça qu'il faut se dire. Il faut croire en soi avant tout. Se dire qu'on est bon, qu'on est super, qu'on fait les choses de mieux en mieux. C'est comme ça qu'on tient. Il faut garder le mental, se dire qu'on est un héros. Prendre de la hauteur par rapport aux malveillances. Je pense que ça marche.

Moi j'ai la foi, une foi immense. Dans les moments difficiles, je me tourne vers Dieu. Je pense qu'il emmène les gens qui se tournent vers lui vers le bien, et je le prie pour ça. Ce qui se passe, c'est sa volonté. C'est lui qui m'aide, qui m'encourage, qui me parle quand ça ne va pas. Parce que les humains peuvent parler, mais tu peux ne pas les comprendre.
Alors que quand Dieu te parle, tu le comprends.

On cherche tous à réussir notre vie. Mais notre vie, c'est ce que nous sommes. Et ce que nous sommes, c'est ce que nous voulons devenir. Nous avons déjà en nous ce que nous serons plus tard. On ne peut pas se mentir. Tout est déjà là. »

REBECCA

23 ans

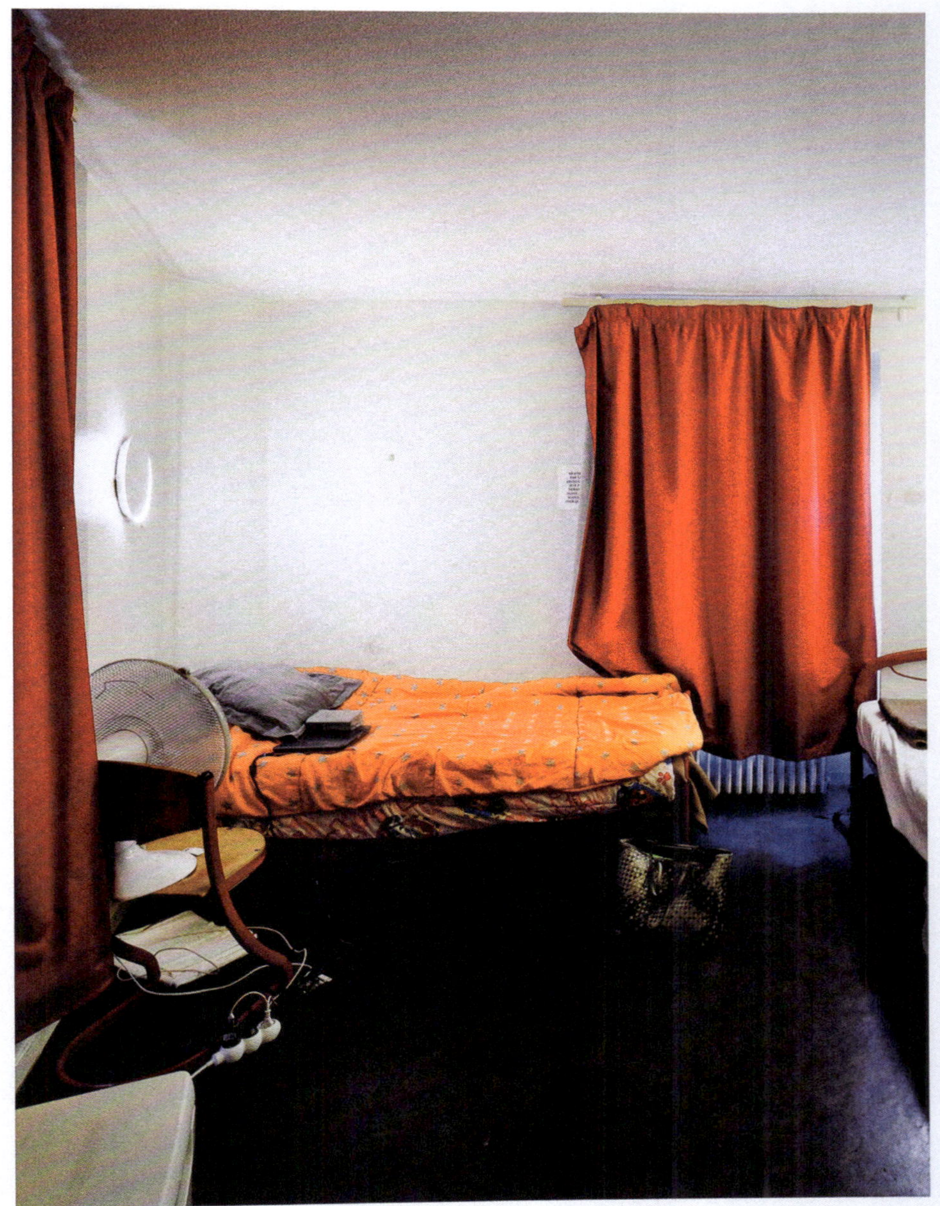

JÉRÉMIE DANON

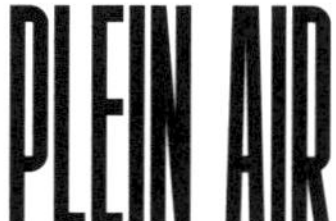

In the series *Plein air*, Jérémie Danon photographs former prisoners in rehabilitation. He took the time to get to know them, to build with them a space of listening and representation where they feel at ease and can find themselves. Together, they weave the fabric of their stories. By his own admission, the visual artist is interested in the individual, their identity, the place that society is willing to leave them.

Working *with* rather than *on* people, he translates into an image a collaborative experience that goes beyond simple documentation. Sitting in front of a green screen, each person is invited to express themselves from the question "Where would you like to be now?" The artist then uses a filmic inlaying process to integrate these testimonies into virtual spaces taken from video games. One after the other, inmates depict their prison experience and their sense of alienation, and deplore the professional and family deadlocks in which they find themselves.

Plein air composes liminal images that de-realize the prison context and the living space that everyone finds once they are out. The film, like the photographs made later with a view camera, produced with the help of the photographer Jules Séverac, offers a fictitious refuge to these individuals who are feeling out of step with the world they find themselves in. These images testify to an impossible return to the heart of an inadequate reality.

Plein air, 2022

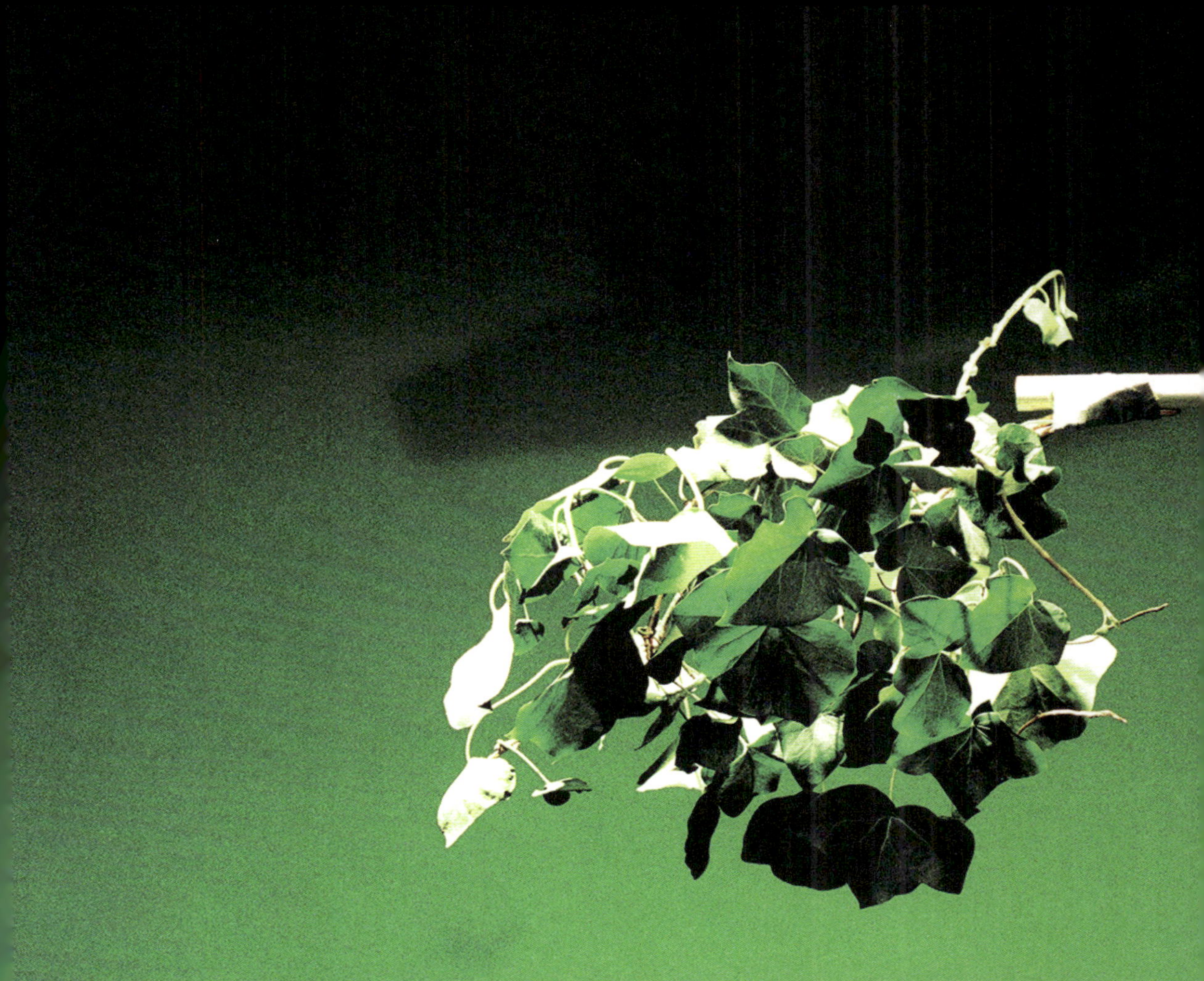

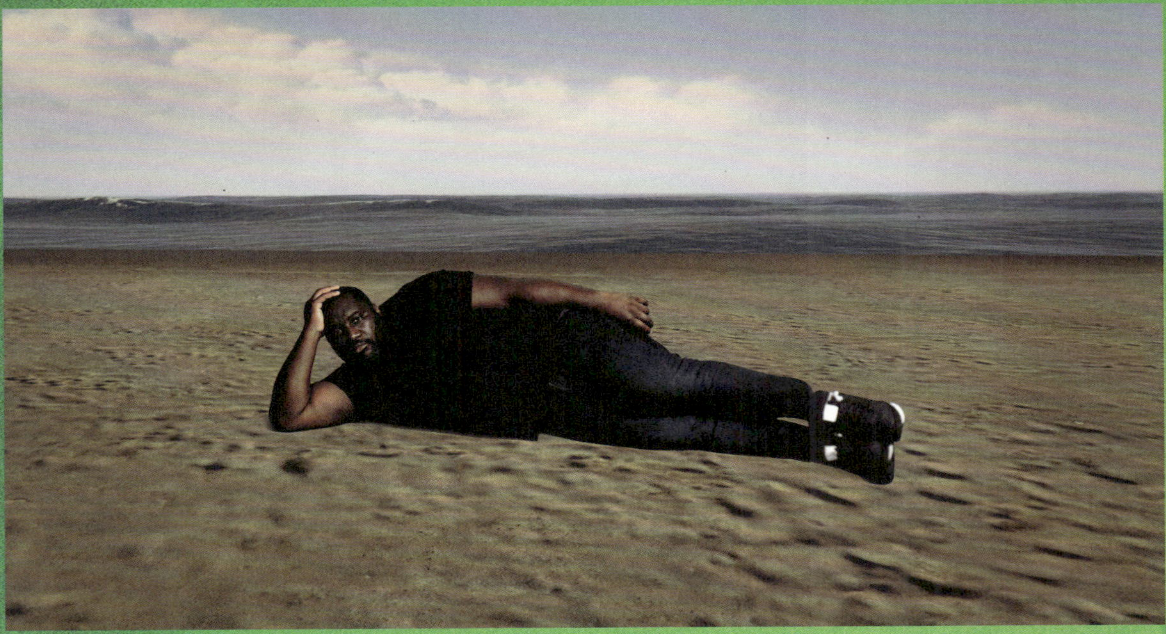

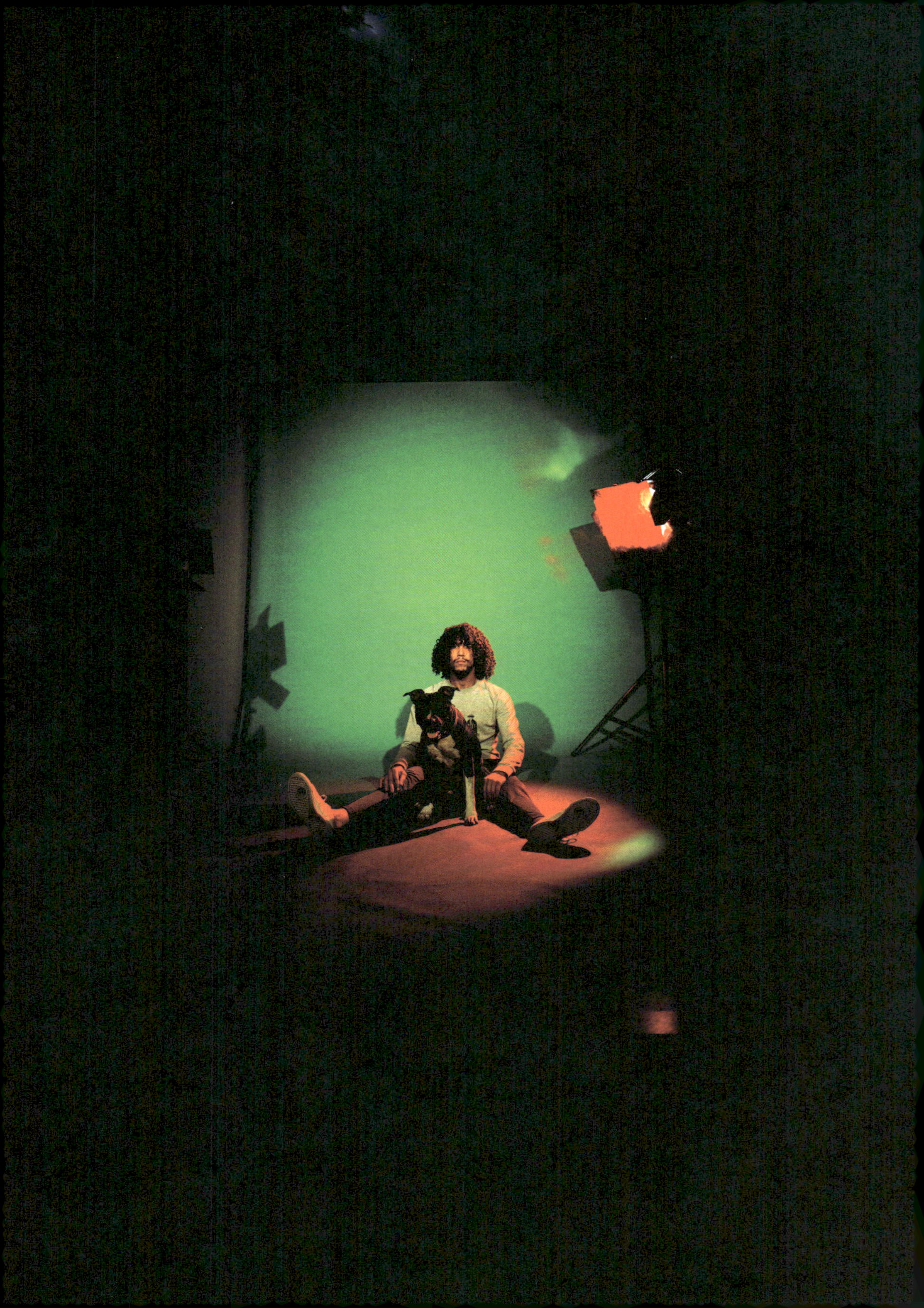

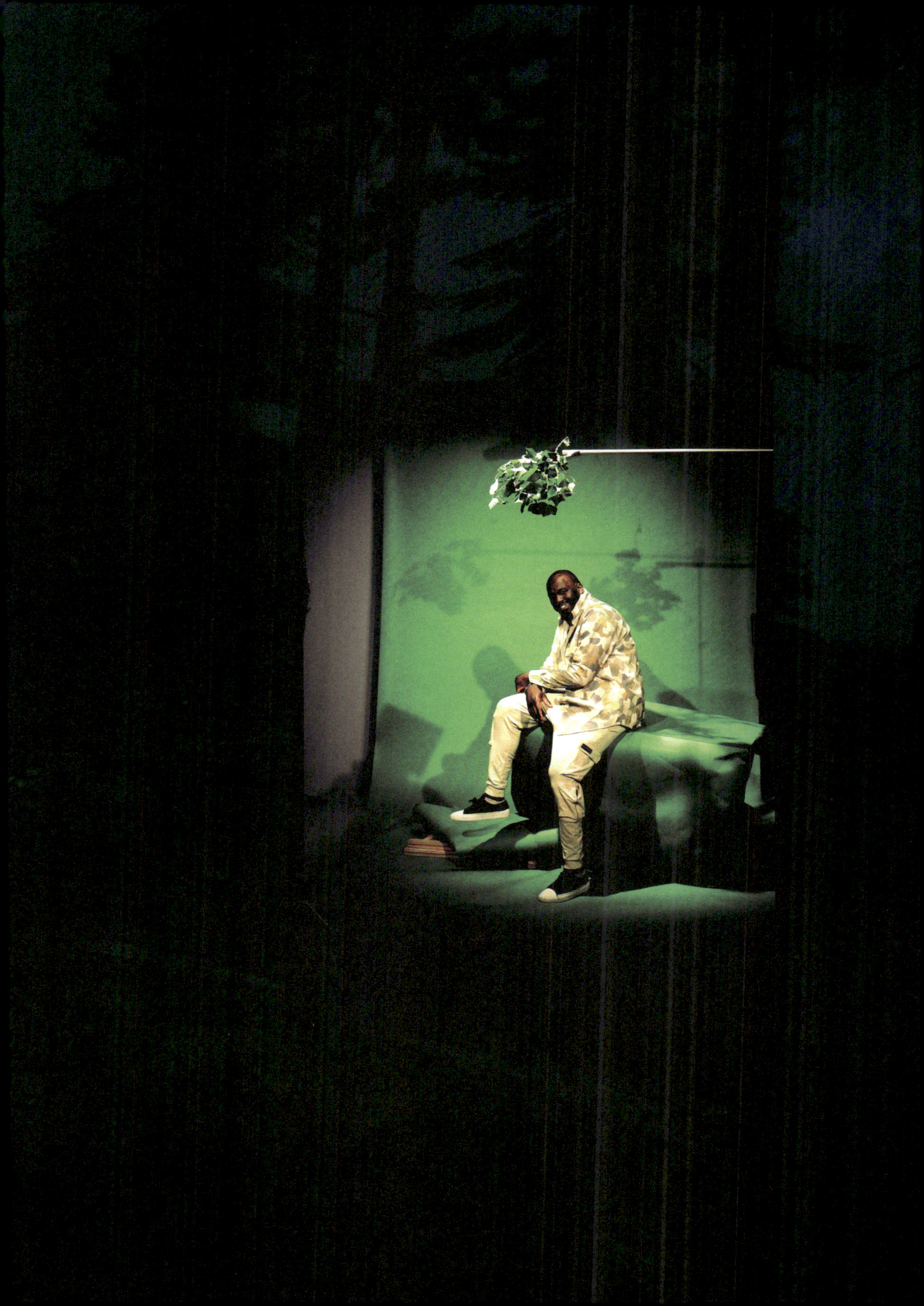

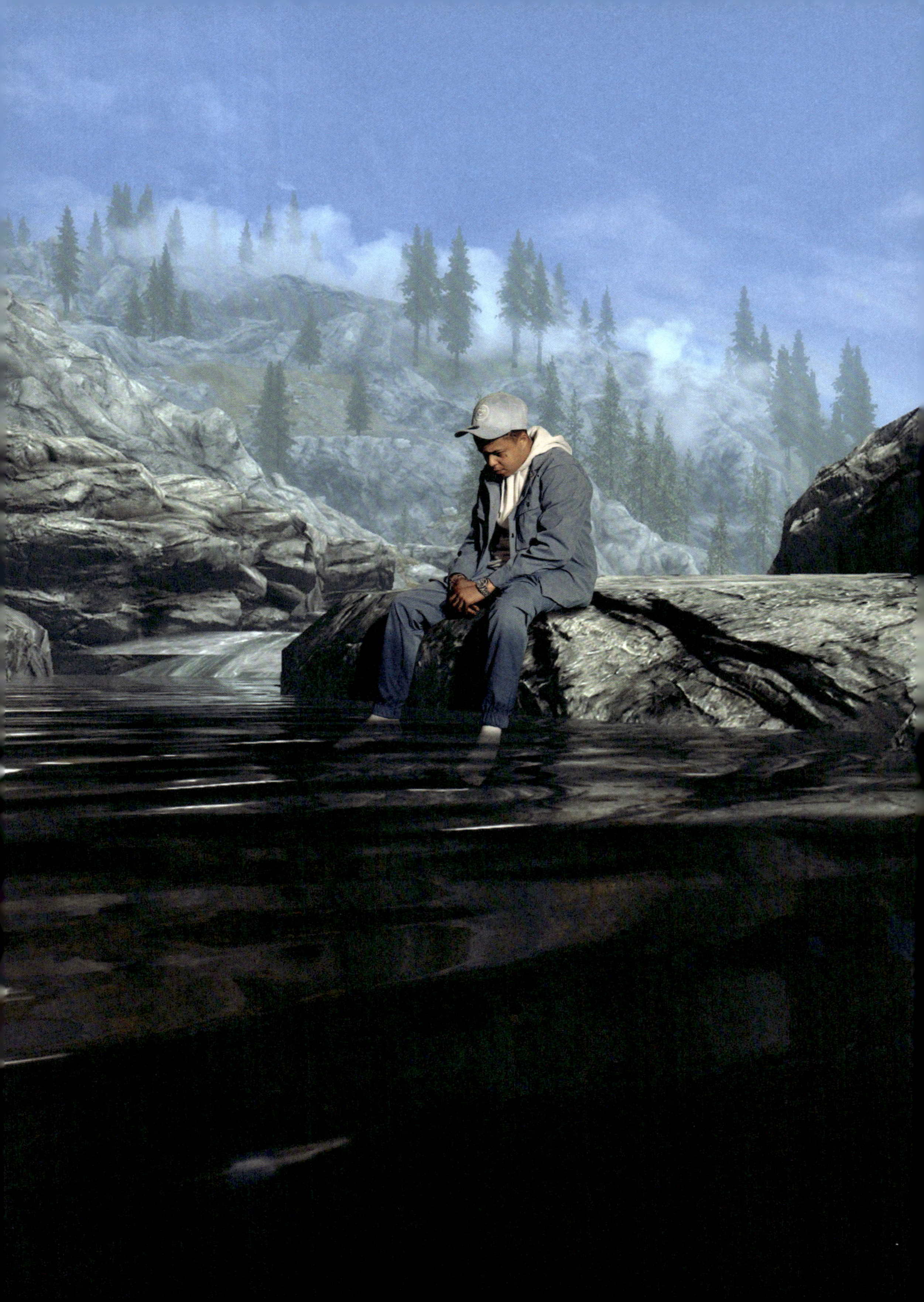

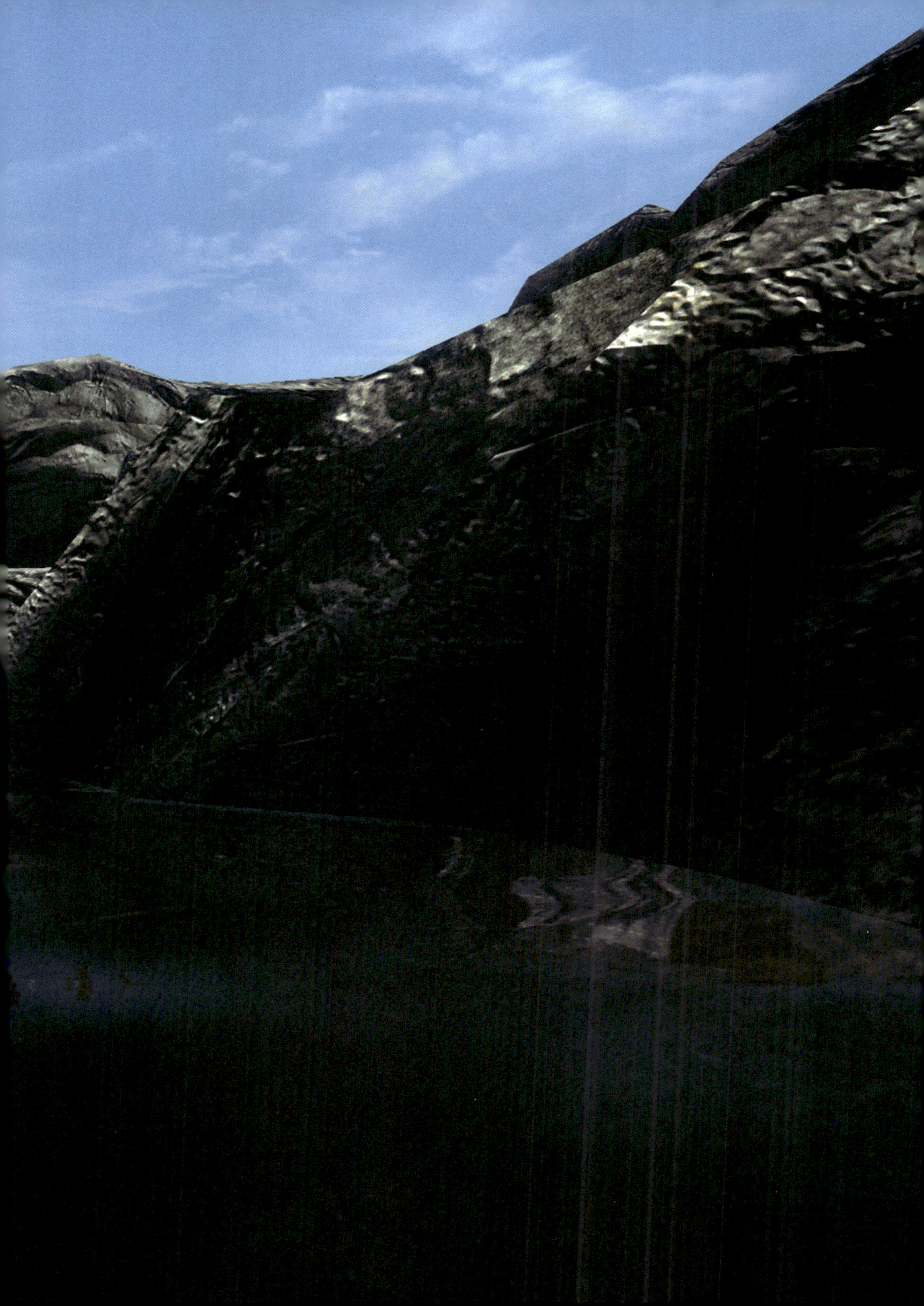

HAYLEY MILLAR BAKER

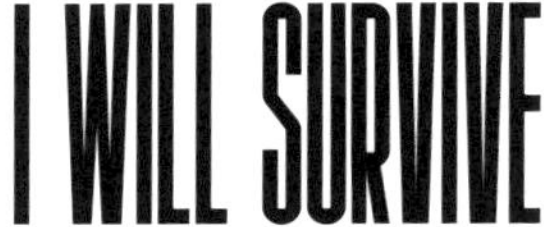

Hayley Millar Baker composes immersive and narrative photomontages that reveal anachronistic temporalities, impossible narratives and recomposed memories. From her "rock and roll" childhood on the outskirts of the western suburb of Naarm (Melbourne), she has retained the sessions of spiritualism that allowed her, her sister and her cousins to ward off the tragic loss of loved ones: "Since then, the spirits are still there, and I know no respite."

Through the surreal abstraction, in black and white, of spaces and times, the photographer, a descendant of the Gunditjmara and Djabwurrung Aboriginal peoples, questions the stories she inherited: stories of genocide and survival, of strength and resistance. Through the multiplicity of enigmatic self-portraits, she deconstructs and reconstructs, in "defamiliarized" landscapes, the memories that time transforms, like so many acts of "decolonial" reappropriation.

Draped in long dark dresses, the splendid silhouettes – charcoal hair and blood-stained hands – replay the gestures, poses and rites of those who haunt Australia's "official" history. As true mediumistic guides, they welcome us to dreamlike places – desert beaches, abundant bush and monumental stones – that trigger a sense of wonder mixed with fright. They designate possible paths and face the horizon without ever revealing the secret of their strange existence. Thanks to them, Hayley Millar Baker preserves the fabric of the stories that forged her, and promises to those who wish it access to a form of sensitive truth.

I Will Survive, 2020

I Will Survive 1, 2020
I Will Survive 2, 2020
I Will Survive 6, 2020
I Will Survive 4, 2020
I Will Survive 5, 2020

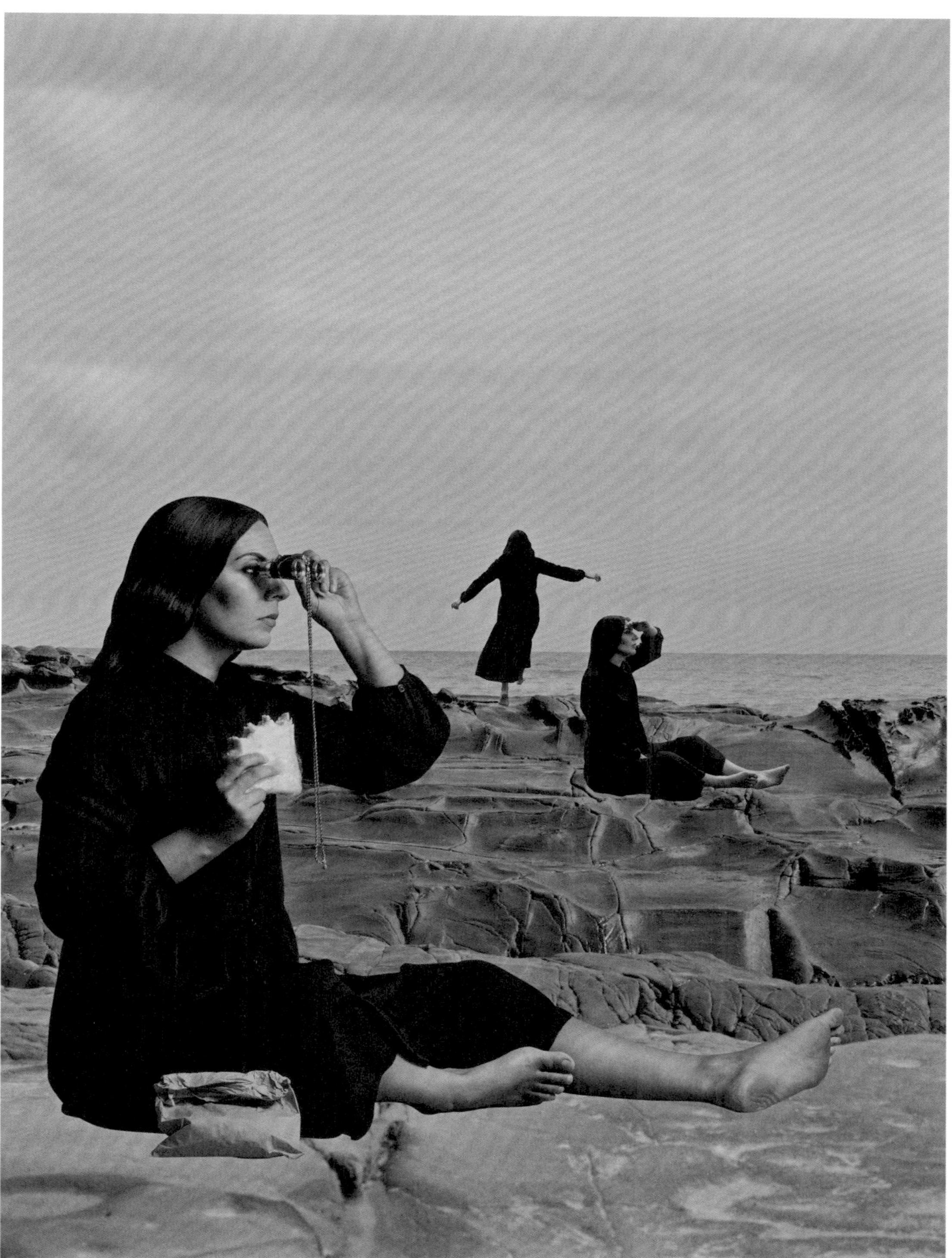

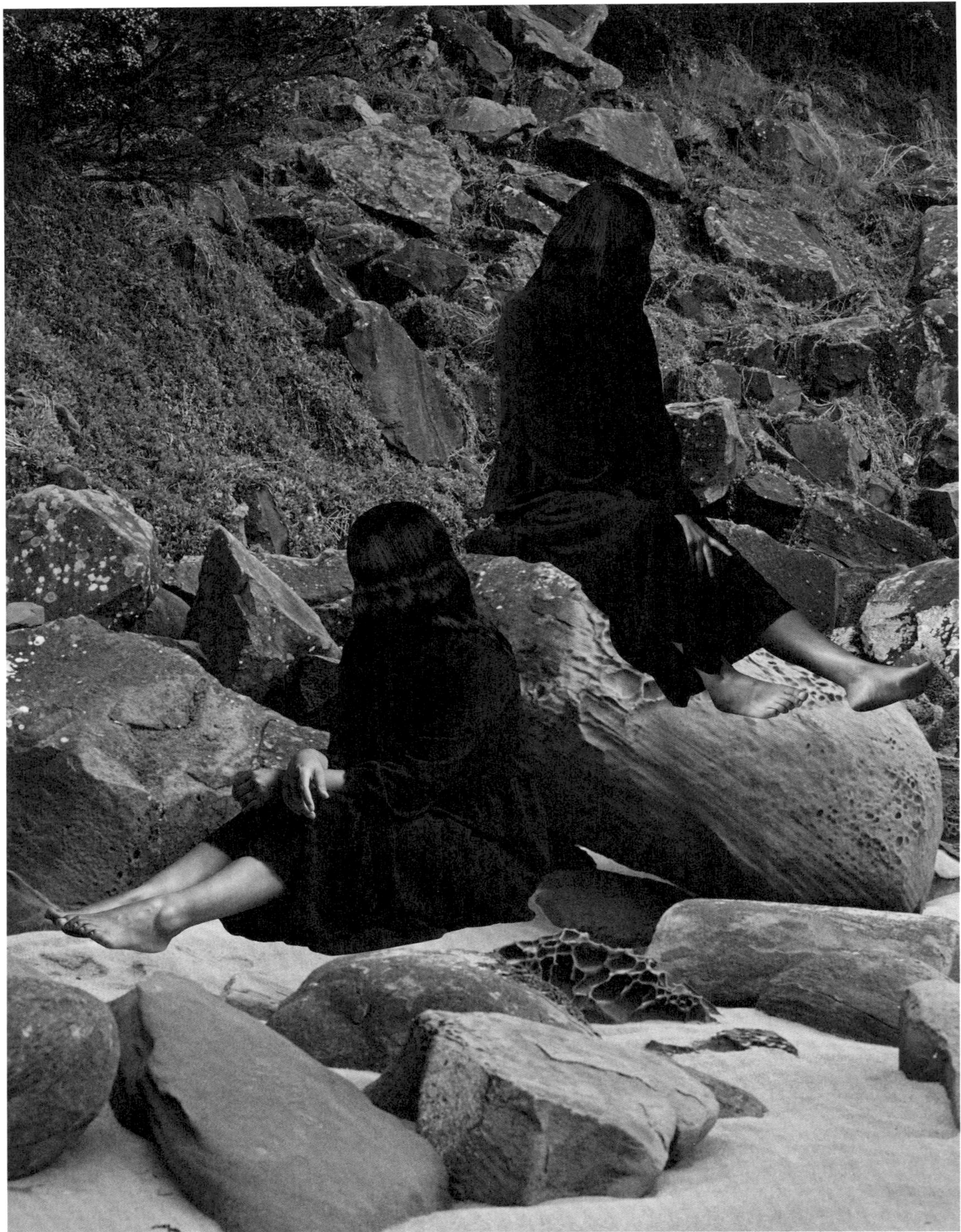

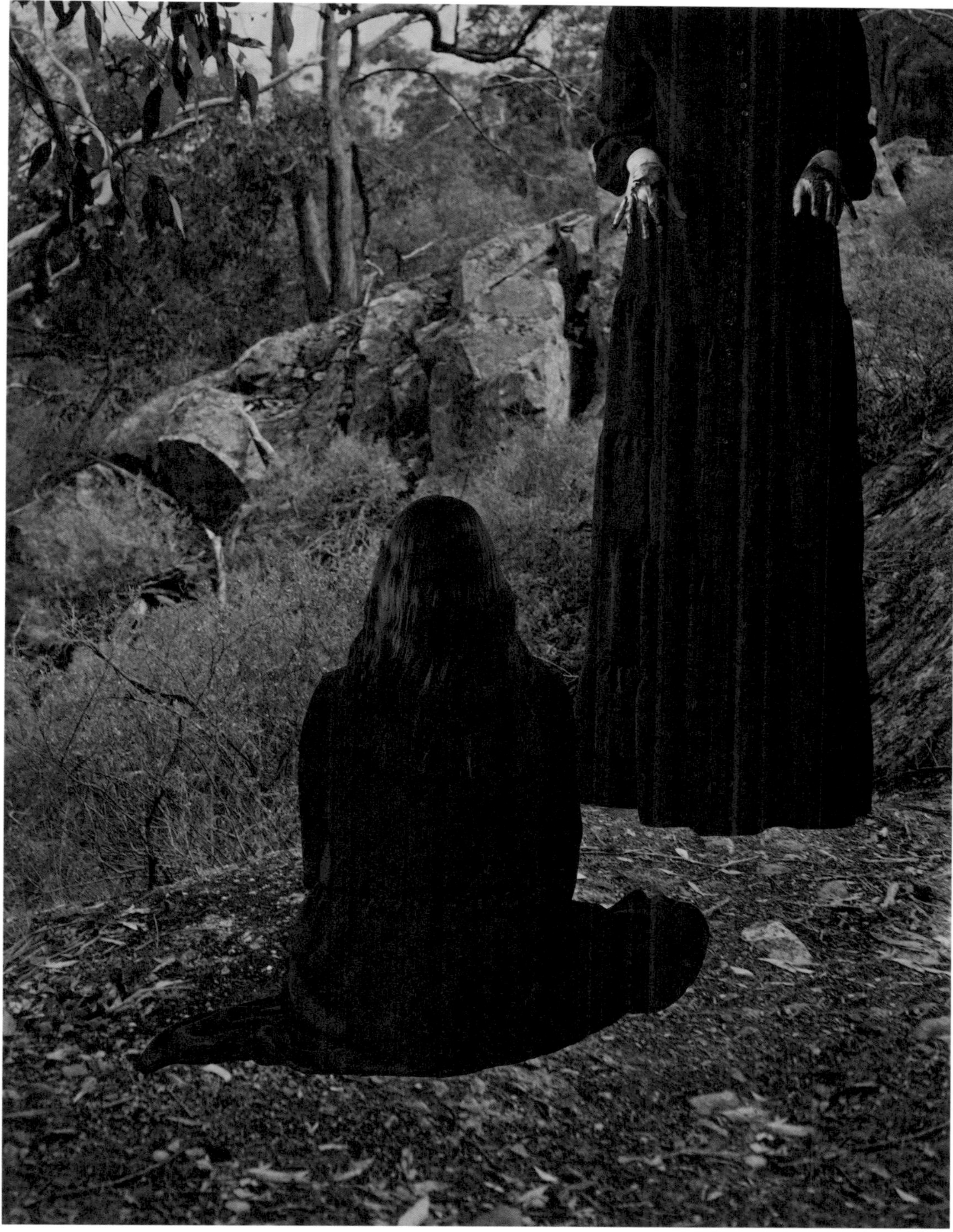

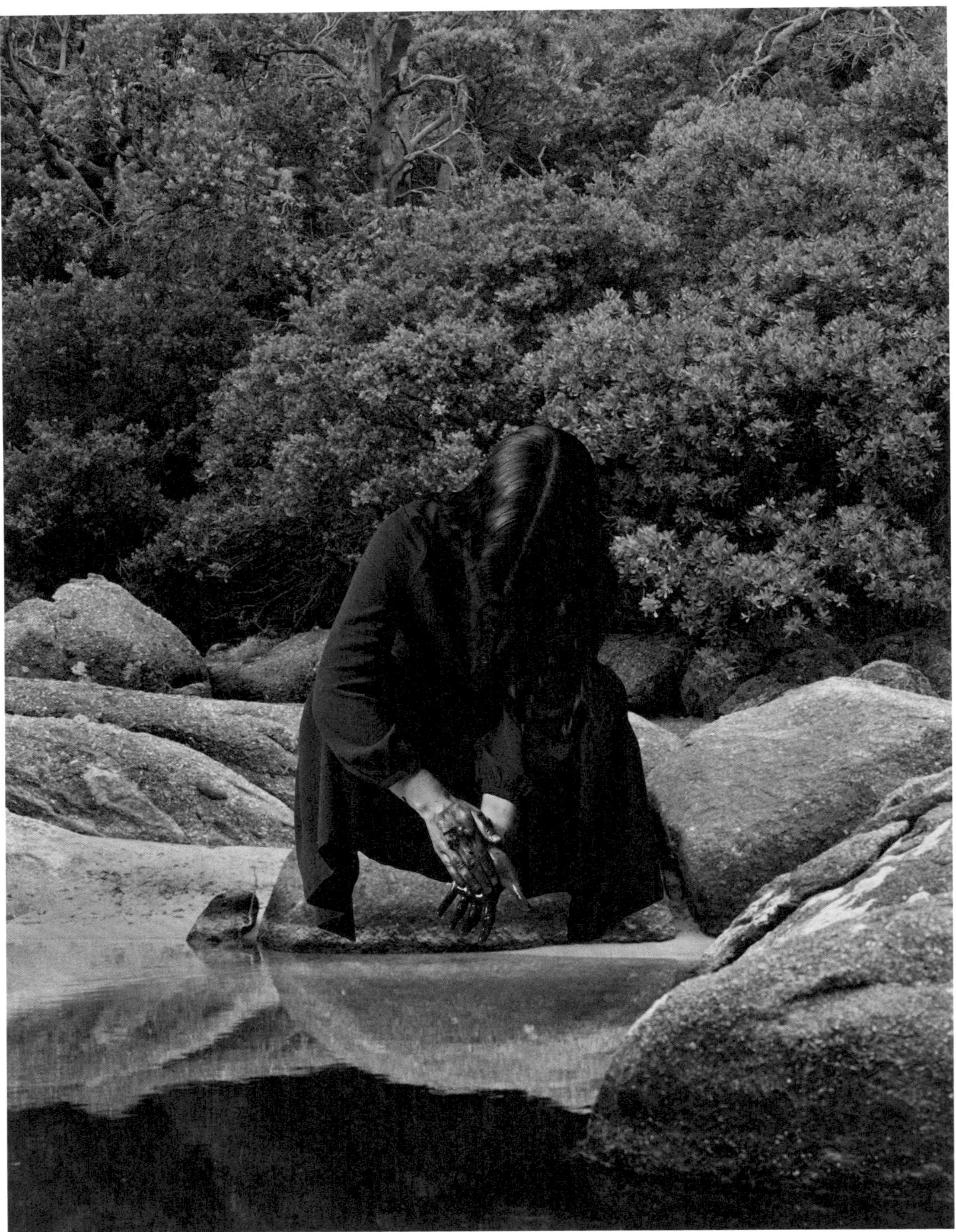

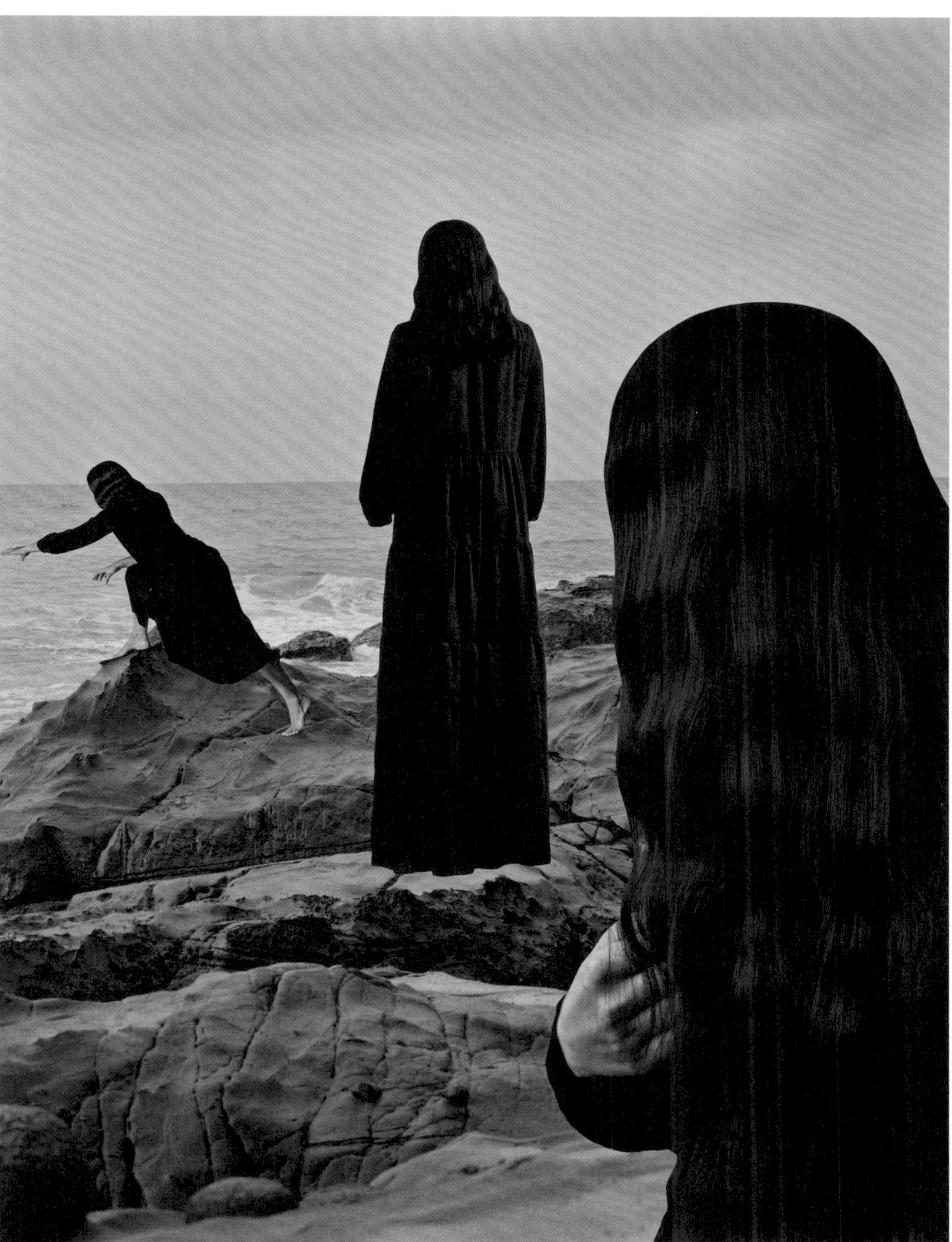

TITLE	MIDLIFE

COVER

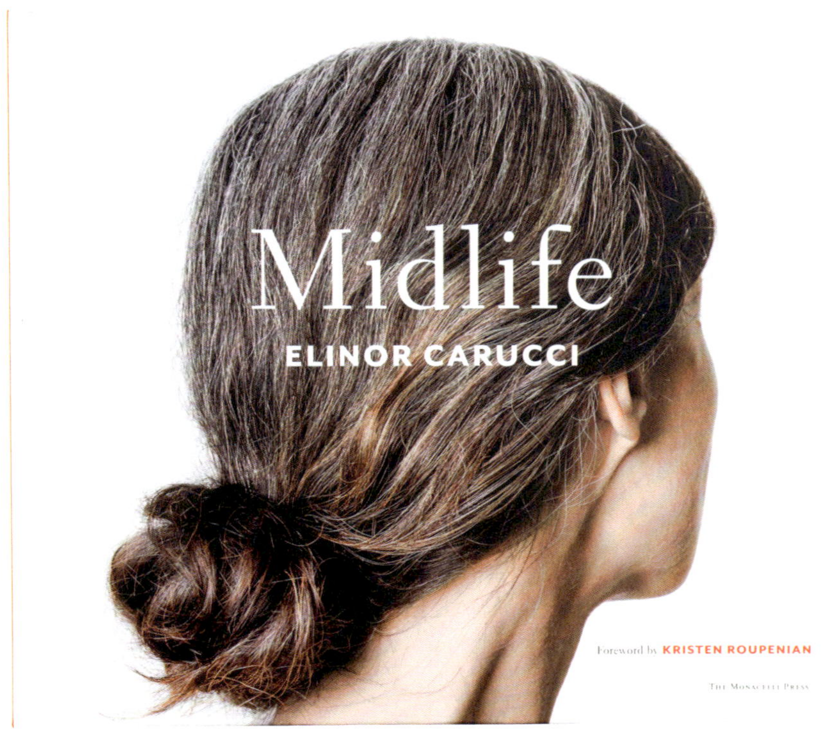

ARTIST	Elinor Carucci
PUBLISHER	The Monacelli Press
MONOGRAPHY	- 132 pages - first published in 2019 - size: 28.65 x 24.84 cm
SUMMARY	Elinor Carucci readily admits that her personal projects bear therapeutic and comforting virtues. With Midlife, the New York-based Israeli photographer explores the dynamics of her family life over the span of three generations, reconsidering the highs and lows marking her midlife. Her photographs, shot on the spot or staged, offer an intimate view of parenthood, life as a couple, illness and ageing. Through a close observation of herself, Carucci tries to understand how, on the eve of her fifties, she redefines herself as a girl, mother and woman. The images are both tender and straightforward; her hair is getting whiter, she needs glasses to read, she is being prepared for a mammogram, she undergoes a hysterectomy, her son and her daughter are growing, she shares the nights with her husband. "I've photographed my mother since I was 15, which has allowed me to understand the importance of sensitivity in my practice." A sensitivity that is also found in her paintings, made with her own blood, which are inserted in this volume. Visceral work in which emotional landscapes are deployed, the subtle variations of becoming.
BIOGRAPHY	Born in Jerusalem in 1971, Elinor Carucci moved to New York in 1995. She works for the press (*New York Times Magazine*, *New Yorker*, *W*, *Aperture*) and teaches at the School of Visual Arts in New York. She has published four fictional autobiographies: *Closer* (2002), *Diary of a Dancer* (2005), *Mother* (2013) and *Midlife* (2019).

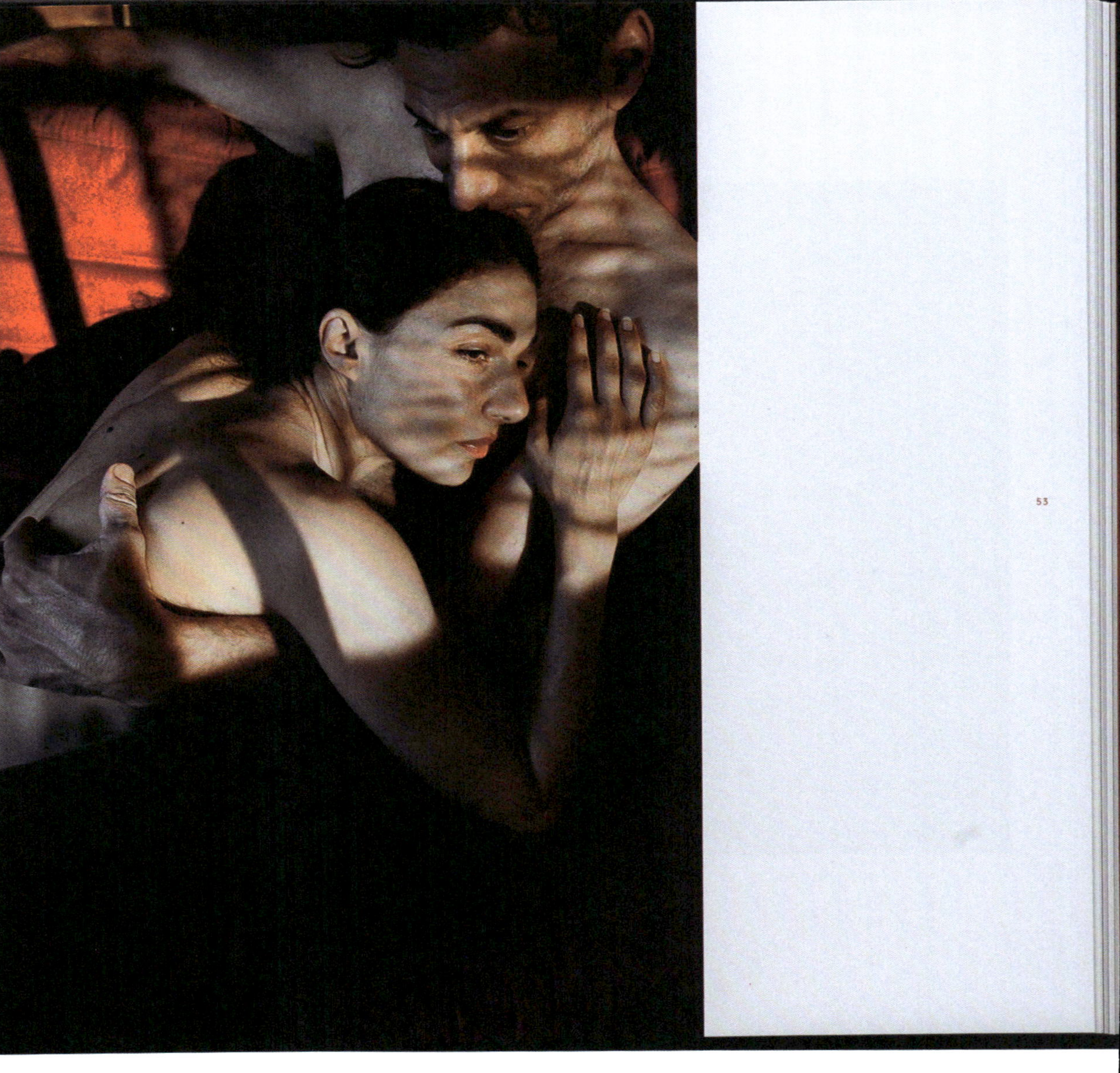

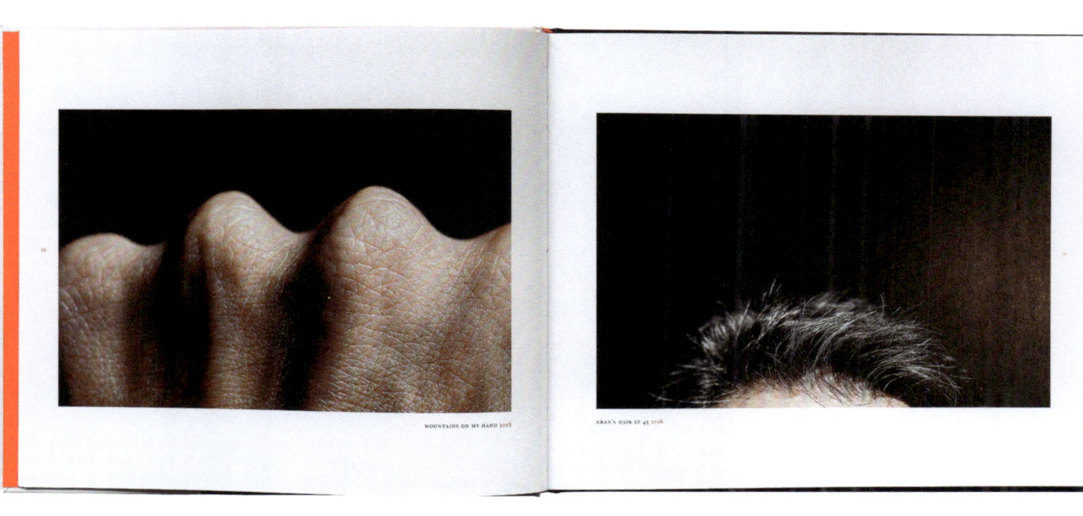
MOUNTAINS ON MY HAND 2016
ERAN'S HAIR AT 45 2016

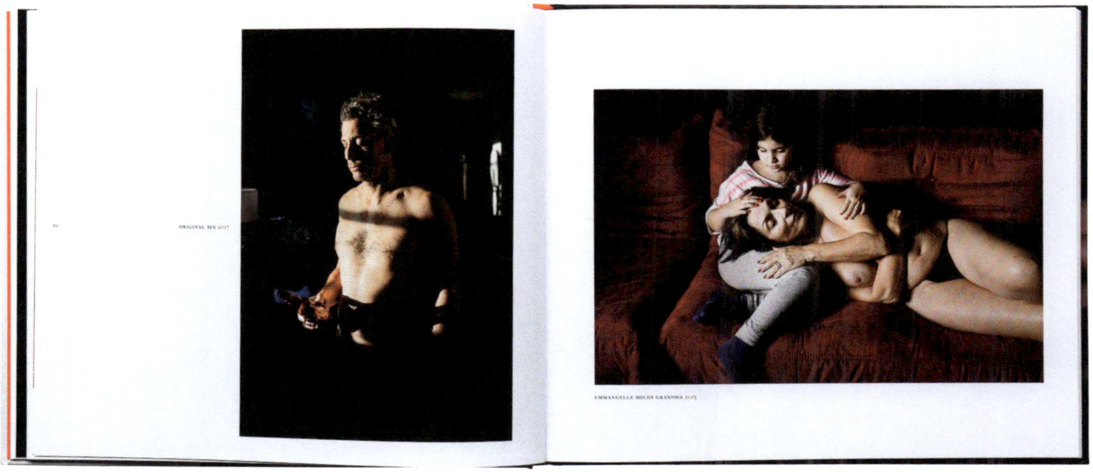
ORIGINAL SIN 2017
EMMANUELLE HOLDS GRANDMA 2015

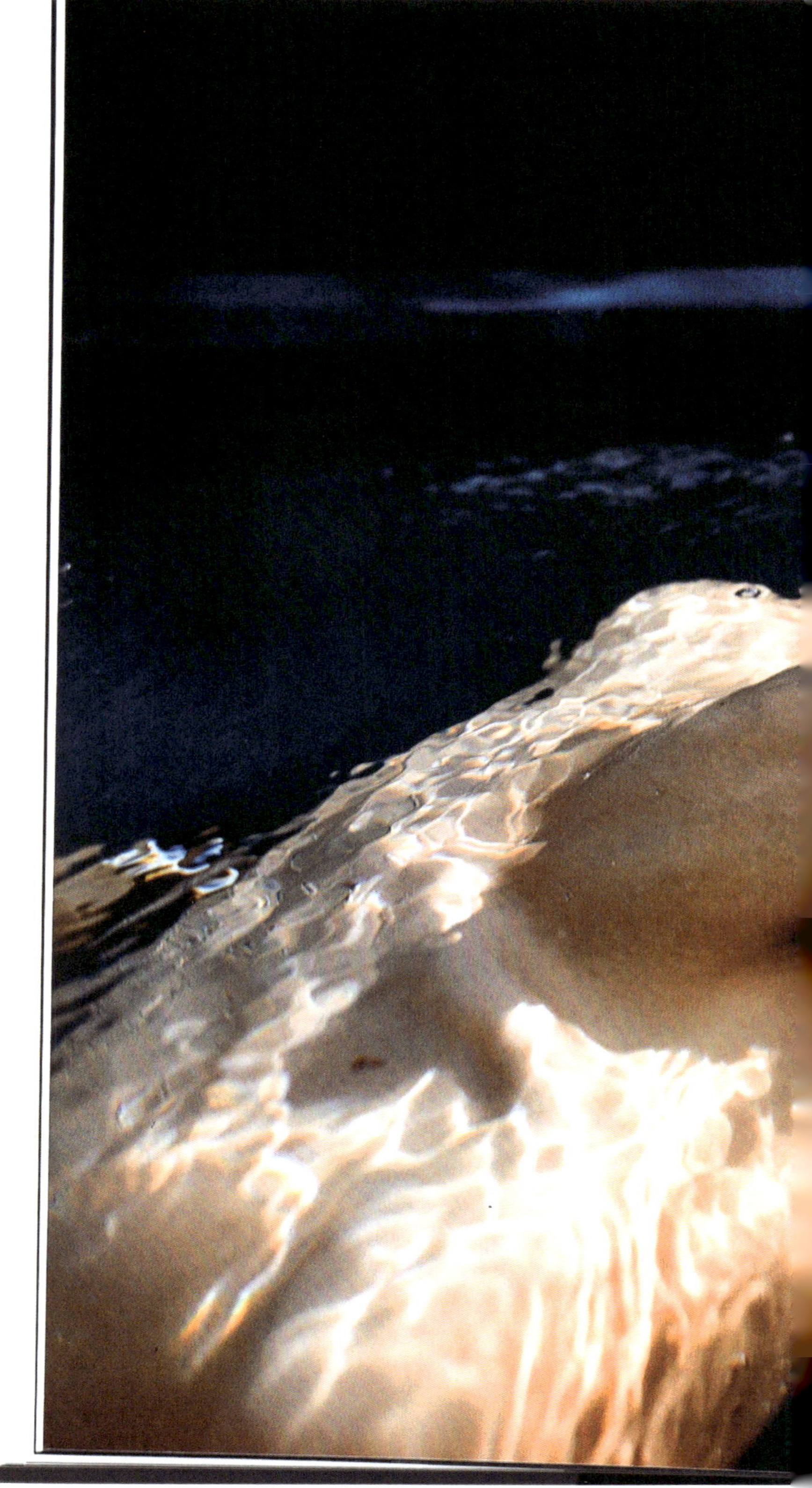

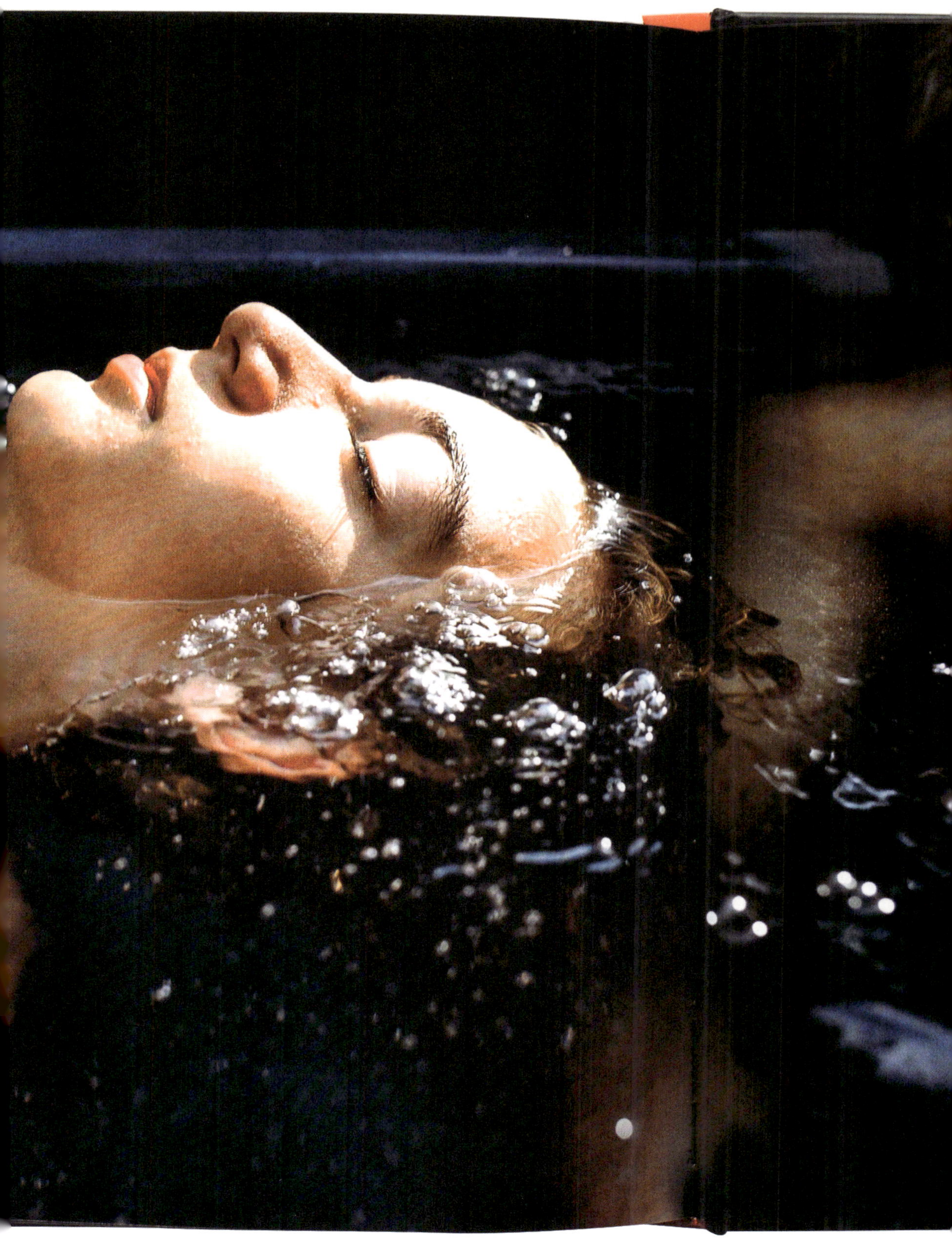

(AFTER)CARE
DANIELA VICHERAT MATTAR

"*El tiempo está después*"[1]
— María Gadú

After what? After, care? After being cared for? After caring? And before? And during? The notion of "(after)care" presupposes that care relations are linear, as if care is a progression from a state of "before care" to "caring" to "after care". In this logic, care is an achievement, a task to be performed, a need to be satisfied. But care is more than that; it is a relationship with – or better, a way of relating with – another (human or non-human) being. So, how to understand and visualize (after)care? And why does it matter for the ways in which we act and do things, like photography? In Spanish (my mother tongue), (after)care is not one word, it comes split as *after_care*. For me this is an invitation to tinker with both words separately before placing them together to understand what they do to one another. Let's start, like everything, with time.

After

According to the Merriam-Webster dictionary, *after* has multiple uses. As an adverb and preposition, it implies following, or a subsequent moment, in time and/or place. As an adjective it means later in time. As an auxiliary verb, it is used to indicate an action that is or has been completed. So, *after* points to a relation that has been established and exists in a progressive manner (a line of time). In this sense, the notion of time is grounded in an Aristotelian definition, considering time as the measure of change.[2] But, what if instead of focusing on the causal relationality of change (something is a trigger for something else to happen *after*) we focus our attention on the engagements and entanglements that allow the causality to happen, looking into the relations that enable them. After all, we are all always, all the time, in relation with otherness – either others who are relatively familiar (imagine your fellow citizens in any given country) or others who are so foreign that one believes not to have anything in common with them (imagine all those strangers with whom we share nothing). In fact, even in solitude, we exist in relation to a given and shared world (a material planet, a historical globe). If we turn our attention to questioning the ways in which we relate to the immeasurability of the otherness with which we share this planet, then *care* matters.

Care

Paradoxically, *care* is defined in the dictionary as a contradictory noun and verb. In both uses, *care* refers to a state of disquiet or feeling of anxiety, attention and responsibility, and at the same time, it can mean a state or feeling of desire, esteem or attention – an inclination towards or concern for something or someone. This paradox has been for decades a point of study for feminist scholarship. At its core the feminist critique reveals how the productive structures of society rest on the exploitation and invisibility of social reproductive work – that is, care work. Reasons for negating, neglecting and devaluing care work are multiple, but most noticeable is the fact that care is a gendered and racialized practice and a normalized disposition.[3] In fact, despite how fundamental care is for the well-functioning of individuals across their lives, in their daily life, and for the reproduction of society as a whole, those who provide care tend to be invisible, and their needs are less recognized than the needs of those privileged enough to be able to pay for care services.[4] This is very visible in many fields of care, from domestic work to health services, where the needs of care givers are subordinated to the needs of care receivers. Some scholars describe this subordination and invisibility as a form of privileged irresponsibility or epistemic ignorance – something one (un)consciously chooses not to recognize in all its importance.[5]

Following the influence of Black feminist works, there has been a recent call to politicize the study of care.[6] What would this imply for the ways in which we define *care*? Many argue that care is not an individual practice but is better understood as a continuous network of relations and negotiations for the support of both care givers and care receivers. A recurrent definition in care theory was elaborated by Joan Tronto and Berenice Fisher in 1990 when they suggested that "[o]n the most general level … caring be viewed as *a species activity that includes everything that we do to maintain, continue and repair our 'world' so that we can live in it as well as possible*. That world includes our bodies, ourselves and our environment, all of which we seek to interweave in a complex, life-sustaining web."[7] In viewing care as this fundamental practice of sustaining life, Tronto identifies four important dimensions:

1. Caring about (resulting from the tension between being attentive and the said epistemic ignorance towards care needs).
2. Taking care of (balancing out the differentials in the power dynamics derived from who, how, when and where the responsibilities for care are placed).
3. Care giving (different degrees of competence and accountability in delivering care in different contexts).
4. Care receiving (different degrees of responsiveness depending on the care needs).

If *care* is anything we do to maintain and sustain life, then *care* is fundamental because life is vulnerable. In fact, inherent to these four dimensions are internal contradictions derived from the unequal distribution of vulnerabilities and how those in positions of power have the prerogative to define what to care about and how to take care, while those in less powerful positions are left with the tasks of care giving and/or care receiving.[8] As a consequence, the assumption of the individual's agency is misleading because even if the responsibility (and accountability) of care giving is attached to those engaged in the (often) menial practice of delivering care, the real power rests in those with the power to define what care is needed when and where, how it is to be delivered, by whom and to whom, and why. In short, as a disposition and practice, care is defined mostly by the processes through which we think, value, recognize and represent what matters (why and to whom). In other words, one *cares* not because things have value in themselves, but rather because they are endowed with value by the care relations invested in them. Thus, how we signify something/someone as a matter of care is an inherently political act. If *care* is the result of processes of engaging with others in the continual maintenance of life, then when is that over? Or what would *(after)care* mean? And who or what could be positioned *after* care? One way of trying to make sense of whether or not there is any real basis to conceiving of a time that is possible *after* care is by connecting it with vulnerability, seeing (after)care as the potential moment when vulnerabilities are fully overcome and the complete autonomy of the self as an individual is achieved.

Vulnerability

Generally, vulnerability is understood as a condition of exposure to different types of risks, either due to conditions integral to one's body or as result of situational circumstances and changes.[9] In either case, the vulnerable individual has a reduced ability to respond to risk situations, whether because they lack assets, capacities or support. Since we are all dependent on structural support in the face of vulnerability at some point in life, it is also logical to argue that vulnerability is a structural condition. In fact, legal theorist Martha Fineman goes as far as describing it as a shared and universal human condition, even if this of course does not suggest that we are all vulnerable in an equal manner.[10] However, the myth of the autonomous (neo)liberal subject stresses a different approach to vulnerability, framing it rather as the result of each individual's actions and decisions, and thus responsibility. This is done with special acrimony when describing groups that are traditionally labelled as vulnerable, like women, racialized peoples, the poor – all identities that place individuals in these categories as publicly unable to make the right choices to overcome "their vulnerability". In this logic, vulnerability becomes a condition of "legibility" over certain bodies that are rendered weak, a burden and inherently susceptible to harm.[11] Agency is denied from those defined and represented as vulnerable; totalizing images of what "they" need become, in a paradoxically pathogenic manner, the justification for forms of paternalistic care. Yet, if vulnerability is what characterizes us as living beings, the narrative about the self-sustained individual misses the extent to which vulnerability is also the result of misrecognizing the profound interdependences of care that make any form of autonomy possible.

Thinking about autonomy as independence in line with the myth of the "self-made" individual overlooks the extent to which any sense and condition of autonomy depends on and is framed by structures – from socio-economic institutions, political-legal forms of recognition and rights enfranchisements, and socio-cultural systems that either recognize or negate the value of care.[12] These structures are never neutral, there is always a perspective that shapes how vulnerability and care are systematically (miss)recognized in relation to the unquestionable value of autonomy as an absolute condition.[13] In other words, what tends to be forgotten is how autonomy is always the result of a network of historical and place-based interdependencies and entanglements based on care relations.[14]

If we take interdependence seriously, as an ontological and existential condition, then the idea that there is some moment when vulnerabilities are overcome, when care is not needed, a moment *post* care when the individual is a complete, self-bounded, autonomous being, seems absurd. Undoubtedly, one of the biggest achievements of modernity is the emancipation of the individual from the constraints of tradition and various types of authority (most noticeably religious and political). What is tenaciously forgotten or neglected from this epochal exaltation of individual freedom and emancipation is the extent to which any experience of total autonomy is illusory, because the autonomous self is never an abstract isolated being. The individual self always rests on a network of interdependencies that support it and make autonomy possible (human and/or non-human, from technology to nature).

In this sense, what characterizes us as living beings is that, in one way or another, we are all care receivers. The problem, though, is that not everyone is ready to recognize the need to also be(come) care givers, and the burdens of care keep on being disproportionally shouldered by women, especially racialized migrant women. Hence, there is an urgent need to change dominant normative images of vulnerability and care. Photography, like British photographer and photo therapist Jo Spence suggests, can play a crucial role in exploring ways to reframe and overturn these normative ideas, so "words and images can take on new and different meanings and relationships and old ideas can be transformed".[15]

Photography

As an artistic practice, photography is neither directly nor explicitly contingent on care giving. Yet, as the works in this issue reveal, in the process of image making care should be taken at every step, especially if you recall the first two dimensions of care discussed above: defining what to care about (making it (in)visible) and how to do it (the exercise of framing). It matters how vulnerability and violence are represented and made visible to the public eye, and who has the power to define them and with what aim. It matters not only as a descriptive task, but mostly to question traditional ways of understanding the roles of care giving and care receiving in contexts of vulnerability and violence. Perhaps this can even help question the prescribed and normalized roles of the photographer and the photographed, especially if the practice of photography is to be understood and transformed as a care act.[16]

I would like to suggest that to act with care requires being open to being transformed by the otherness of others. To develop skills to become aware of the order we unconsciously impose when looking at alterity, from the moment we direct our attention and lens (or choose to ignore, as a form of privileged ignorance). To conceive of photography as a practice of care, it is necessary to tinker constantly with imagination, compassion and action – all forms of engagement in which we can actively resist the temptation of seeking to attain and represent a complete and total image of alterity. In this sense, considering care both as a disposition *and* a practice, the positionality of the photographer is from the onset one that negotiates with(out) care the otherness that is to be photographed.[17] As a practice that mediates reality, photography holds relative power to define, give shape to, represent and frame vulnerability and care, either as experiences to be overcome (so there will be a moment *after* them), or as inescapable and constitutive conditions of being alive (thus partial and unfinished). In doing the latter, there is no space for abstract and neutral representations of alterity, because what is at stake is precisely the recognition that all points of view are interconnected, each with a given perspective and specific aim.

What I am contending here is that care, as an idea and a practice, is by definition incomplete. It is a constant invitation to explore the question of what matters, when, why and for whom, and what position one has in all of it (or in other words, how are we implicated in what we see and how we do it). The fact that a photograph is always, and by definition, taken from somewhere, for someone and for some purpose, raises far-reaching questions about the personal position, the direct and relational accountability and the capacity of the photographer to negotiate how to frame and represent fragments of the world in which we are all entangled. A caring way to do so requires beginning by resisting the tendency to do so in an abstract, apparently neutral, and totalizing manner.[18] A caring way demands recognizing difference in its incommensurability and the inescapability of our participation in it.

(After)care

So far I have attempted to argue that the (after)care question is not a temporal one – after care, what? – but a procedural one about how to care; how to do so in ways that recognize that "the needs of" and "to care" are at the core of life's infinite interdependencies. To politicize and democratize care implies thinking of it as an affective disposition that connects the self to others (or, in other words, how self-care can never be carried out without care for another). Care implies immersing ourselves in feeling/thinking *with* – instead of feeling/thinking *for* – others. Mobilizing care as a goal requires us to be aware of the extent to which we are involved in the acts of preservation and maintenance of individuals, communities and different social worlds.[19] To help with this, then photography can mobilize new forms of imagining, reimagining, thinking and acting "other-wise" rather than "self-wise" with care.[20]

My attempt here has been to invite you to think how, in the care/vulnerability dance, there is no *after*. If this is so, then there is only time to care. All the rest comes after.

Daniela Vicherat Mattar (Santiago, 1974) is Associate Professor of Sociology at Leiden University in The Hague. Her research, teaching and publications gravitate around 3Cs: Cities, Citizenship and Care, how they are thought, imagined, contested and experienced. Currently she is senior fellow at Mecila (Maria Sibylla Merian Centre Conviviality-Inequality in Latin America) based in São Paulo, where she is working on the project *The Union of Disunion: Spatialising the Inequality-Conviviality Nexus* in Chile, looking at the history and experiences of Plaza Dignidad/Italia/Baquedano in Santiago.

1 "Time is after" – My translation.

2 In philosophy, time, although dominant, is not only conceived as the measure of change following Aristotle and Heraclitus. Another line of thought, following Parmenides and Zeno, contends that change is just a mental illusion of the totality of life, hence time is just an idea of the mind. See Adrian Bardon *A Brief History of the Philosophy of Time* (OUP, 2013).

3 For instance, in its 2020 report "Time to Care", Oxfam estimates that out of the 67 million domestic workers worldwide, about 80% are women, with about half of them lacking minimum wage protection, and more than half having no legal protection on their working hours – patterns exacerbated by the internationalization of the domestic work industry and traffic, which follows a south/north pattern, clearly framed by acute racial and class inequalities. Alison Jaggar calls our attention to how this system rests on logics of coerced consent that make it even more difficult to dismantle. See Alison Jaggar "We Fight for Roses Too: Time-Use and Global Gender Justice", *Journal of Global Ethics* 9/2 (2013), 115–129.

4 Joan Tronto *Moral Boundaries: A Political Argument for an Ethics of Care* (Routledge, 1994), 116.

5 See Riikka Prattes " 'I Don't Clean Up after Myself': Epistemic Ignorance, Responsibility and the Politics of Outsourcing of Domestic Cleaning", *Feminist Theory* 0/0 (2019), 1–21.

6 On the politics of care see the work of Deva Woodly. Important is also the work of Beatriz Nascimento on the Brazilian quilombos as places of resistance and care, or the decolonial feminist work of Maria Lugones and Rita Segato.

7 Joan Tronto *Moral Boundaries: A Political Argument for an Ethics of Care* (Routledge, 1994), 103.

8 Ibid. 144.

9 See Catriona Mackenzie, Wendy Rogers and Susan Dodds (eds.) *Vulnerability: New Essays in Ethics and Feminist Philosophy* (OUP 2014).

10 See Martha Fineman "The Vulnerable Subject: Anchoring Equality in the Human Condition", *Yale Journal of Law and Feminism* 20/1/2 (2008).

11 Erinn Cunniff Gilson eloquently describes how the association between femininity and vulnerability is also at the core of women's susceptibility to harm and violability. See "Vulnerability and Victimization: Rethinking Key Concepts in Feminist Discourses on Sexual Violence", *Signs: Journal of Women in Culture and Society* 42/1 (2016), 71–98.

12 In the words of Susan Dodds, "we are inherently vulnerable to dependency". See Susan Dodds "Dependence, Care, Vulnerability" in Catriona Mackenzie, Wendy Rogers and Susan Dodds (eds.) *Vulnerability: New Essays in Ethics and Feminist Philosophy* (OUP, 2014), 194.

13 In other words, my contention here is that neither autonomy nor neutrality can be fully attained, because both are dependent on the relationships that make them possible (often defined in terms of power inequalities that enable a single individual and/or their perspective to be conceived of as the desirable and universal one).

14 The privileged irresponsibility and epistemic ignorance I discussed above can here be understood in relation to this "self-made" fiction that enables an individual to neglect and dismiss the care relationships that make that sense of autonomy, undermining in turn the value of care work and care giving.

15 See Jo Spence's exhibition "Libido Uprising" (1–31 August 2019), https://www.richardsaltoun.com/viewing-room/6-jo-spence-libido-uprising/

16 An example of this practice can be the seen in the graduation work of Federica Iozzo at the KABK in 2021, the production of a care album. For more information see https://graduation2021.kabk.nl/students/federica-iozzo

17 I want to thank the comment of my student Eline Koopmann, who suggested on an early version of this essay that I should think about photography as an act and practice of negotiation.

18 I am aware that photographers hold relative power to do this in as much as they are also conditioned by their own vulnerabilities, positionalities, possibilities and relationships with their patrons. However, there is a strong care potential in framing and producing images of others and the world.

19 Hi'ilei Julia Kawehipuaakahaopulani Hobart and Tamara Kneese "Radical Care: Survival Strategies for Uncertain Times", *Social Text* 38/1/142 (2020), 1–16.

20 Kathleen Lynch "Love Labour as a Distinct and Non-Commodifiable Form of Care Labour", *The Sociological Review* 55/3 (2007), 550–750.

JOANA CHOUMALI

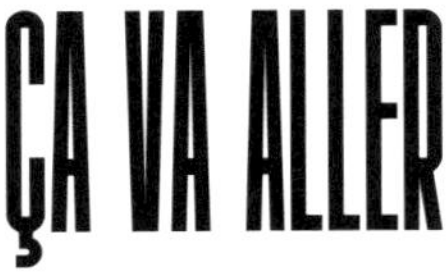

When she returns to Grand-Bassam, Côte d'Ivoire, after the 2016 terrorist attacks, Joana Choumali does not recognize the refuge city she cherished. The air quality has changed and the once bubbling life of the streets seems numbed by sadness, stuck in suffering and pain. All is loneliness and melancholy. Like the other survivors, she feels an immense and inexpressible sense of loss.

In order to reconnect with her "defamiliarized" environment, Choumali begins a "dialogue of hope" between the places and the people who cross them. She goes out at dawn to capture suspended moments on her iPhone: men and women alone, motionless or moving, deserted landscapes. For her, "walking in the morning is like walking on a blank page where everything can be printed".

By embroidering on the photographic medium of her work, Choumali revives her pieces and weaves a chronicle of fractures. Coloured stitch after coloured stitch, by the repetition of restorative gestures, she sutures her wounds. At the same time, she perpetuates the patience of her grandmother, who sewed *n'zassa*, colourful patchworks composed of disparate scraps of wax.

The artist also confronts a cultural taboo in a country where one does not express personal feelings, where mental health issues are mocked or even ignored. Ça Va Aller (It's going to be okay), the title of the series, is the Ivorian expression commonly used to politely close conversations that touch on trauma or emotional struggles.

Ça Va Aller, 2019, mixed media
© Joana Choumali, courtesy Sperone Westwater

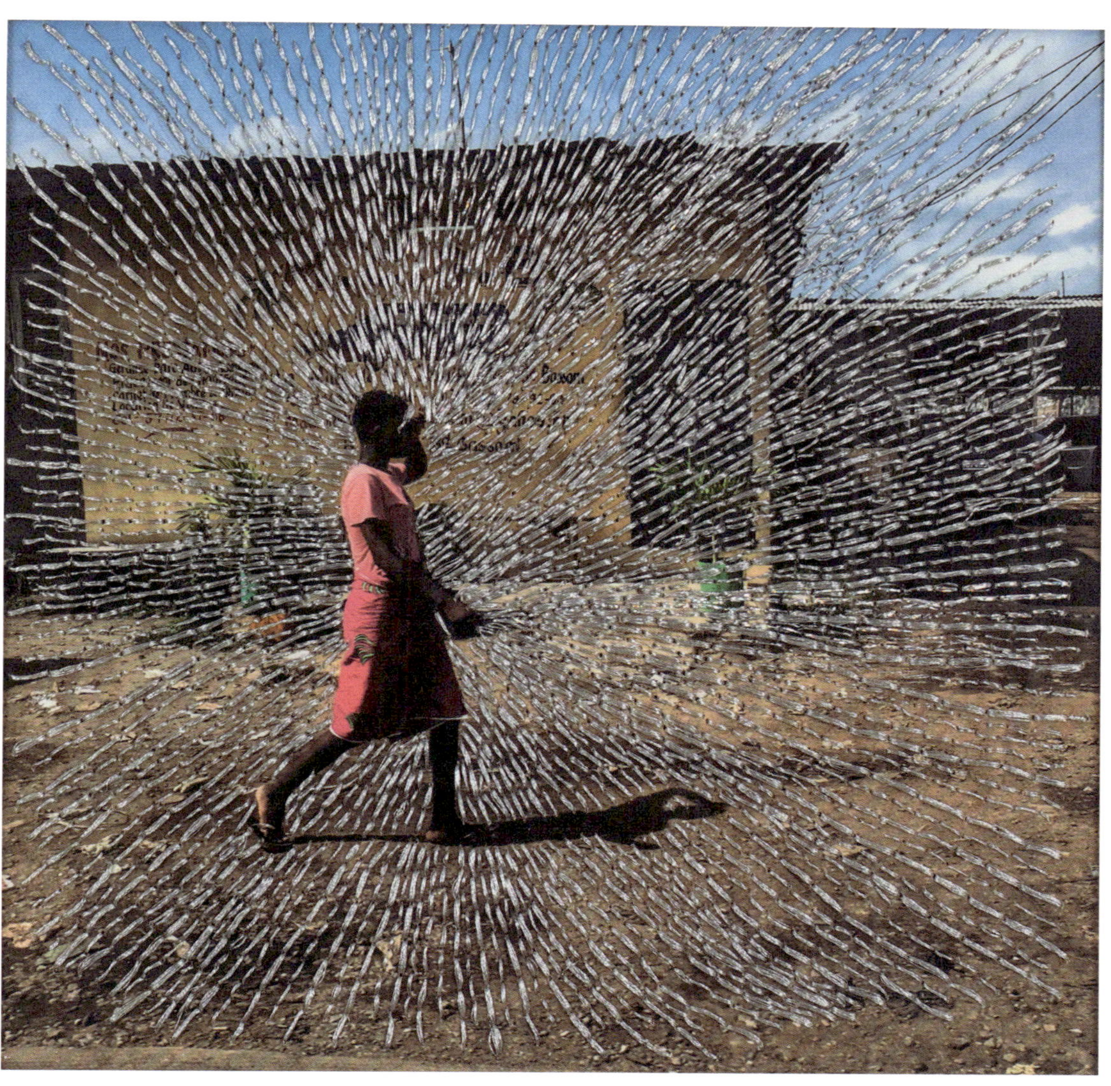

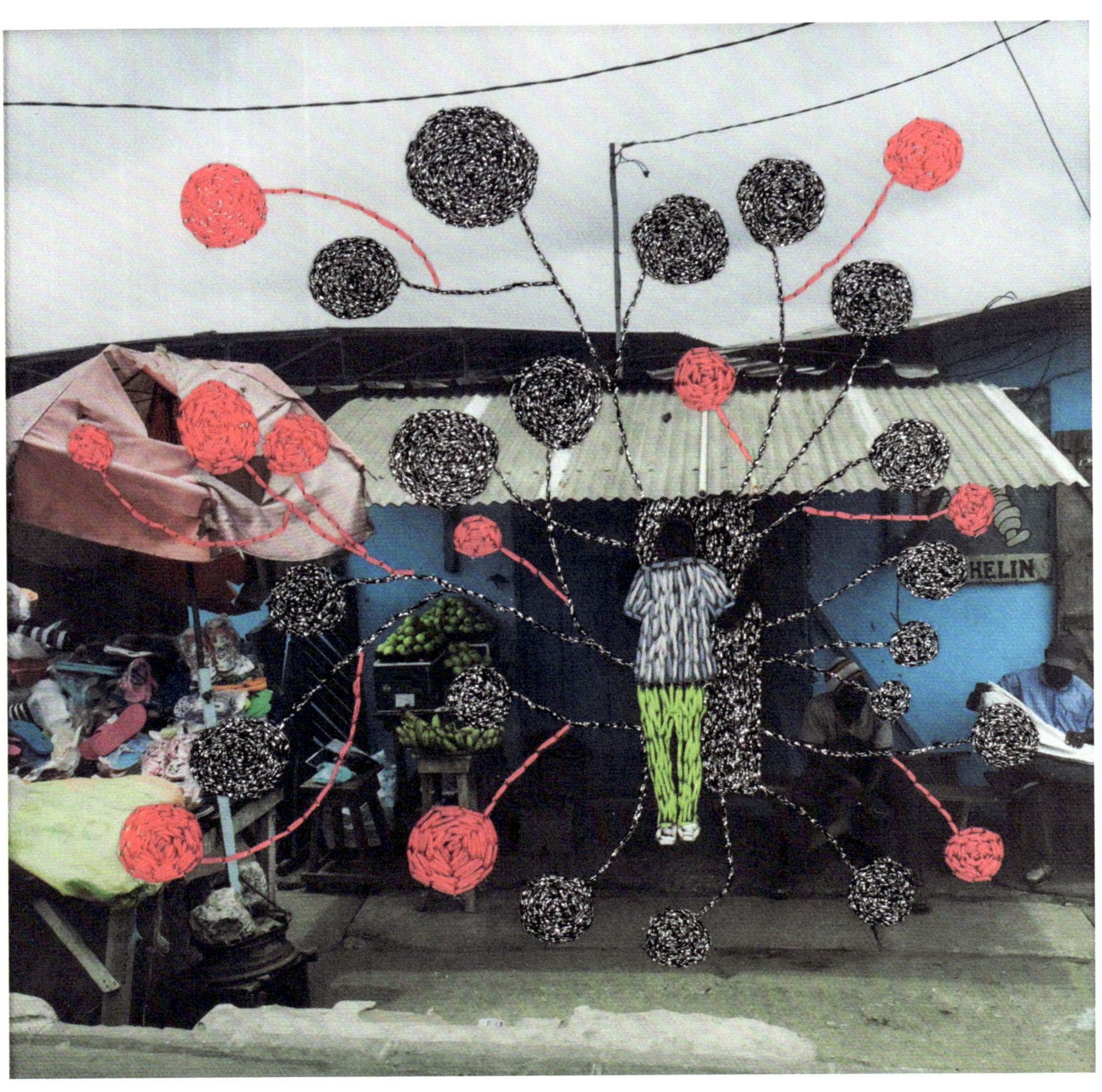
HELIN

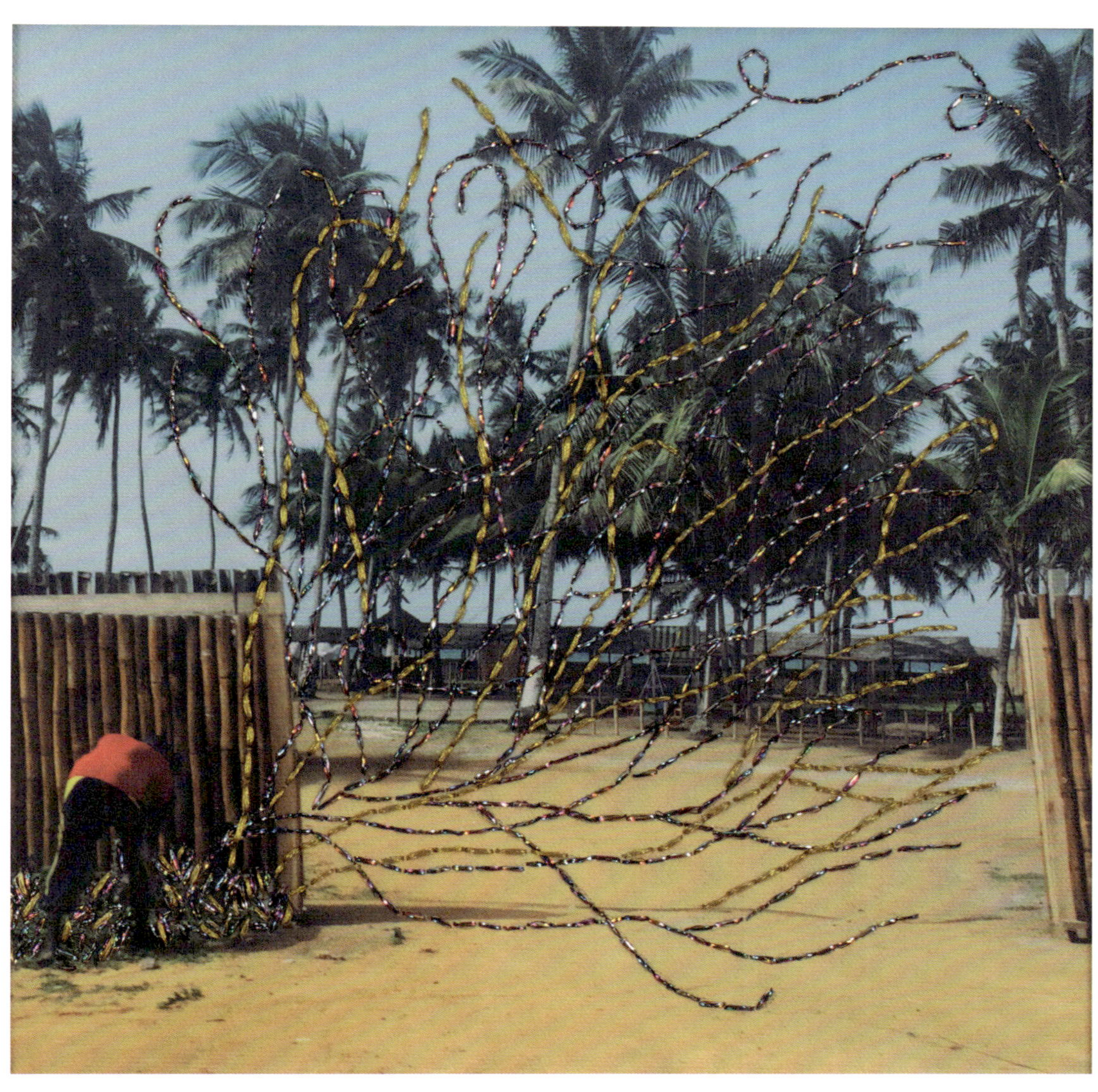

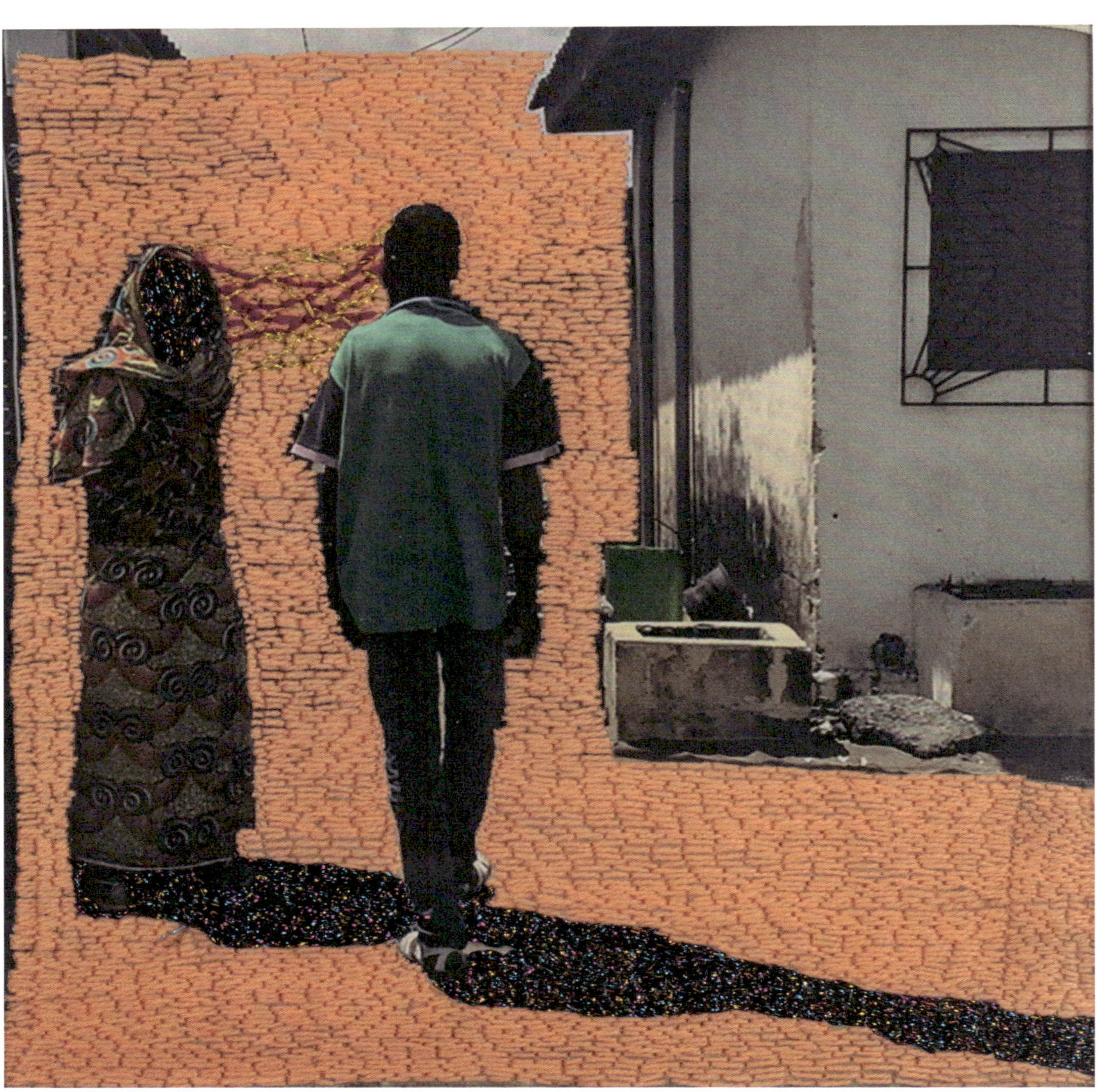

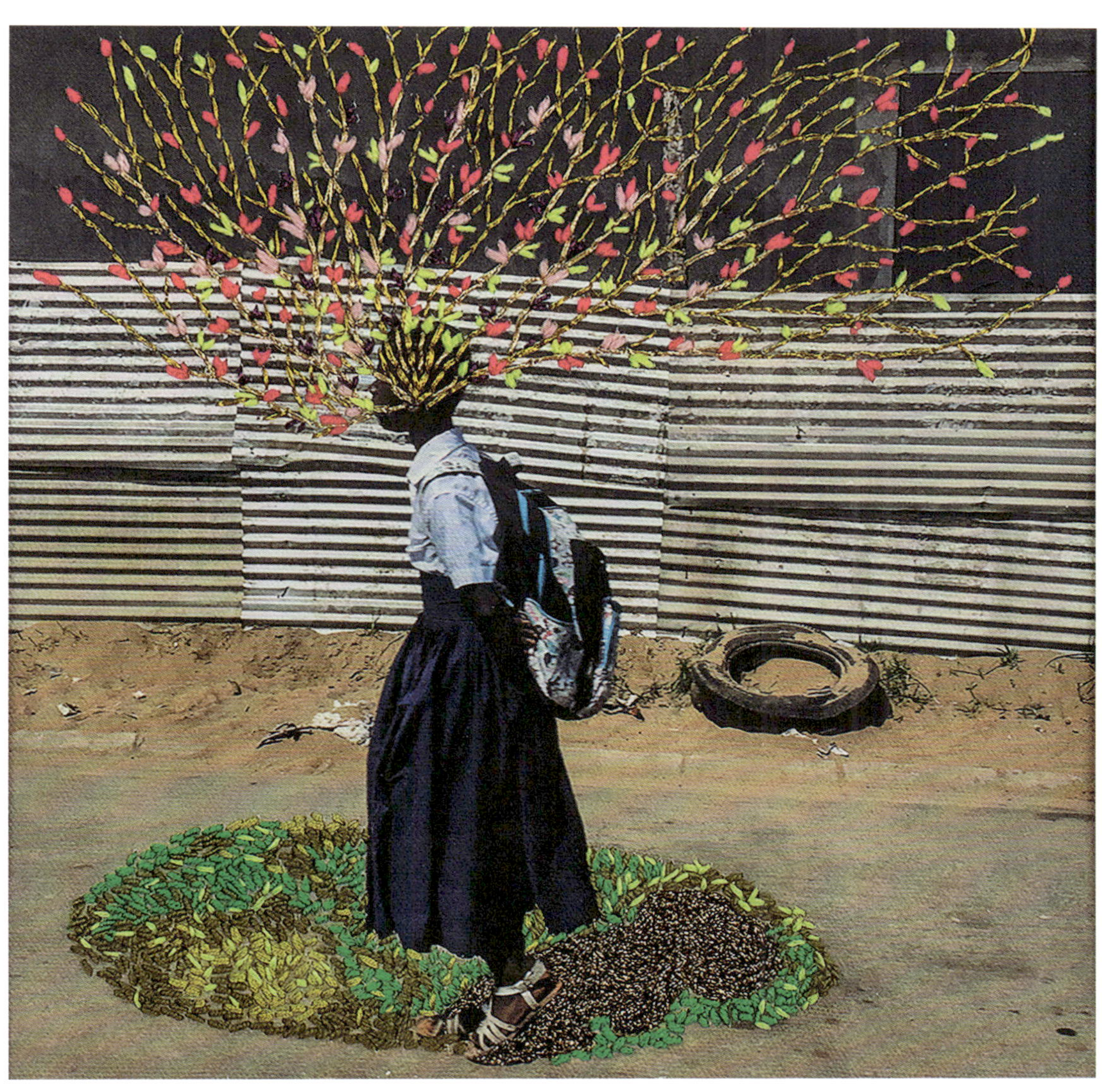

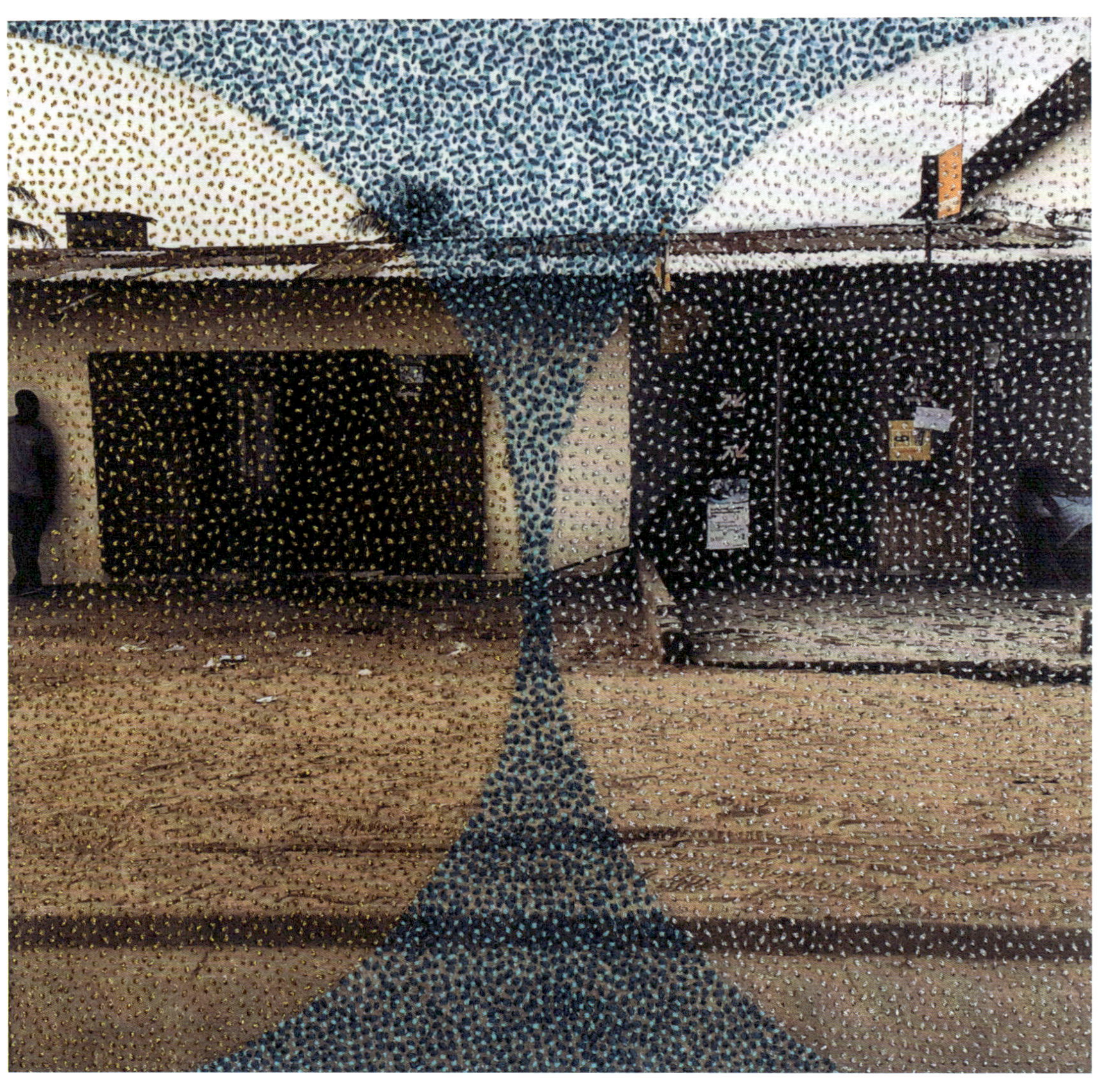

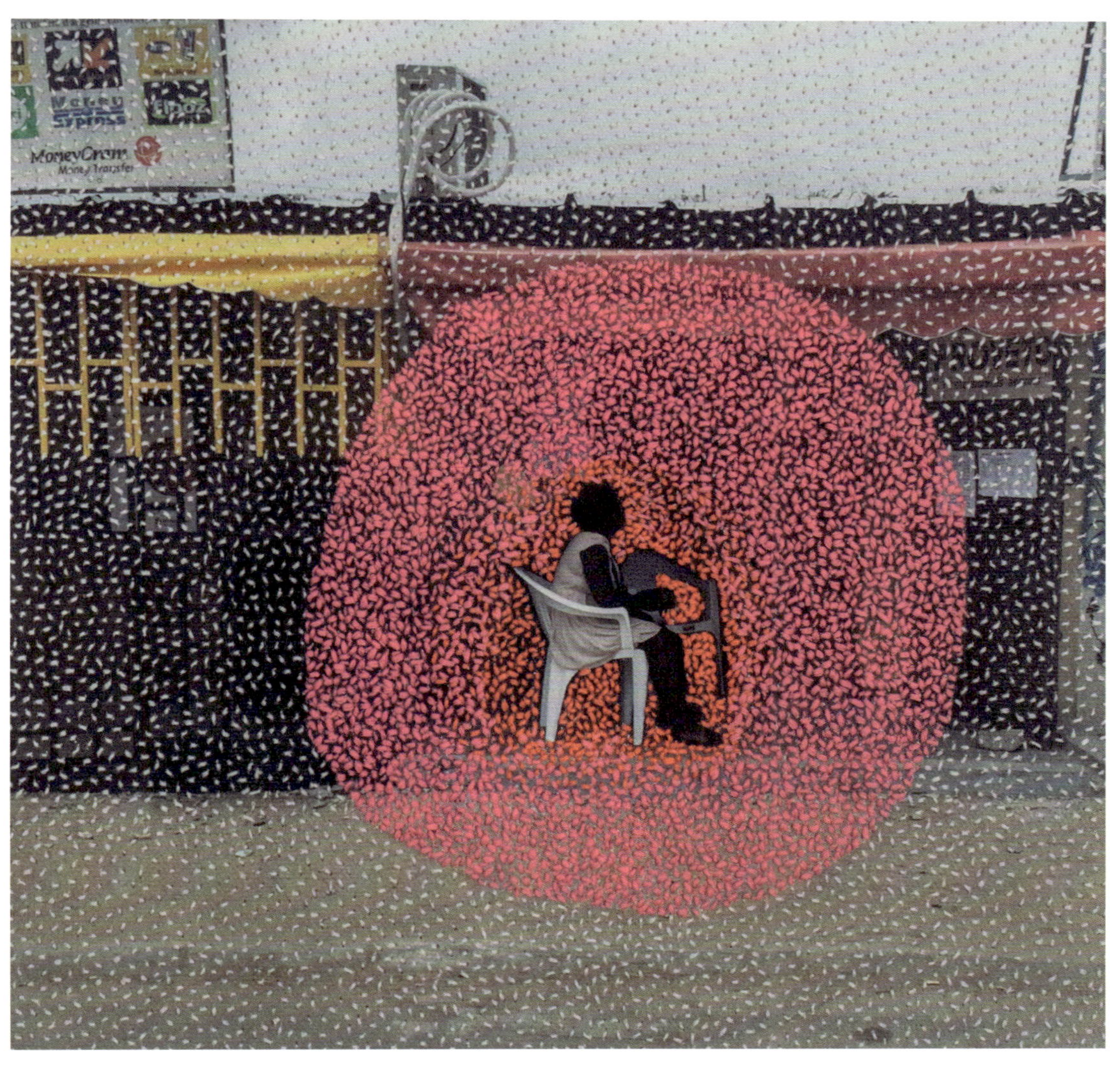

TITLE

JARDÍN DE MI PADRE

COVER

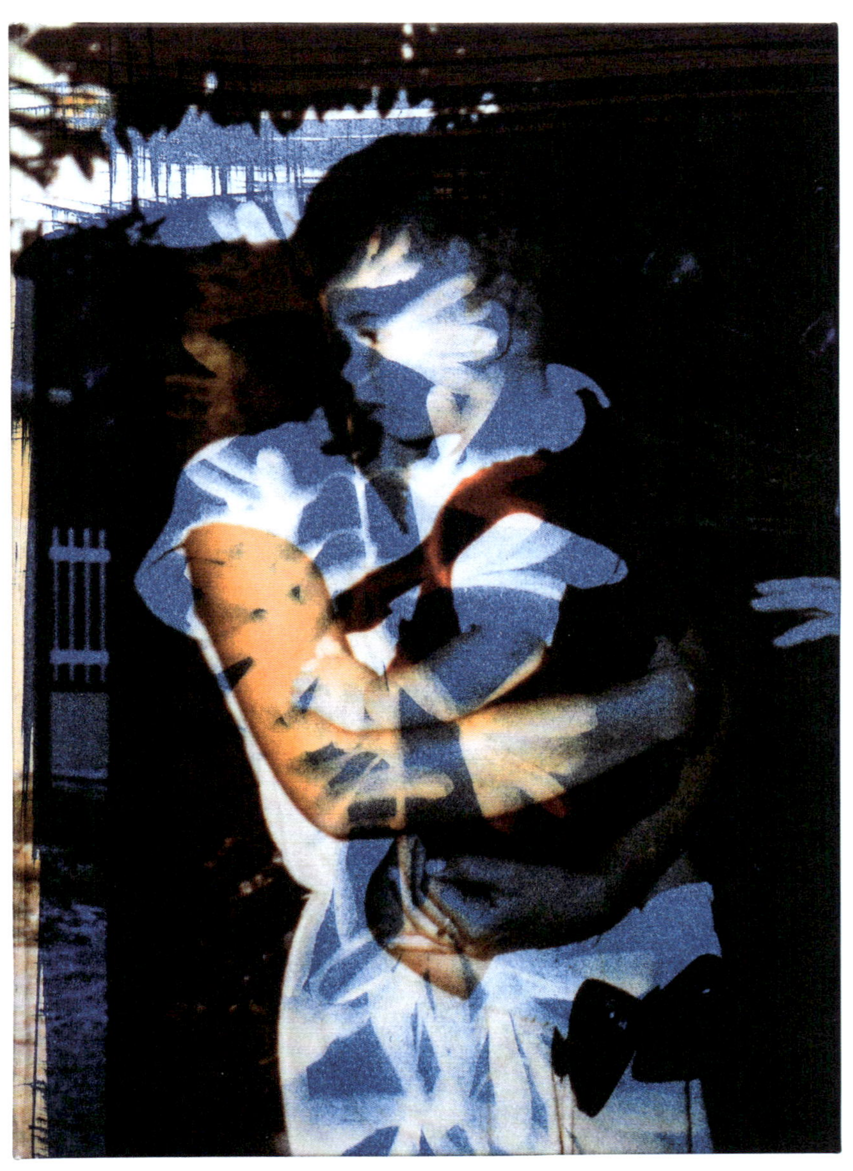

ARTIST	Luis Carlos Tovar
PUBLISHER	Editorial RM
MONOGRAPHY	- 240 pages - first published in 2020 - size: 19.8 x 28 cm
SUMMARY	On 20 February 1980, Jaime Tovar was kidnapped by the FARC (Revolutionary Armed Forces of Colombia) and sequestered in Caquetá, in the Amazon rainforest. A Polaroid proving that he was still alive was sent to his family. Jealously kept in his most secret and personal files, this photo is part of the family saga. Jaime's son, Luis Carlos Tovar, has never seen it. It is at the heart of this foundational absence, probing the difficulty of understanding his father's silence, sorrow and pain, that the Colombian artist anchors his work. *Jardín de mi padre* (My father's garden) tries to reconstruct a denied memory, the traumatic experience of captivity. During his detention, Jaime Tovar collected butterflies, leaves, flowers and grains that he preserved between the pages of the revolutionary books he was forced to read – Karl Marx's *Capital*, Ernesto Che Guevara's *The Bolivian Diary* and Lenin's *What Is To Be Done?* His harvests allowed him to cultivate his memories and fight for his survival. On his return from captivity, he set out to create a garden that reminded him of the Amazonian lagoons. Somewhere between an outdated family album, an entomological notebook and an archive file, Luis Carlos Tovar's book opens a dreamlike space-time that aims to reweave the undone bonds and make visible all the contrasting affects contained in the absent image.
BIOGRAPHY	Born in 1979 in Bogotá (Colombia), Luis Carlos Tovar works at the crossroads of photography, engraving, collage and video installation. Combining post-photography and archival work, his projects explore geographical discontinuity and post-memory. He teaches and facilitates workshops with vulnerable populations and refugees. He lives in Paris and Bogotá.

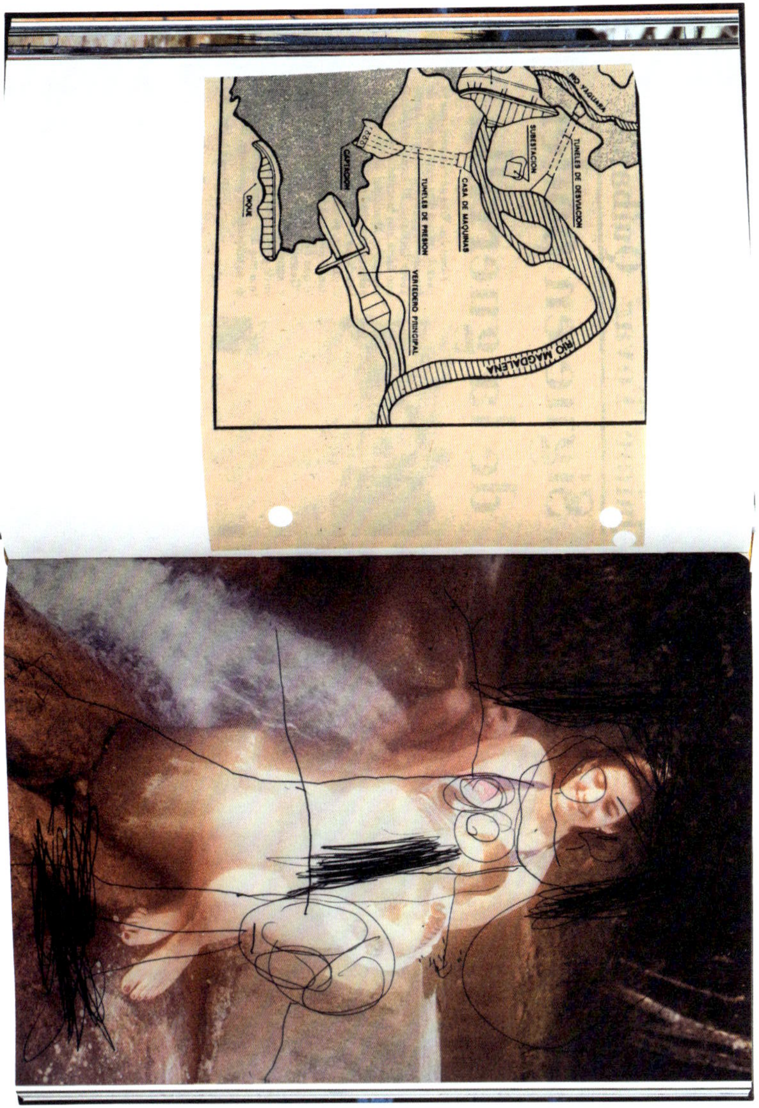

RIO YAGUARA
TUNELES DE DESVIACION
SUBESTACION
CASA DE MAQUINAS
TUNELES DE PRESION
VERTEDERO PRINCIPAL
RIO MAGDALENA
CAPTACION
DIQUE

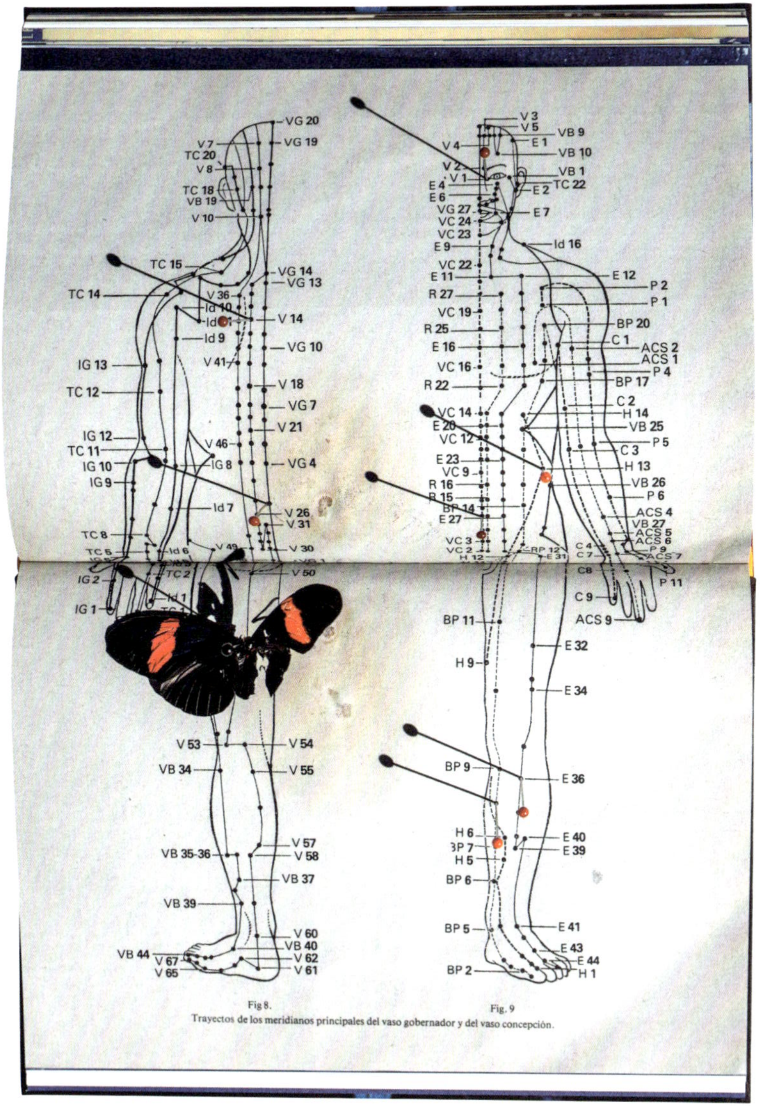

Fig 8.

Fig. 9

Trayectos de los meridianos principales del vaso gobernador y del vaso concepción.

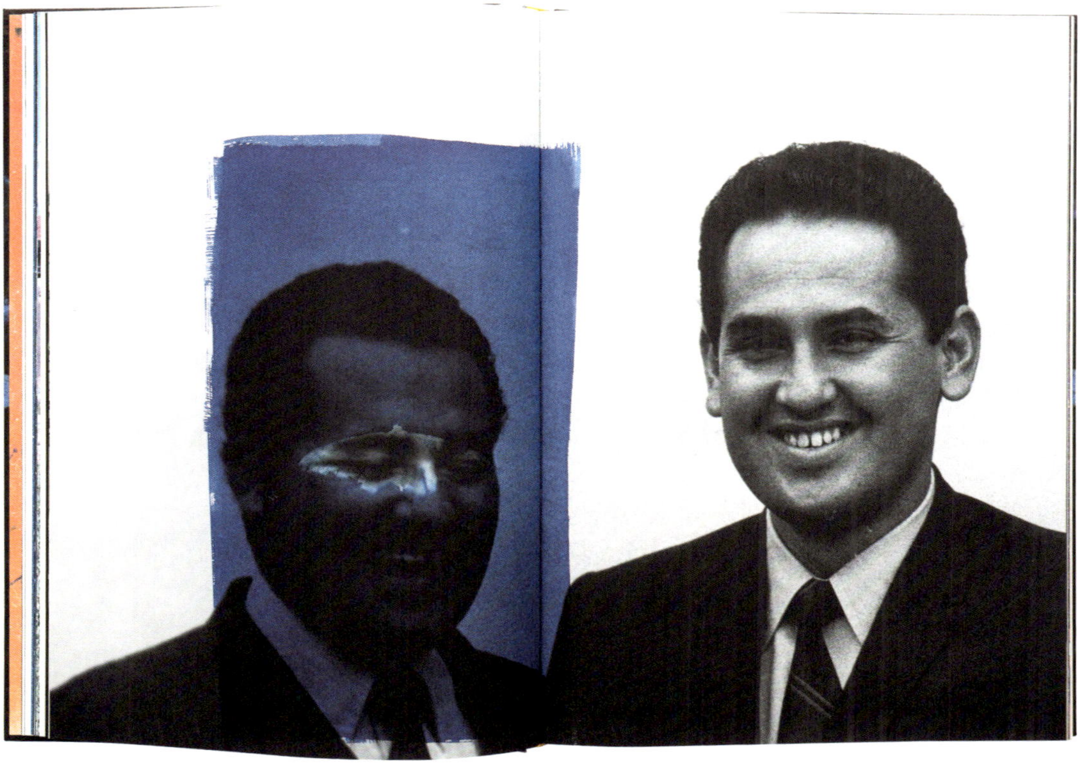

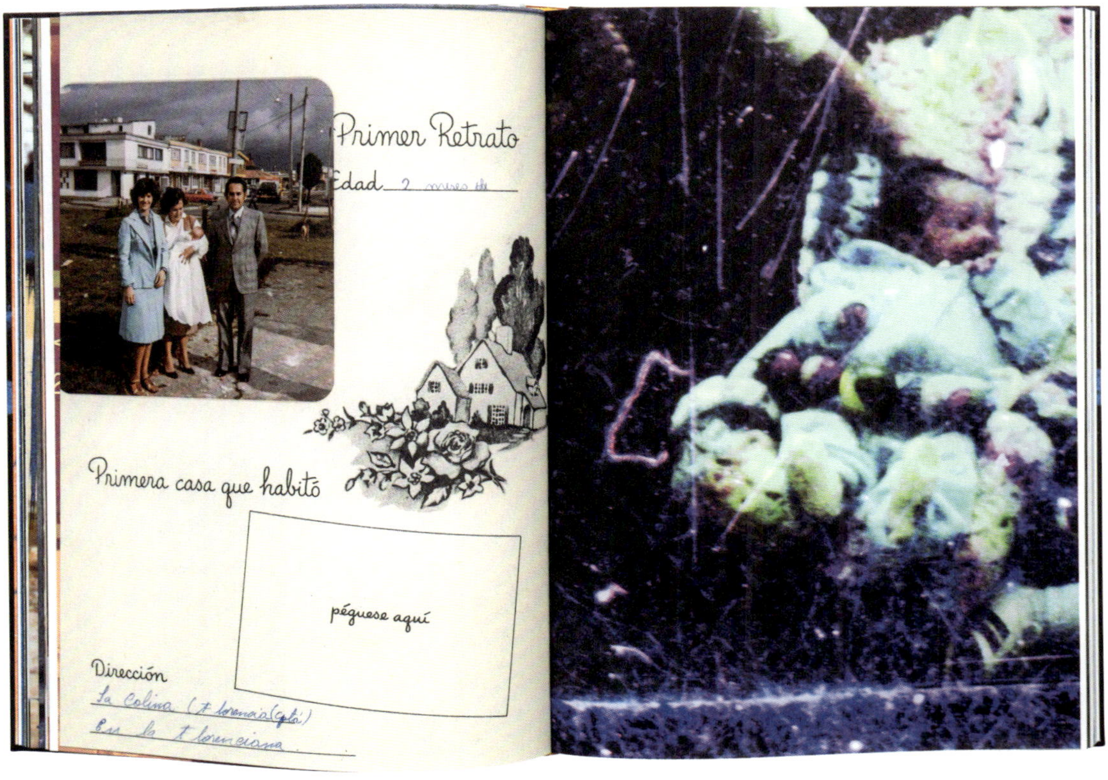

Primer Retrato

Edad 2 meses de

Primera casa que habitó

péguese aquí

Dirección

La Colina (Florencia (Cota))

En la Florenciana

Jaime Tovar Quibano

Sigue en poder de la guerrilla

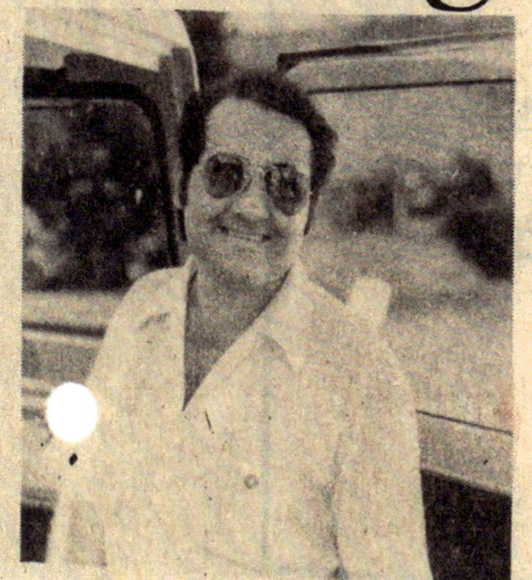

Florencia. Tras un cautiverio que y pasa de quince días sigue en poder d fuerzas irregulares el industrial Jaim Tovar Quibano. El joven profesion que fuera alto funcionario en la adm nistración Municipal de Medellín hubiera desechado muy buenas opo tunidades para trabajar en Colombia el exterior, se ubicó en el Caquetá e donde forjó una pequeña industria e lo que hoy es la importante empres "Gasesoas Florencianas". Dinámic y supremamente dil··ente se co virtió en el nervio de su empresa fre te a sus dos hermanos hasta derive de su empresa de gaseosas, la emb

(Pasa a la Pág. 4a

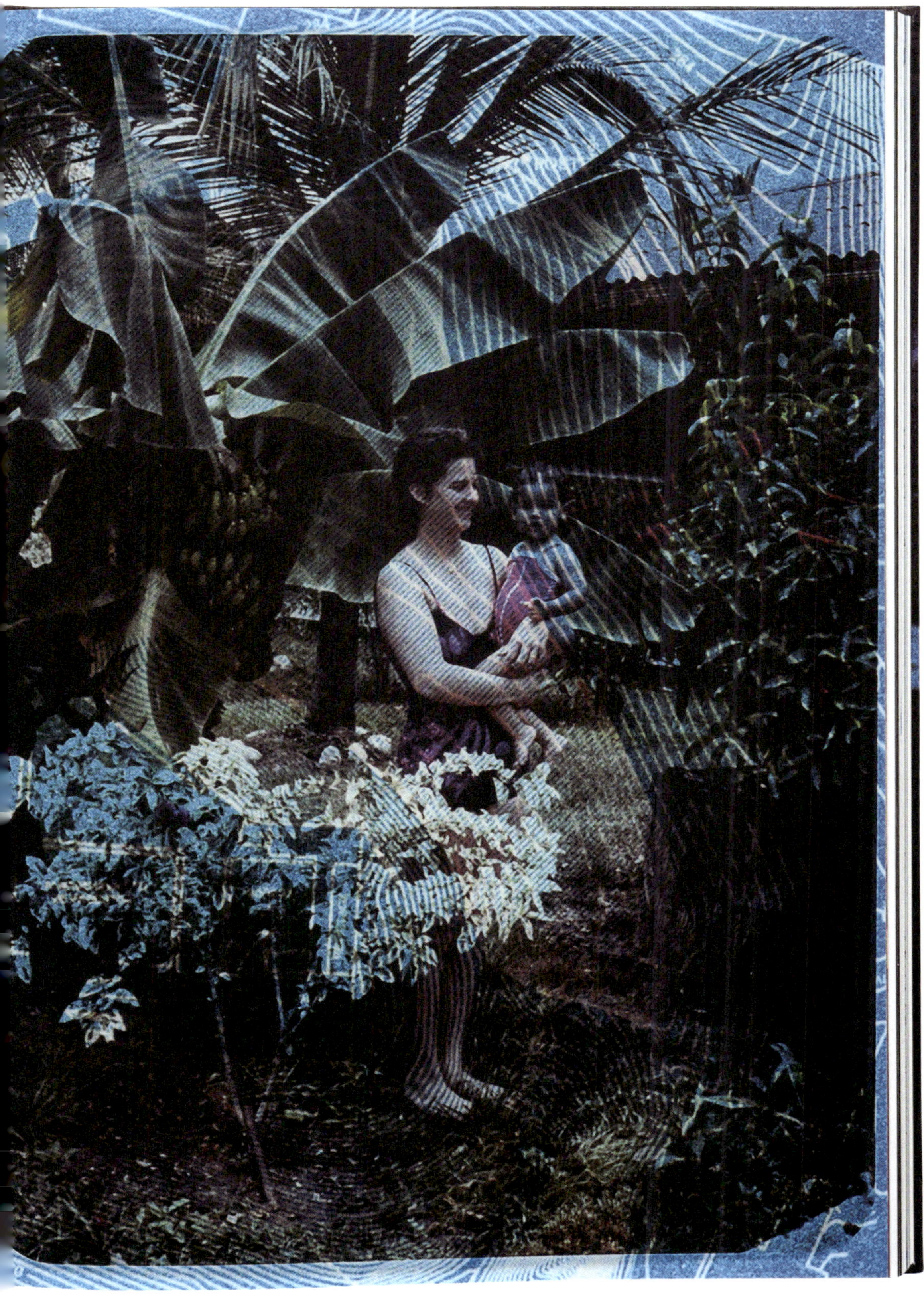

MAX PINCKERS ET AL.

UNHISTORIES

In Max Pinckers' *Unhistories*, photography is a dialogue with history: it shows the vestiges of colonial conflicts, it documents "the life of an oversight"[1] imposed on Indigenous populations and proposes to constitute the archives of the history to come. Photography is also collaborative and, in the case of *Unhistories*, put at the service of the memory of Mau Mau fighters, members of the Land and Freedom Army who, from 1952 to 1960, rose up against the British Empire in Kenya.

Faced with the incomprehensible lack of photographs in the colonial archives documenting the British atrocities – archives that were intentionally destroyed, hidden or tampered with by the authorities of the time – Pinckers proposes to (re)visualize the struggle for independence from the personal point of view of those who survived the colonial violence. *Unhistories*, which mixes patchy archives, symbolic vestiges of the past, images of former mass graves and testimonies from veterans, claims to be decolonial and revisionist. Together with the National Museums of Kenya and members of Mau Mau War Veterans Association (MMWVA), the photographer delivers a collective response aimed at healing – but without erasing – the still gaping wounds of colonial violence.

Through the reconstruction of traumatic scenes, the "re-photographing" of places of confinement and torture and the portraits of those who were at the forefront of the rebellion, Pinckers makes a restorative instrument of the photographic medium that makes it possible to tell their truths to the powerful. He is among the few photographers who, through their practice and the dialogues they engage in, question their privileges and the symbolic power they exercise as white and Western individuals, as much as their position in the face of our shared colonial legacies.

Unhistories, 2015–ongoing
© Max Pinckers in collaboration with the Mau Mau War Veterans Association and the National Museums of Kenya

1 "The life of oblivion" is a concept developed by philosopher Jacques Derrida to describe the living appropriation of forgotten presences, grasped in their very loss and transfigured into new presences.

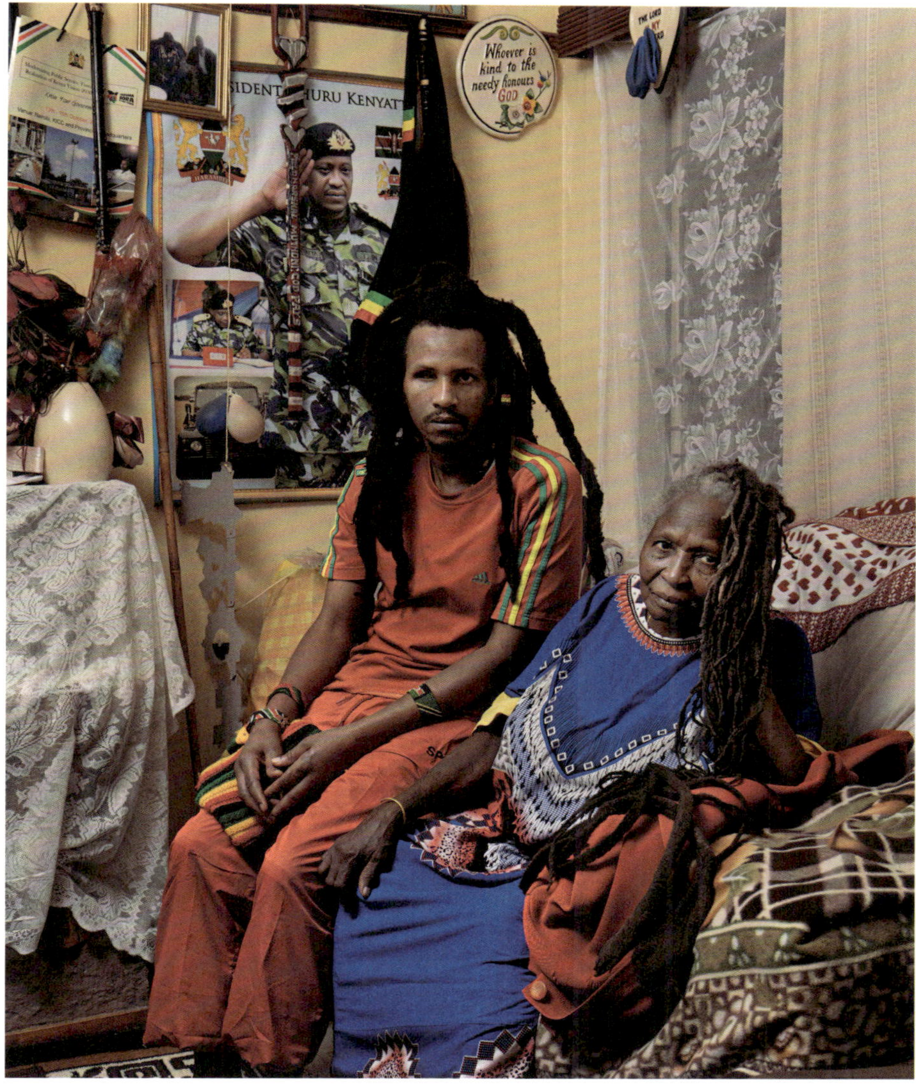

Field Marshal Muthoni wa Kirima at home with her grandson Bernard Mungai Kamande, Nyeri, 2019.

Muthoni wa Kirima (b.1930) attained the rank of field marshal. She entered the Aberdare Forest in 1952 and was never caught, although she still has a bullet lodged in her hand. She was nicknamed "Nina wa Thonjo" (weaver bird) by Dedan Kimathi because of her ability to weave brilliant war strategies. She was one of the last Mau Mau who laid down their arms at the flag of free Kenya at Ruringu Stadium in 1963, where she met Jomo Kenyatta.

She still has the same dreadlocks she had when fighting in the forest, which she calls "the history of Kenya". They are a symbol of her dissatisfaction with the new governments and she vows only to cut them when the deserved compensation is given to the Mau Mau veterans. "I emerged from the forest after 11 years but was never given even an inch of land. I have nothing to show for those 11 years, not even a needle. It was only the sons of the supporters of the white men who benefited from the blood and sweat of our battered bodies."

"I am still in the forest," she says. She wants the "protruding bones of fallen heroes in shallow graves in Mt Kenya forests" collected and buried honourably. "The bones of my fellow freedom fighters are, like me, crying in the forests. We ventured into the forests to free the country from the grip of the white settlers. We thought that those we left behind schooling would fight for us, but things turned out differently." The erasure of Muthoni and others like her from Kenya's history books depresses her as she cites how unfortunate it is that "only white people" visit her enquiring about her story.

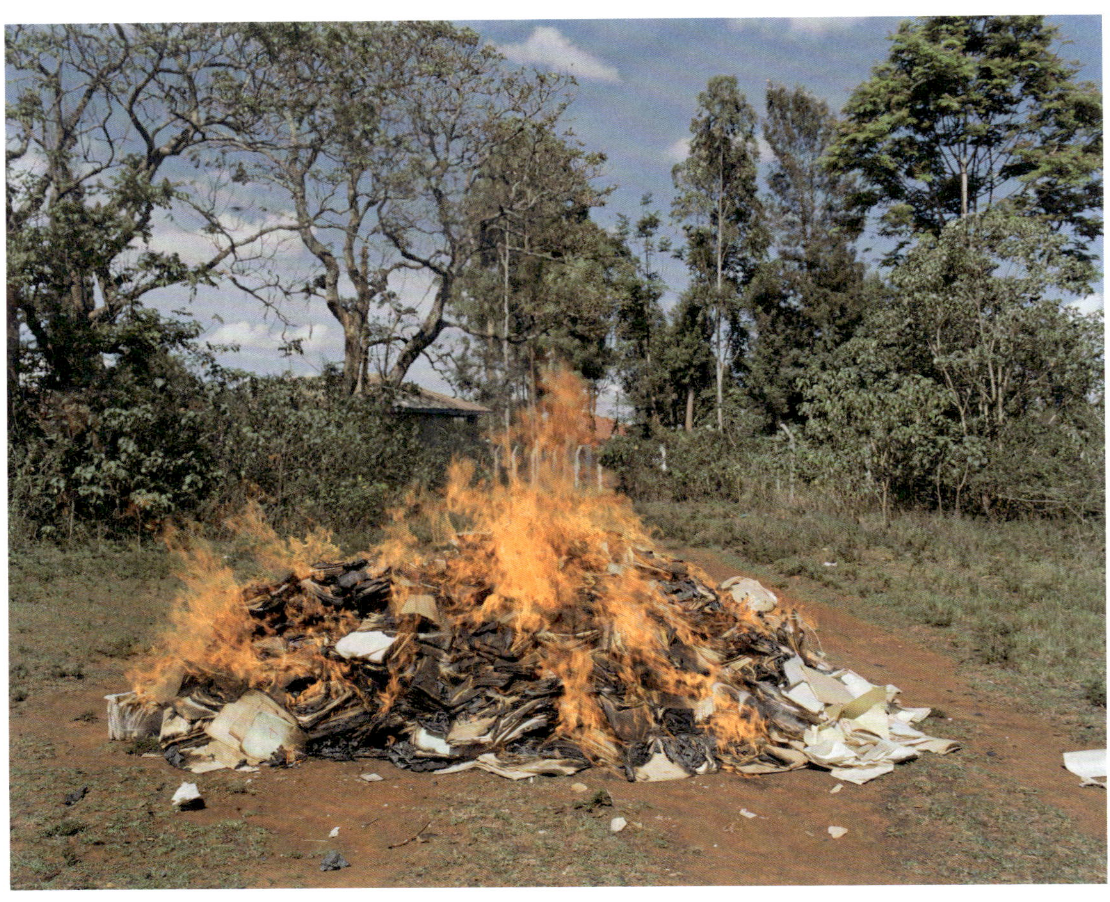

A burning pile of documents that were found in a stock in the Nyeri County Archives in Kenya. According to the National Museums of Kenya, these were duplicates of colonial-era documents held at the Nairobi National Archive, 2015.

In 2011, during the negotiations for compensation of Kenyan victims of abuse, the unrelenting efforts of lawyers and expert witnesses led to the discovery and release of thousands of secret files held by the Foreign and Commonwealth Office (FCO) at the highly secured government facility Hanslope Park. The FCO was forced to reveal the existence of some 1,500 government files secretly removed from Kenya on the eve of independence, a process known as "Operation Legacy". They provided many unseen documents which described in detail the systemic torture of detainees during the emergency, and the knowledge of those abuses by British government officials in London and Nairobi. These "Migrated Archives" are just a small part of a much larger collection of documents that were either destroyed or have disappeared. The FCO subsequently announced that it held files from all 37 former colonies, a collection of about 20,000 items, now commonly referred to as the "Hanslope Disclosure".

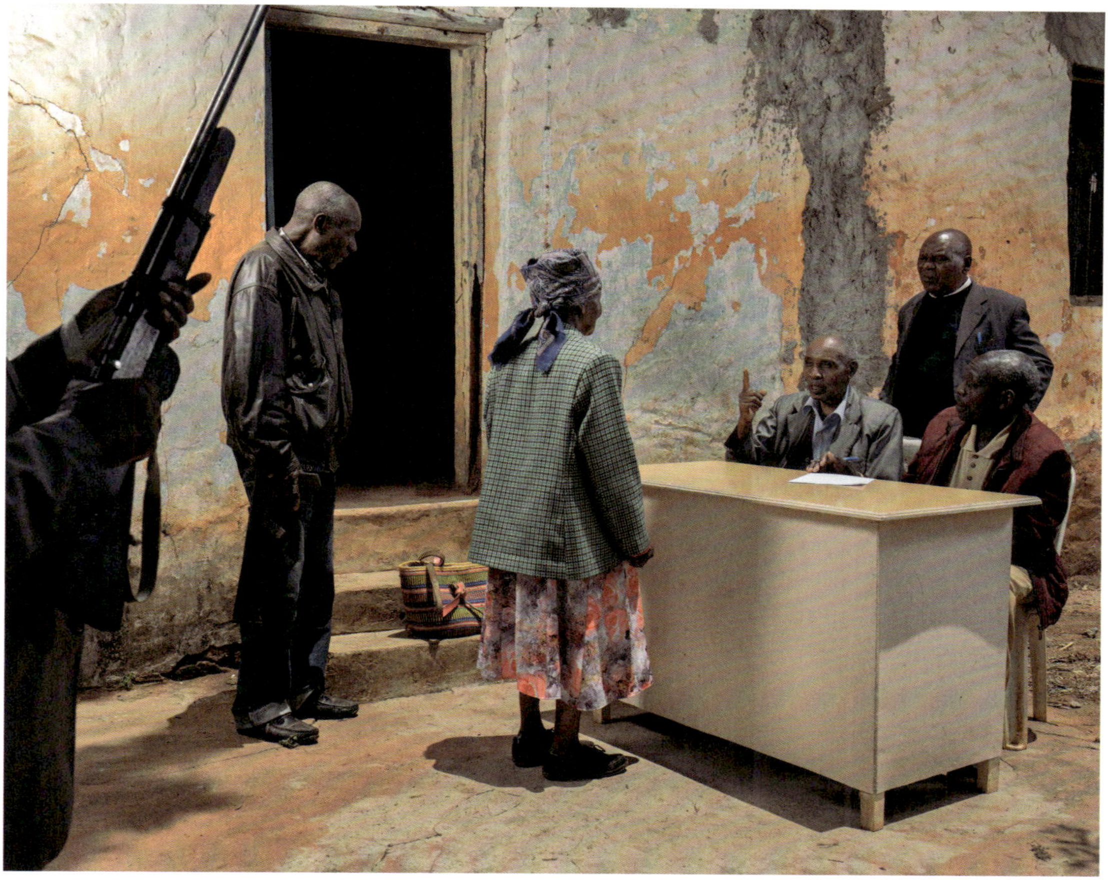

© Max Pinckers/MMWVA

Beninah Wanjugu Kamujeru demonstrates how she was interrogated, Murang'a, 2019.

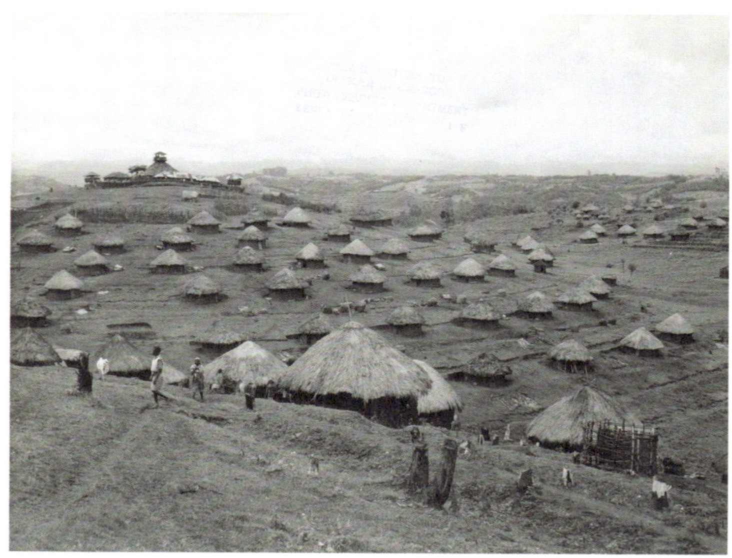

Colonial Office: Kenya Information Service: Photographs, CO1066/9: "Kikuyu villages and Home Guard posts", 01 Jan. 1953–31 Dec. 1955, The National Archives, Kew, UK.

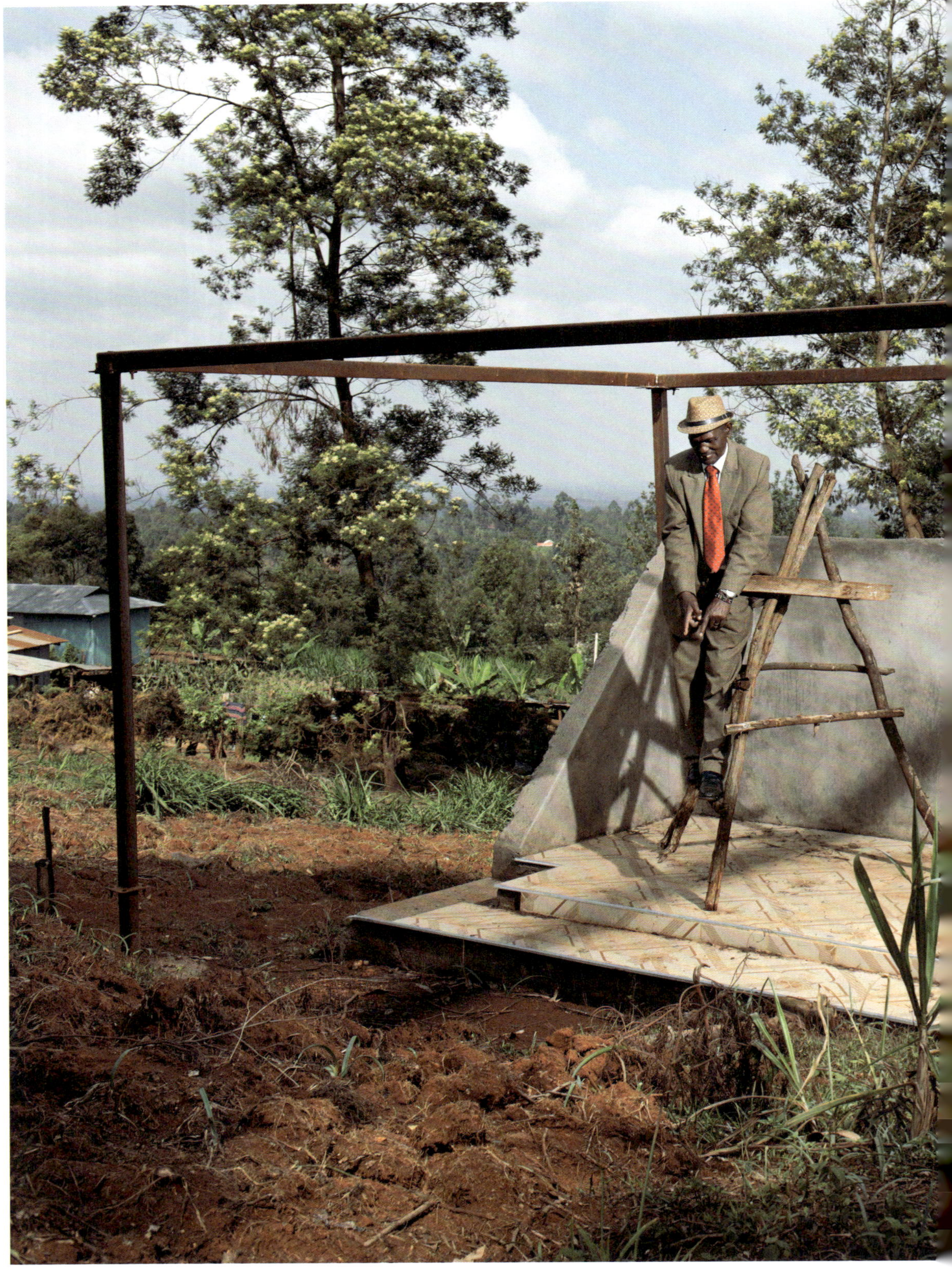

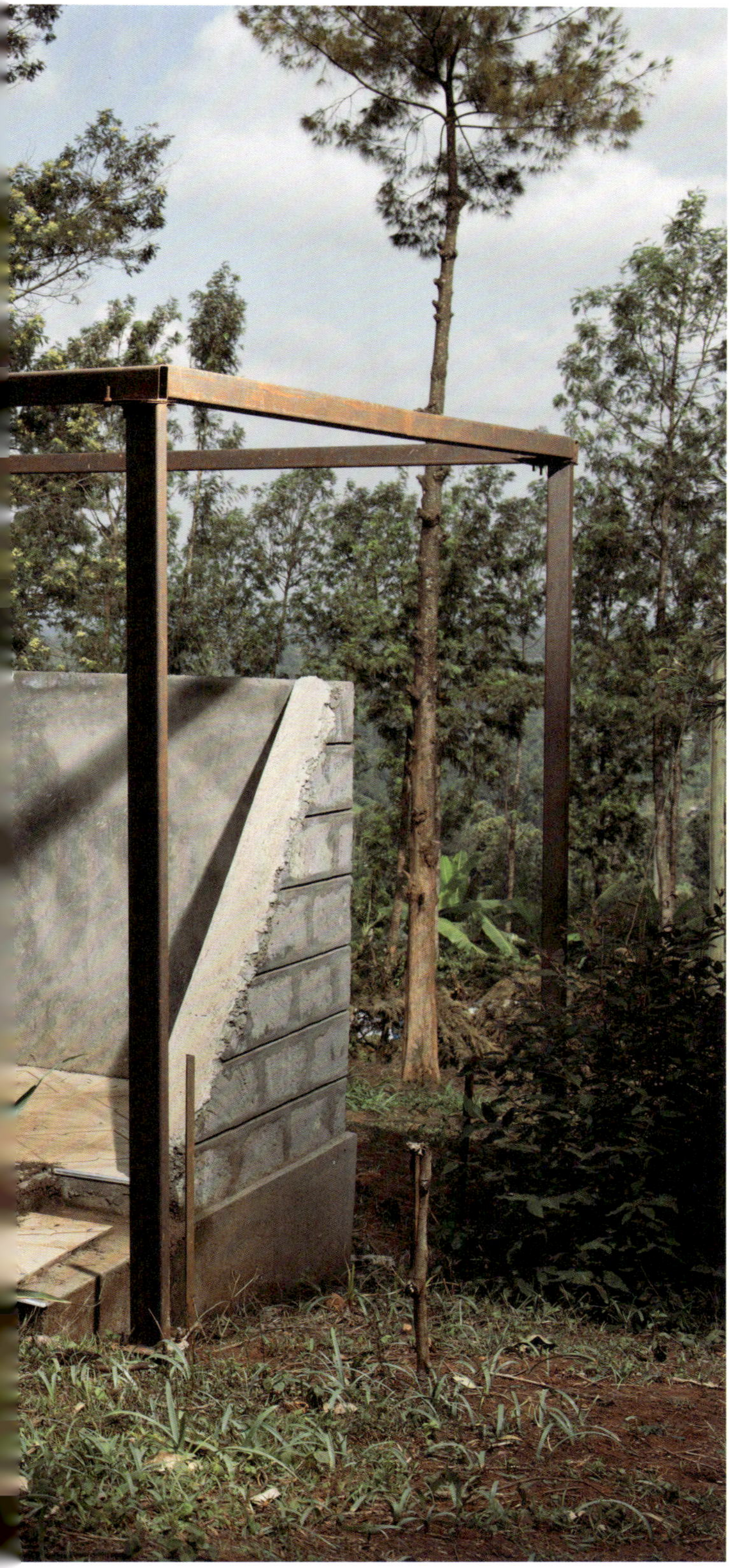

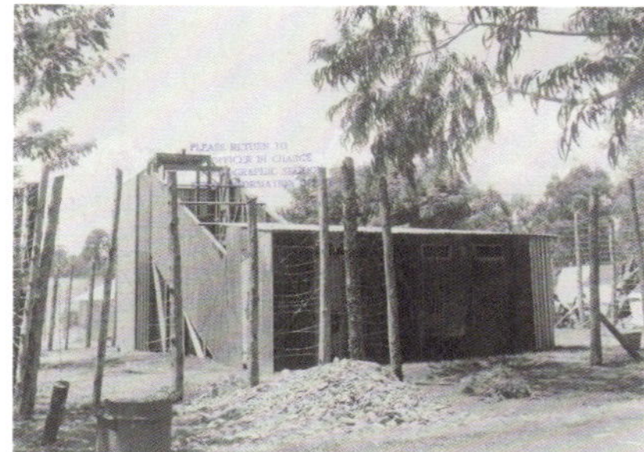

Colonial Office: Kenya Information Service: Photographs, CO1066/9: "Kikuyu villages and Home Guard posts", 01 Jan. 1953–31 Dec. 1955, The National Archives, Kew, UK.

Mburu wa Gitou shows where the mobile gallows once stood and a monument is being built, Githunguri, 2019.

"The gallows stood here and this cemented block is where the bodies would drop dead before they were wrapped up and hauled out. During the hangings there was a Catholic Father at the door. He prayed and after the conviction, he would sign, break the pen and wash his hands. Fifty-seven people were hanged here.

The hangings began at 11 at night and we could hear them saying: "We have gone, we have died and you have been left. Never let go of this land, for it is what we die for." They all died with a fistful of soil in their hand.

Once hanged, the bodies were not disposed of immediately – they were seen by everybody so that people would be afraid. So that they would stop the war. But they would dare not surrender. The bodies were hauled into a truck in the morning. The army trucks rode away with legs dangling from the back.

The monument serves as a reminder of those who were hanged in this nation, who died for independence. We can come for prayers here. The design of the monument is made in collaboration with the National Museums of Kenya, and we will engrave their names on the wall."
— Mburu wa Gitou, 2019

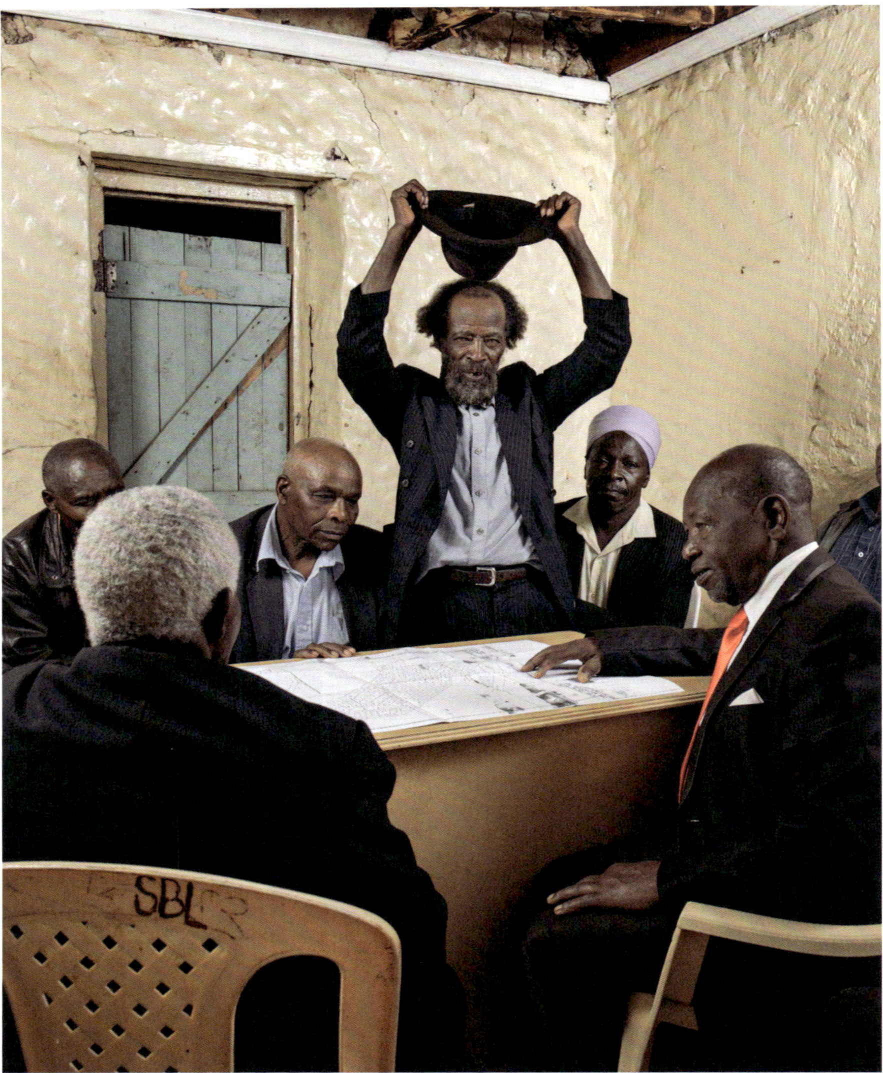

Peter Irungu Njuguna demonstrates how buckets of soil had to be carried during forced labour in emergency villages, Murang'a, 2019.

"In the whole of Central Province the British installed a villagization programme for women and children. The villages were surrounded by a fence, a trench with spikes, and Home Guards in watchtowers. You'd leave early in the morning to go for forced labour, either digging roads or digging trenches; just out of spite so that you are continuously engaged.

At 5pm you had one hour to leave the compound and search for food. One hour to go and look for food to feed your family. If you were late in coming back, you were arrested and taken to detention at the inner post, because it was alleged that you were helping Mau Mau on the outside. When in detention you were beaten and whipped and you would sleep outside. In the morning you would be forced to carry a basin full of sand on your head for 12 hours, with your hands up, without putting it down."
— Peter Irungu Njuguna, 2019

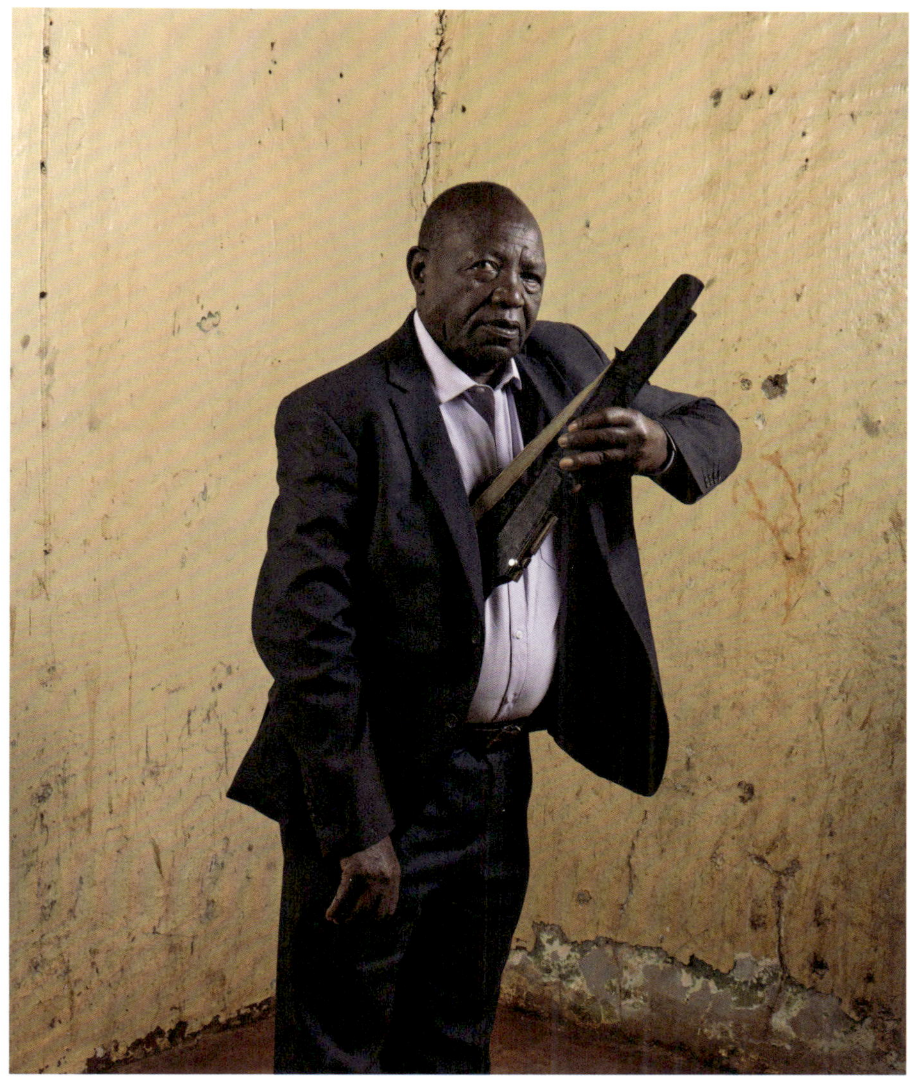

Paul Mwangi Mwenja, home-made gun maker, demonstrates the concealment of a gun, Murang'a, 2019.

"During the struggle for independence I was a student at a school where the King's African Rifles were staying. They were fighting for the British, but the soldiers became our friends. They showed us everything, and that's when I learned how the gun works.

I began making home-made guns. You could only use one bullet at a time. You'd take out the cartridge and put in another. We used these guns to hunt European soldiers. When we'd get one – we would ambush or hide beside him in the bush and shoot him – we'd take his gun. That way we'd gain a gun. A new gun.

We used water pipes to make these guns. And then we were using door locks. We would sharpen the tip of the door lock and use a spring or elastic rubber to hit the bullet, so that oxygen would get in and the bullet fires. The guns we were making could be taken apart while travelling. In order to hide it in the *kabuthi*, the jacket, you could break it up into two pieces, and when you wanted to be in action you could put it together again. It was easy to travel with."
— Paul Mwangi Mwenja, 2019

TITLE

THE RESTORATION WILL

COVER

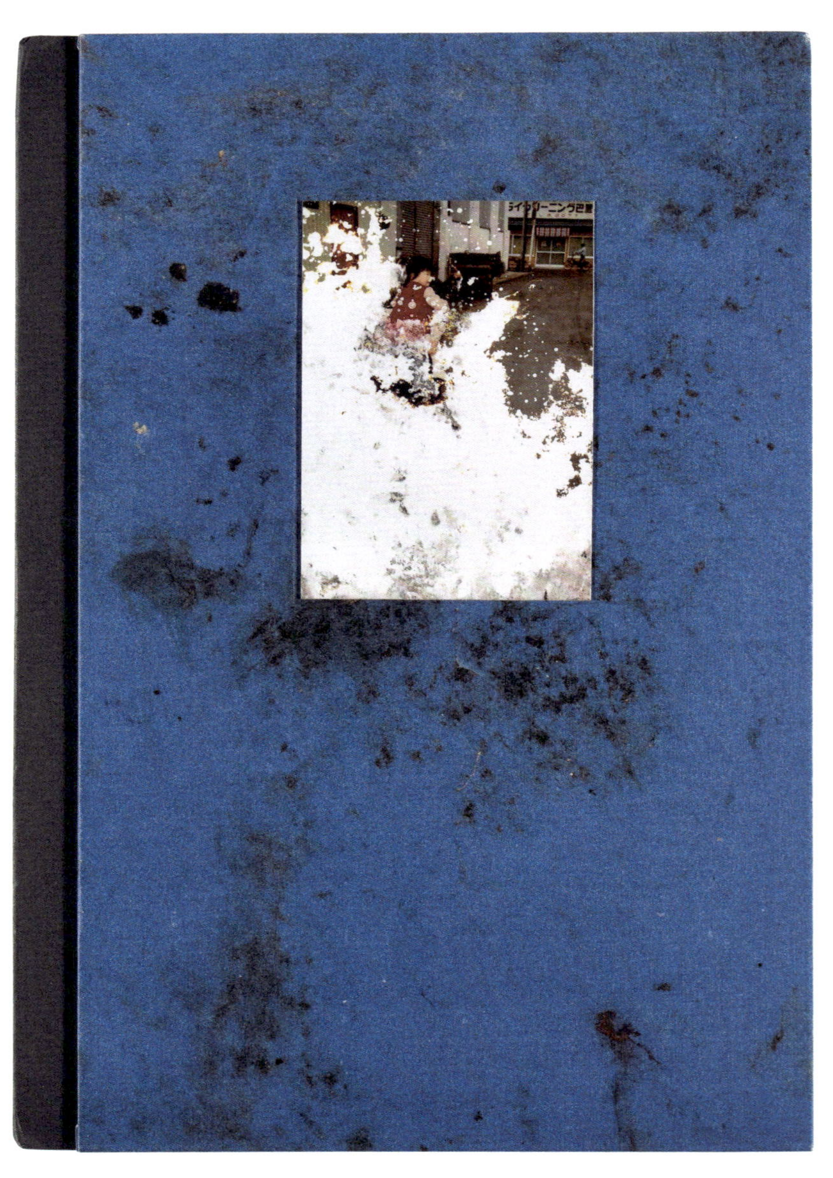

ARTIST	Mayumi Suzuki
PUBLISHER	Ceiba Editions
MONOGRAPHY	- 104 pages - first published in 2017 - size: 19 x 27.5 cm
SUMMARY	On 11 March 2011, Mayumi Suzuki's native Onagawa was devastated by an earthquake and then a tsunami. Her parents, Atsuki and Katsuki Suzuki, are missing. The family business, a photographic studio, is destroyed except for part of the darkroom. Within seconds, the childhood home, the living and working spaces, have vanished. Under the rubble, Mayumi finds her father's camera, his portfolio and a family album that she manages to extract from the mud: "One day, I tried to photograph a landscape with my father's muddy lens. The image came out dark and blurry, like a vision of the deceased. As I took it, I felt that I could connect our world to that of the afterlife." Combining ghostly black-and-white landscapes with damaged family photos (with white smears, torn, erased) and views of the ruined village, Mayumi Suzuki tells the story of an intimate and collective devastation. She tells us of shared memorial scars as the recollections of what was – the peaceful life of this fishing village – slowly fade away to give way to obsessive fear. *The Restoration Will* testifies to her desire to repair and temporarily revive a life annihilated.
BIOGRAPHY	Born in Onagawa (Japan) in 1977, Mayumi Suzuki grew up in the photographic studio-house founded in 1930 by her grandfather. She became a photographer after the disappearance of her parents in 2011 and defines herself as a visual storyteller. With *The Restoration Will*, she engages in a conversational endeavour that addresses survivors to better ensure the survival of the disappeared. She lives in Tokyo.

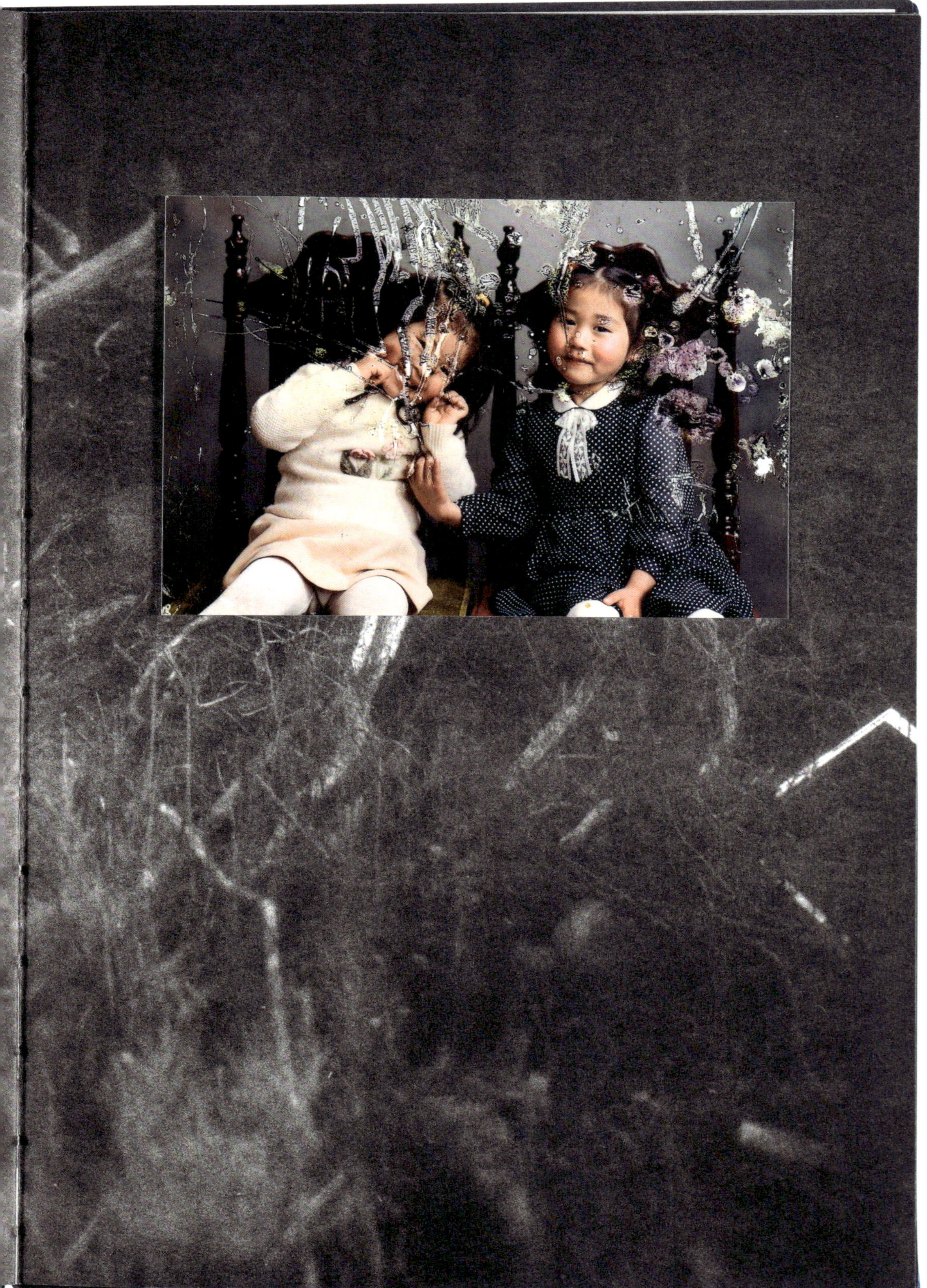

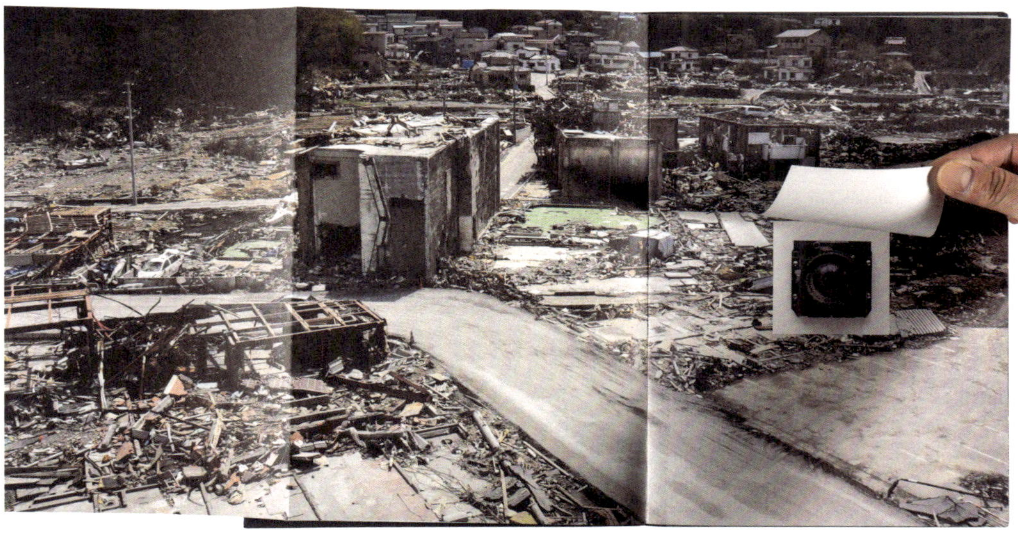

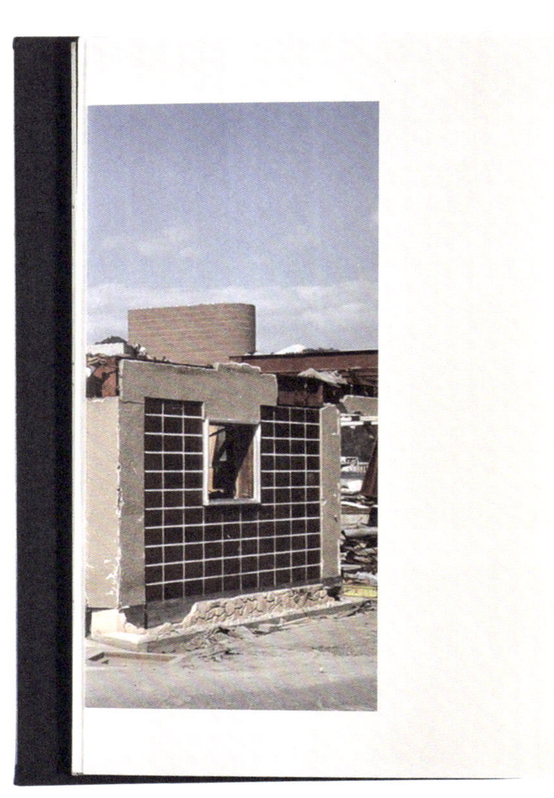

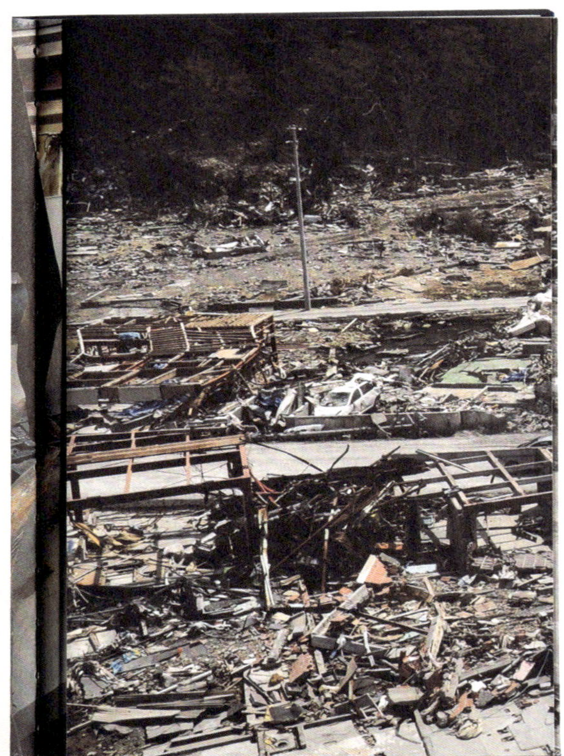

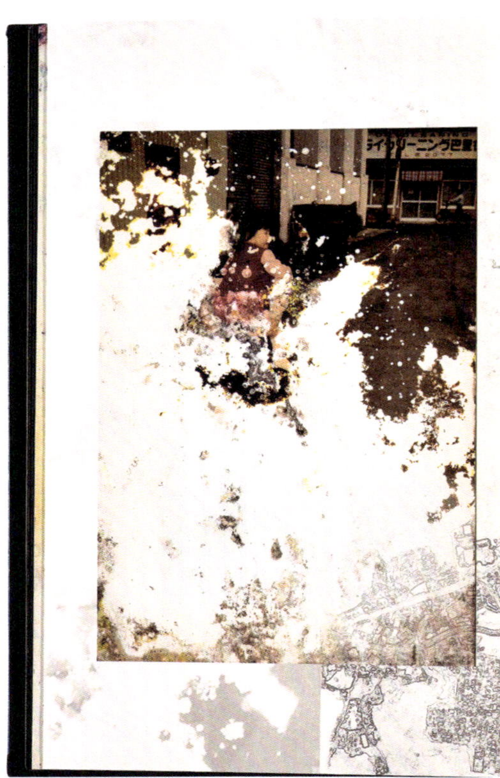

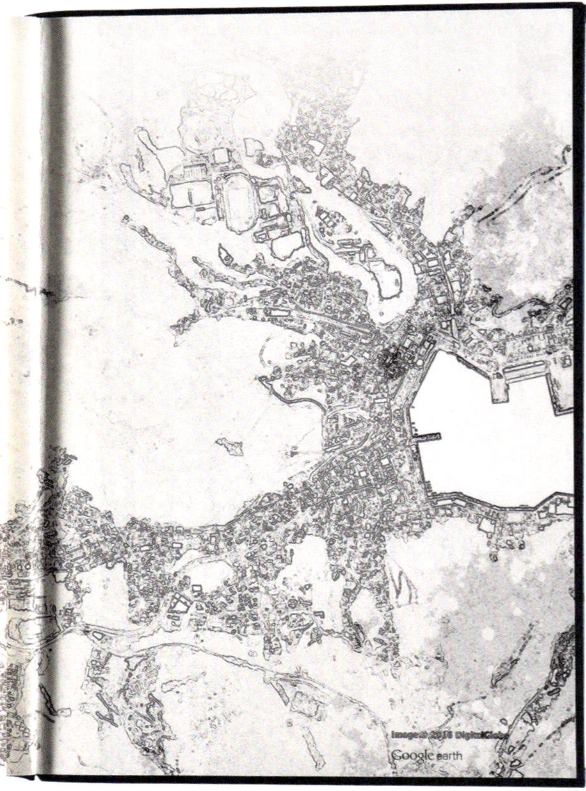
Google earth

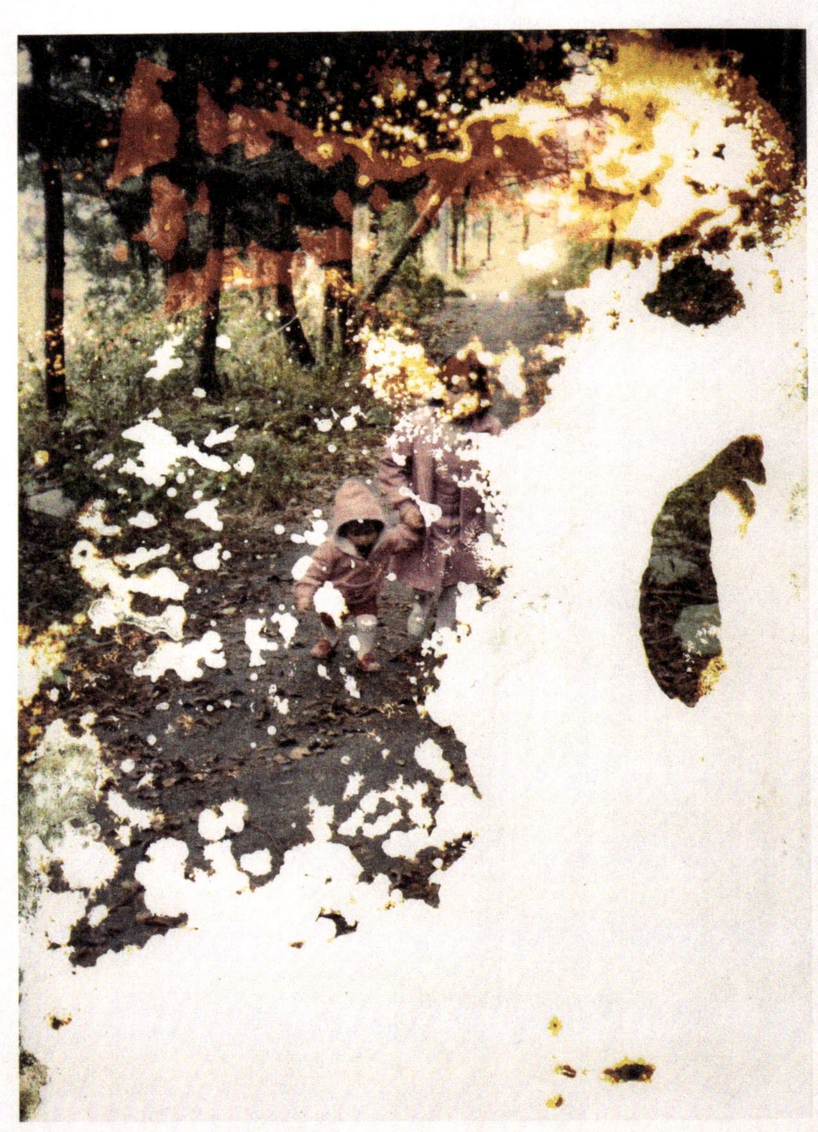

HOW WOULD YOU CONSIDER (AFTER)CARE IN YOUR WORK?

Ana Vallejo, *Neuromantic*, p. 10
(After)care is one of the most essential practices for our mental well-being and something that I tend to put aside when I get carried away by the worries and responsibilities of daily life.

For a long time, I sought acceptance and validation through my work. Much of my internal work has been learning that my art does not define my worth.

The alchemy of art making shouldn't be forced. It can be impulsive, but it also needs pacing, patience and persistence. It's a gift for others, yet it shouldn't carry the weight of expectations. It's most honest when it's devoid of ego and serves a deeper purpose.

Every day I try to be more structured. I am now learning to create with more depth and honesty in less time. I am learning to say no. I am learning to set boundaries so I can find time to rest and regenerate.

It's not an easy nor linear process and sometimes I regress and fall back to burnout. Yet one tweak at a time, I build my practice and (after)care routines to find sustainability in my life.

Hayley Millar Baker, *I Will Survive*, p. 48
I Will Survive is multi-layered conceptually and physically. It challenges memory and looks to the notion of constructed memory based on our ability to accept or deny certain experiences, how our minds protect us from fear or how they inflate things for storytelling purposes.
My photographs lay bare multiple possibilities and scenarios to a particular experience or memory that has been founded in truth, revealing just enough information for the viewer to take over the narrative and decide which road the narrative takes. This approach allows me to care for the foundation story with privacy and respect, as it is often connected to my Indigeneity and family biography, and it gives the viewer the opportunity to seek truth – if they are capable and willing to find it.

Hoda Afshar, *Agonistes*, p. 18
Agonistes is based on the experiences of several men and women – whistle-blowers – who chose to speak out about cases of institutional misconduct and abuses of power. It describes their shared fate and struggle – their heroic and often tragic attempts to navigate between the two forces of morality and the law – and the great personal costs they suffered as a result.

The word "agonist" – from the Greek agon – describes one who is engaged in a public contest or struggle. But here, it suggests too the agony that one who is engaged in such a battle for truth and recognition must suffer. Thus, what I have tried to depict in these images is at once the heroism of these men and women and the suffering and trauma that is forever recorded in their bodies.

Kitra Cahana, *Still Man*, p. 104

In the aftermath of my father's brainstem stroke I moved into the ICU with him, sleeping on a mattress on the floor of his room, tending to his body around the clock. I was in my early twenties and I struggled with the weight of caregiving. Using our experiences in the ICU and later in a rehab facility and then in long-term care as the material content of our artistic collaboration became my solace. Interpreting our lives into objects of beauty and meaning is what lifts and sustains me through the difficult and even tragic. It gives me a role to play, an outside eye to interpret my life through. After an explosion we find the means to piece ourselves back together. We learn the unique language of our own survival. For me I survive through creating an artistic interpretation of a lived experience. To me this is the meaning of (after)care.

Margo Ovcharenko, *Country of Women*, p. 156

Working on a project called *Country of Women*, I wanted to see what women loving women looked like in different countries of the former Soviet Union 30 years after its failure. I wanted to share something that is unique for Eastern Europe. I strived to photograph whoever came forward after placing my ad in queer magazines. I found that uniqueness came through working together with my subjects on posing and touch. Intimate contact in these images was the most important part not only shown between partners but also in the closeness of my camera in capturing skin textures, softness and strength of bodies. Seeing images of women who look like oneself and to whom one might relate is no doubt a healing experience. But I didn't want to sugar-coat what it's like living in countries that have long histories of homophobia and of making queer women invisible. (After)care for me in these images was accepting the battles and tribulations of each person by allowing their bodies to express themselves.

Max Pinckers, *Unhistories*, p. 80

How can one visualize the past by photographing the present with a future audience in mind? The "in-person" re-enactment, or demonstration, allows us to speak about the past in the present tense, and about the present in the future tense. In *Unhistories*, survivors demonstrate their past experiences in which they claim their roles as heroic victims instead of terrorists to create communal images as a response to the trauma of colonial violence. Zigzagging through history's multi-directional ghost notes, *Unhistories* interweaves fragmentary colonial archives, architectural and symbolic remnants from the past, mass grave sites and the testimony of people who experienced and survived the war themselves. It is a visual historiography in which ambiguity, uncertainty and speculation are inherent in the retelling and reclaiming of unresolved historical narratives based on memory, photography and physical traces.

Robert Andy Coombs, *CripFag*, p. 118
With a physical disability like mine, there is a lot of care involved in everyday activities, and more specifically with sex. I need help in foreplay with undressing, getting in bed and positioning. I need help during sex by telling my partner what I want to do or what I would like them to do. Most importantly I need help post-sex with (after)care – cleaning up and getting dressed and back into my wheelchair. I've had my fair share of potential partners tell me that I would be too much for them because they would be doing all the "work". With my work I hope to change the narrative of care as "work" by photographing activities that could be considered mundane and photographing them in a fun and sexy way.

Masina & Gal, *GH. Gal & Hiroshima*, p. 142
For us, the word "care" has become too subtle. We did not seek to revive the violence, but to retaliate. As Jota Mombaça says: redistribution of violence as self-care. Our photography is delicate but does not think about delicacy. Nor do we blunt the narratives. In some of the photographs, we took the stones found on the street where Hiroshima was stoned and wrapped them in foam, childishly, with string and knots, aware that this softening does not undo the wounds left; but the mastery over memory, the act of shaping memory, is a gesture of exercising sovereignty. If necessary, we moulded everything. We would react. The series *GH* is a delayed reaction, not a flashback.

Jérémie Danon, *Plein Air*, p. 42
Thanks to the privileged relationship I have with the models, a space for listening and representation is created in which they feel comfortable. They and I know that I can't put myself in their shoes; I don't pretend to do anything other than to listen to them. With this principle in mind, I want them to think together about the form that their story will take. It is important that everyone plays a central role in the architecture of their own representation; this involves testimony and the conception of personal settings. Through my projects, I always try to work not *on* people but *with* them.

Sometimes they are close to me, sometimes they become close to me. In the "after", these links do not fade, and their presences, physical as well as symbolic, infuse the projects at each stage of their dissemination. I particularly like to express my gratitude to them, to save a place for them at my side when I am invited to speak. Finally, as part of my last solo show, I wanted to publish a catalogue of which they were the subject and which was specially intended for them; yet another way to integrate them totally into my artistic practice.

TITLE

SMALL WARS

COVER

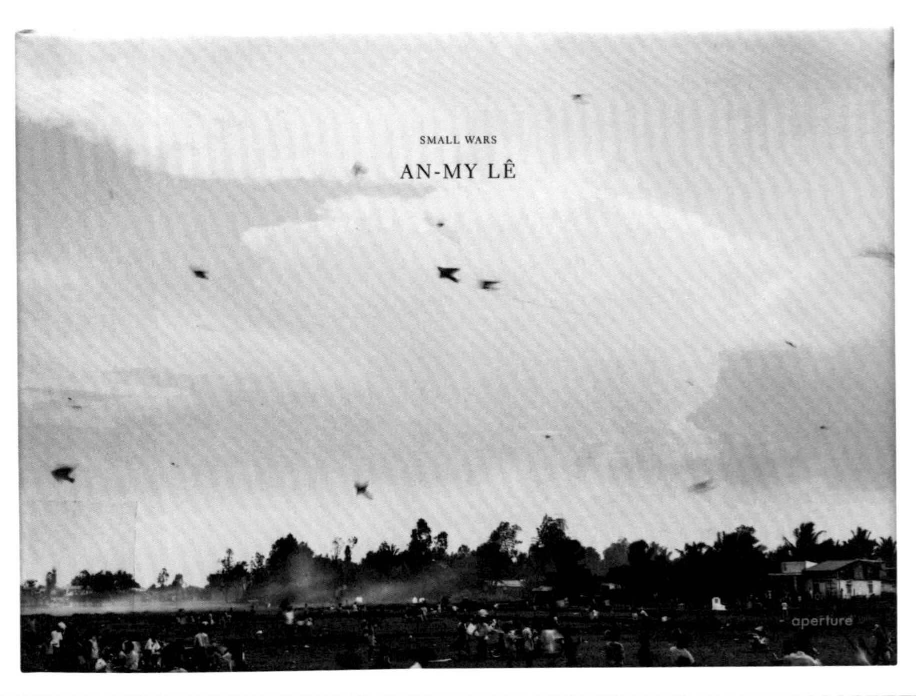

ARTIST	An-My Lê
PUBLISHER	Aperture
MONOGRAPHY	- 128 pages - first published in 2005 - size: 29.85 x 22.23 cm
SUMMARY	An-My Lê photographed the Vietnam War in the forested landscapes of the northern United States, documenting the work of those who reconstruct – to better (re)live and analyse – historical battles. Sometimes she appears in some of the images, in the role of the translator or, ironically, as a member of the Viet Cong army. The series, situated between intimacy and documentary, questions both the complexity of her Vietnamese American identity and the personal dimension of the conflict, and soothes family and collective wounds. The camera provides her, she says, with "multiple shields against the painful memory of the war, while allowing [her] to get as close as possible to try to understand it". Her images, taken with a view camera, have the same clarity as those of the American pioneers who photographed the devastated landscapes of the Civil War (Mathew Brady, Timothy O'Sullivan or Alexander Gardner). They are also reminiscent of the infinite number of films, documents and reports circulating in the media and within families. Her exploration of a Vietnam that is both truthful and imaginary questions how we remember, glorify and reinvent war after it has taken place.
BIOGRAPHY	Born in Ho Chi Minh City (formerly Saigon, Vietnam) in 1960, An-My Lê spent her childhood between France where her family had taken refuge, Vietnam where she returned in 1973 and the United States where she emigrated permanently in 1975. Her work focuses on the environmental and cultural impact of war. She lives in Brooklyn, New York, and teaches photography at Bard College.

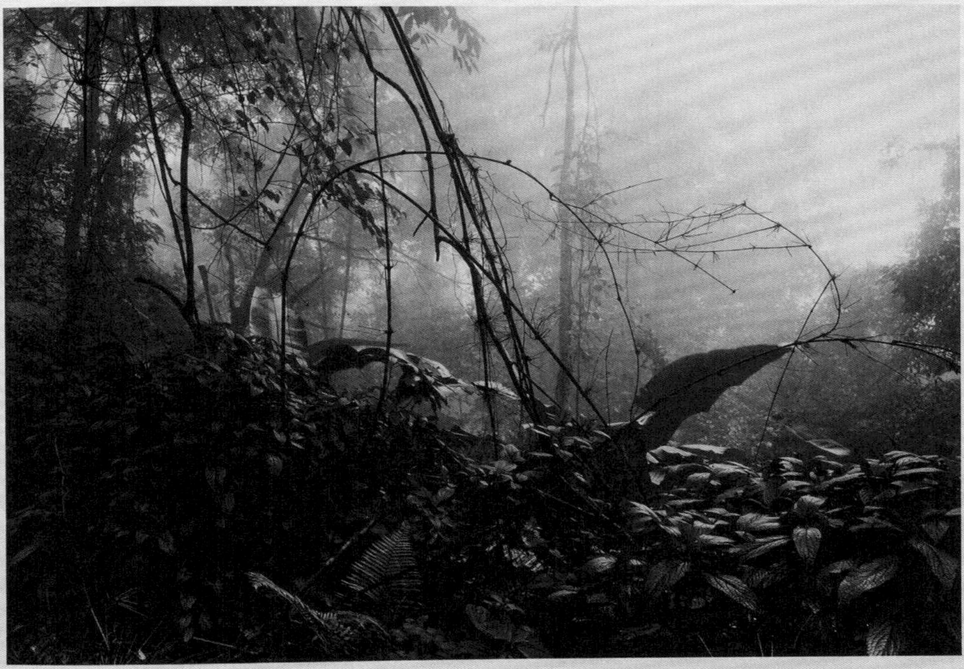

21 Untitled, Ba Vi, 1998

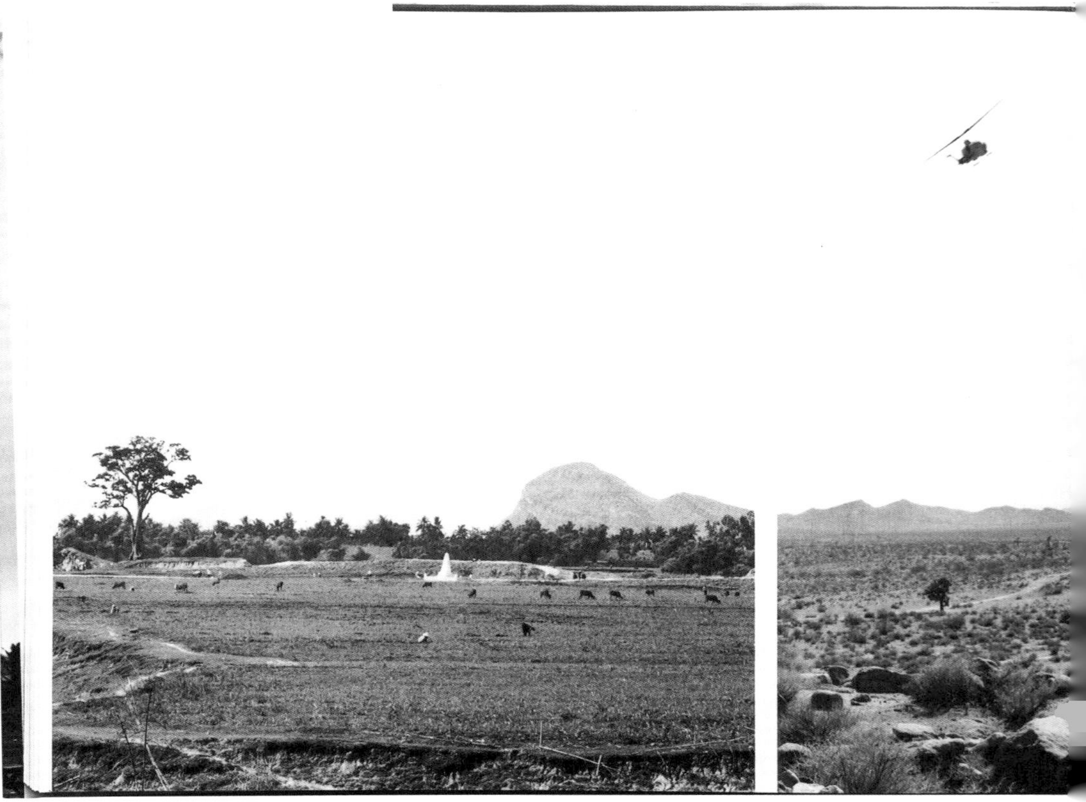

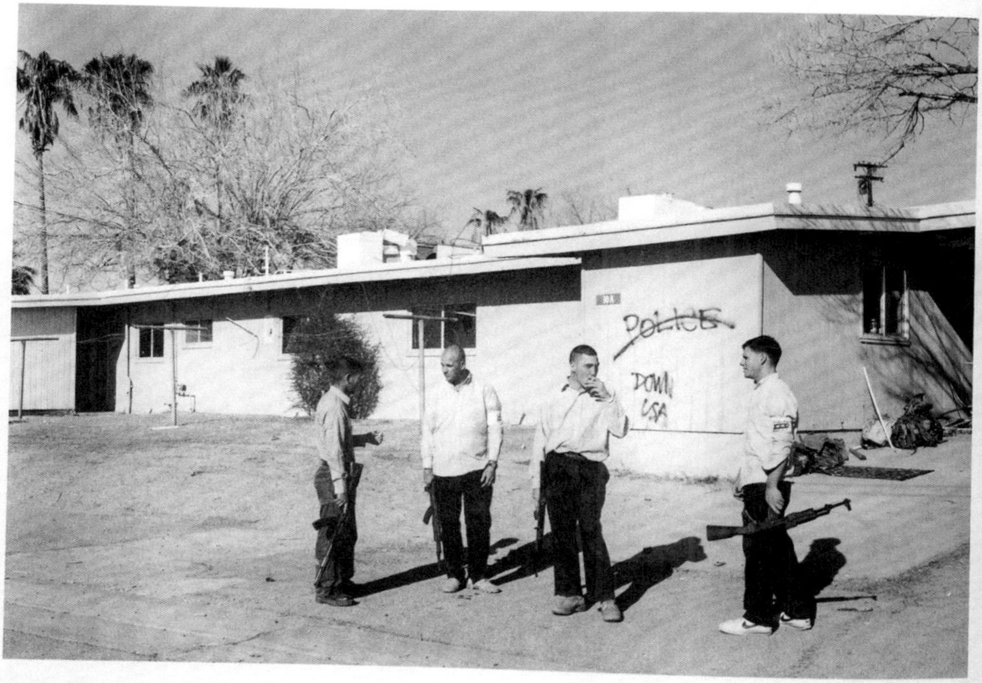

Security and Stabilization Operations, Iraqi Police, 2003–4

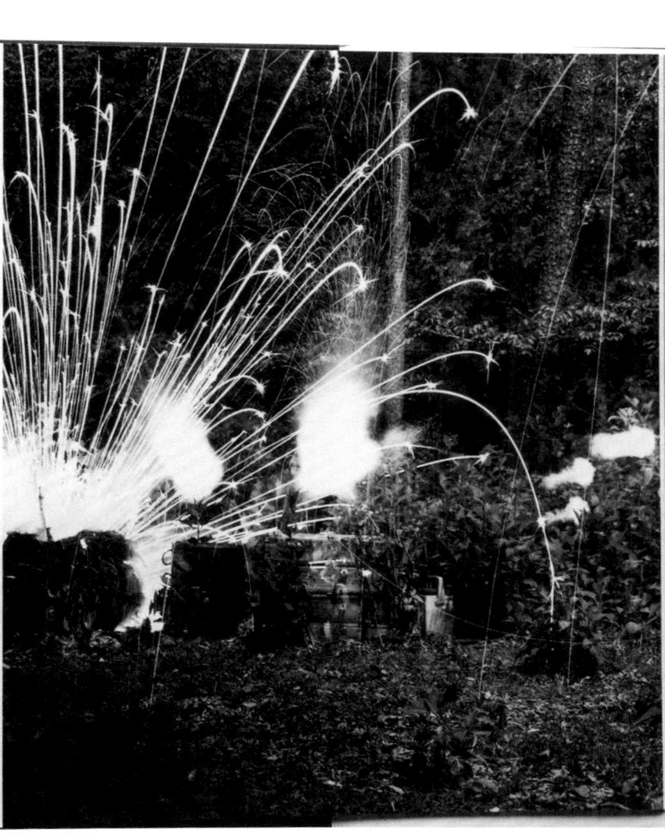

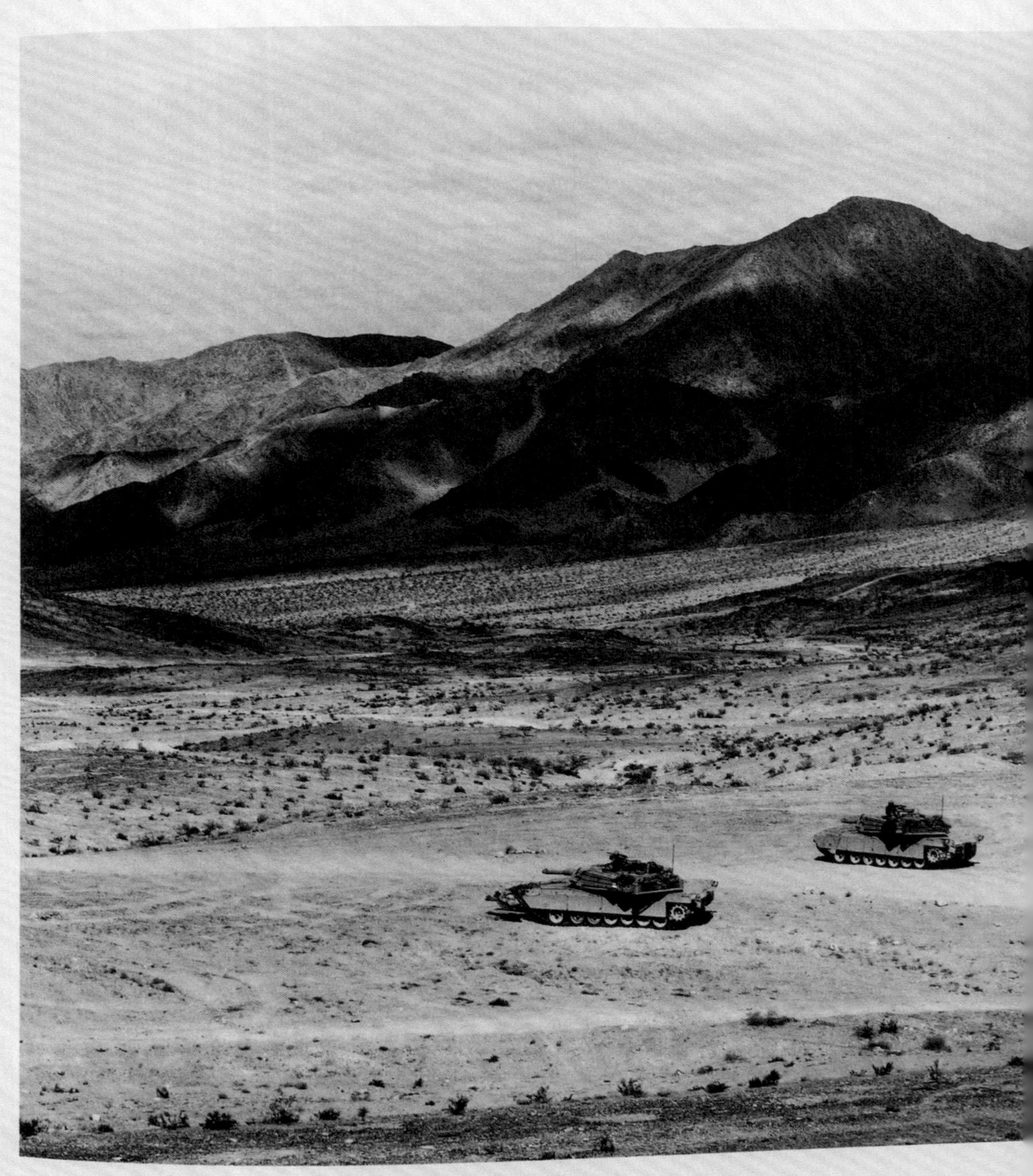

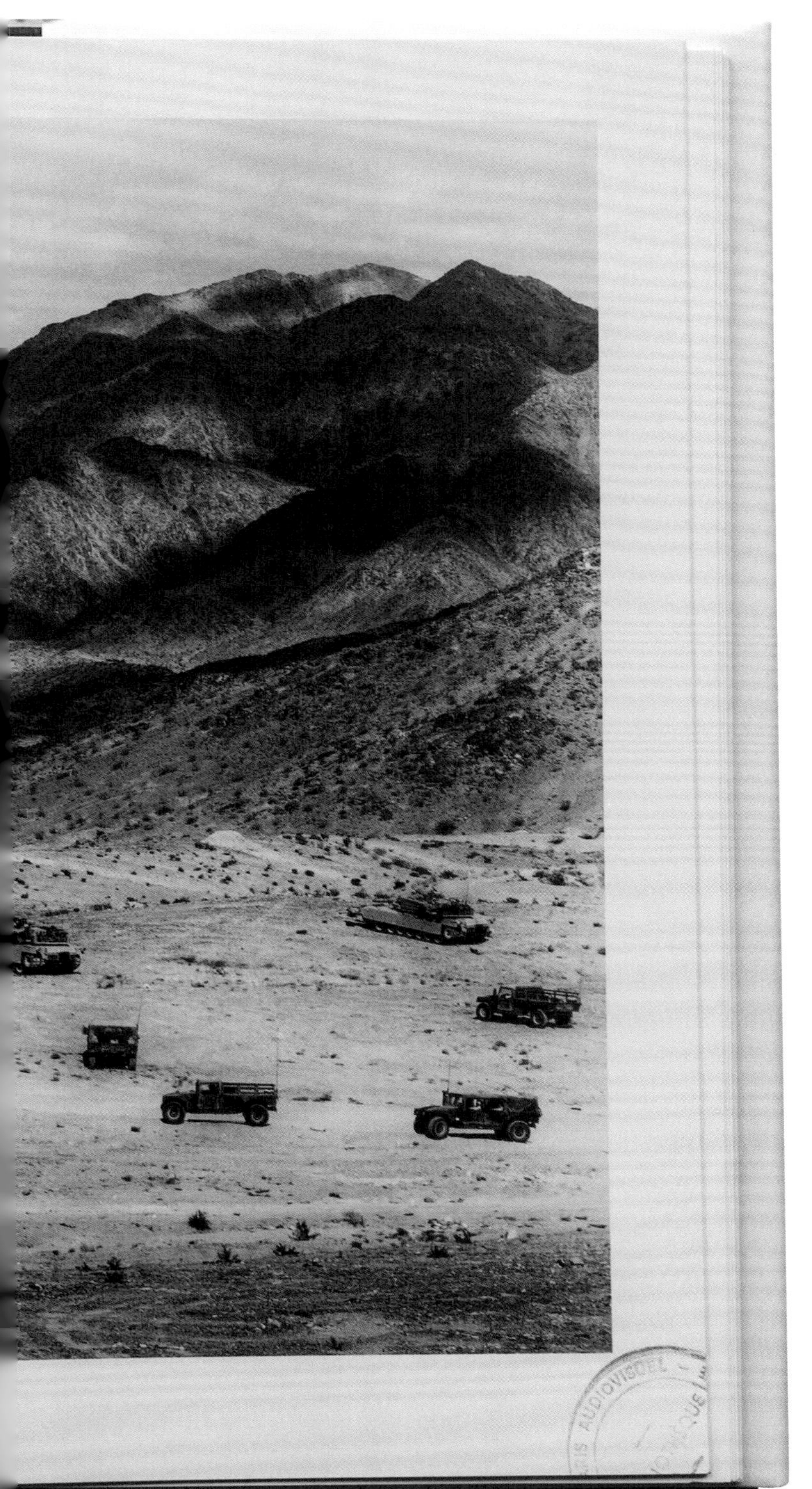

KITRA CAHANA

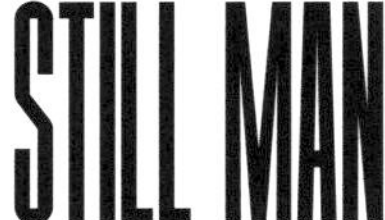

"Let me take you into a dream, into my reality." When her father, Rabbi Ronnie Cahana, became paralyzed except for his eyes, Kitra Cahana spent her days and nights at the hospital. Ronnie communicated by blinking his eyes while his family recited the alphabet, one letter after another. As he slowly came back to life, Kitra took out her camera to record the first nods, the recovery of his breathing, the furtive movements of his limbs, as parents would have done for their child. *Still Man* is the testimony of this rebirth.

The series presents the floating life, the in-between. Kitra Cahana was careful to retain in the image the care and love that surrounded her father, the "cocoon of feelings" that she was able to recreate with her mother, brothers and sisters. Through transcribed texts, the recorded paternal voice and photographic experiments, together they invented the common language of their survival. Ronnie Cahana says: "There is a sacred way to ask for help. And that's what I'm learning: to say, 'I need you. I need your hands. I need your presence. I need you to feel good.' Holiness is reached when the body feels loved."

Borrowing from both religious iconography and chronophotography, the series seeks to translate the experience of confinement from within, to convey the ineffable and spiritual significance of such a space of co-healing.

Still Man, 2011–ongoing
© Kitra Cahana

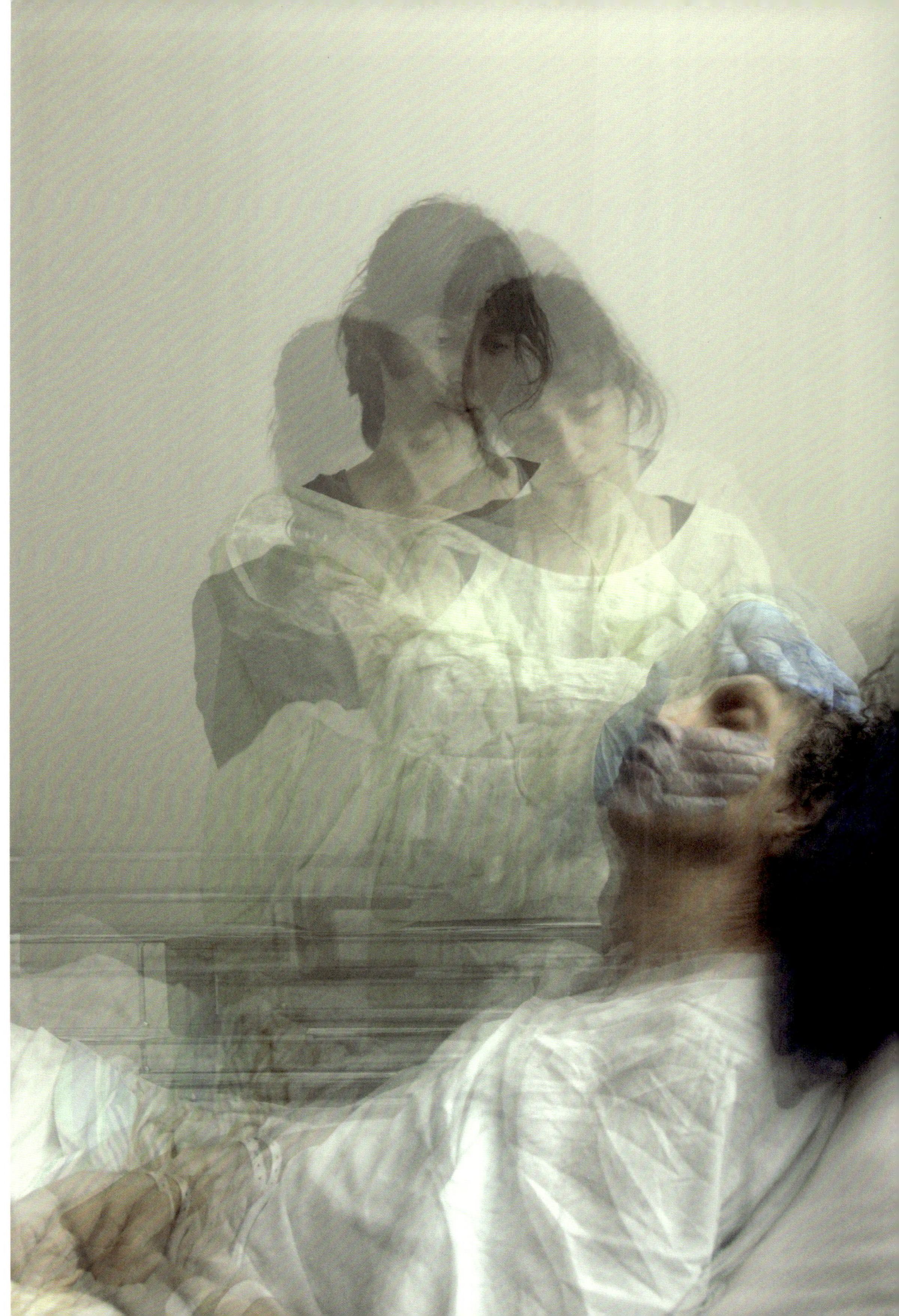

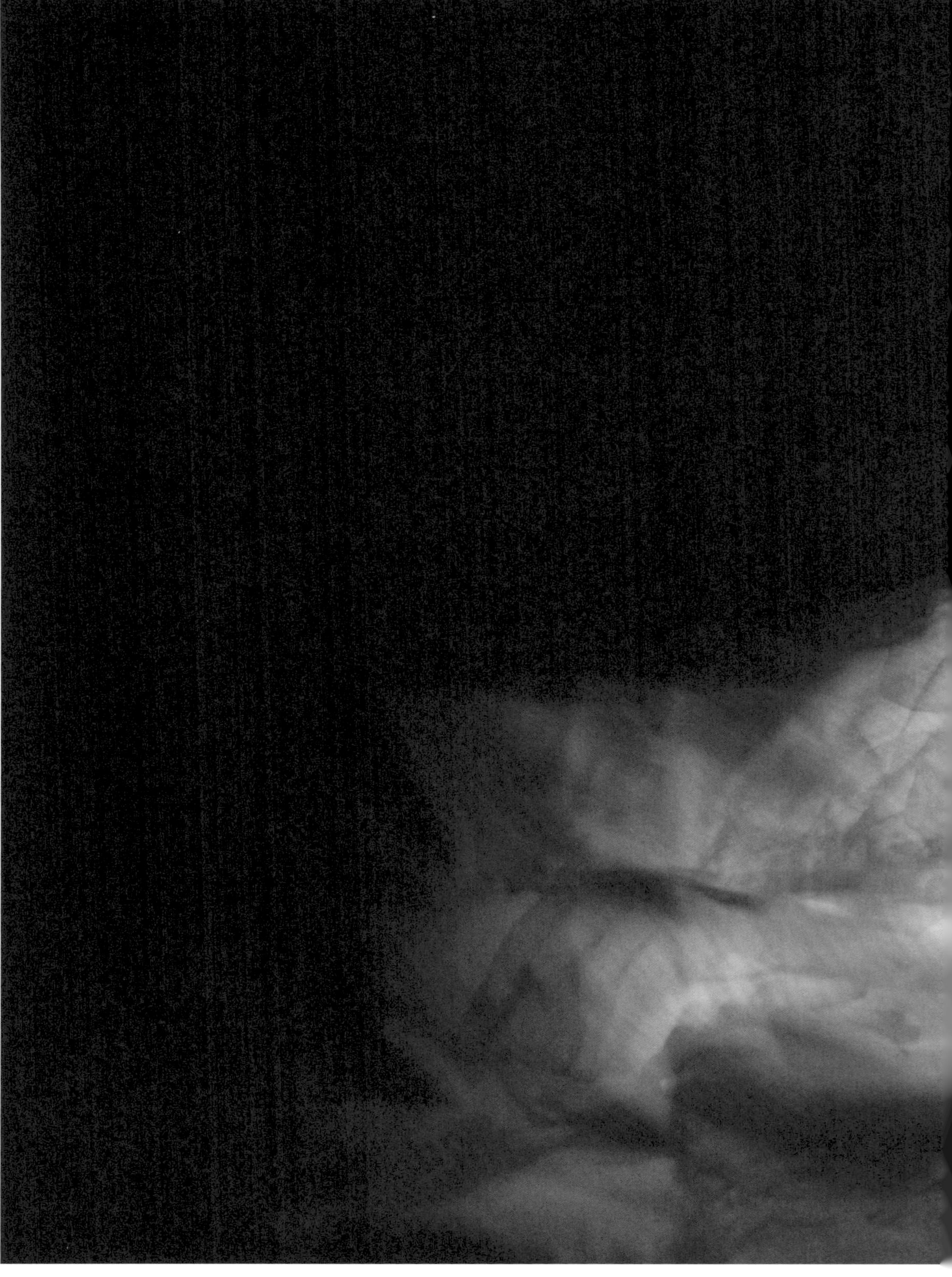

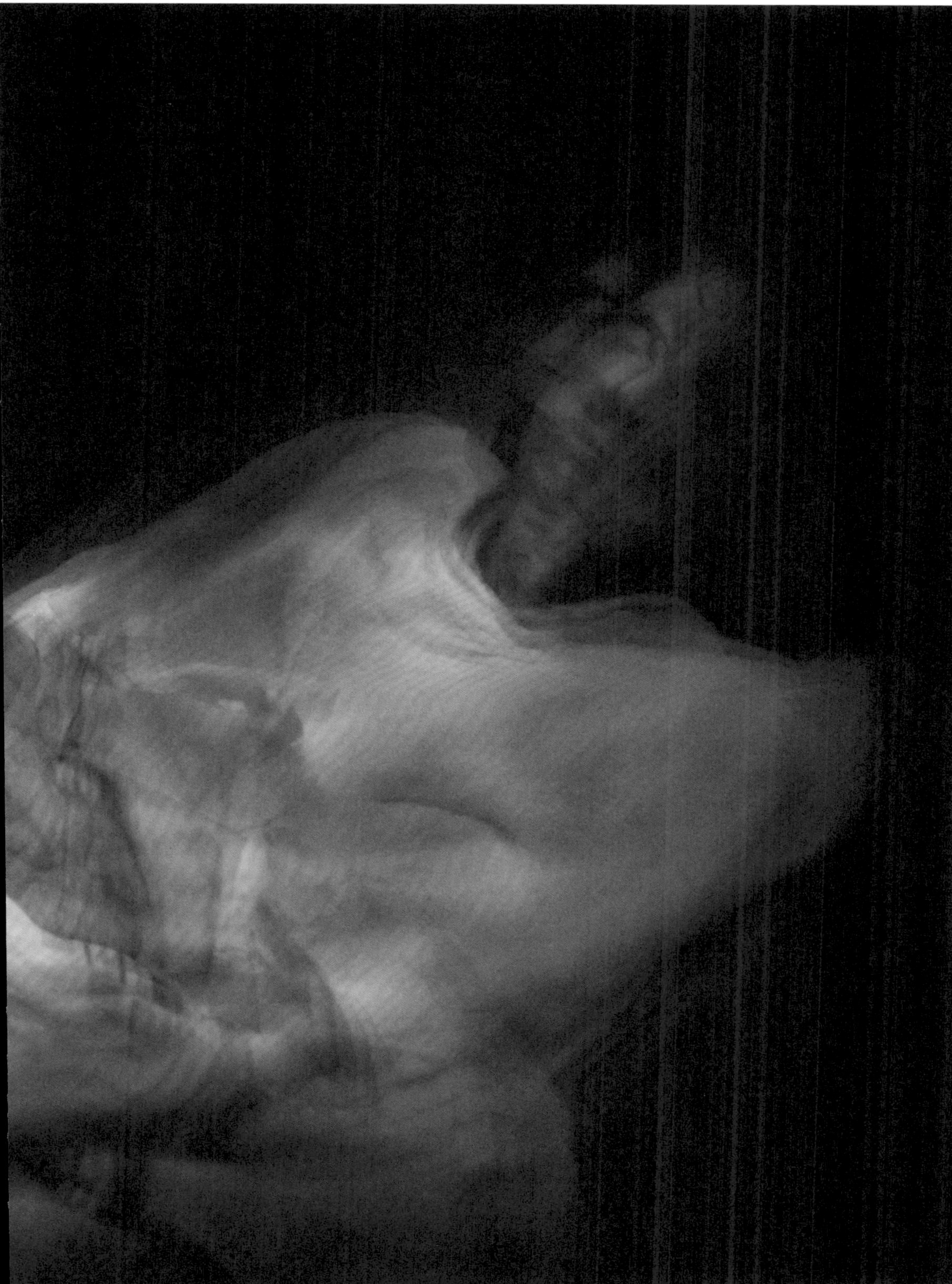

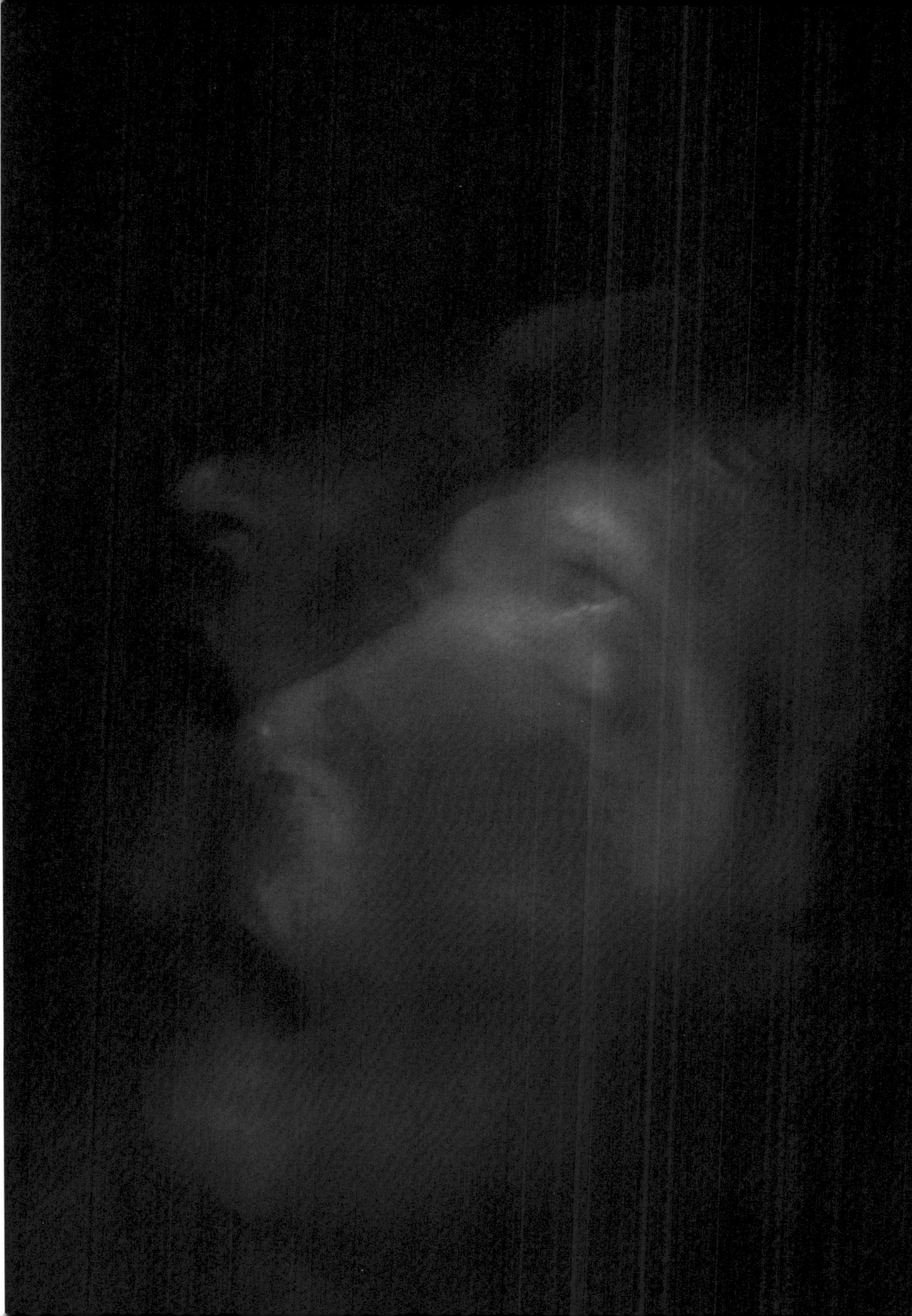

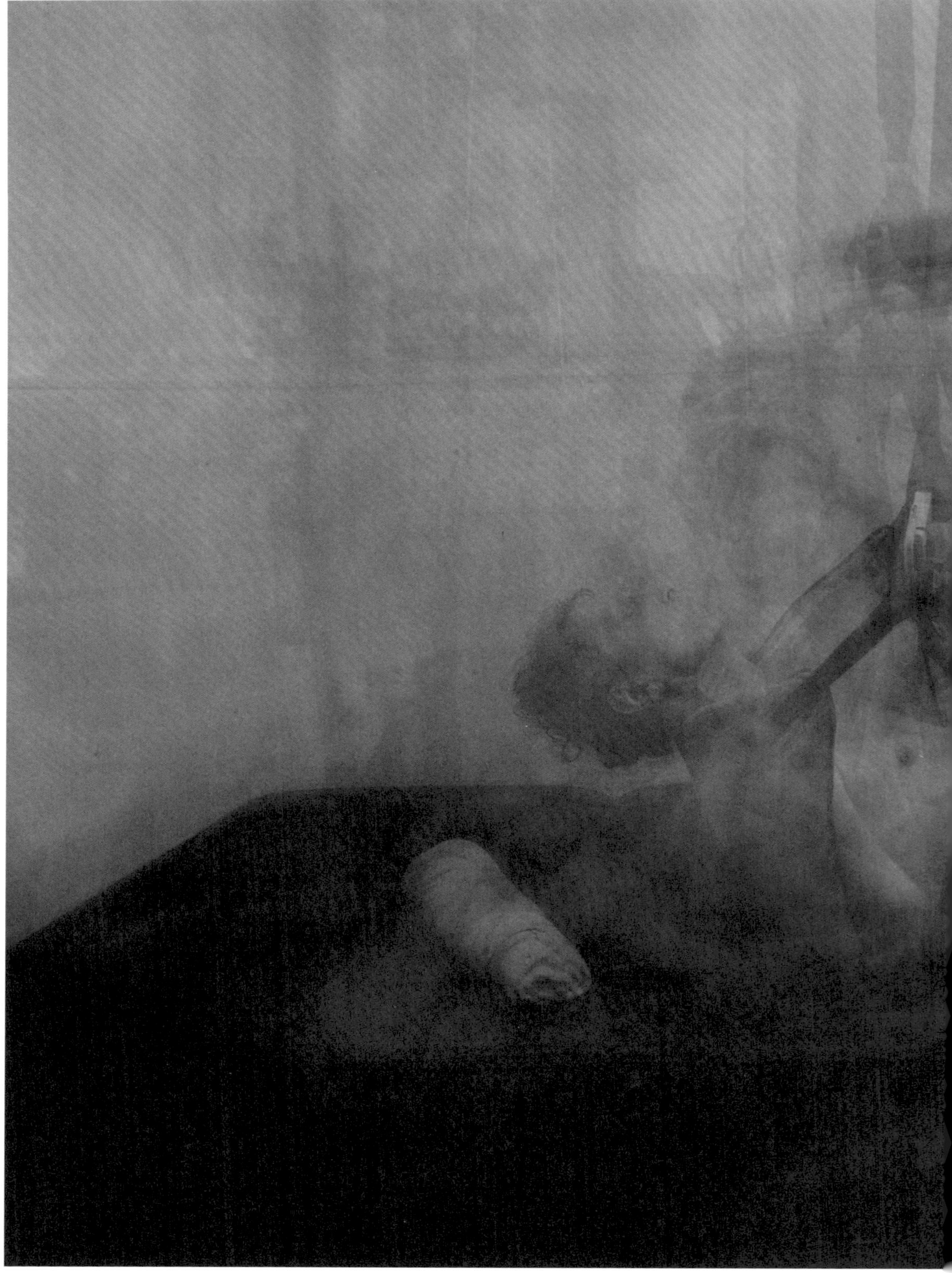

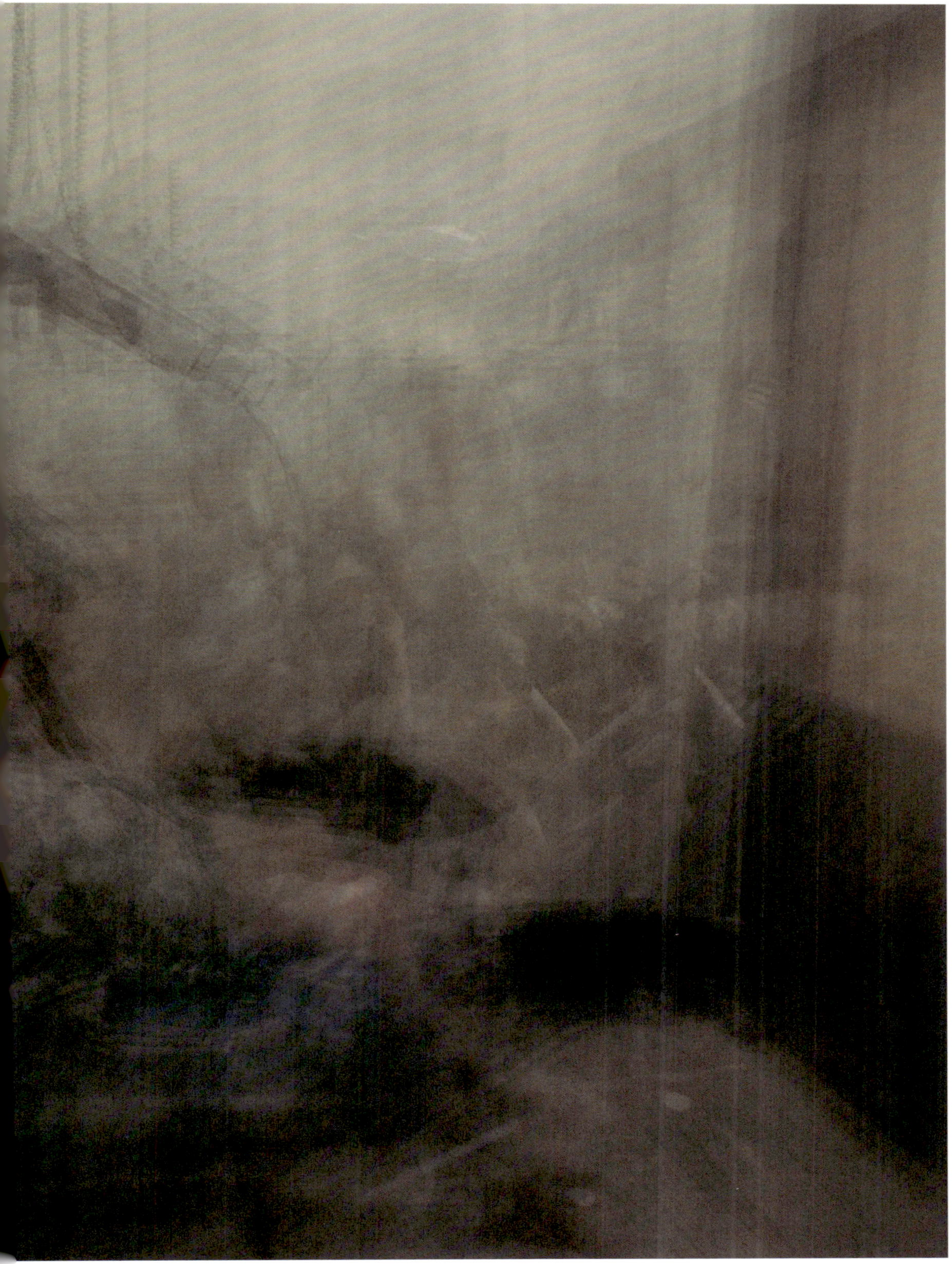

TITLE

DRY

COVER

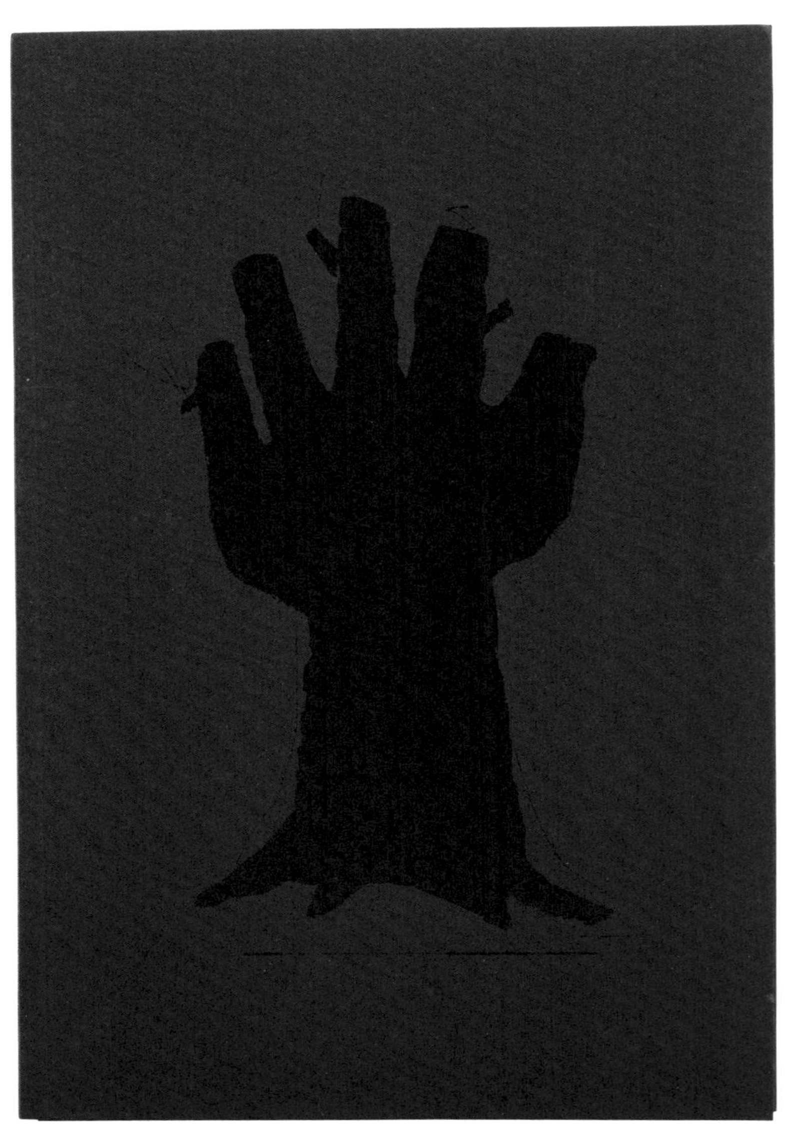

ARTIST	Abdo Shanan
PUBLISHER	Self-published
MONOGRAPHY	- 104 pages - first published in 2022 - size: 15.2 x 22.8 cm
SUMMARY	Born in Oran to a Sudanese father and an Algerian mother, Abdo Shanan grew up in Libya. This cultural hybridization gave rise to an identity disorder. Until the age of 18, he was convinced that he was Algerian like his mother, while his father insisted on his Sudanese ancestry. At the age of 28, he decided to settle in Algeria and began to question his sense of belonging through the photographic medium. Whether portraits, objects or landscapes, colour or black and white, his images hit right to the point. They embody what psychoanalyst Karima Lazali calls the colonial trauma, the way in which "coloniality" has produced memory erasures – absence and disappearance of memory, of speech – that falsify the meaning of history. In addition to his somatic images, Shanan gathers in a booklet excerpts from his investigation into the psychological and political consequences of colonial oppression in Algeria. Together, they tell of the bruises and survivals; they replay the painful failings to better expose them and, thereby, reflect on them. *Dry* is a dark folder that contains within its three-flap jacket images and texts designed to arouse discomfort and embarrassment: "I want you to doubt everything you've been told about national identity and what it means to 'belong'. For what do these social constructs mean anyway?"
BIOGRAPHY	Born in 1982 in Algeria, Abdo Shanan studied telecommunication engineering at the Sirte University (Libya) before dedicating himself to photography. He turned to reportage photography following an internship in 2012 at the Magnum Photos agency in Paris. In 2015, he co-founded the collective of Algerian photographers "220".

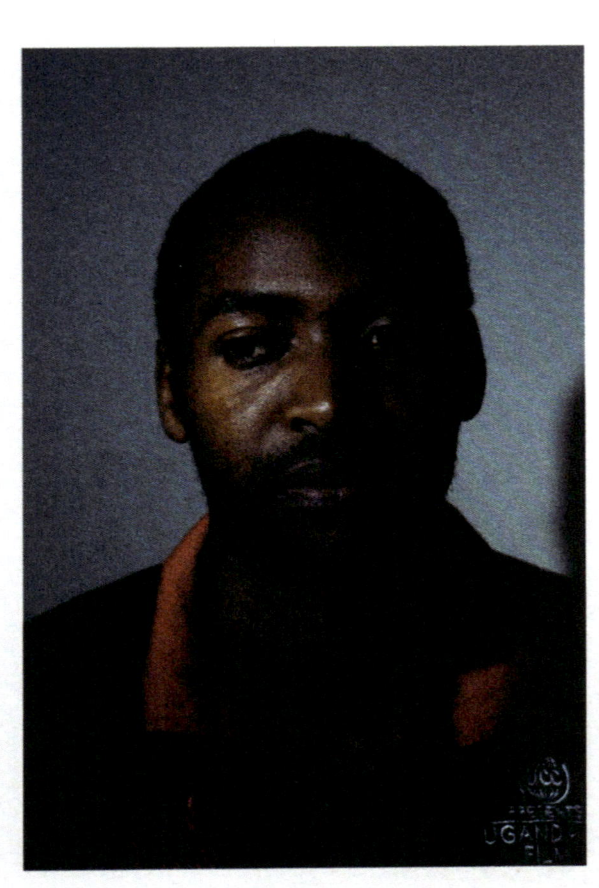

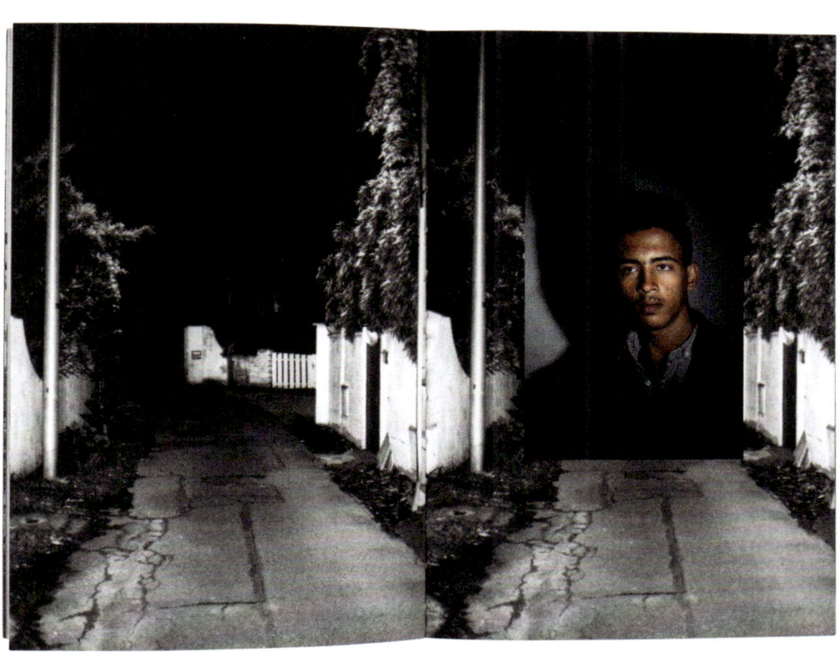
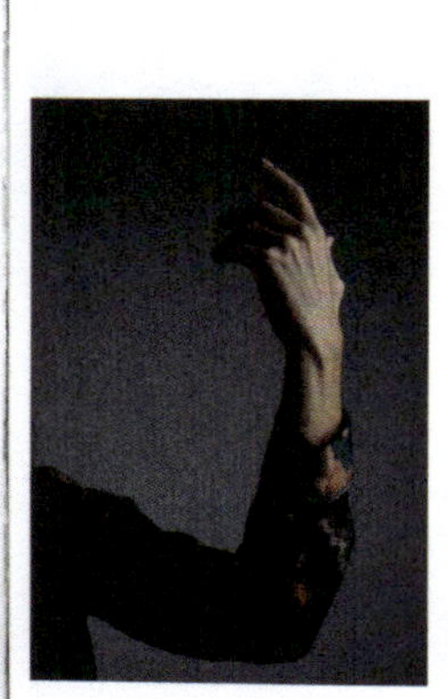
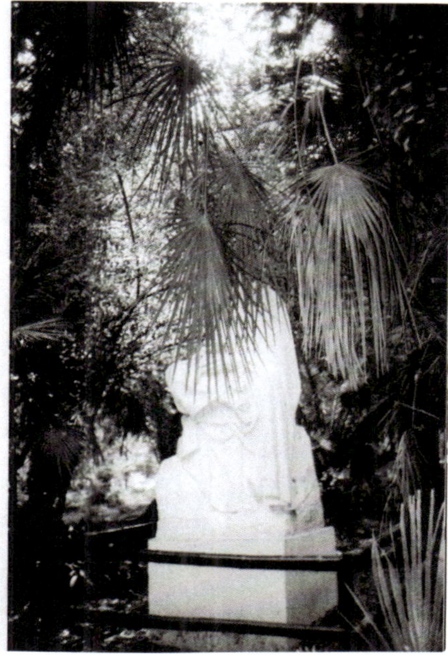

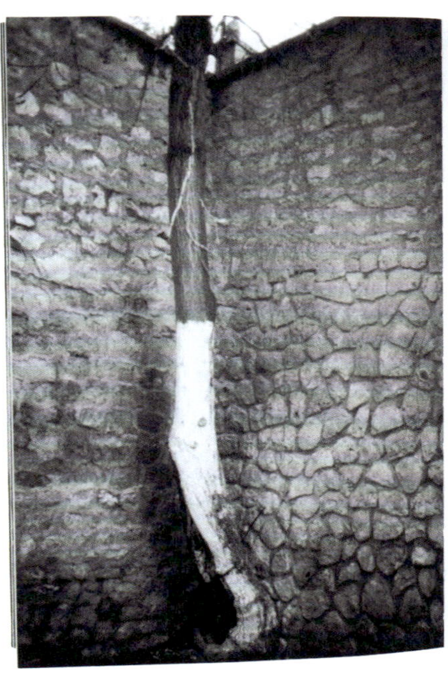
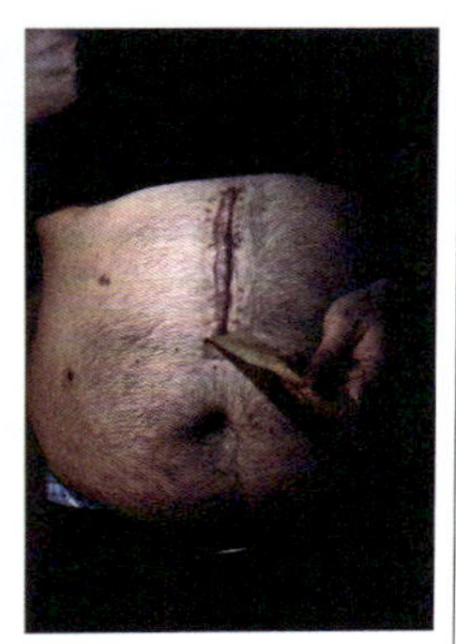
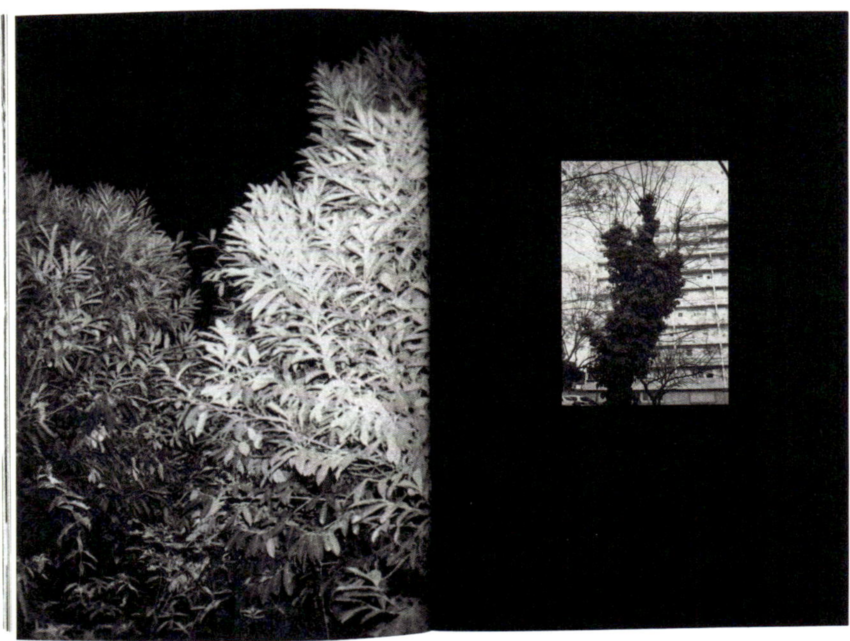

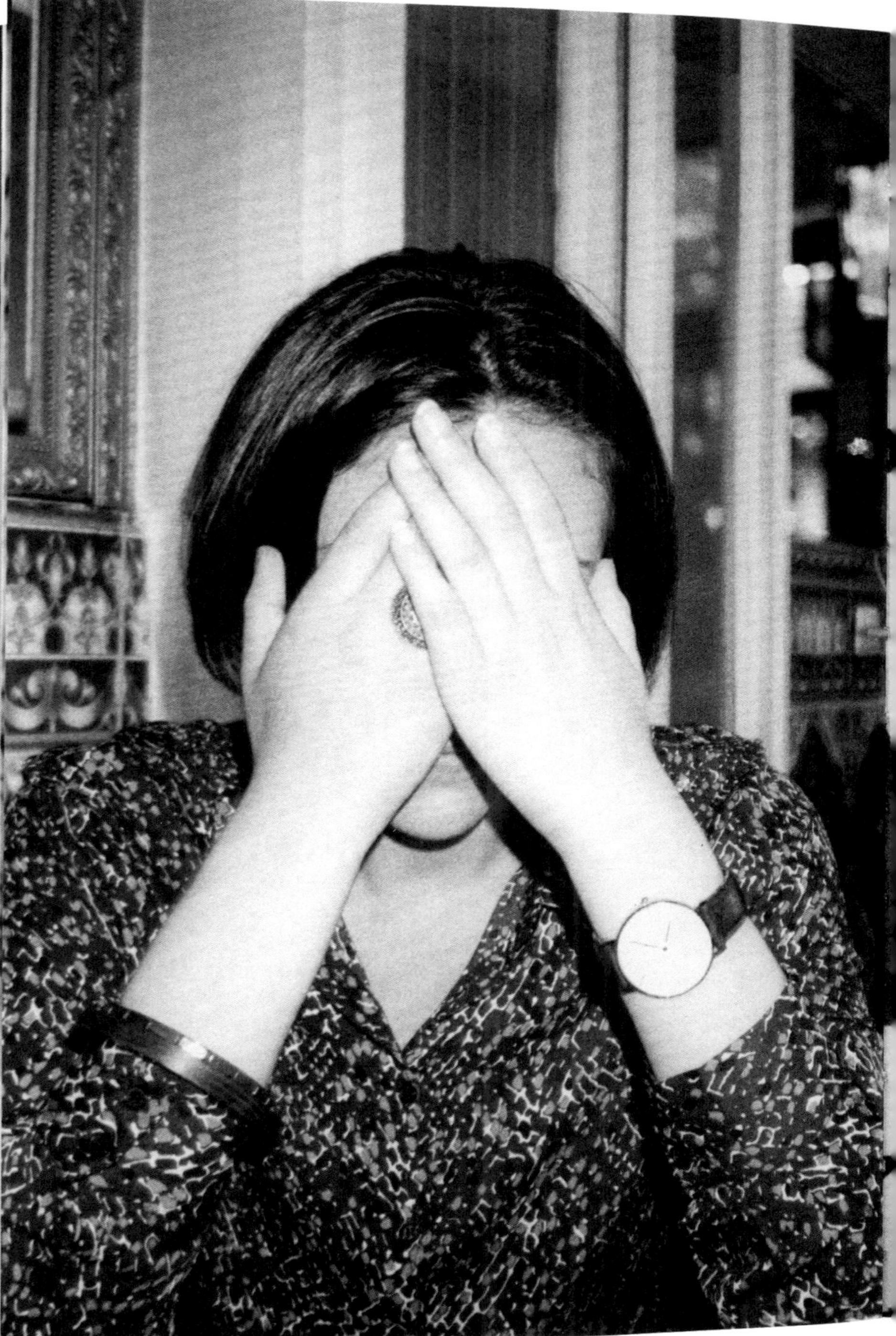

ROBERT ANDY COOMBS

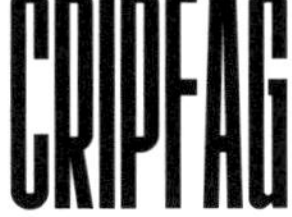

Robert Andy Coombs' blue gaze is piercing. He scrutinizes us without blinking, in turn serene and playful. He calls out to us and enjoins us to support his gaze, to look again, to look better. To insist.

"With a physical disability like mine, you need a lot of care on a daily basis and especially for sex. I need help during foreplay to undress, get into bed and position myself. I need help during intercourse to tell my partner what I want to do or what I would like him to do. And above all, I need help after sex, to clean up, get dressed and get back in my wheelchair," says Coombs, whose *CripFag* series aims to contradict "validist" narratives and, perhaps, promote other narratives. His photographs educate those who continue to deny existences like his own.

Through the images, frontal and attentive photographs of his love life, Coombs provides a provocative response to the medical profession, unable to consider or represent the sexuality of a semi-paralyzed queer man. Photographing his *crip*(pled)*fag* existence allows Robert Andy Coombs to turn the stigmas around and make visible, in a deeply embodied manner, adventures both real and fantasized. Highly vulnerable and reinforced by this exposed vulnerability, the quadriplegic photographer politicizes *care* and gay sexuality. He politicizes the tenderness, care and pleasure that are at the heart of his intimacy, his banal daily life.

CripFag, 2017–ongoing
© Robert Andy Coombs

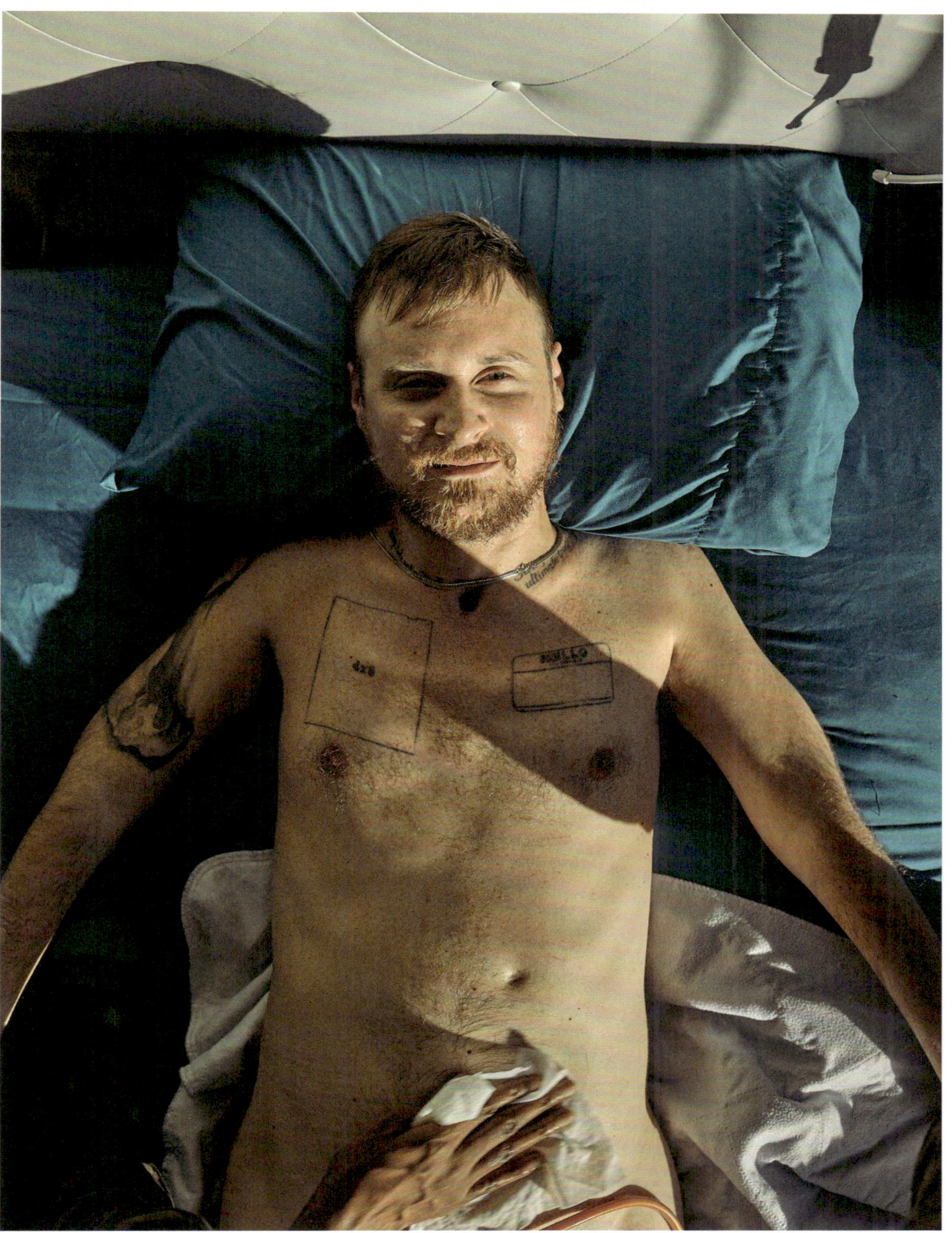

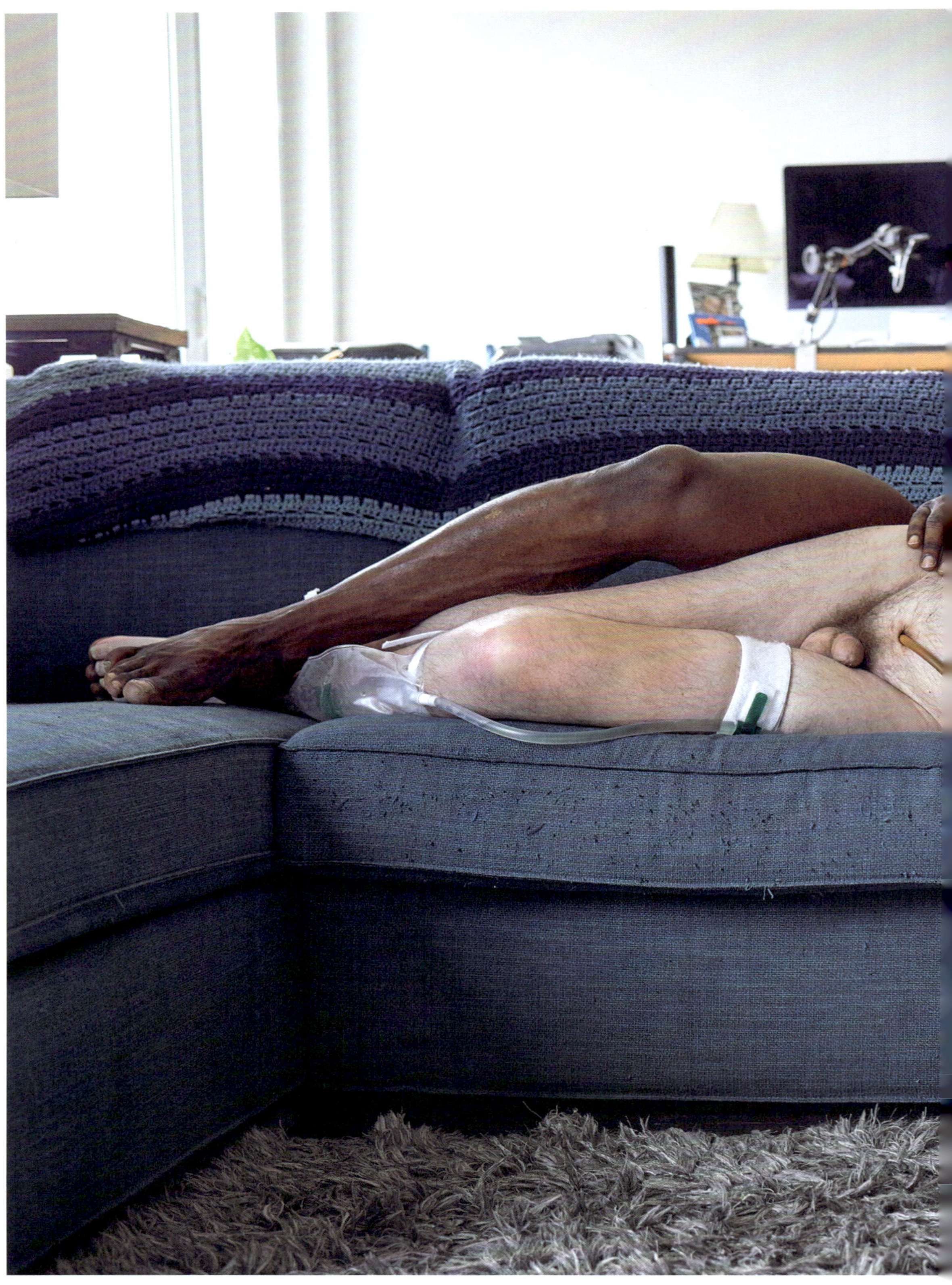

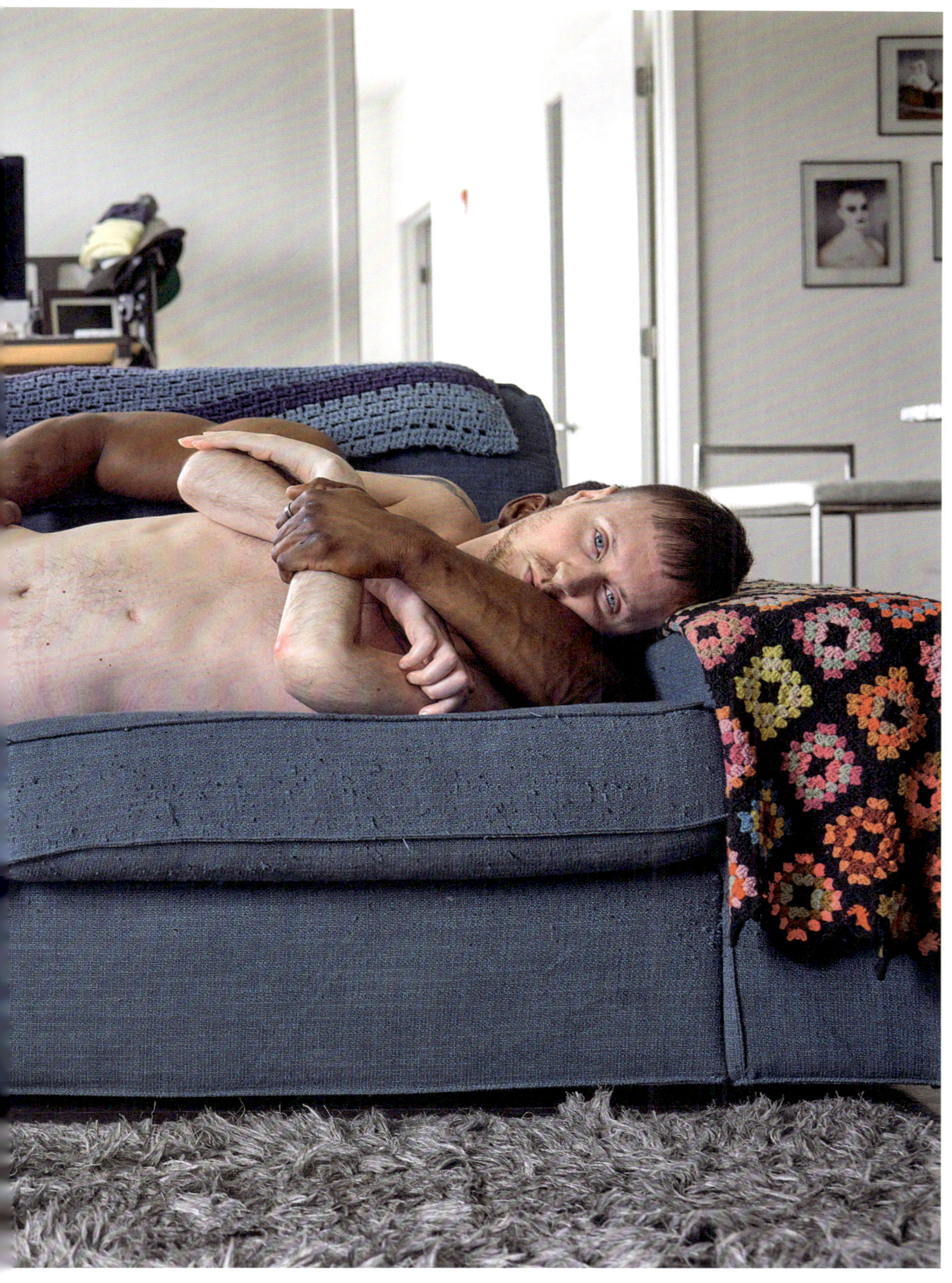

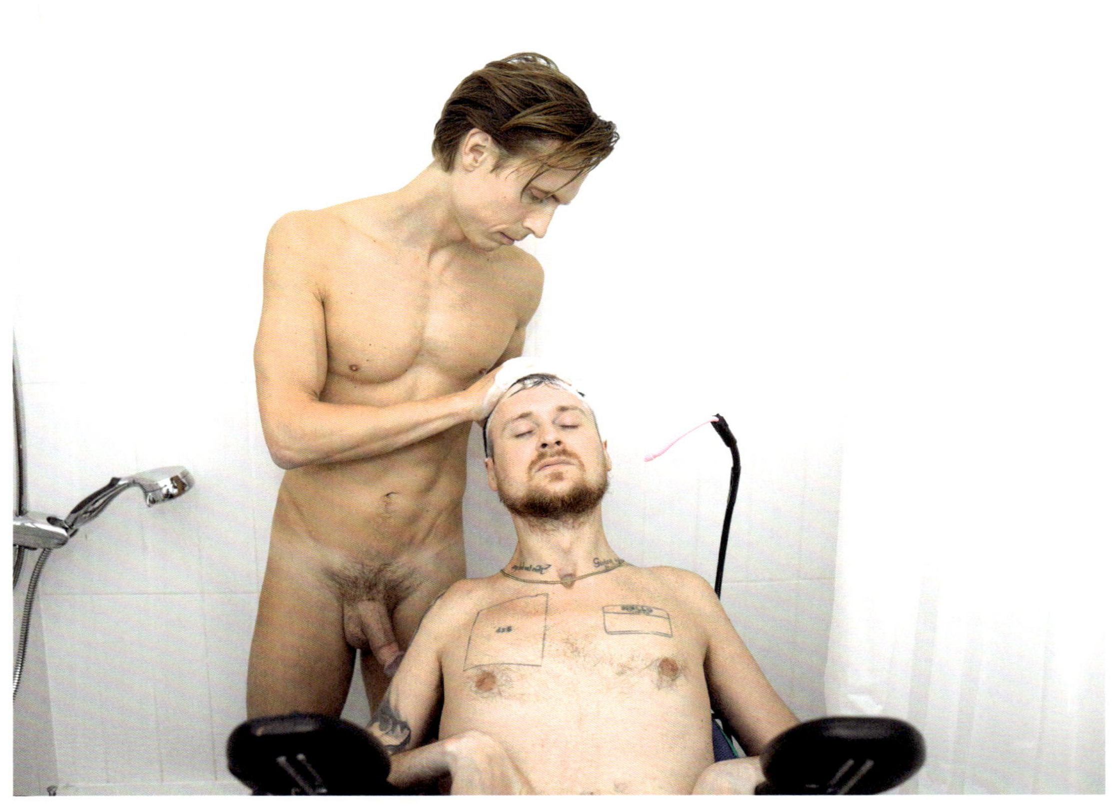

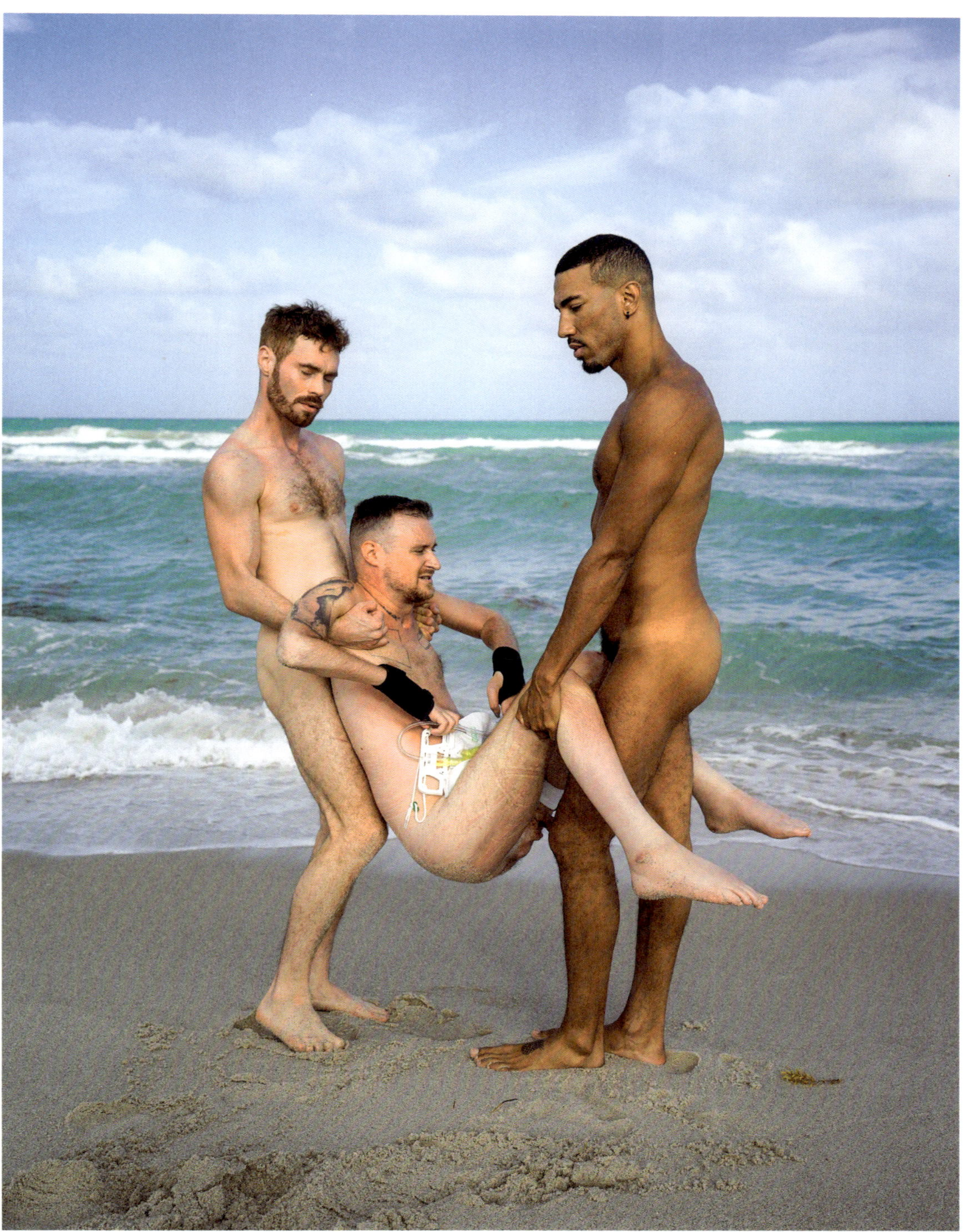

TITLE

SICK IN BED

COVER

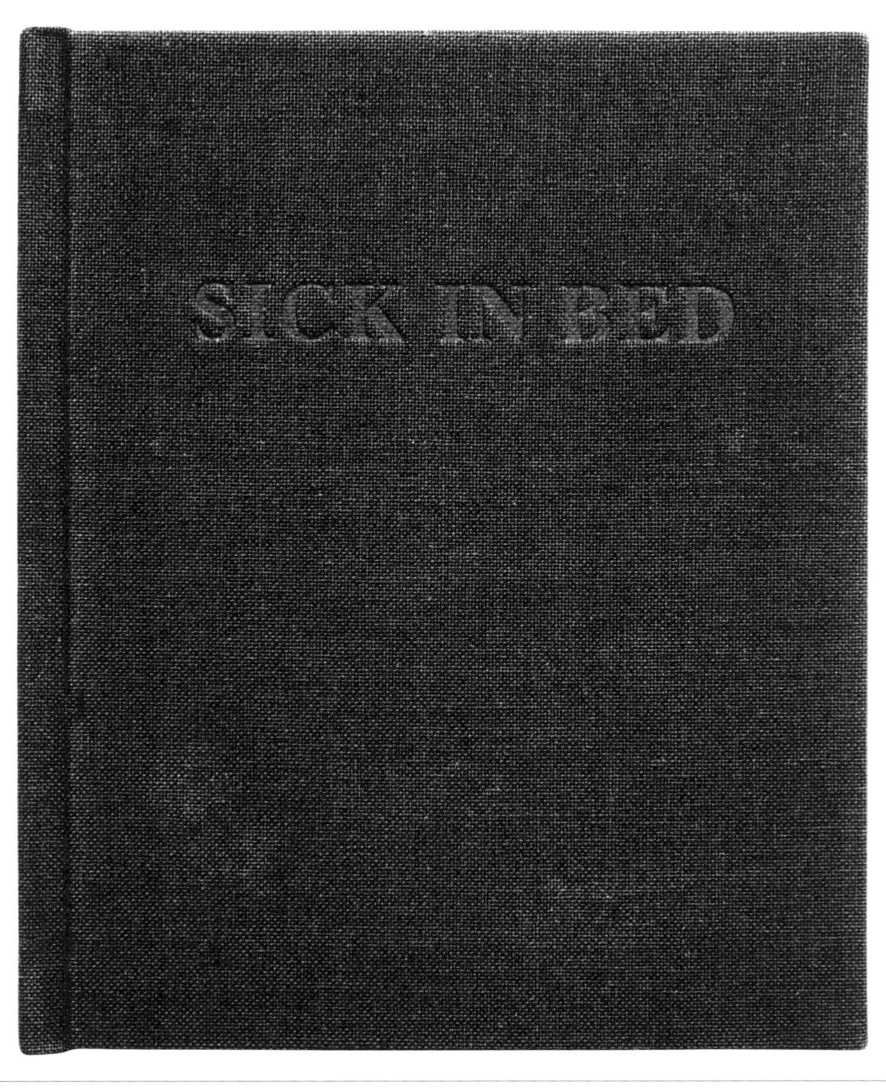

ARTIST	Cheryl Newman
PUBLISHER	Self-published
MONOGRAPHY	- 88 pages - first published in 2018 - size: 11 x 14 cm
SUMMARY	Through her collection of vernacular photographs, Cheryl Newman probes the photographic gaze to question it. She examines the unequal power dynamics between the photographer and his or her subject, especially when the person photographed is a woman with disabilities and health problems that have confined her to her bed. “When my daughter Mimi turned 20, she developed a disability. I started taking pictures of her, but it was painful because I felt like I was becoming complicit in the general voyeurism towards people with disabilities,” explains the London photographer. Through portraits of anonyms, she reconnects with the experience lived with her daughter: the confrontation of an uncomfortable photographic voyeurism and vulnerable patients, deprived of agency. Thus, the point is to reveal the visual impulse that puts into tension the viewer and the suffering, gendered and objectifiable, bedridden body. The accumulation of photographs reveals the spectatorial device that encloses the subject in a frozen setting, while dramatizing the illness and conditioning our gaze. The images say nothing about the knowledge of the bedridden people: the unspeakable experience of their body, a carnal and embodied knowledge acquired in the solitude of disability, of illness. The succession of images testifies to the empathy of the artist, who knew how to see and recognize those whose suffering and identity we do not know.
BIOGRAPHY	For over 15 years, Cheryl Newman was the director of photography at *Telegraph Magazine*. Now an independent curator for the Gaia Foundation and co-founder, with photographer Siân Davey, of the Dartington Workshops supporting photographic practice, she explores her personal history through archival and family photographs. Cheryl Newman lives in London.

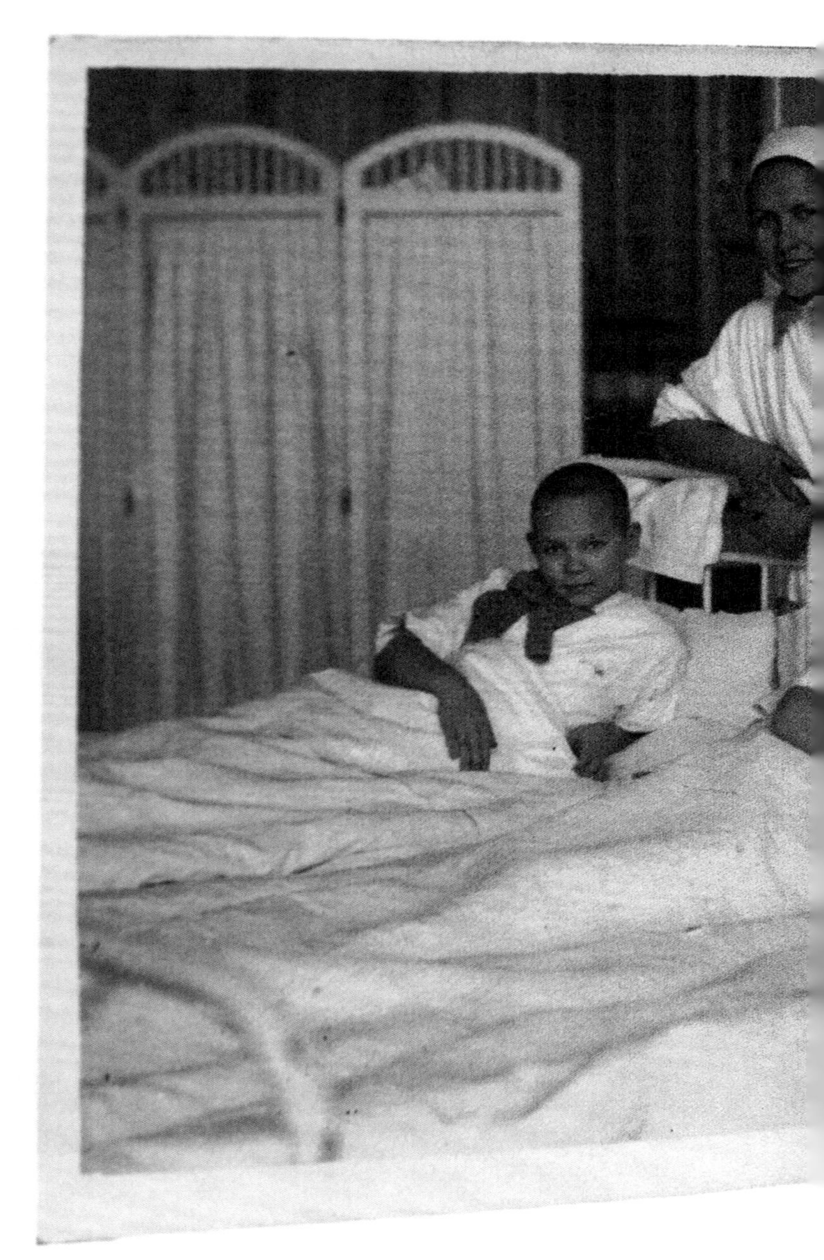

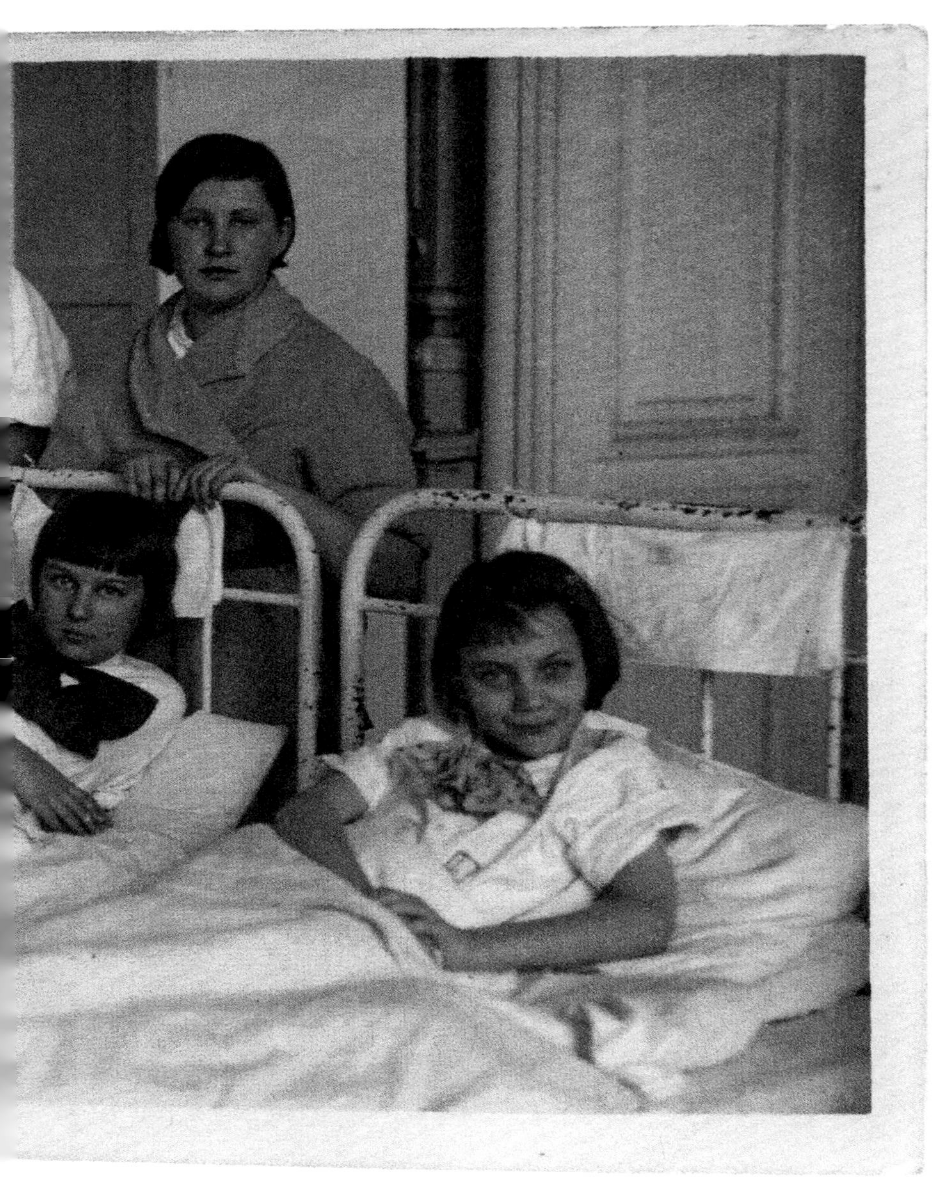

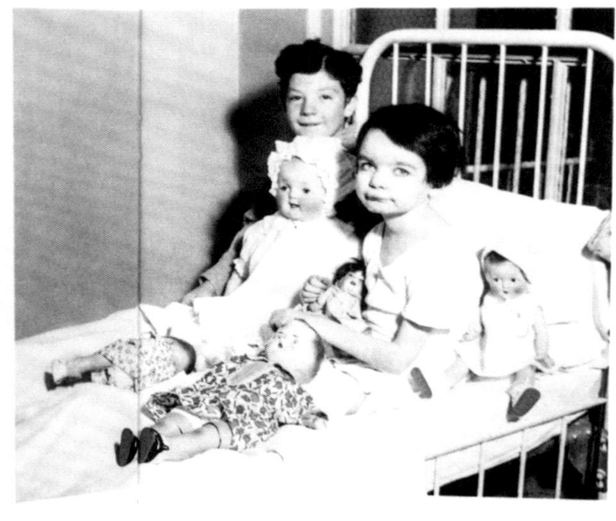

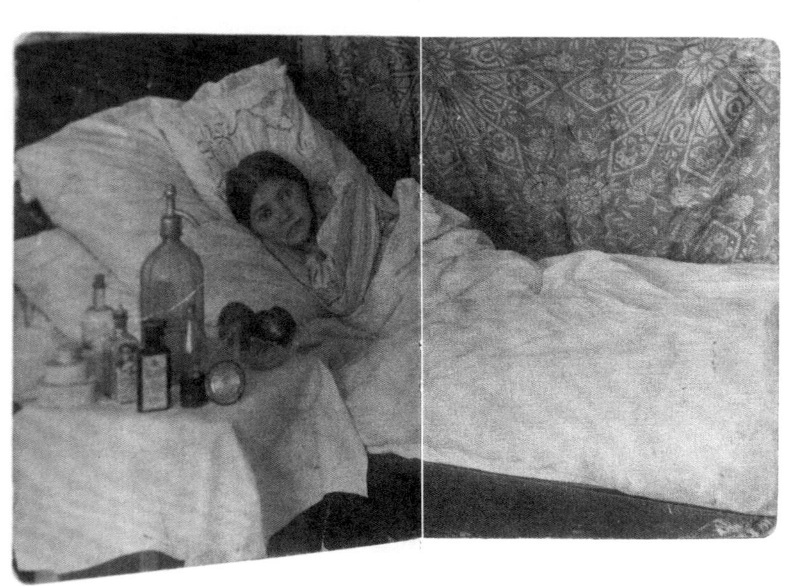

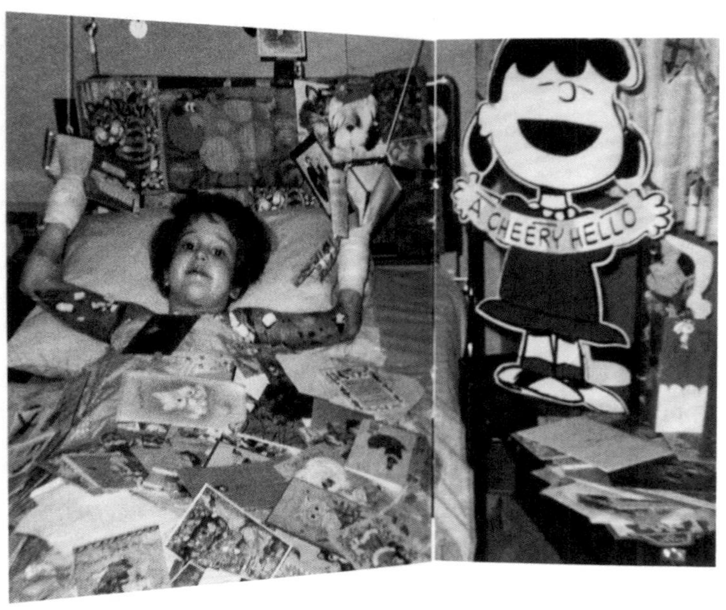
A CHEERY HELLO

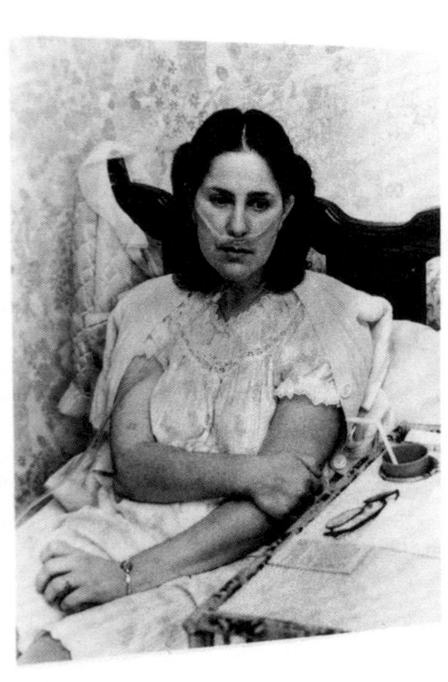

CARMEN WINANT

A BRAND NEW END: SURVIVAL AND ITS PICTURES

A Brand New End: Survival and Its Pictures, 2022 © Carmen Winant, commissioned by The Print Center, Philadelphia
Moon Faces Demons, 2022, photo: Jaime Alvarez
Women's Blueprint for Survival (1), 2022
Violence is one of the ways that men have learned to cope with stress, 2022
Bus shelter poster, 2022
Bus shelter poster, 2022

On one of the custom t-shirts that North American artist Carmen Winant found in the archives of the Philadelphia association Women in Transition (WIT), a woman who was a victim of domestic violence wrote: "Though no one can go back and make a brand new start, anyone can start from now and make a brand new end."

A Brand New End, borrowing from the last words of this quote, works with the documentary holdings of the WIT, founded in 1971, and of the National Coalition Against Domestic Violence, based in Denver since 1978. Winant appropriates, transposes and recontextualizes their archival images in order to highlight the women's liberation movement and the achievements of social workers. The artist questions the images, what they say about abused lives and how they can be used as pedagogical tools, as weapons in the struggle for autonomy and self-representation.

Taking up the aesthetics typical of associations' offices, Carmen Winant documents the feminist strategies of survival and revolt. The series gathers her collages – colourful DIY-style patchworks, her photographs of customized t-shirts and a constellation of newspaper clippings whose accumulation reflects the discourse of the media on domestic violence. *A Brand New End* makes it possible to heal wounds in joy and camaraderie.

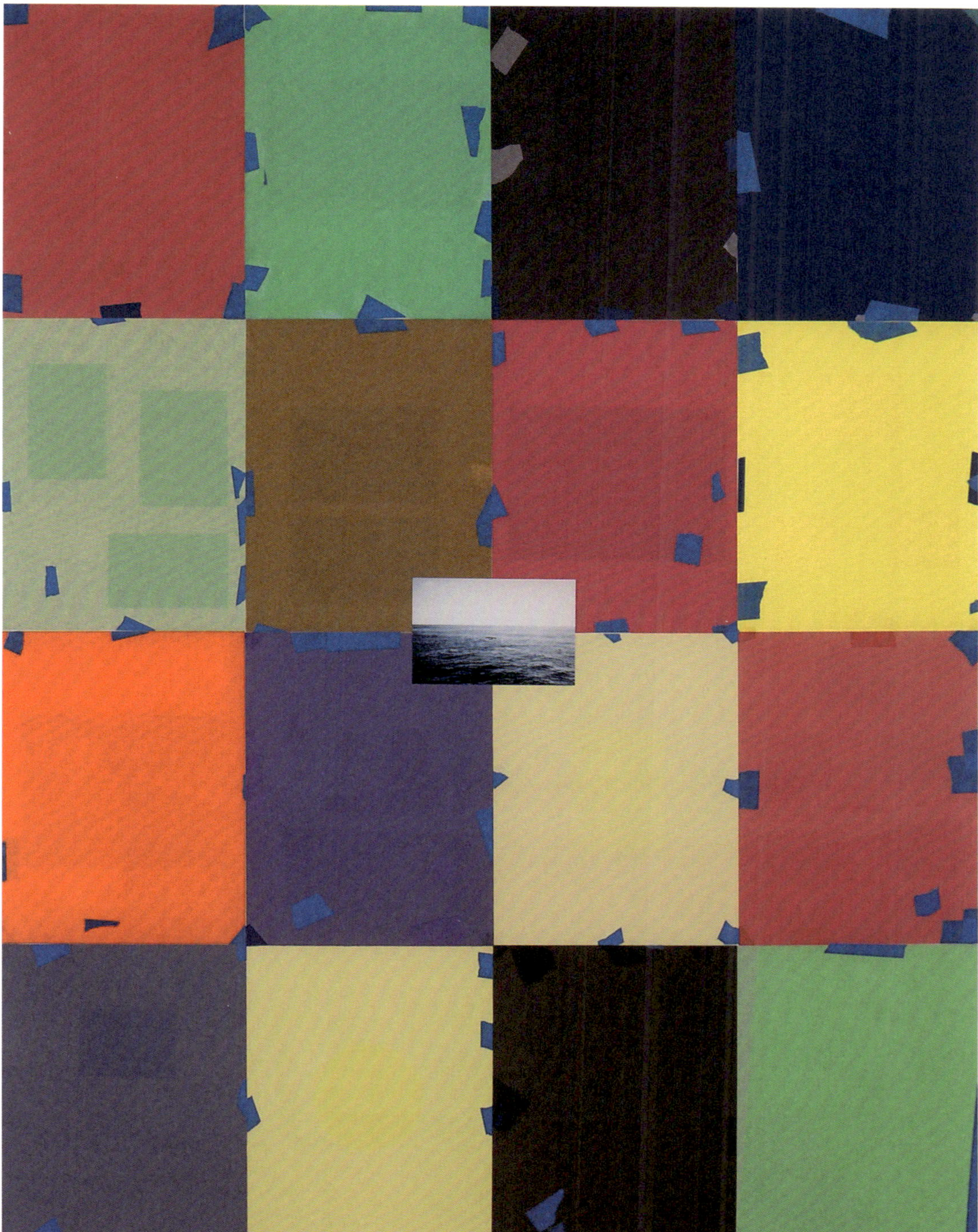

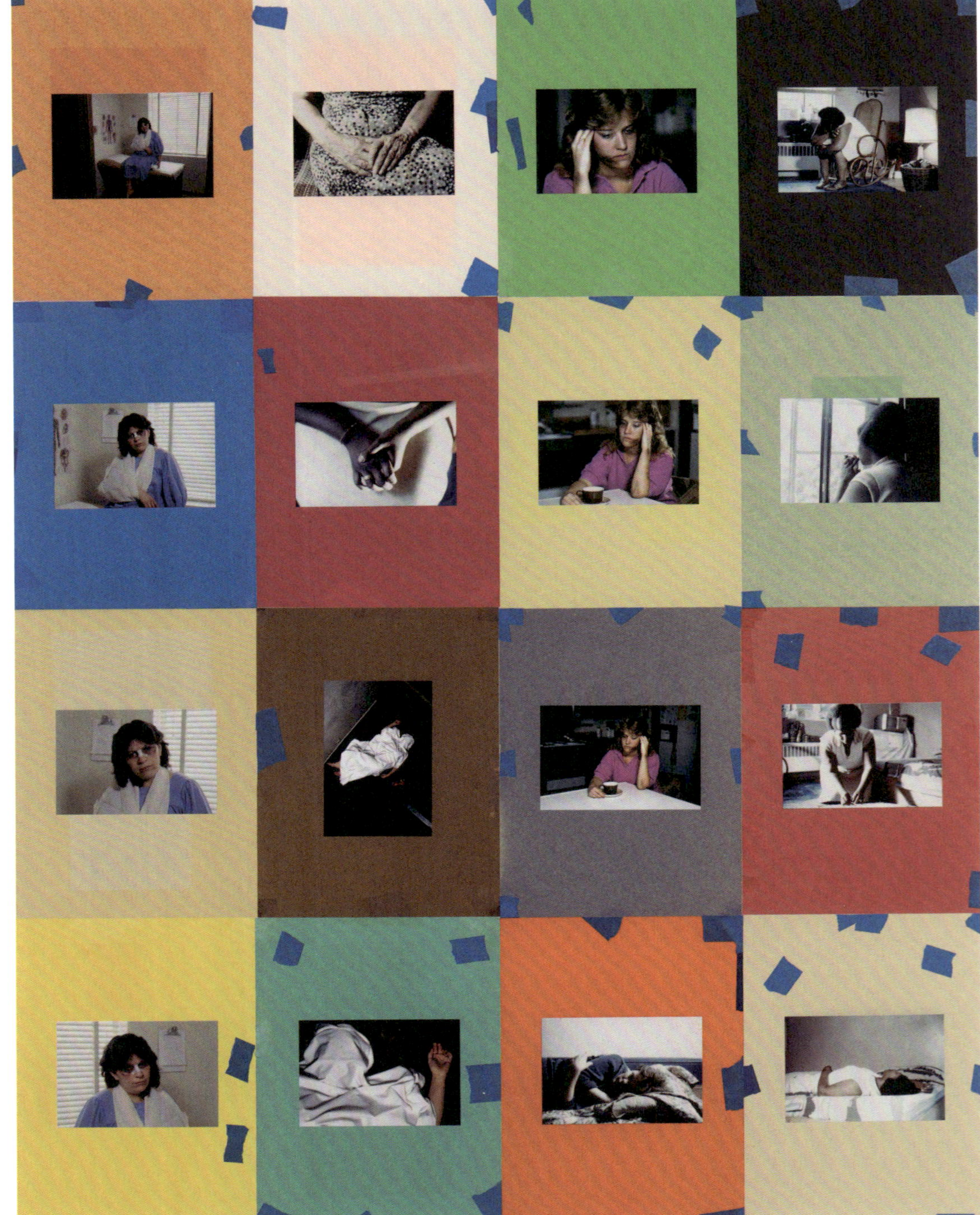

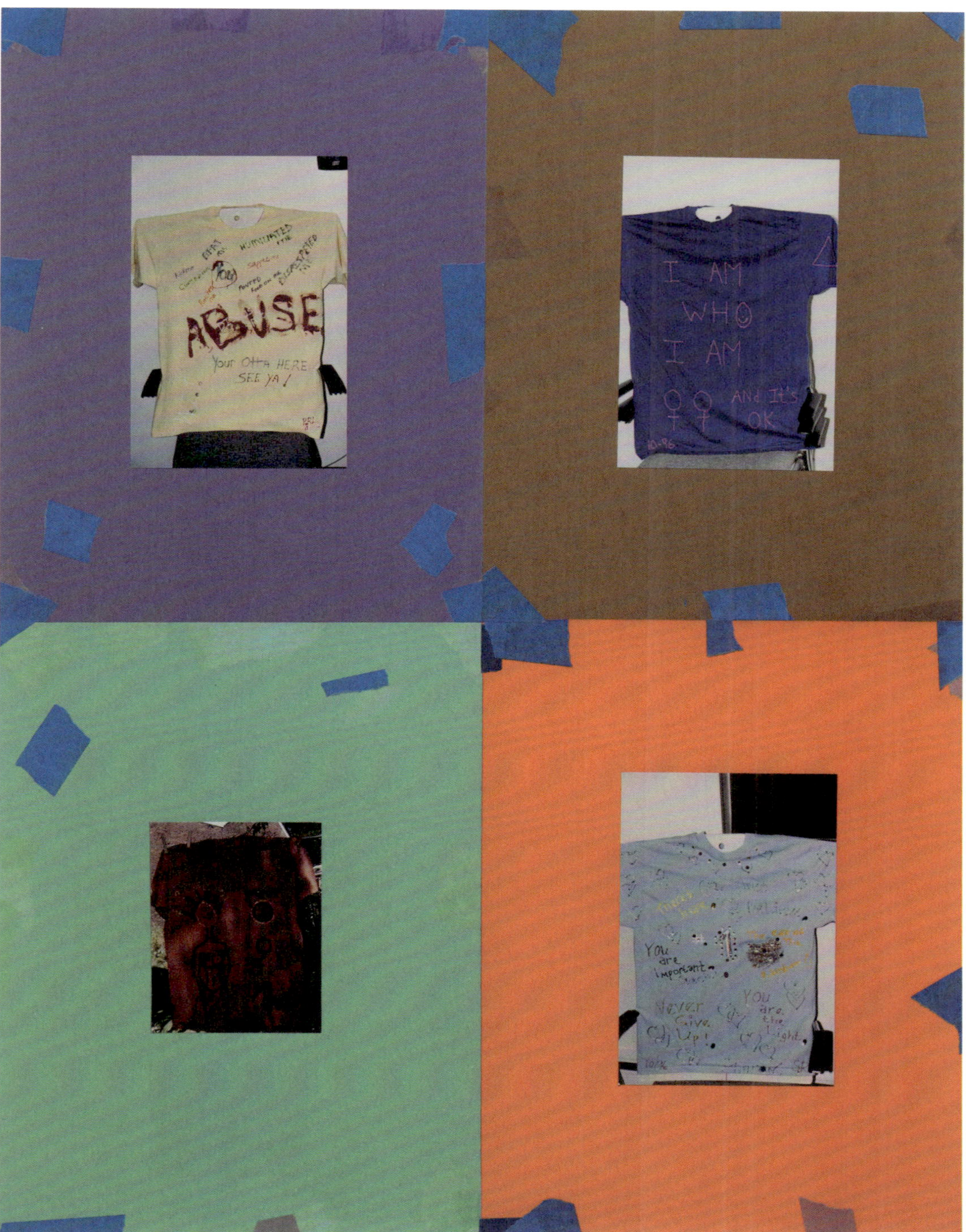
ABUSE
Your Outta HERE
SEE YA!
I AM
WHO
I AM
And It's
OK
You
are
important
Never
Give
Up!
You
are
the
light

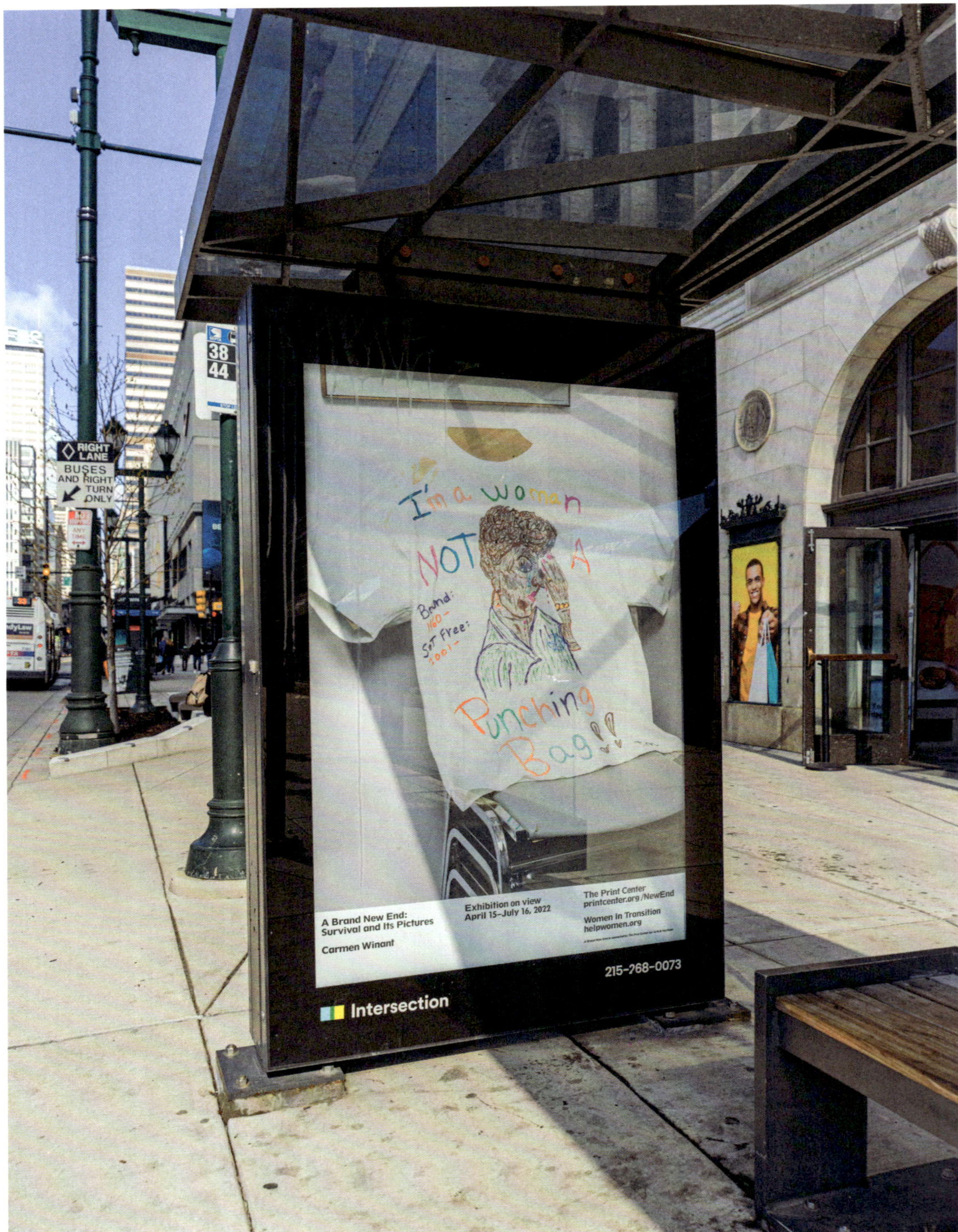
RIGHT LANE
BUSES AND RIGHT TURN ONLY
38
44
I'm a woman
NOT A
Brand:
Set Free:
Punching Bag!!
A Brand New End:
Survival and Its Pictures
Carmen Winant
Exhibition on view
April 15–July 16, 2022
The Print Center
printcenter.org/NewEnd
Women In Transition
helpwomen.org
215-768-0073
Intersection

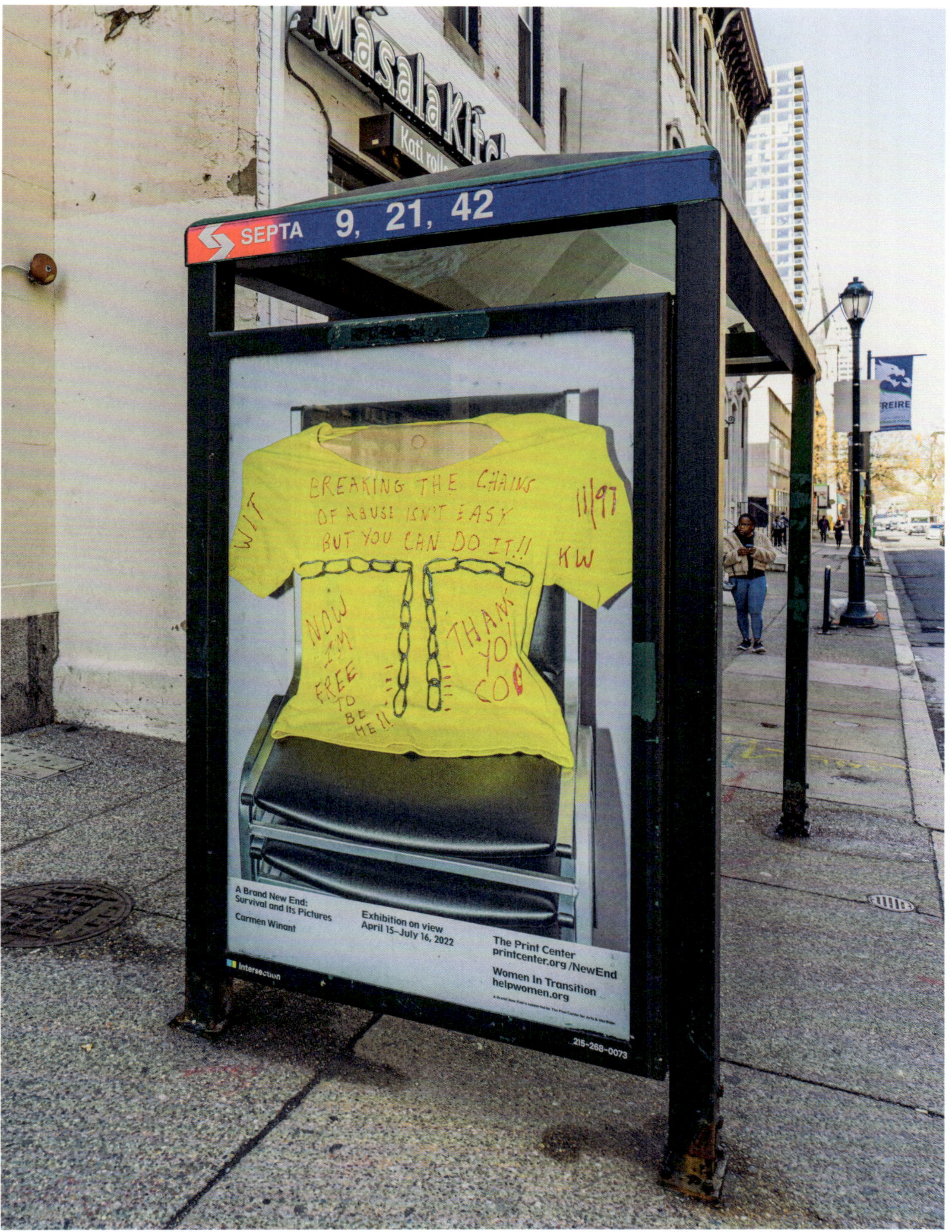
Masala Kitch
SEPTA
9, 21, 42
BREAKING THE CHAINS
OF ABUSE ISN'T EASY
BUT YOU CAN DO IT!!
WIT
11/97
KW
NOW I'M FREE TO BE ME!!
THANK YOU CO
A Brand New End:
Survival and Its Pictures
Carmen Winant
Exhibition on view
April 15–July 16, 2022
The Print Center
printcenter.org /NewEnd
Women In Transition
helpwomen.org
Intersection
215-268-0073

NETWORKS OF MUTUAL CARE

CARMEN WINANT & LAIA ABRIL

IN CONVERSATION

When Californian visual artist Carmen Winant released her project on gendered violence, entitled *A Brand New End: Survival and Its Pictures* (2022), she reached out saying how this project had been extensive and somewhat revelatory for her in terms of how she regards questions of care. As such, it was obvious that we had to continue this conversation for this issue of *The Eyes*.

When digging into organizational archives, she mentioned how she expected to find barbarity as she turned to the subject of domestic and gendered violence, but what she so often found were networks of mutual care.

This conversation took place in the context of the US Supreme Court formally overturning *Roe* v. *Wade* on 24 of June, concluding that the constitutional right to abortion, sustained for over 50 years, was no longer valid. As such this dialogue took an even deeper meaning.

Last year, artist Christian Patterson approached both of us to show some of our work in his Garage gallery, given the political situation regarding restricted access to abortion that was already happening in Texas (see image on p. 141). It was then that we came up with the idea of combining our work: Carmen's piece on one side would show an archival depiction of the *Roe* v. *Wade* victory, and on the other side there would be one of my images from a DIY abortion piece showing a coat hanger. So it almost felt like a very weird déjà vu.

LAIA: I just read that in Poland one of the subjects of my book is facing three years in prison for helping other women with access to abortions.

CARMEN: I'm sure they'll be locking people up right and left here too …

LAIA: Which makes the question I was planning to start this interview with so difficult … What is for you the role of art in this political situation we're living in?

CARMEN: It's such a hard question. I feel that if you'd have asked me even a week ago, I would have had a different answer. Even if I've always felt conflicted about the role and function of being a political artist, this week I feel a kind of despair and need for real radical action. So much of my work is about looking back or reaching back towards other people's bravery – about people who have risked so much to make progressive social feminist change happen, and my admiration for them. But in a lot of ways I don't risk anything myself. So I've been frustrated and I've been thinking about how to make art functional.

LAIA: That's already the case with your latest project on gendered violence, *A Brand New End: Survival and Its Pictures*. You mentioned the "networks of mutual care" as "the bedrock of feminism" and how we could "build these worlds where none other exist; to help us imagine another way forward that is based in reciprocity and threatlessness."

CARMEN: "Functional" has different meanings for different people. A big part of this new show we opened in Philadelphia was putting the work up in bus shelters along with the information from the hotline organizations (see images on pp. 134 & 135). As well as, in the exhibition, having material you could take away, that is likewise serviceable, that you can use in your life. So I'm thinking how art can literally in this way reach people, and if it's not too grandiose to say, can even save people. But I wonder if that's enough and I wonder about my responsibility now, with everything that's going on, and if I've been risking enough. What do you think about this?

LAIA: The other day, I was invited to take part in a round table with Pilar Aymerich – an iconic feminist photographer from Barcelona – and even in her eighties, she is still strong and hopeful, and it made me realize: would things be even worse if artists were not actually doing this work? And I think about your work, which has always had this very uplifting element, as well as being very vulnerable. How did you decide to switch to this new heavier topic, how do you think this will evolve for you?

CARMEN: First of all, I surprised myself as well! As you've said, I tend to gravitate towards these moments of explosive radical feminist joy, and I think I do that because I want this for myself. I have this impulse to collect these moments; I want to feel their residual effects. So there's a kind of optimism and a little bit of hope to imagine that another world is possible. I'm always looking for proof positive of that. Many domestic support organizations don't have archives, that's not their priority, for obvious reasons. So when I ended up finding these collections, I was at once thrilled and terrified. I thought, this is not what I make work about. It was filled with horror, but it also had inside of it (as all feminist projects have to, I think) a kind of joyfulness. So much of this project was about the support systems themselves, entangled with the survivors and the politics, but also the support staff – who are themselves survivors – building whole new social networks of care. There was something about that … maybe "joyful" is not the right word given the context, but "powerful" … and it really resonated with me in a larger way regarding the whole practice.

LAIA: How did you deal with the impact on your own well-being? Especially when faced with the more heavy aspects of the project?

CARMEN: There was a tremendous amount of tragedy. I didn't allow myself to really feel it as I was going on, I fully dissociated. We have previously talked about this in terms of how to get through the work, and people do that in different ways. I didn't cry or anything, I just moved forward, and as soon as the project was out, I just completely lost my shit, I cried for two weeks. I'm still getting over it, to be honest. I suppose you must deal with this on a regular basis in your work, but I don't, I go around it, and I think it was important for me to confront it, absorb it into the work, and also to balance it with this sort of community and care, that was so important.

LAIA: When working with traumatic archives, where do you find relief in the process? Is it when sharing with others part of the process, maybe even during talks or exhibitions?

CARMEN: I would imagine, based on how you talk about your work, that this is something you think about a lot: interpersonal connections and points of collaboration as you work. It requires so much trust, going into somebody's home, opening up their drawers and looking through their material, them opening up to you, being in collaboration with you, being vulnerable … So when I talk about the results of the work, showing the images, the installation, that's not possible. In fact, 90% of the work is about building trust with other people and demonstrating a kind of reciprocity. Over time it has become so clear to me that, while people might describe me as an archive artist, I think of what I do as being a kind of a social practitioner … So much of my work is meeting people! I build relationships with them, not only in the service of the work, but in the service of life … creating a sort of friendship, but also sharing a political agenda.

LAIA: Is it where you find meaning?

CARMEN: One of the archives in the show, an umbrella organization for domestic violence, has this archive that was 110 boxes in a storage unit in Downtown Denver (Colorado, USA). After many conversations, they gave me the key to the storage unit – quite incredible that they had that kind of trust in me ... It became clear that they wanted to do something with it, maybe place it in a public library, maybe organize it. They needed volunteers or a grant. So now, a whole new project has begun. The show is about to come down, and now, I'm engaged in this new chapter. I can only speak for myself, but if the end goal is to only get to the exhibition, then that has become a bit too shallow, not enough, not substantial enough. Building relationships with people, sustaining relationships that yield in different ways over time, and not only to my end and needs, has become very crucial, even if that's not the work that most people see.

LAIA: You mentioned the label "political art", which I use too, and we've also talked about how the label "activist" is very different in the US than in Europe. However, would you say that your practice is growing towards activism?

CARMEN: That's interesting, because the sort of obvious response is to go back to the beginning of our conversation when we were discussing whether what we are doing is enough. But on the other hand, another way of being an activist is what you're talking about in terms of care; even though it's a much "quieter" way of being an activist. I wonder about these ongoing networks of care, between artist and archive: what can those yield? I've become interested in both avenues and I have to think about those because I have two small children and I'm engaged in constant and ongoing care work, which in my country, like in most countries, is invisible and valueless. So I think about the work that I do at home as a kind of activist work ... how I raise my sons is my own personal resistance. I think about my artworks, and the ongoing networks of mutual investment, as a kind of way to care for people. Not very dissimilar to being a mother, like: "I'm here for you every day, I'm not going away, I'm not going to only take what I want and leave." That extends into how I teach and how I make art, which in the USA, we certainly would never talk about when referring to being an activist.

LAIA: And how does "care" look like in your practice today?

CARMEN: It makes me think of Mierle Laderman Ukeles, the American artist I mentioned to you during our Zoom conversation for *Foam Magazine* in February 2021. She's someone who's been a really important influence on me. One of the things that she talked about early on is the sort of irony of the conundrum of care: "Care is work that produces no results." Of course, my children are growing older and they're healthy, but ultimately there's a kind of maintenance aspect to it. However, regarding art, there are no slides that I can show in my PowerPoint that demonstrate that I have a relationship with the people I collaborate with or that we're checking in on each other. So there's something invisible to that work. In a certain way, I feel like the concept and reality of care are sometimes in conflict with each other, and with my desire to be an artist, because that requires producing results that often detract time and energy from how I care for myself, how I care for my children – because there's no support structure for that. There's so much investment that has to go into it. And as Mierle has said so many times about care, it's thrilling, it's boring. This is a kind of root concept, a contradiction: in the demand of care work and the demand to make art.

LAIA: I guess there's a kind of pragmatism around care that we're not really talking about. I remember a female artist colleague telling me about the difficulty of getting approval for babysitting fees when making work budgets. Sometimes it's even

understanding that from a professional perspective – care could mean for curators or editors to grant more time.

CARMEN: Absolutely. I mean, just what you say, first and foremost about childcare, is so important. I too write that into every grant proposal, every budget, and if they don't fund me because of it, or if they don't want to cover that aspect, that's not acceptable. I also go to great pains to just talk about being a parent and having small children every time I do an artist talk. At one point I couldn't travel because I had a small child and he was waking up 10 times a night to breastfeed. That's a political stance, but it's also just a practical stance. I need childcare more than I need a studio assistant, more than I need material costs. I talk about that all the time with students. I don't think when I was a student I ever heard anyone talk about how they function as an artist with small children.

LAIA: Or even the combination of having those children and a career. These things might seem so obvious, and even naive, but sometimes they're the ones that can make the difference. But this is also linked to the theme of this issue of *The Eyes*, finding artists who have been doing projects from a caring perspective. But as you said, we need a whole structural revolution in this field in order to be able to do that and keep being artists.

CARMEN: You're right. And it seems so glaringly obvious. I'm convinced that the only thing that will save us is women's strikes, basically. Otherwise, the patriarchy will continue to reinforce itself. We need to leave it with no choice. I'm thinking a lot about what it means to be asked to work with or about care.

Carmen Winant is an artist and the Roy Lichtenstein Chair of Studio Art at The Ohio State University. Her work utilizes installation and collage strategies to examine feminist modes of survival and revolt. Winant's recent projects have been shown at the Museum of Modern Art, SculptureCenter and Museo Universitario Arte Contemporáneo. Winant is a 2019 Guggenheim Fellow in Photography, and the mother to two sons, Carlo and Rafa, whom she shares with her partner Luke Stettner.

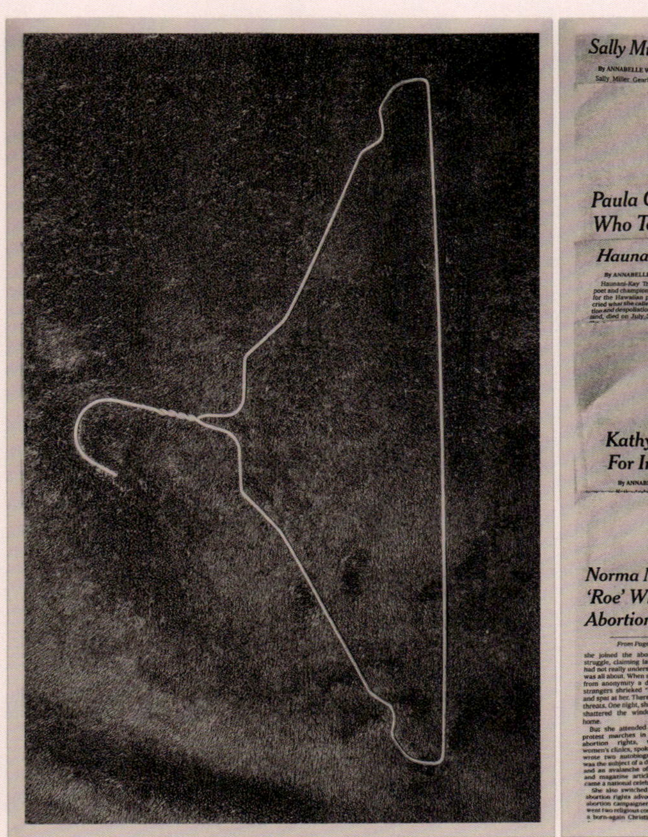

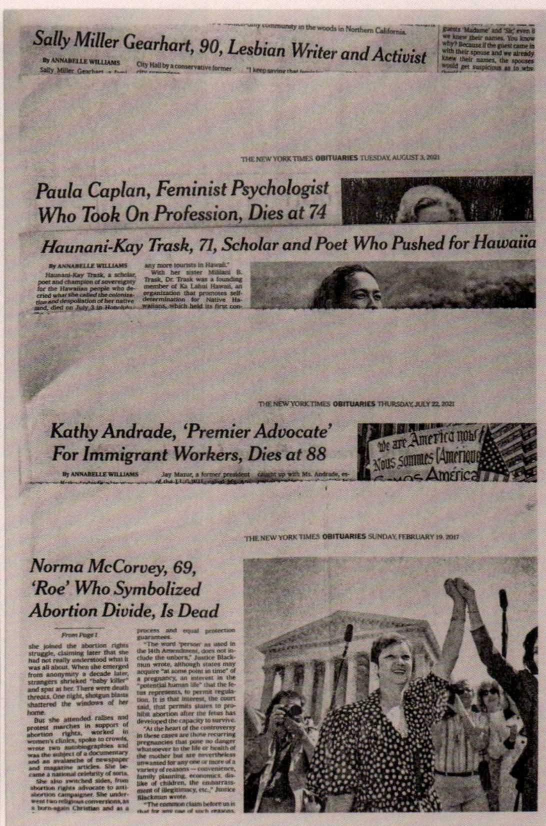

community in the woods in Northern California.

Sally Miller Gearhart, 90, Lesbian Writer and Activist

By ANNABELLE WILLIAMS

City Hall by a conservative former

guests 'Madame' and 'Sir,' even if we knew their names. You know why? Because if the guest came in with their spouse and we already knew their names, the spouses would get suspicious as to why

THE NEW YORK TIMES **OBITUARIES** TUESDAY, AUGUST 3, 2021

Paula Caplan, Feminist Psychologist Who Took On Profession, Dies at 74

Haunani-Kay Trask, 71, Scholar and Poet Who Pushed for Hawaiia

By ANNABELLE WILLIAMS

Haunani-Kay Trask, a scholar, poet and champion of sovereignty for the Hawaiian people who decried what she called the colonization and despoliation of her native land, died on July 3 in Honolulu.

any more tourists in Hawaii."

With her sister Mililani B. Trask, Dr. Trask was a founding member of Ka Lahui Hawaii, an organization that promotes self-determination for Native Hawaiians, which held its first con-

THE NEW YORK TIMES **OBITUARIES** THURSDAY, JULY 22, 2021

Kathy Andrade, 'Premier Advocate' For Immigrant Workers, Dies at 88

By ANNABELLE WILLIAMS

Jay Mazur, a former president

caught up with Ms. Andrade, es-

THE NEW YORK TIMES **OBITUARIES** SUNDAY, FEBRUARY 19, 2017

Norma McCorvey, 69, 'Roe' Who Symbolized Abortion Divide, Is Dead

From Page 1

she joined the abortion rights struggle, claiming later that she had not really understood what it was all about. When she emerged from anonymity a decade later, strangers shrieked "baby killer" and spat at her. There were death threats. One night, shotgun blasts shattered the windows of her home.

But she attended rallies and protest marches in support of abortion rights, worked in women's clinics, spoke to crowds, wrote two autobiographies and was the subject of a documentary and an avalanche of newspaper and magazine articles. She became a national celebrity of sorts.

She also switched sides, from abortion rights advocate to anti-abortion campaigner. She underwent two religious conversions, as a born-again Christian and as a

process and equal protection guarantees.

"The word 'person' as used in the 14th Amendment, does not include the unborn," Justice Blackmun wrote, although states may acquire "at some point in time" of a pregnancy, an interest in the "potential human life" that the fetus represents, to permit regulation. It is that interest, the court said, that permits states to prohibit abortion after the fetus has developed the capacity to survive.

"At the heart of the controversy in these cases are those recurring pregnancies that pose no danger whatsoever to the life or health of the mother but are nevertheless unwanted for any one or more of a variety of reasons — convenience, family planning, economics, dislike of children, the embarrassment of illegitimacy, etc.," Justice Blackmun wrote.

"The common claim before us is that for any one of such reasons

MASINA & GAL

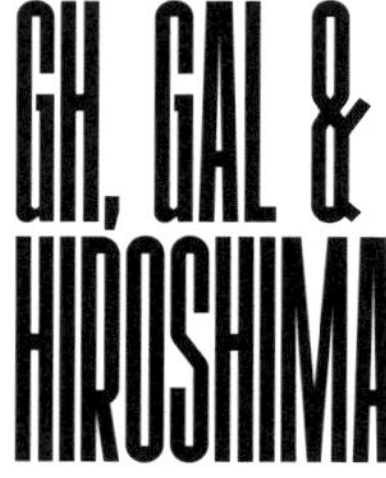

At the age of 10, Hiroshima was stoned for being too androgynous. As a child, Gal wore heels and then, as an adult, asserted her trans identity. By their very existence, the duo disrupts and overturns the norms of the heterosexist regime that reigns supreme in Brazil. Proud to choose life to extract themselves from the shame, they handle their personal stories with great care and, in the in-between of genders, acquire a defensive autonomy. Their series *GH* expresses self-love and systemic violence, and with poignant sensitivity defends stories that they refuse to downplay.

Gal Cipreste Marinelli and Rodrigo Masina Pinheiro (nicknamed Hiroshima because they were born on the same day as the bomb) turn melancholy into strength and build a combative work, which they see as a vengeful and curative counterattack. Together, they create an art of reaction that aims to redistribute the violence received in order to regain a certain ontological sovereignty: "For us," they admit, "the concept of care is now too subtle."

A few stones bloom on a still-life. Between the bare legs of one of the artists, an array of sharp blades juts out. There is a playground climbing frame in the shape of a boot, a foot covered in soot, stiletto heels. A hand shatters with a hammer stones collected in the childhood neighbourhood. A wooden chair crosses its front legs with impunity. A cluster of rocks covered in protective foam expresses childhood abused, childhood to be protected. These bodies no longer perform what gender assigns to them.

GH, Gal and Hiroshima, 2019–ongoing

Implant, 2020
GH, 2020
Bait, 2020
Gal, 2019
Arch (or When They Spoke Again), 2020.
Fence, 2021
Sculpture of Asphalt and Foam Made for a Child, 2019

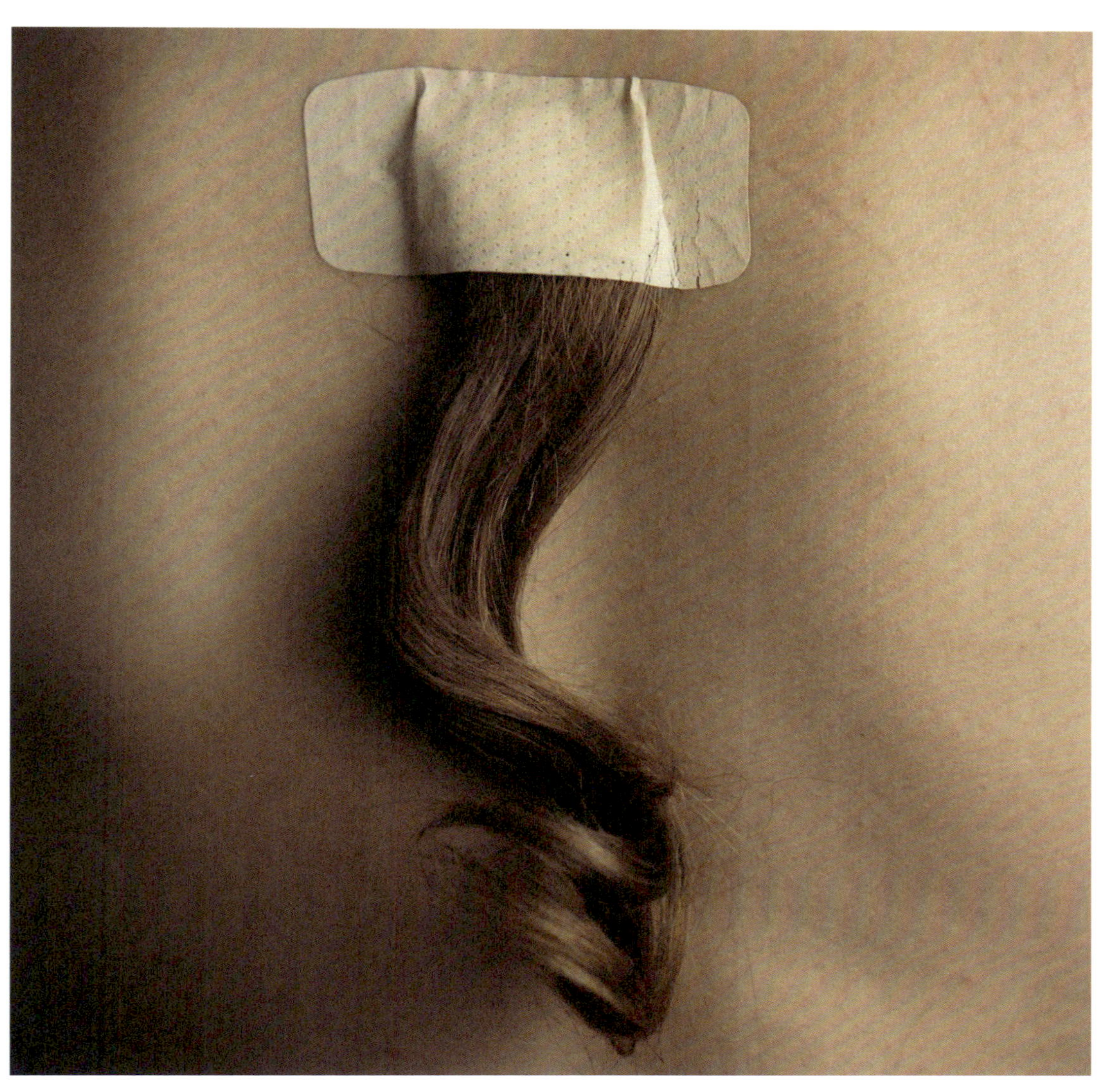

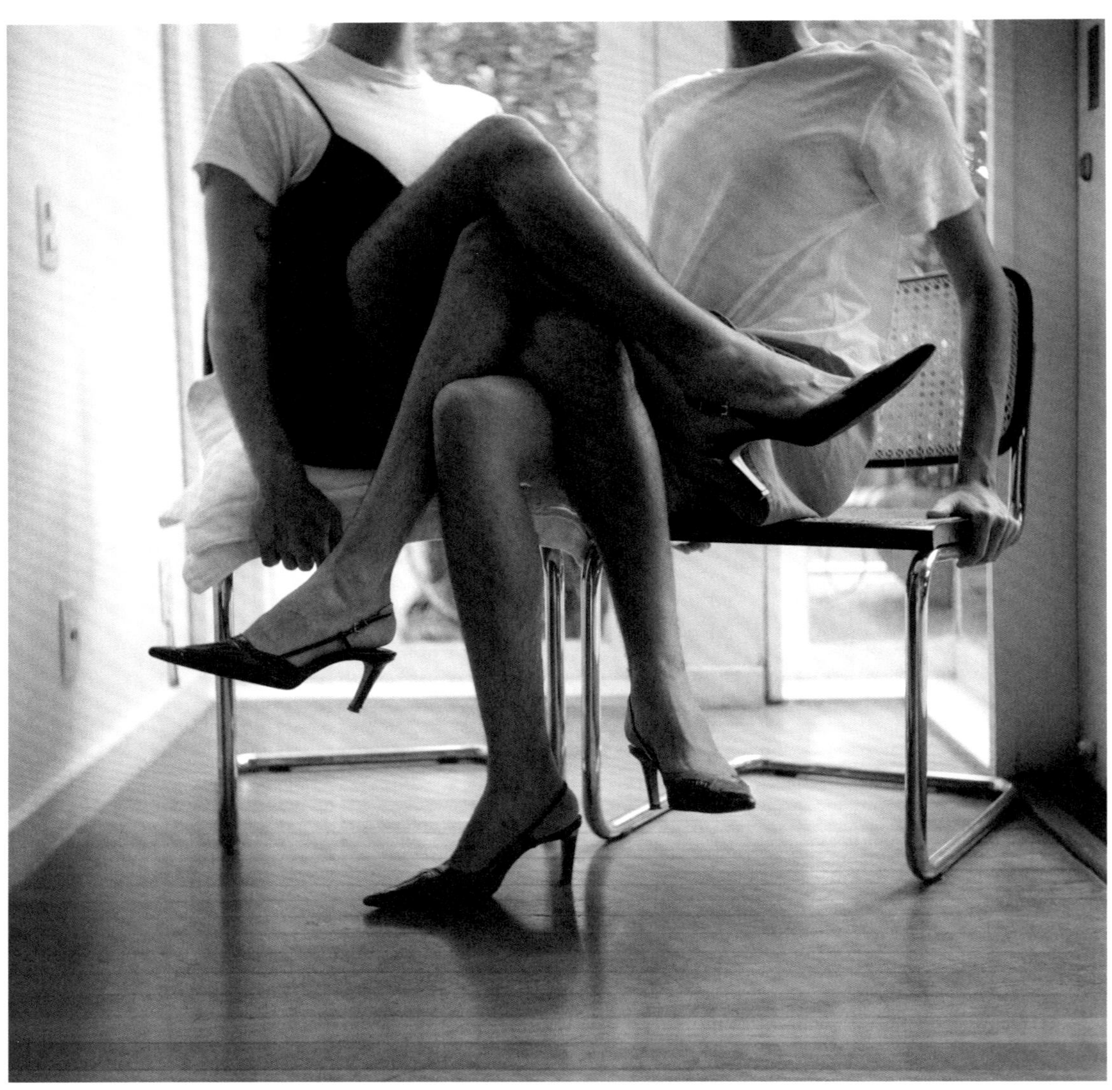

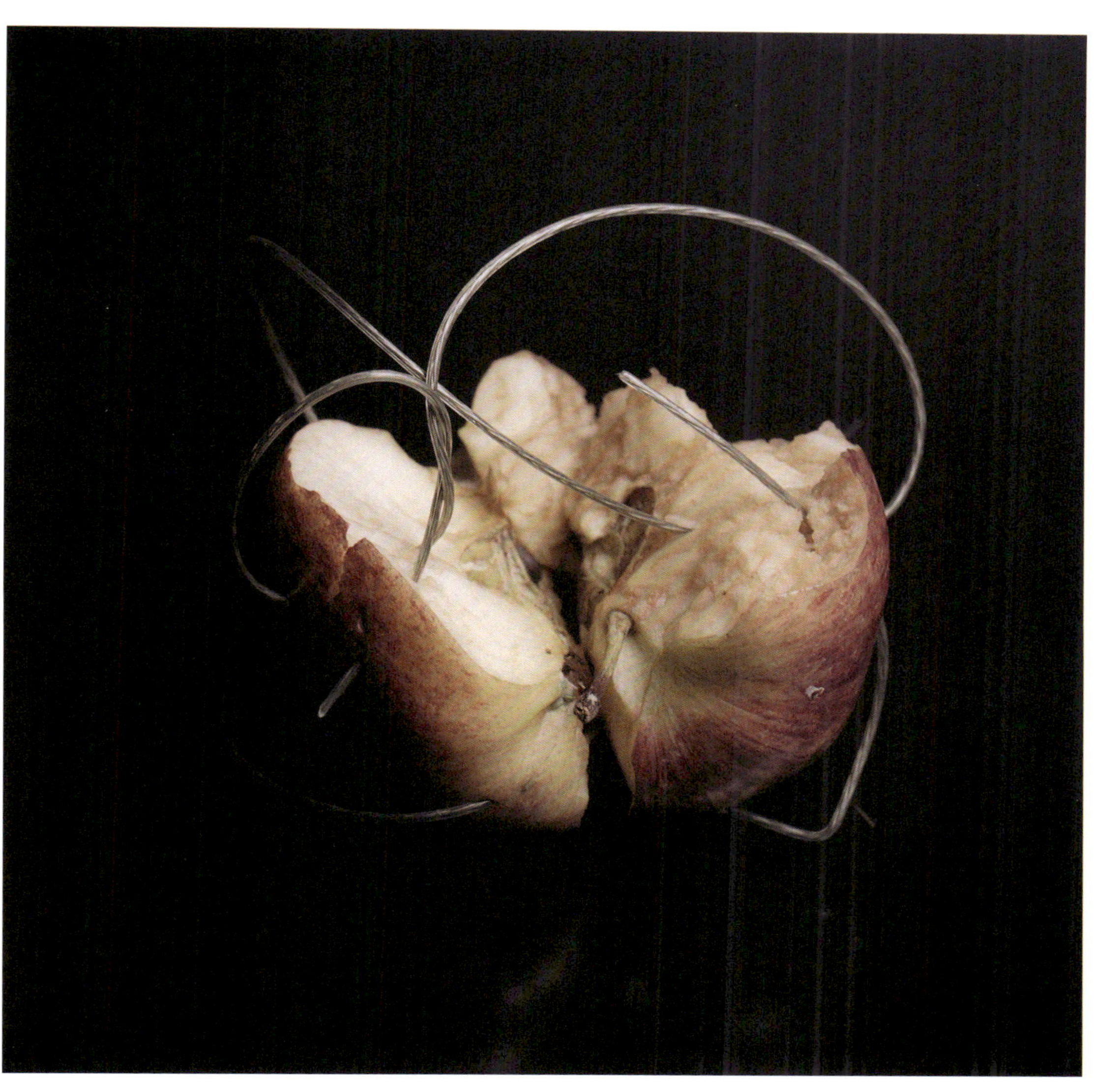

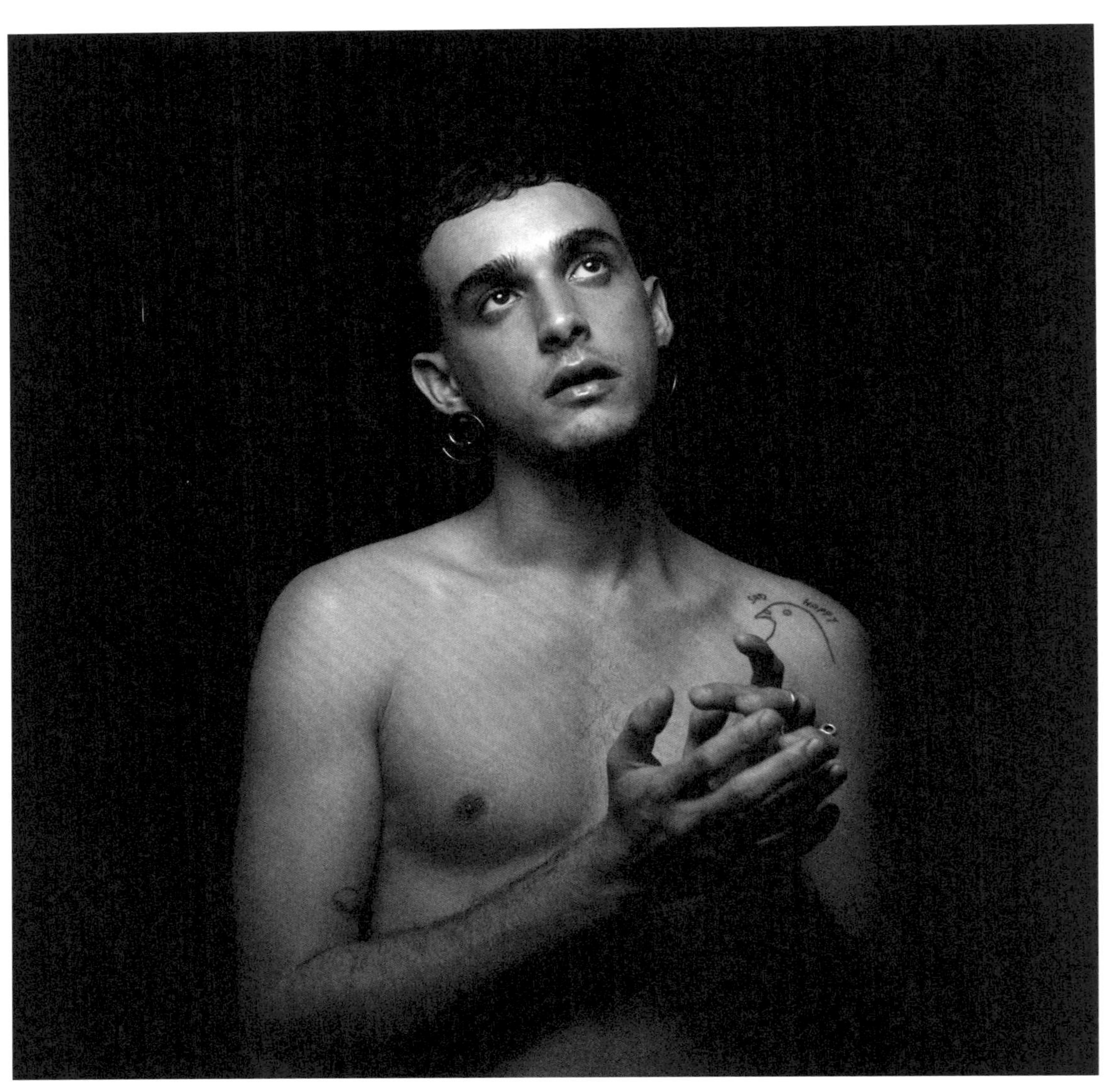

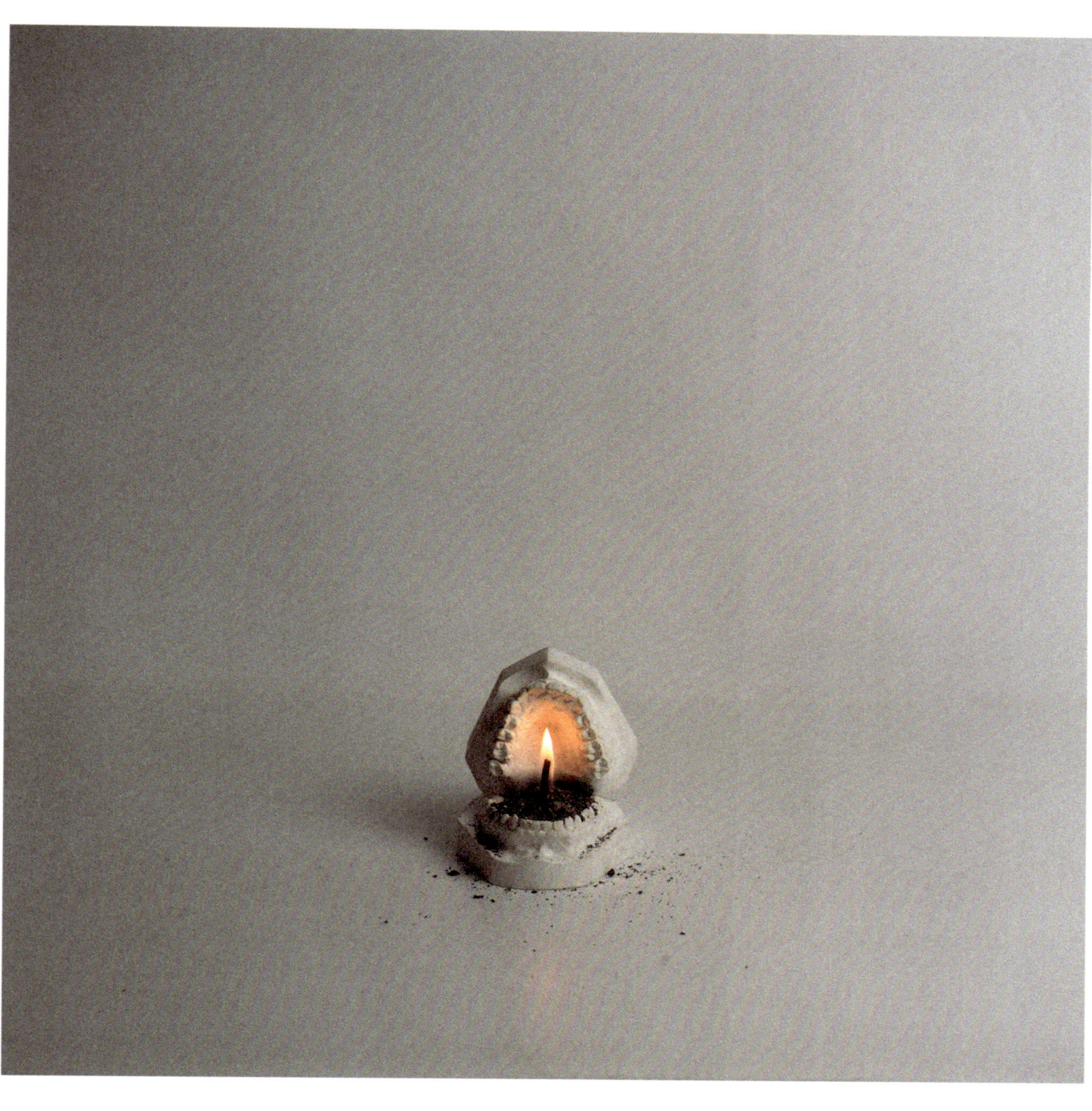

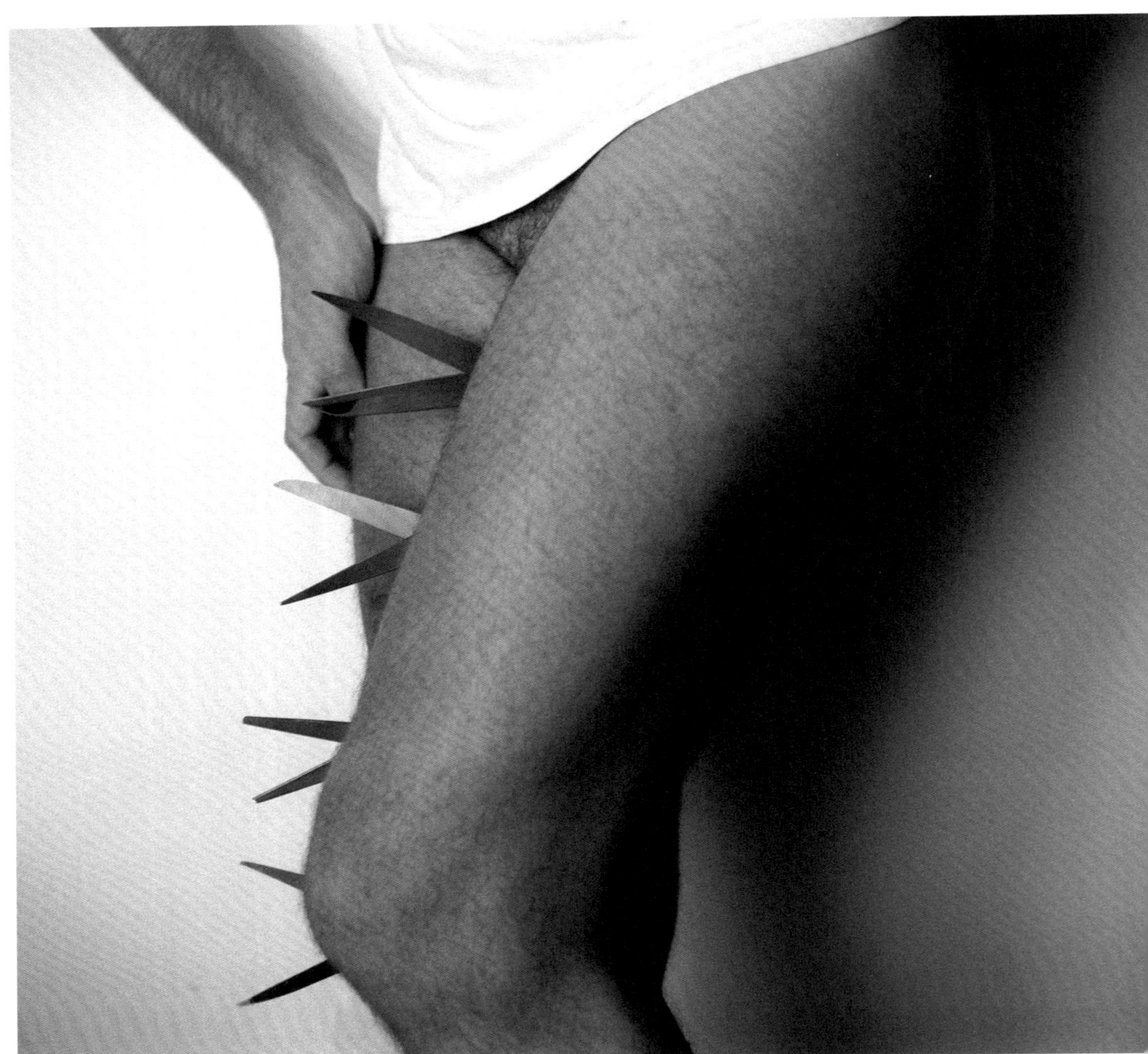

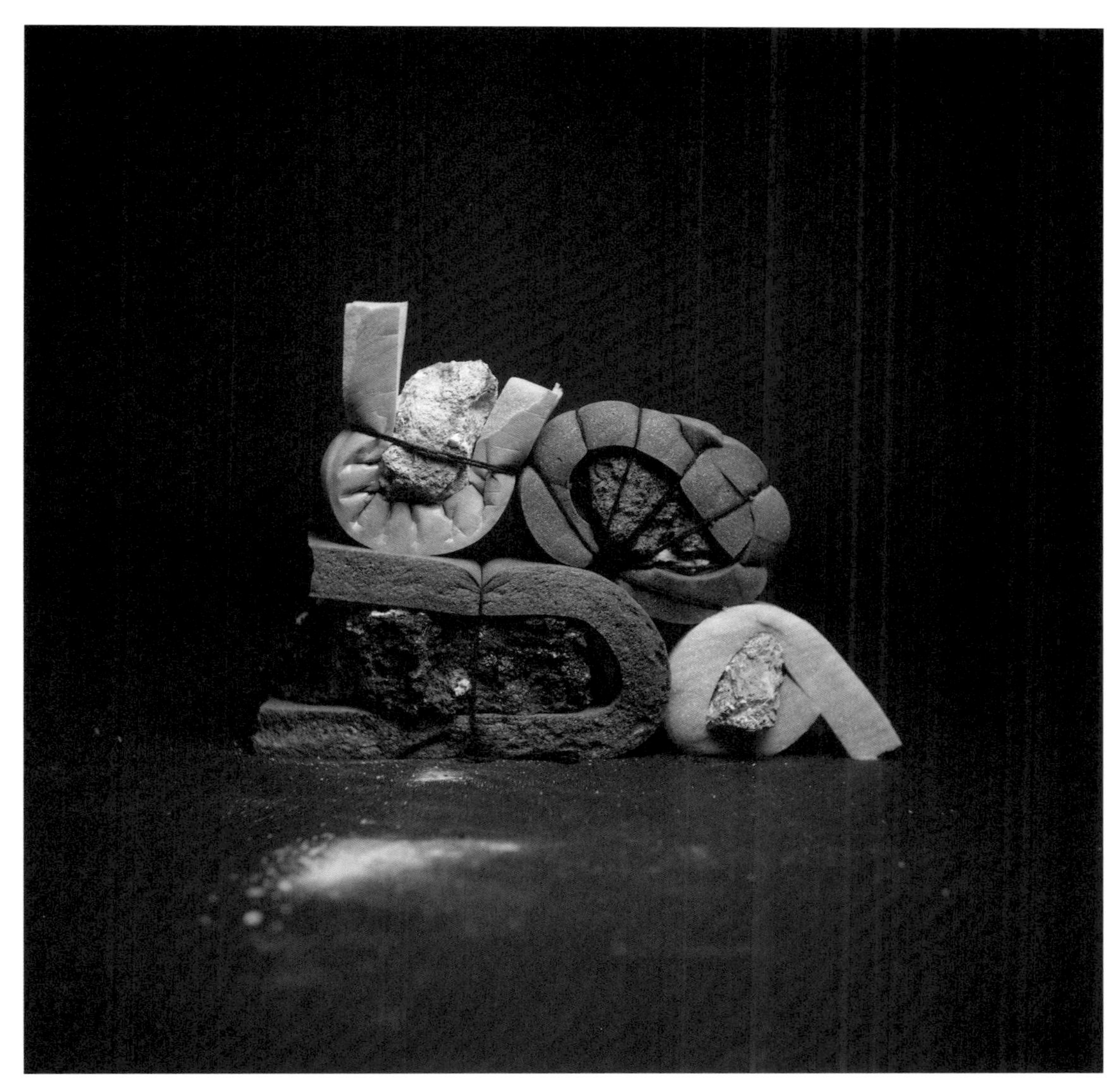

TITLE

WHERE MY HEART SETTLES DOWN

COVER

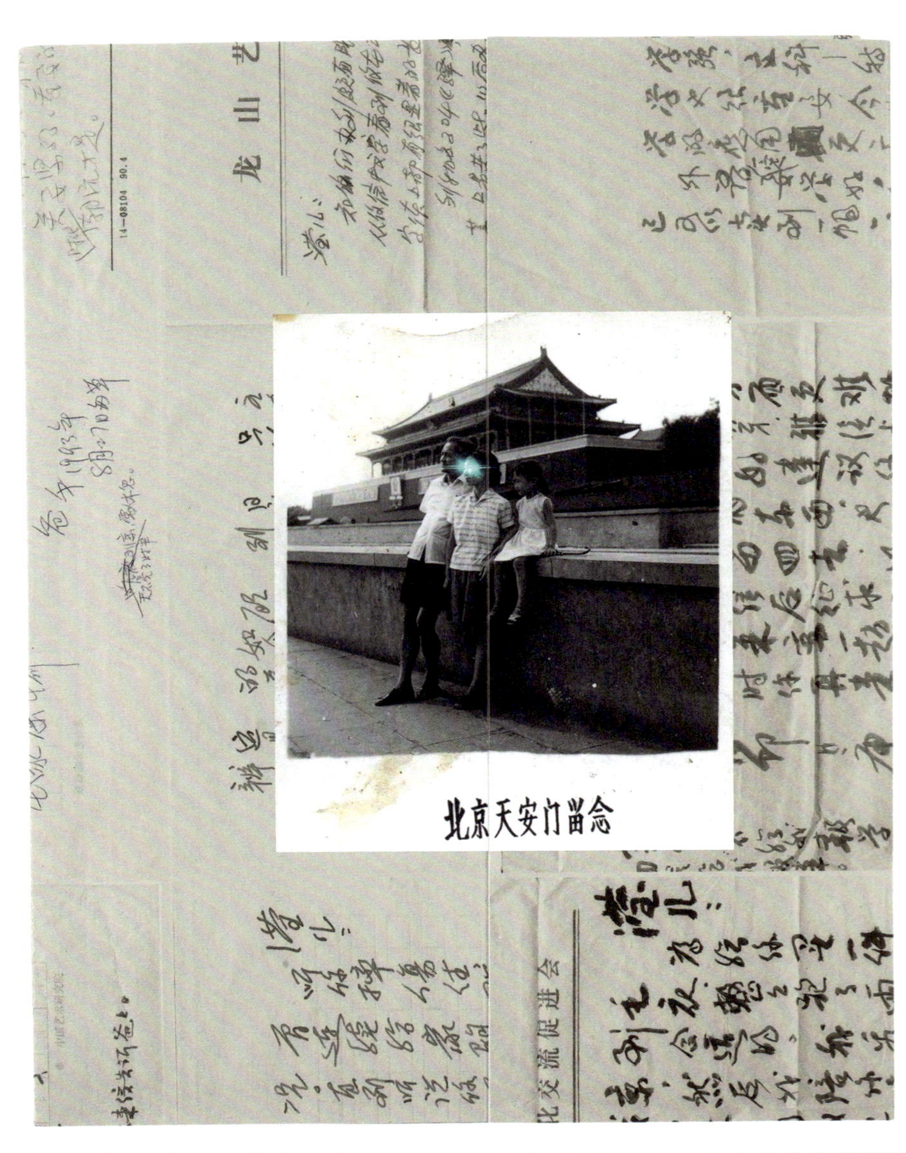

ARTIST	Wang Yingying
PUBLISHER	Jiazazhi
MONOGRAPHY	- 168 pages - first published in 2022 - size: 17 x 25 cm
SUMMARY	In the 1960s, Wang Yingying's father was accused of being an anti-revolutionary intellectual and was sent to Wangqiao, where he was forced to do manual labour. Rehabilitated after the great Cultural Revolution, he returned to work in Beijing to try to rebuild his marriage damaged by the separation. Forty years later, his daughter Wang returns to the family's native region to re-arrange the puzzle of a generation fractured by Mao Zedong's revolution. To delve into *Where My Heart Settles Down* is to go through the diary of a rediscovery, that of a forgotten place of childhood. Dated short texts punctuate the sequence of images – archives, colour photographs of places, of people lost from sight, and pencil drawings. The photographer invites us to contemplate a "defamiliarized" environment: the city of forced exile or the time when her parents were not separated. Her words convey the emotion of an impossible return, of a mourning doomed to endure. *Where My Heart Settles Down* is a sobering view of the devastating consequences that historical events can have over intimate destinies. With gentleness and subtlety, the book sketches the double portrait of a father and his daughter who have become partly strangers to each other. Photography thus offers a benevolent space where the tormented heart of those who suffer can finally settle.
BIOGRAPHY	Born in 1976, Wang Yingying became a photographer at the age of 38, after a career as a civil servant and head of a state-owned company. She undertook an autobiographical and introspective work through photography and documentary cinema that focuses on the representation of women and their interiority. She lives in Hangzhou, China.

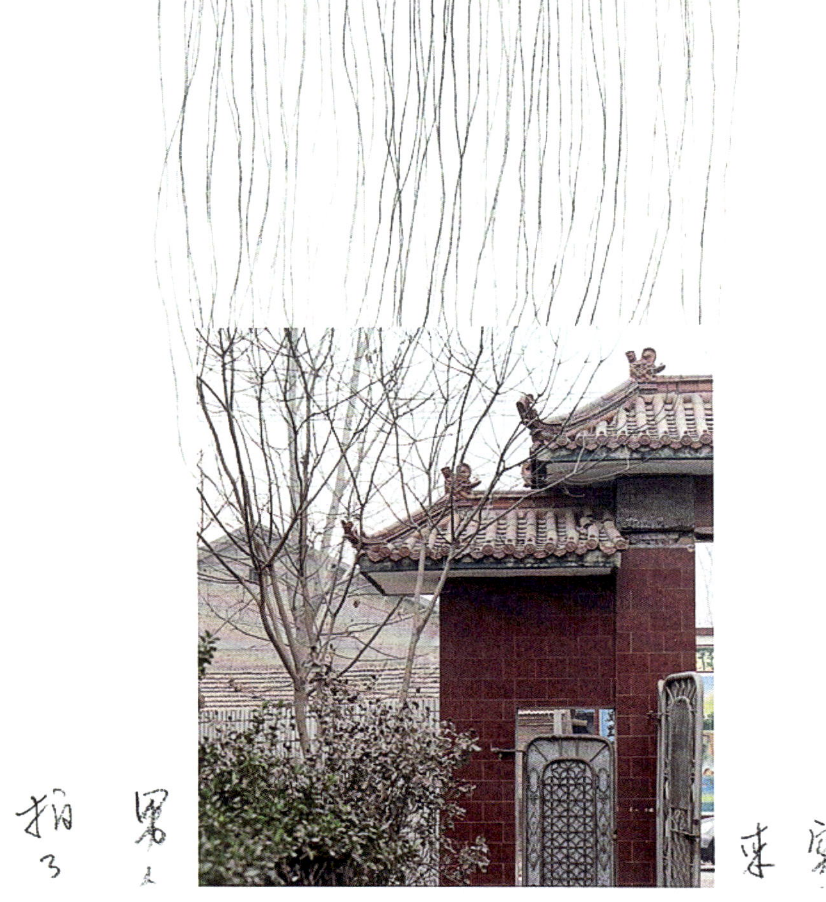

All the men at the funeral suddenly knelt and began to cry. It wasn’ t done with much sorrow but was just a part of the ceremony. Before long, the crying suddenly stopped. The men stood up together, beating the dust off their clothes. Everything calmed down.

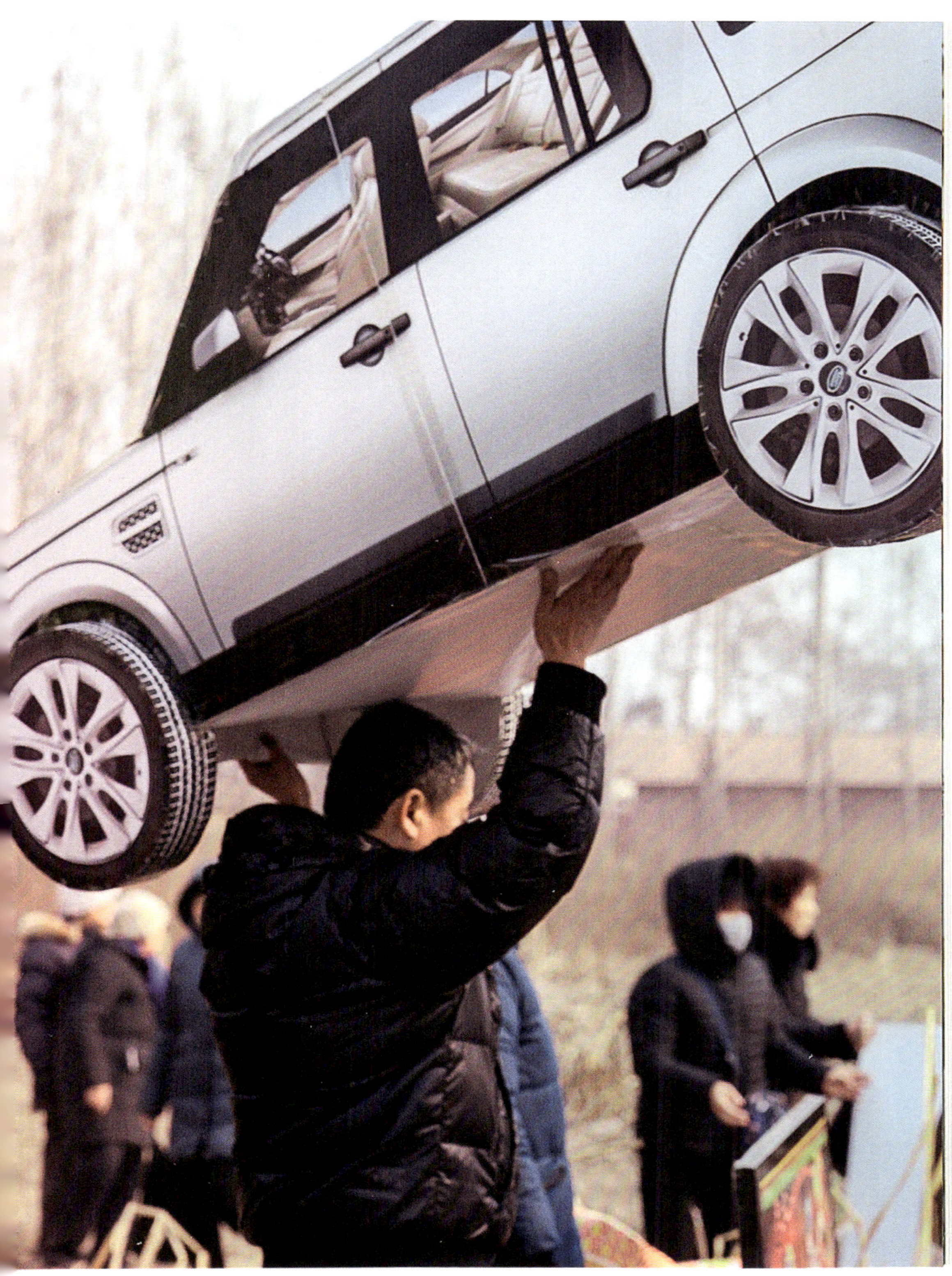

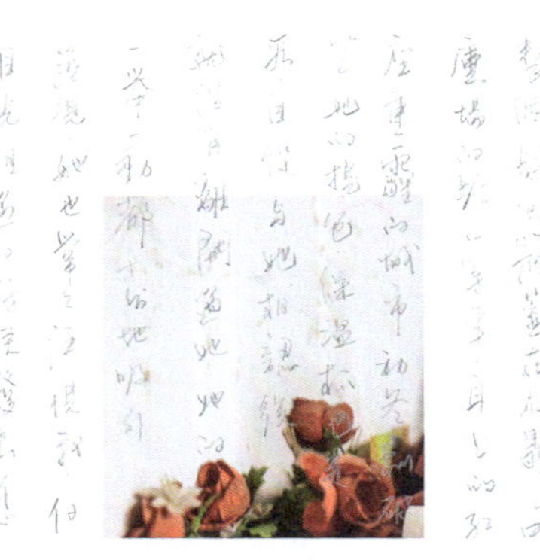

The whole county town was covered in smog. Nanny Jinfeng was waiting for a bus at a road crossing by the square. Her garnet coat was like flare piercing the thick fog of early winter. Her handbag and her thermo-mug also looked very nice. Since I first met her, I could not take my eyes off her. Her features, dress, and every movement attracted me. Meanwhile, I noticed that she also looked at me, examining me carefully. When our eyes met, we both burst into smiles with love, kindness, and understanding.

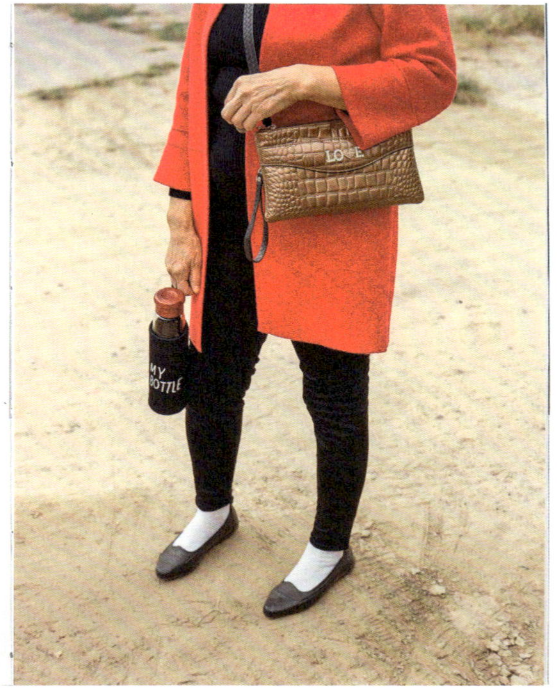

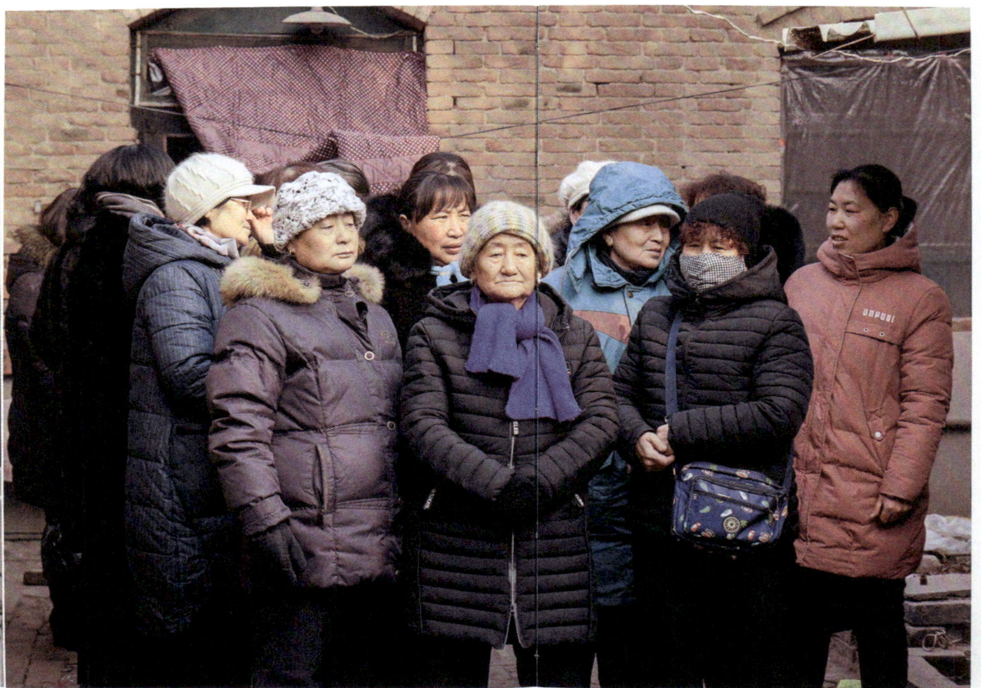

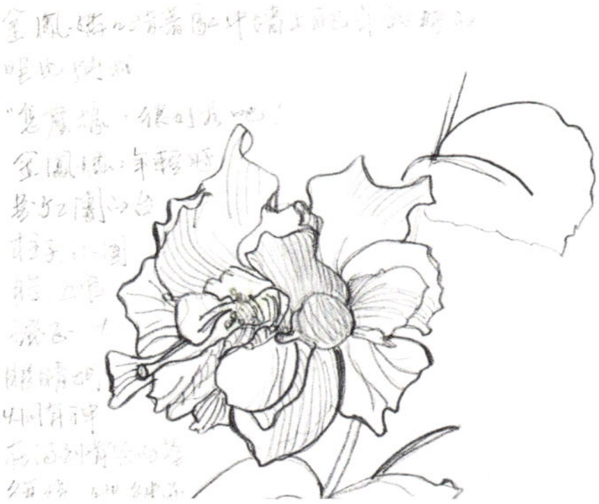

Nanny Jinfeng pointed at her picture on the wall, taken when she was young, and asked me: "What do you think? Pretty?"

When she was young, Nanny Jinfeng used to be the leading light of her cultural troupe. She had a petite face, prominent features, and vivacious eyes.

After confirming my agreement, she said, "You see, you drank my milk; of course, you will be as beautiful as me!"

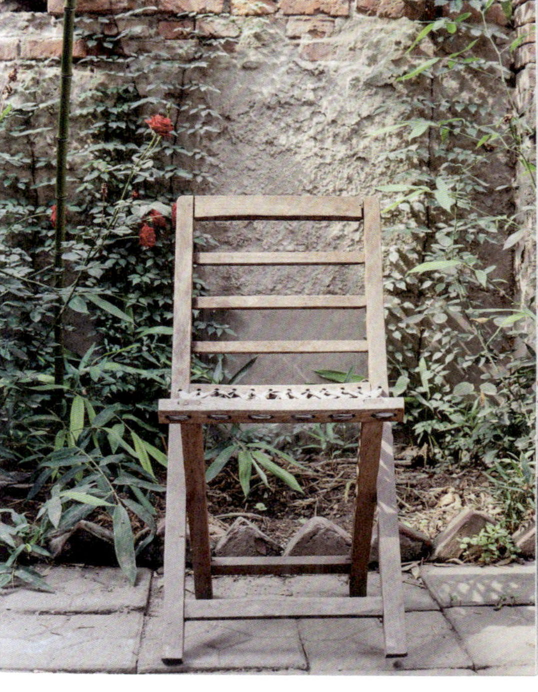

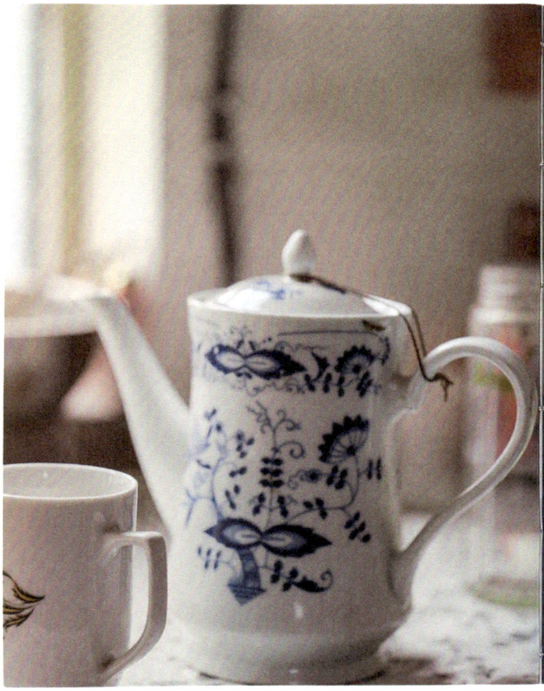

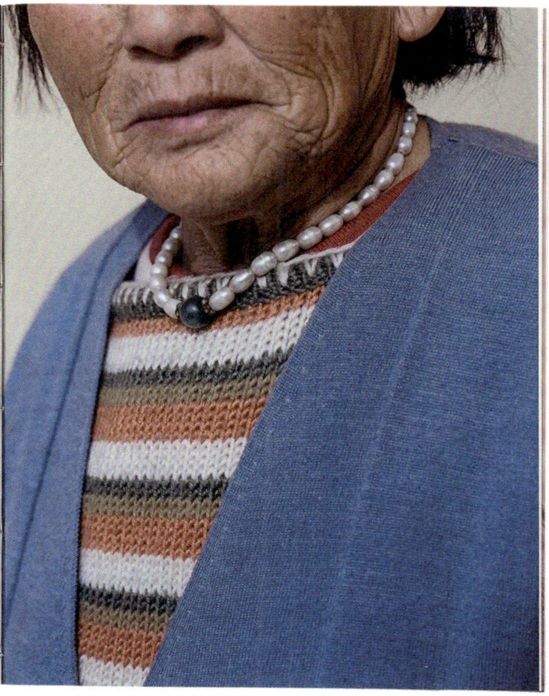

MARGO OVCHARENKO

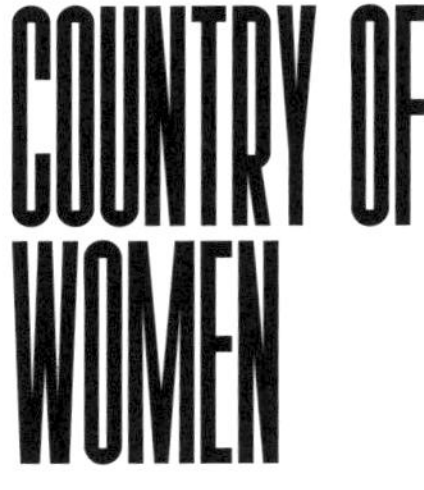

It started with a classified ad published in the queer media of various Eastern countries. Tired of the invisibility and invisibilization of queer women, and the lack of visual memory regarding them, Margo Ovcharenko decided to begin the construction of an eloquent photographic legacy. This series of sober and powerful portraits proposes to counter the disenchantment of a generation.

In the series *Country of Women*, women show themselves, sober and proud, with a clear and unrepentant eye. Close-ups and details accentuate the dive into an intimacy that reassures and empowers. Margo Ovcharenko discovered photography at the age of 15 as a means of exploring her sexuality and body, of interacting with the world. Through her portraits, the artist creates a photographic space where empathy and affirmation predominate, where the gazes – hers, those of her models and ours – join forces to build a close-knit community in the face of what's to come.

Gestures, posture and expressions compose a place of sharing and speaking. With strength and gentleness, fingers are entwined, bodies relax, gazes assert themselves. Tangible, they invite the touch. Inspired by the Soviet sports aesthetics, Ovcharenko revisits their asexual postures and insists on the carnal, the corporeal, the tensions that cross this community of women. In the intimacy of bodies that brush and embrace each other, she offers a place of repair where images make it possible to identify oneself and reconnect with others.

Country of Women, 2018
© Margo Ovcharenko
Nastasya and Oksana, 2016
Mirro, 2016
Untitled, 2016
Masha, 2016
Untitled, 2016

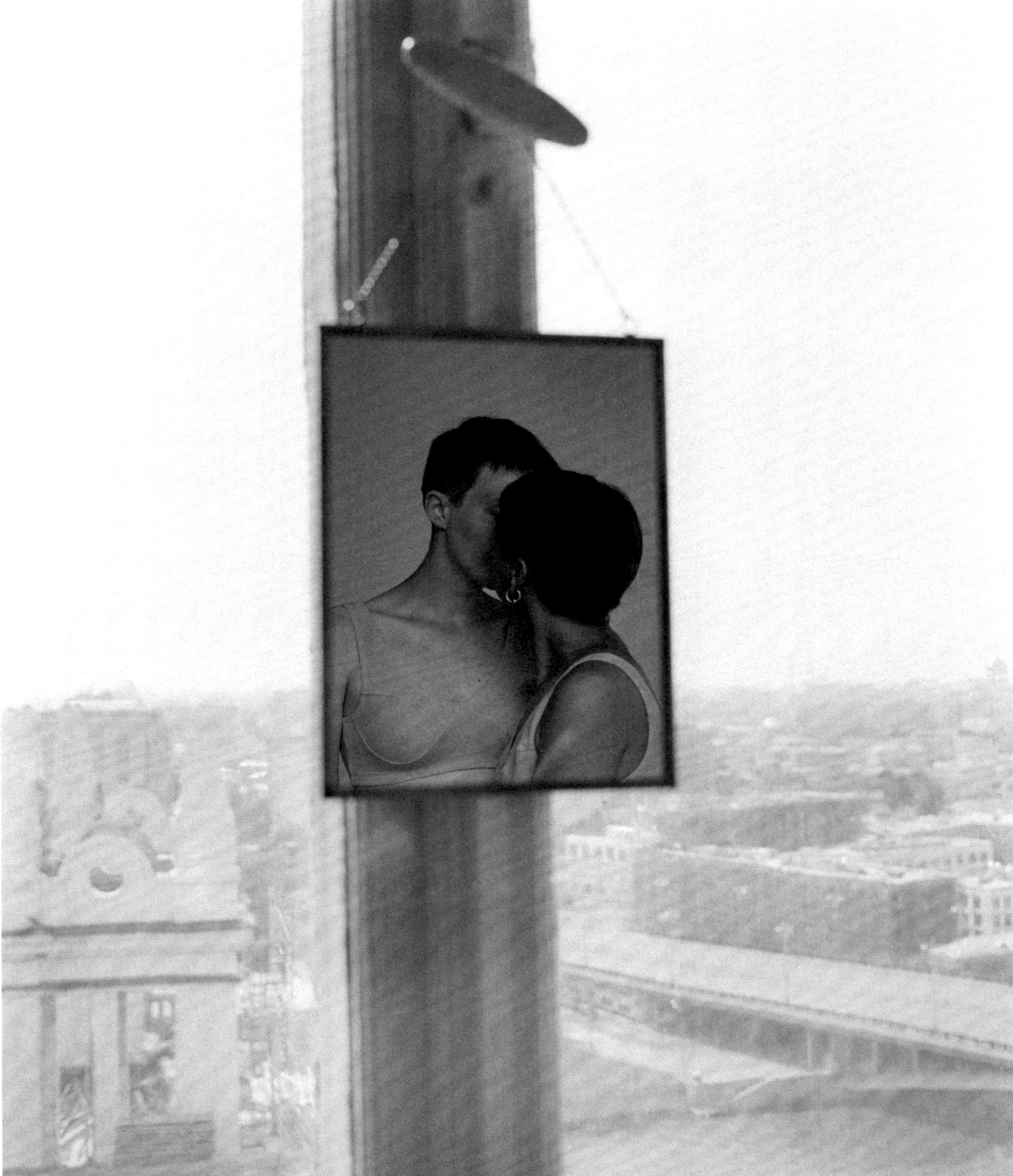

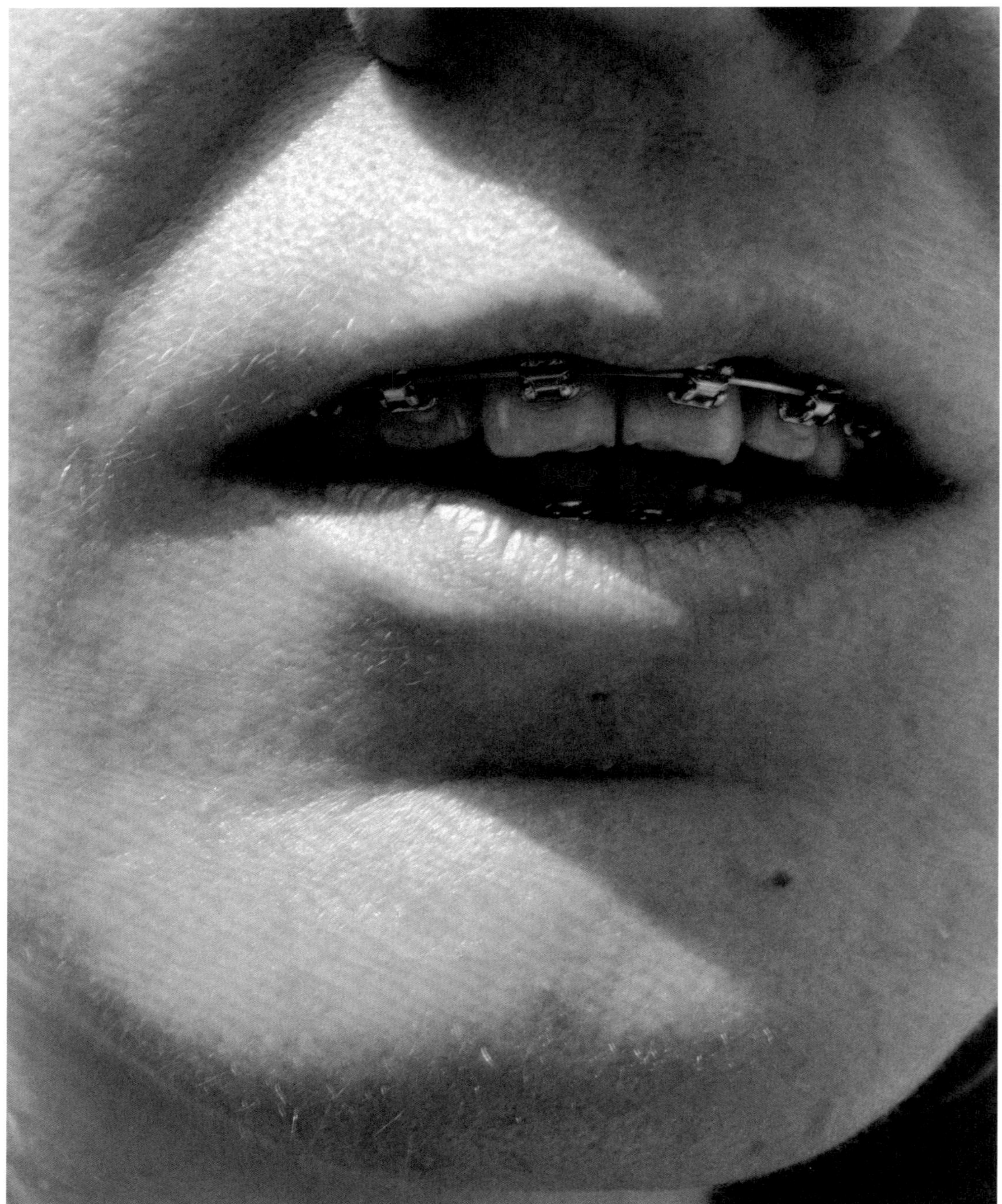

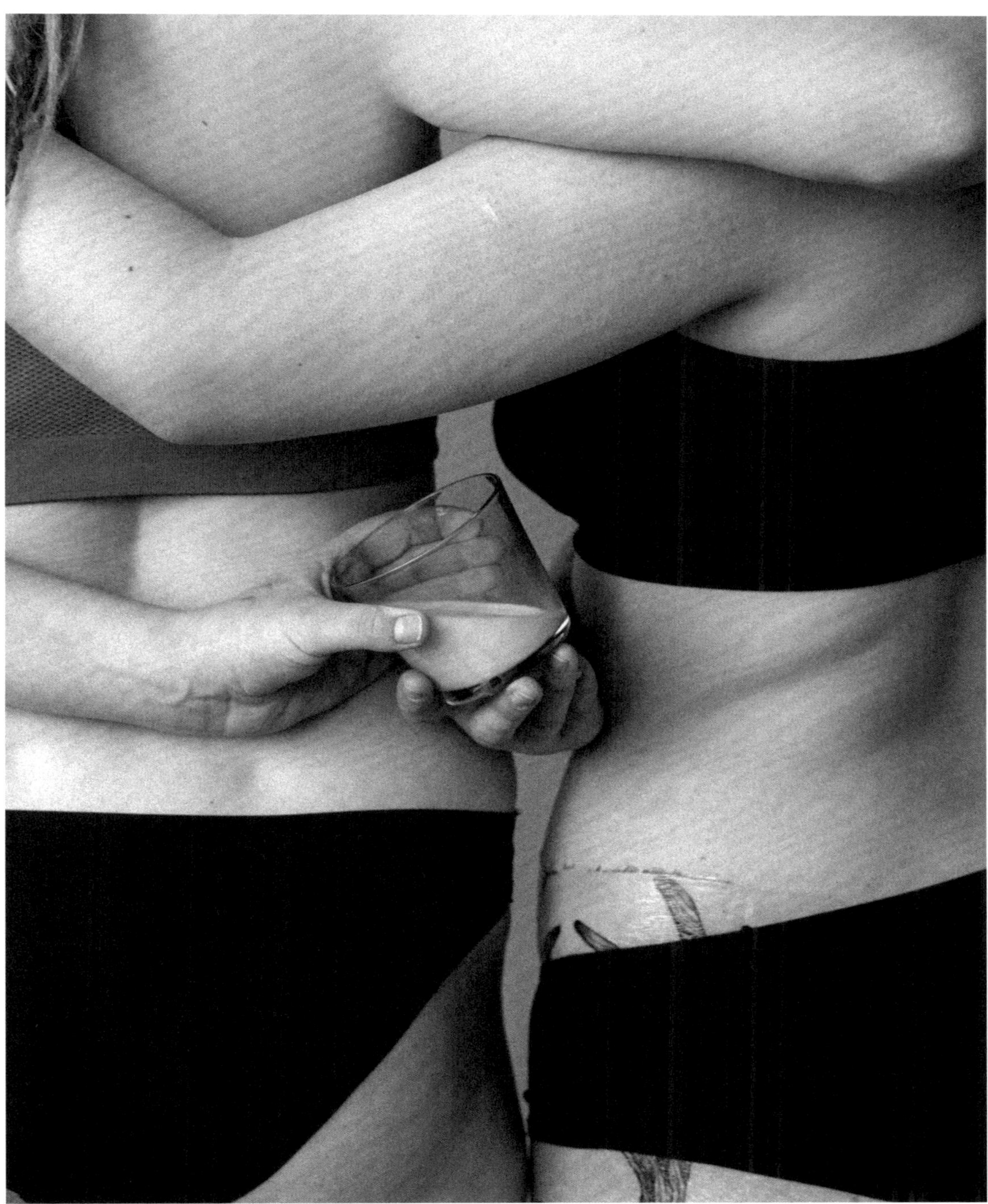

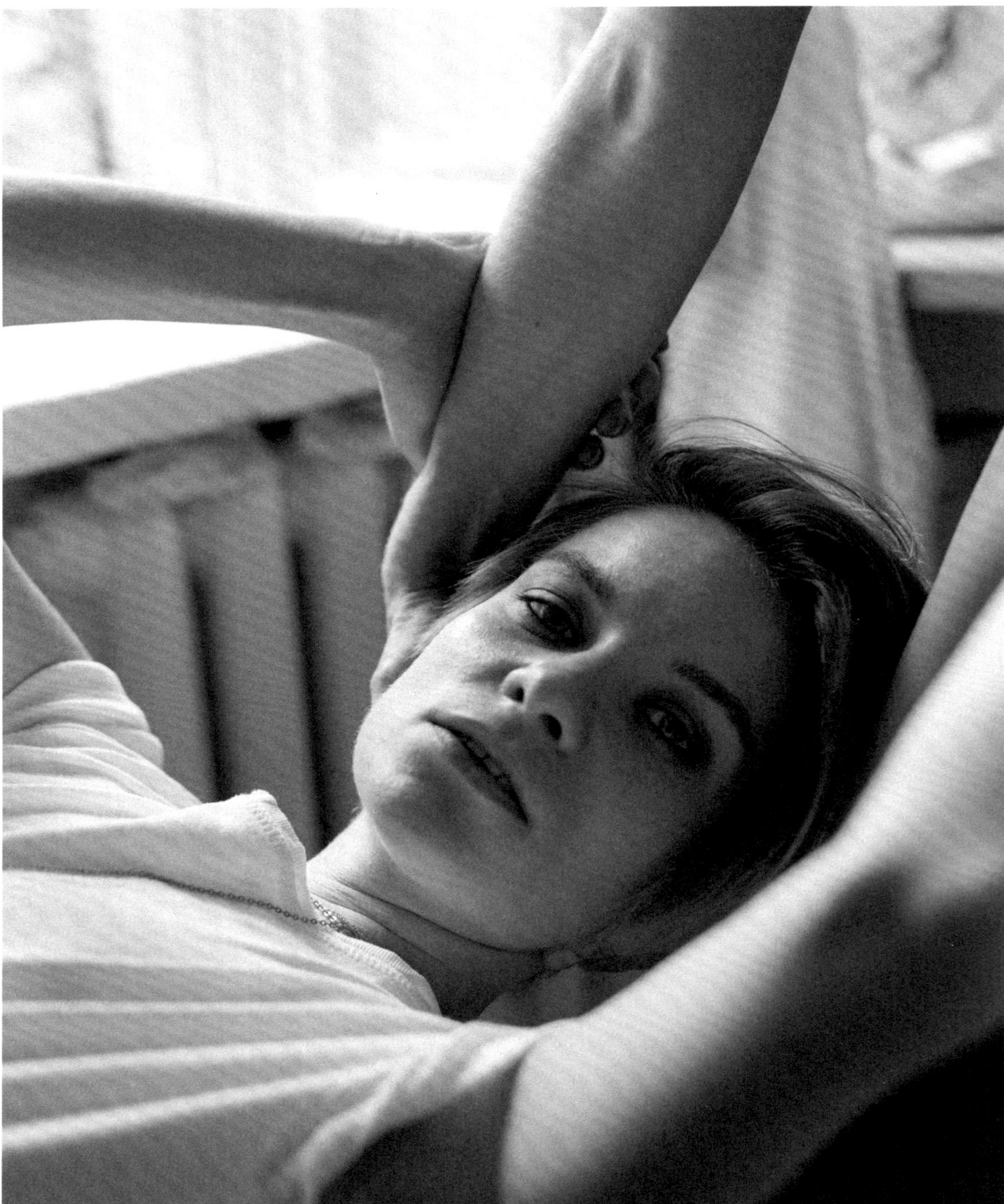

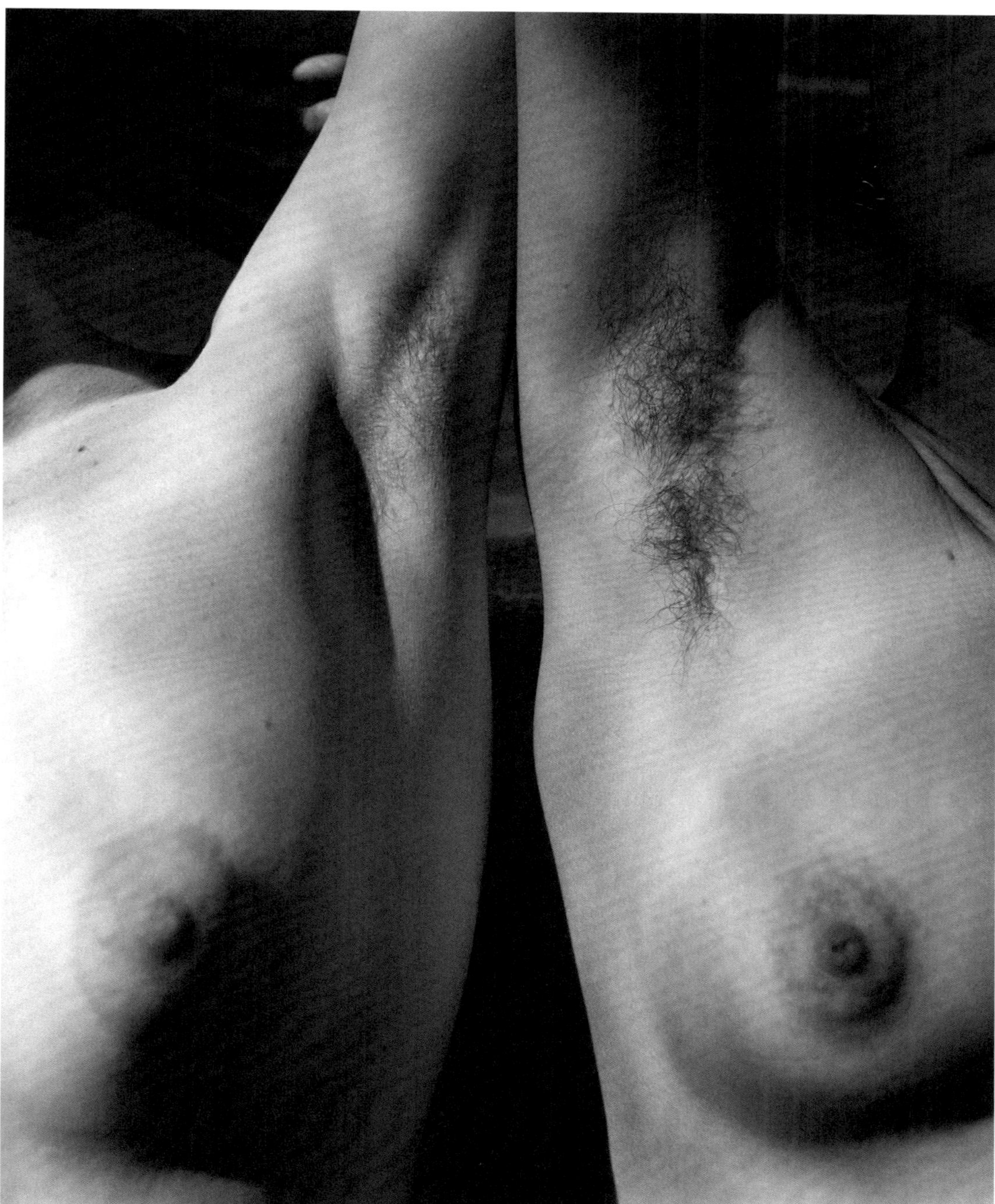

LAIA ABRIL'S INSPIRATIONS

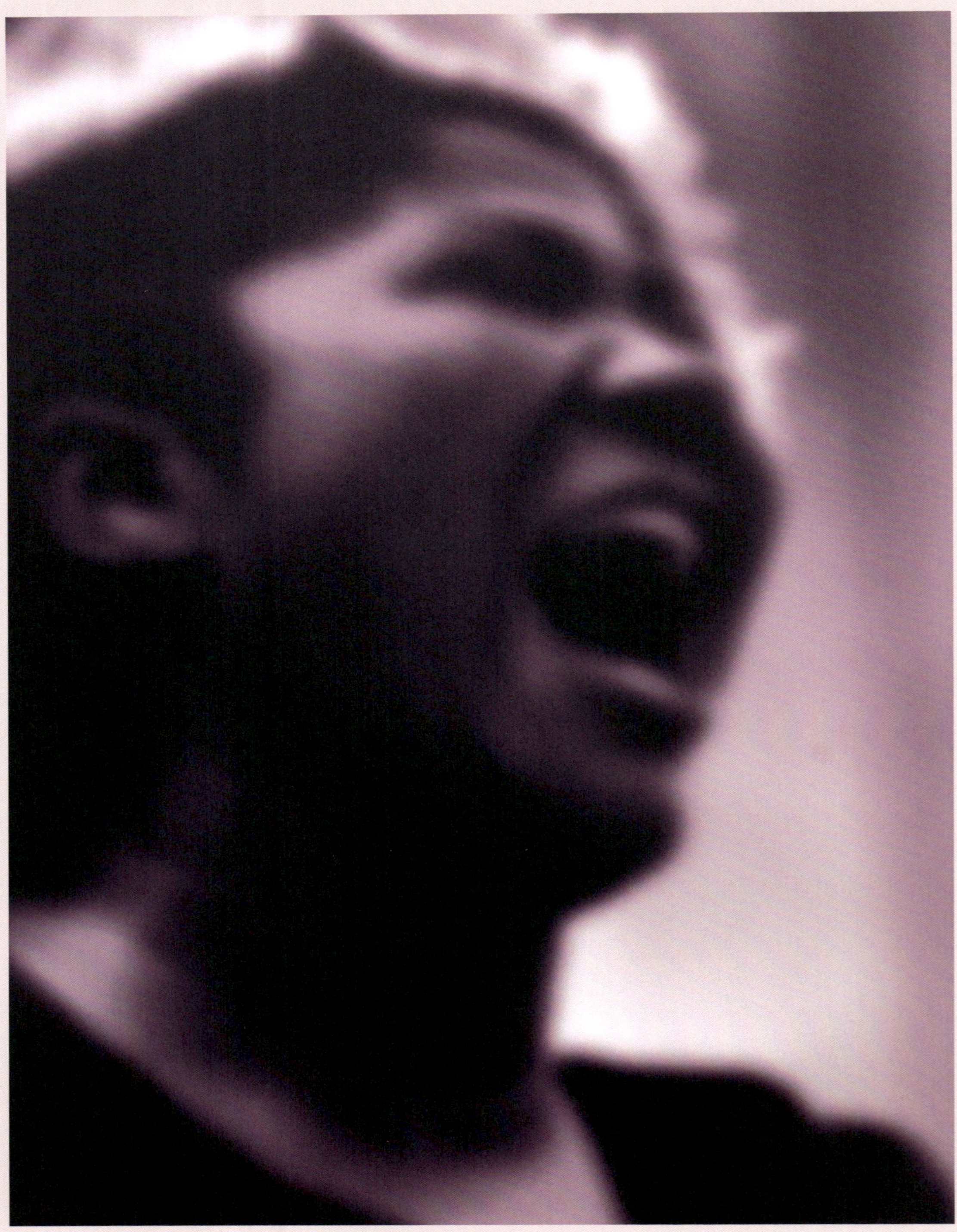

As a research-based photographer and visual artist, Laia Abril wouldn't consider starting a new project or even bringing it to completion without undertaking a thorough investigation of the subjects in question. Inspired by this, this section is a visual overview of Laia's modus operandi as applied to the theme of "(after)care". This section provides historical references and key names that populated the many conversations around the making of this issue. From Abigail Heyman to Carrie Mae Weems or the Guerrilla Girls, these are the trailblazers that inspired us and are, today, enabling us to keep the conversation going on the notion of care.

ELENA ALMEIDA

SONIA ANDRADE

PILAR AYMERICH I PUIG

LOUISE BOURGEOIS

TANIA BRUGUERA

CABELLO/CARCELLER

SOPHIE CALLE

JUDY CHICAGO

ĀGNES DĒNES

RINEKE DIJKSTRA

VALIE EXPORT

ESTHER FERRER

GUERRILLA GIRLS

NAN GOLDIN

ABIGAIL HAYMAN

BARBARA HAMMER

LYNN HERSHMAN LEESON

EVA HESSE

GRACIELA ITURBIDE

FRIDA KAHLO

MARY KELLY

BARBARA KRUGER

TERESA MARGOLLES

SUSAN MEISELAS

ANNETTE MESSAGER

FINA MIRALLES NOBELL

SHIRIN NESHAT

JO RACTLIFFE

ROSÂNGELA RENNÓ

PIPILOTTI RIST

ULRIKE ROSENBACH

MARTHA ROSLER

DORIS SALCEDO

TARYN SIMON

JOE SPENCE

NANCY SPERO

MILAGROS DE LA TORRE

AGNÊS VARDA

REMEDIOS VARO

HANNAH WILKE

LORENA WOLFFER

FRANCESCA WOODMAN

Mahalia, 2010
© Carrie Mae Weems, courtesy the artist and Jack Shainman Gallery, New York

Next spread: *Pesquisas (Inquiries)*, 2016
© Teresa Margolles and Galerie Peter Kilchmann, Zurich, photo © Richard-Max Tremblay, installation, 30 colour prints of photographs of street signs showing missing women that cover the walls of Ciudad Juárez, Mexico, from the 1990s until today, 100 × 70 cm each, altogether 301 × 704.5 cm, installation view: Teresa Margolles

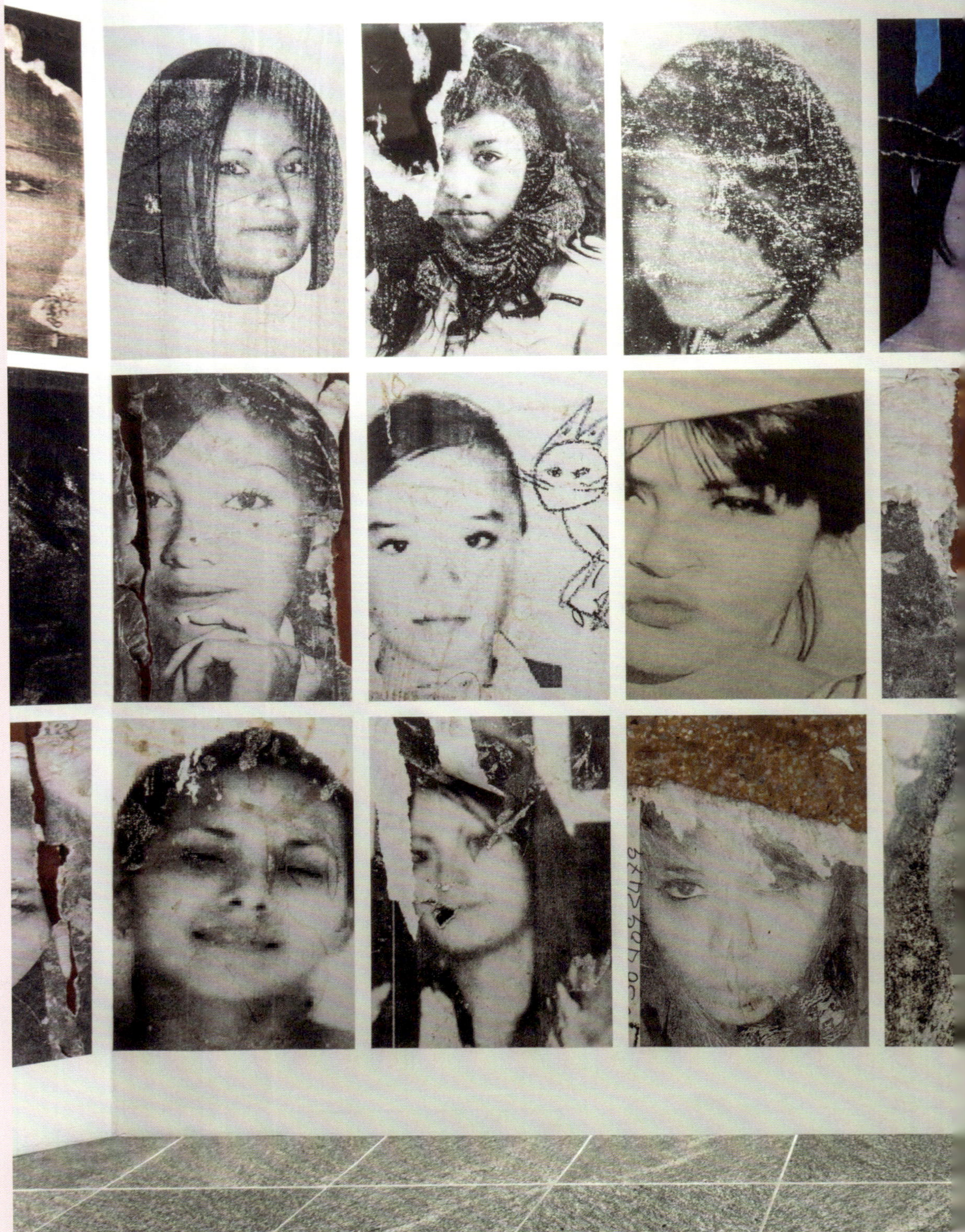

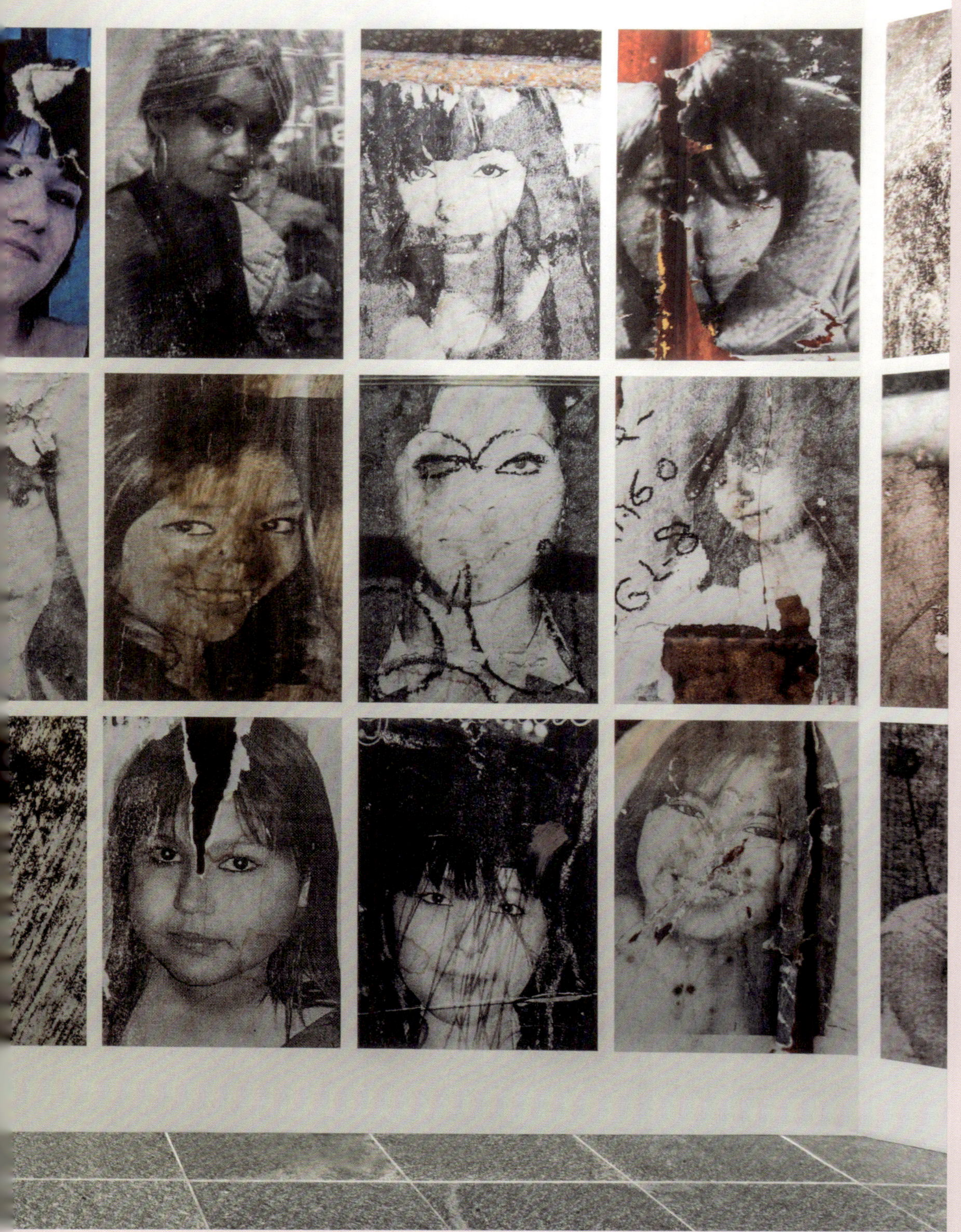

At first I didn't want my husband in the delivery room because I didn't want him to see me that exposed. And I was afraid he would never want to make love with me again.

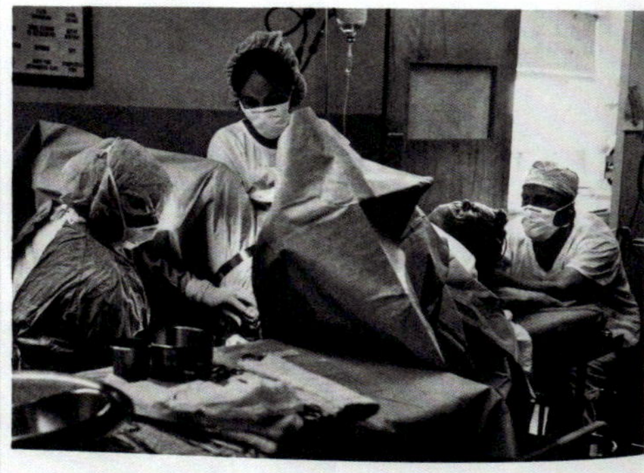

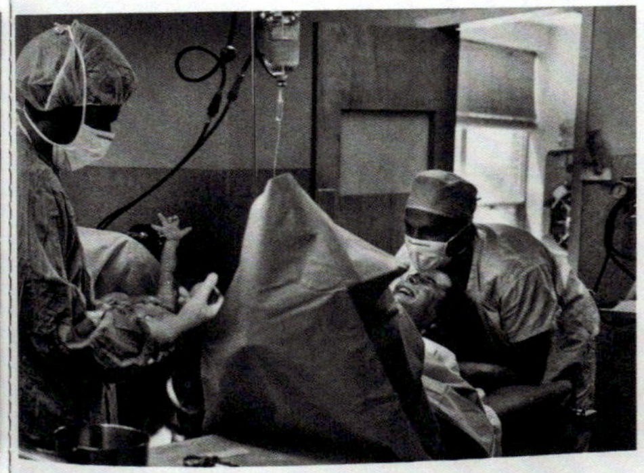

Nothing ever made me feel more like a sex object than going through an abortion alone.

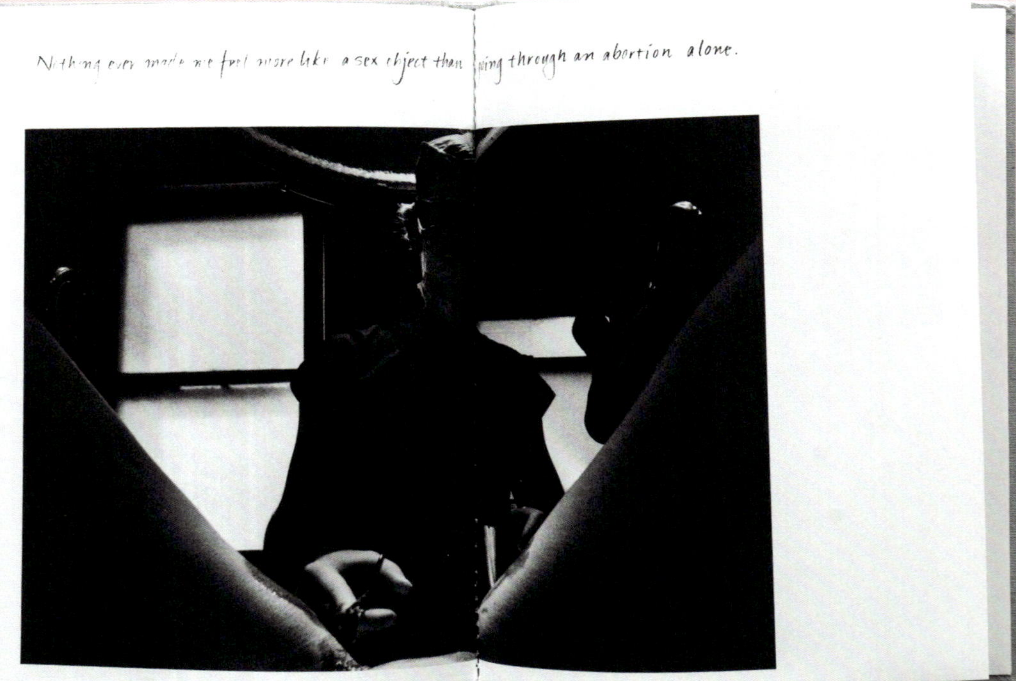

© Abigail Heyman, *Growing Up Female*, Holt, Rinehart & Winston, 1974

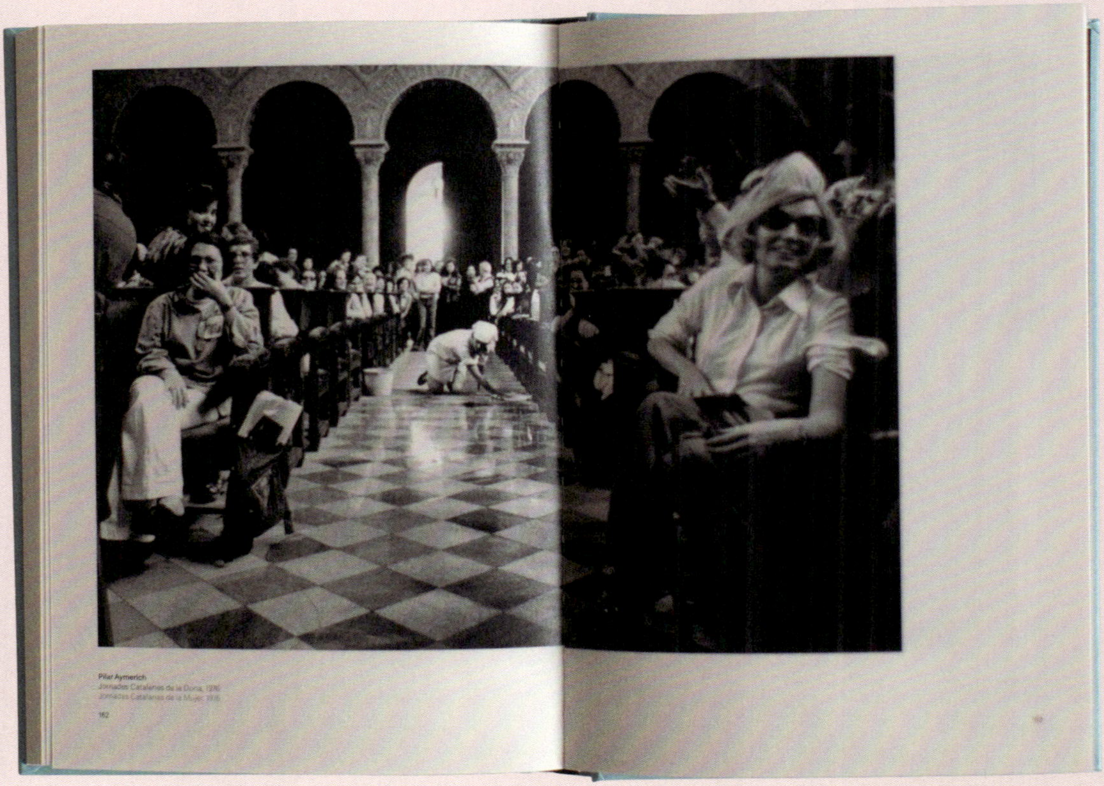

«Marduk va atrapar Tiamat al seu cau, i va fer entrar els vents que l'acompanyaven dins el cos de Tiamat, i quan va tenir la panxa prou inflada hi va tirar la llança i l'hi va clavar al cor, i li va arrencar les entranyes i amb una maça li va aixafar el crani. Es va plantar damunt el cos d'ella i amb un ganivet el va partir com si fos un llenguado en dues meitats, i d'una d'elles en va fer el mantell del cel.»

Aquest antic mite sumeri, que es remunta a un dels orígens de la cultura humana, 5.000 aC, ja posa de manifest la por, l'odi i la crueltat envers les dones. L'odi expressat en el desmembrament de Tiamat s'absol en aparença amb la idealització de Tiamat com a cel. L'elevació de Tiamat a l'inassolible és una versió sublimada de la por.

Encara avui, «Tiamat» pateix aquesta mena d'atacs en presons d'arreu del món. També els homes pateixen abusos sexuals a les cambres de tortura del món modern, però les dones són el principal exemple i l'objecte desitjat d'aquesta àvida atenció.

Nancy Spero, 1985

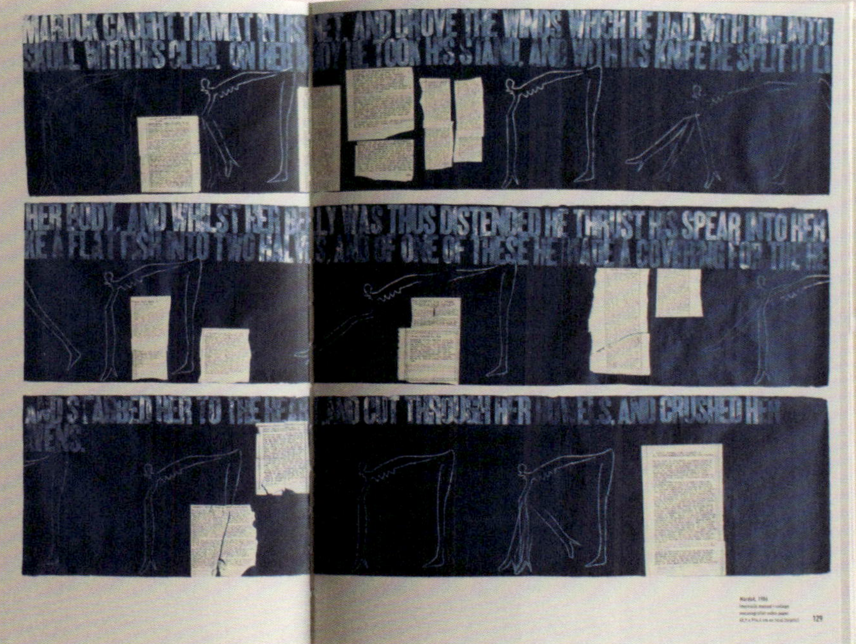

Marduk, 1986

129

Pilar Aymerich
Jornades Catalanes de la Dona, 1976
Jornadas Catalanas de la Mujer, 1976

162

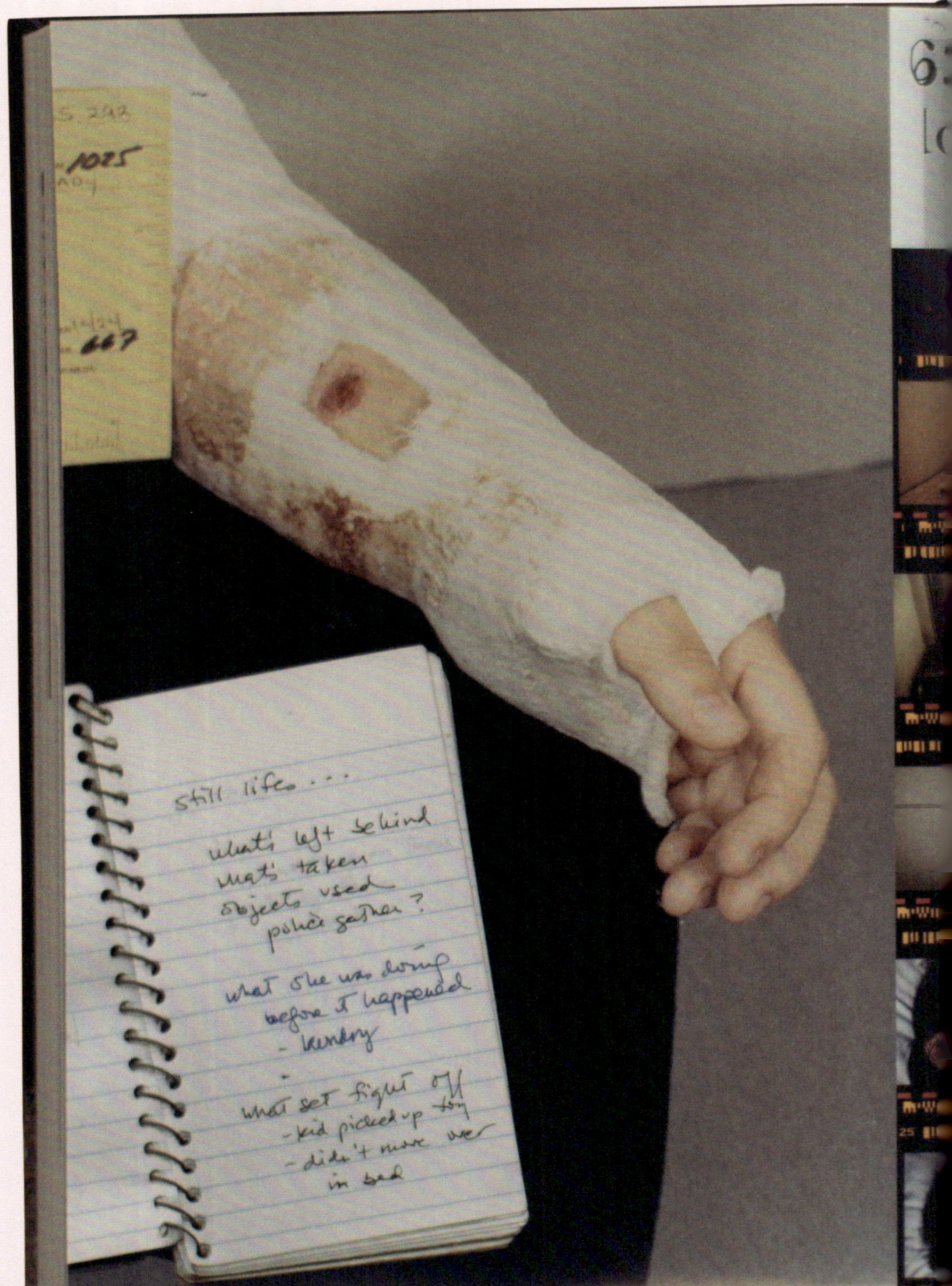

© Susan Meiselas, *Mediations*, Damiani, 2018

SFPD 377

of males between 11 and 20
time for homicide in the US
ed their mother's batterers

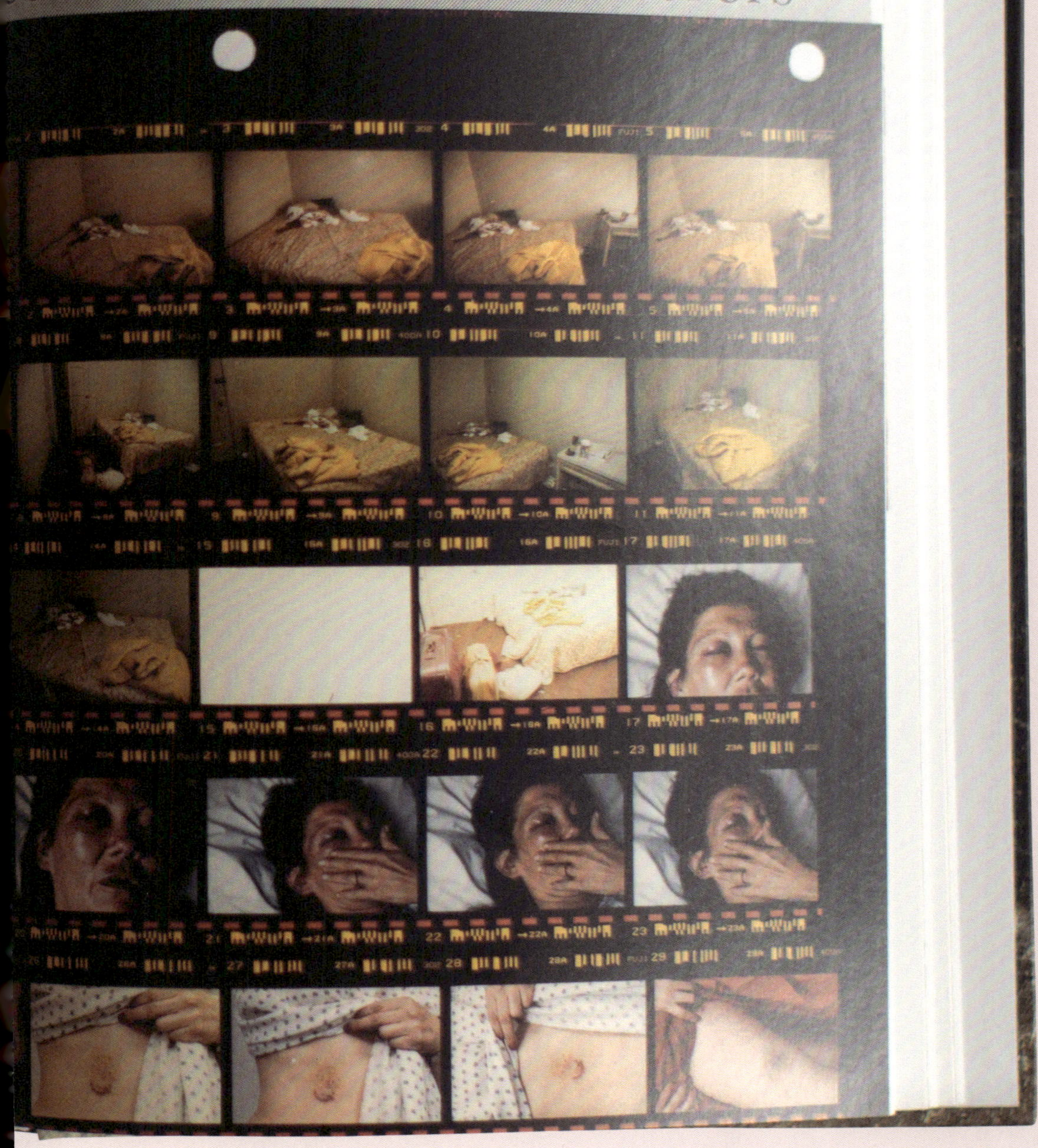

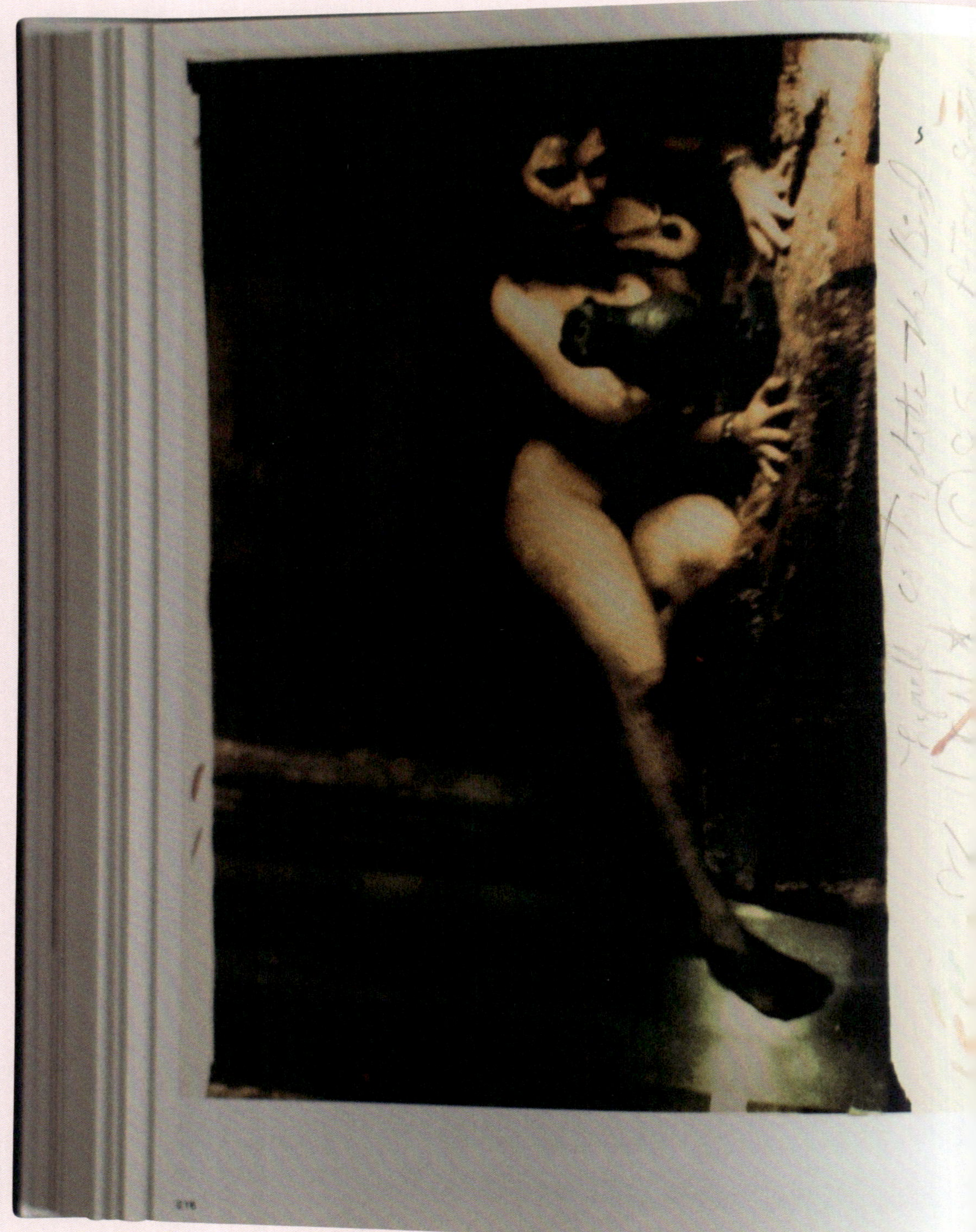

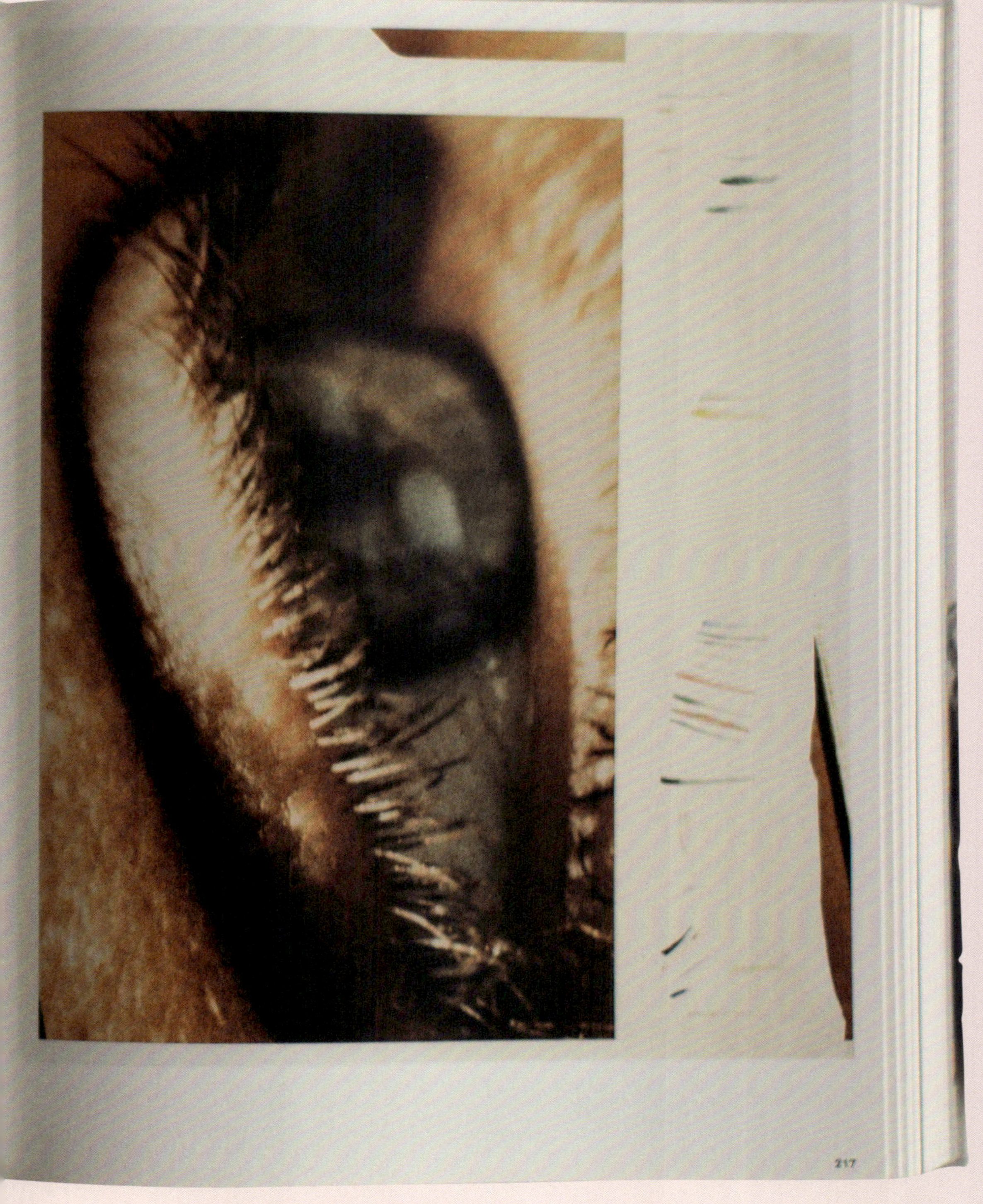

Interim Part I: Corpus 1984

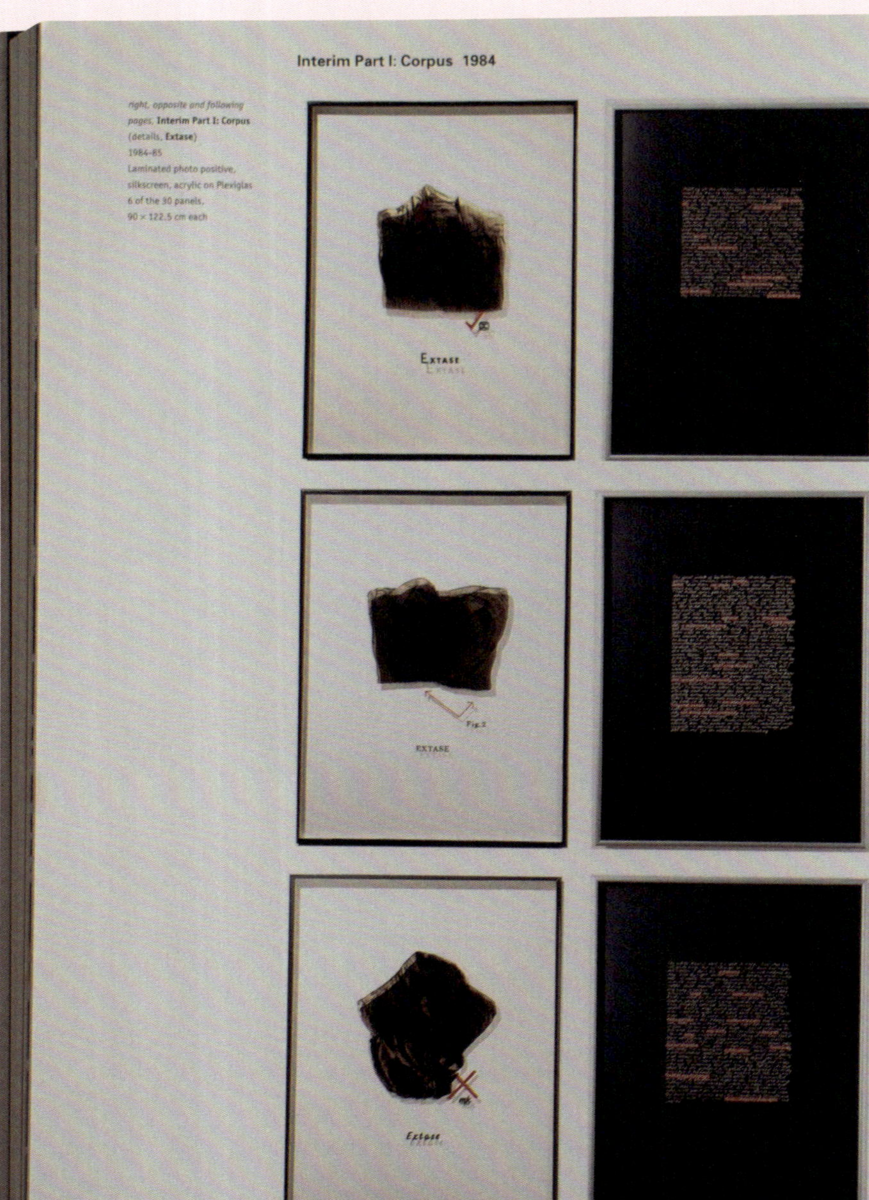

right, opposite and following pages, **Interim Part I: Corpus** (details, **Extase**)
1984–85
Laminated photo positive, silkscreen, acrylic on Plexiglas
6 of the 30 panels,
90 × 122.5 cm each

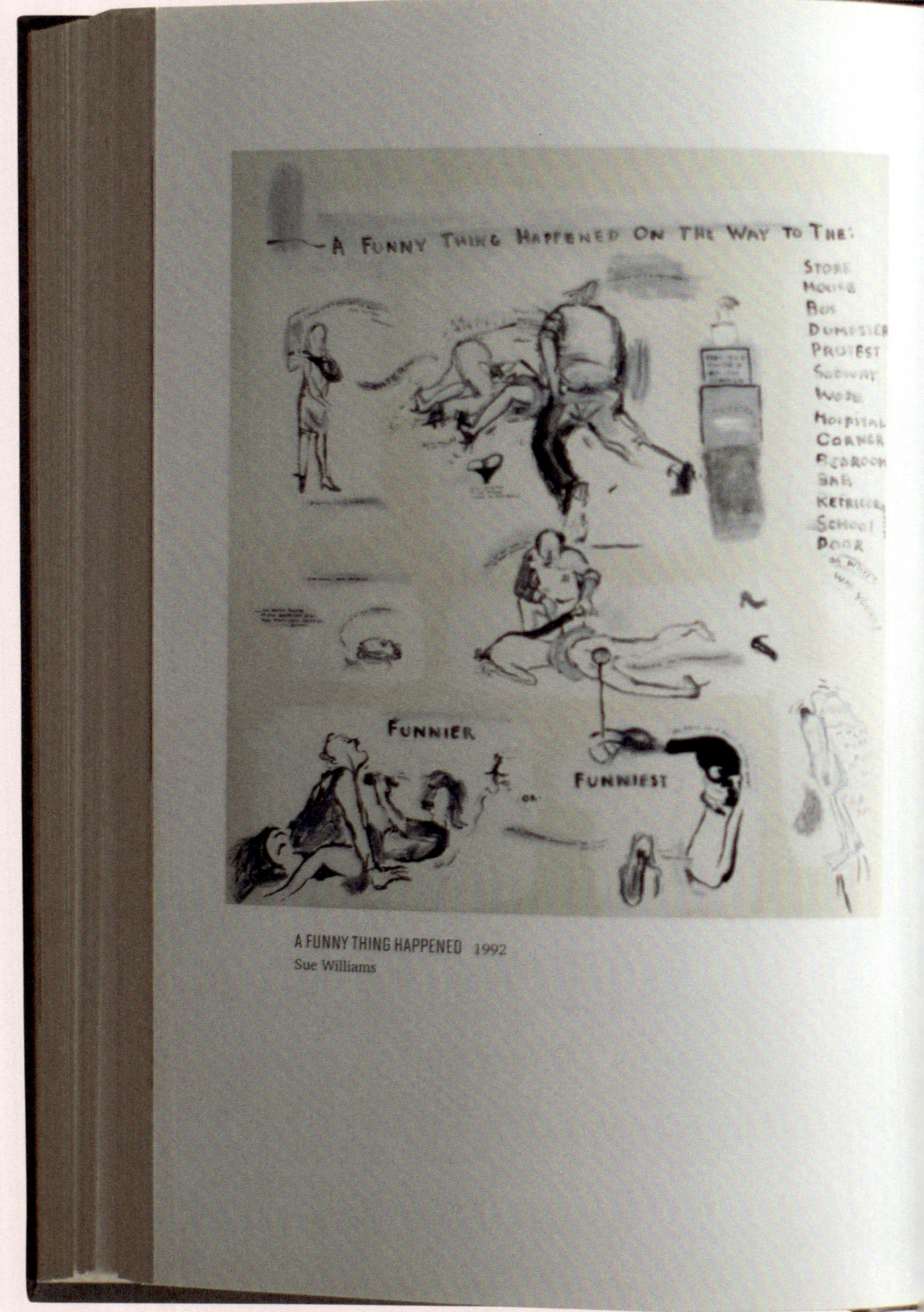

A FUNNY THING HAPPENED 1992
Sue Williams

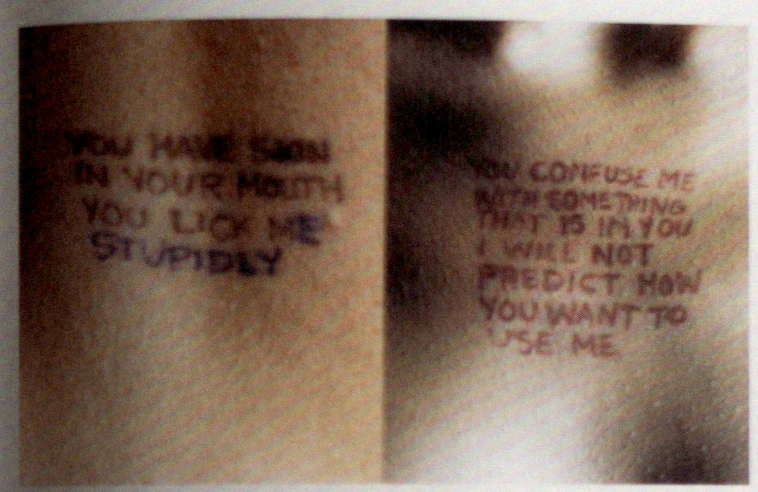

LUSTMORD 1993
Jenny Holzer
Ink on Skin. Originally published *Süddeutsche Zeitung*, Germany.

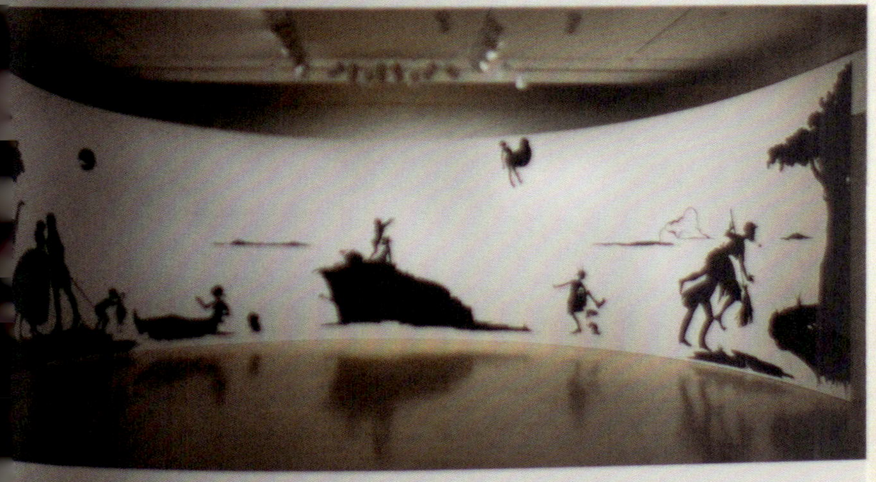

GONE: AN HISTORICAL ROMANCE OF A CIVIL WAR AS IT OCCURRED B'TWEEN THE DUSKY THIGHS OF ONE YOUNG NEGRESS AND HER HEART 1994
Kara Walker
Cut paper on wall. Approximately 156 × 600 in (396.2 × 1,524 cm)

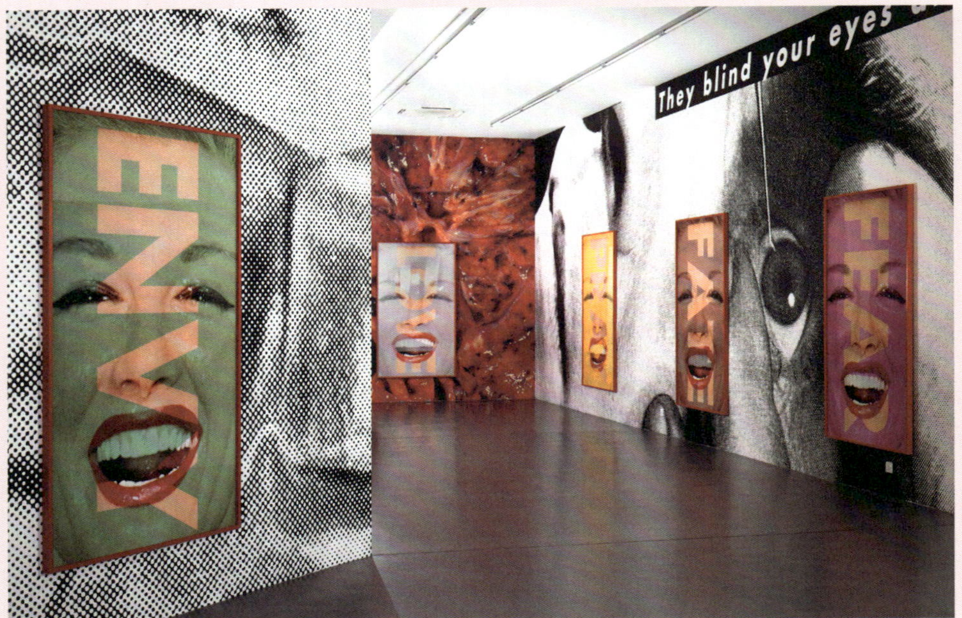

Installation view, Sprüth Magers Lee, London, 29 May–31 July 2003

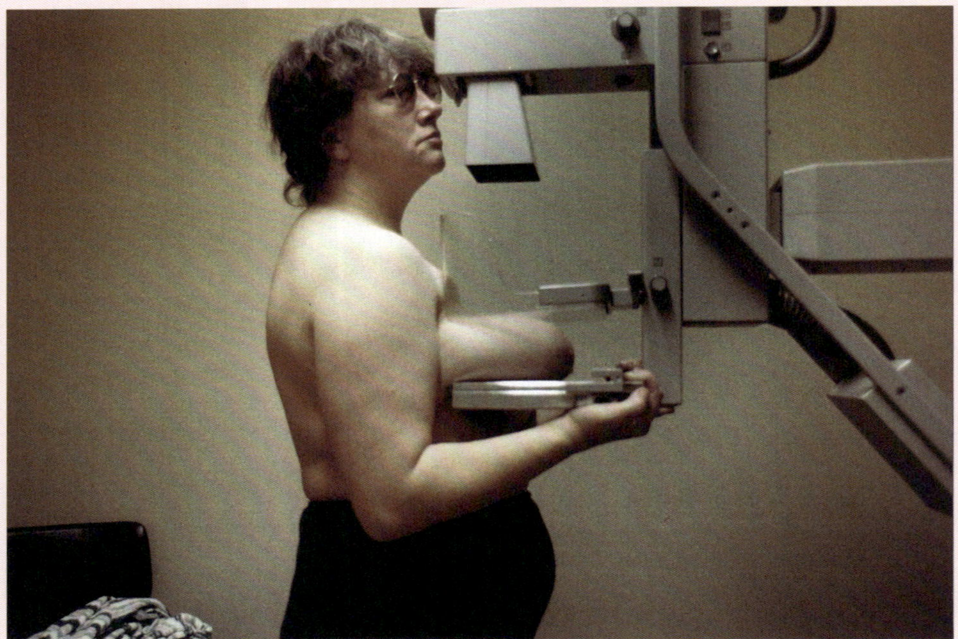

The Picture of Health

Republicans do believe in a woman's right to control her own body

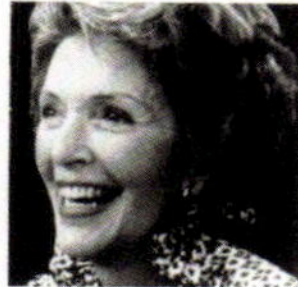

Dyed hair & make-up

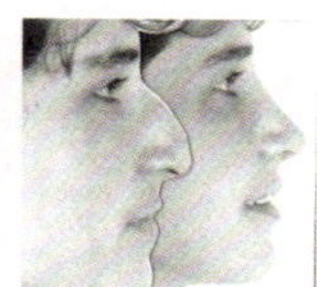

Nose jobs

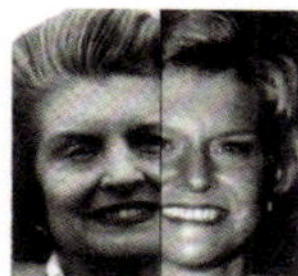

Face lifts

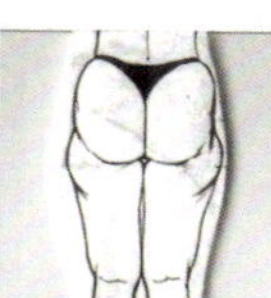

Liposuction

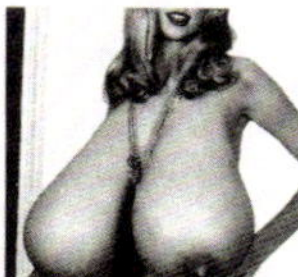

Breast implants

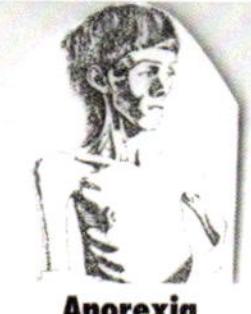

Anorexia & Bulimia

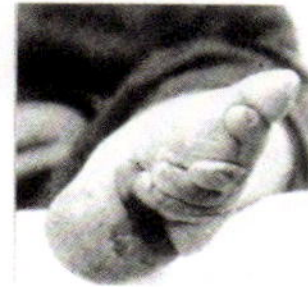

Foot-binding

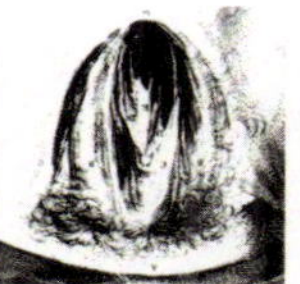

Clitorectomies

A PUBLIC SERVICE MESSAGE FROM THE GUERRILLA GIRLS 532 LaGUARDIA PL. #237, NY 10012

Guerrilla Girls, Republicans Do Believe in a Woman's Right to Control Her Own Body, 1992

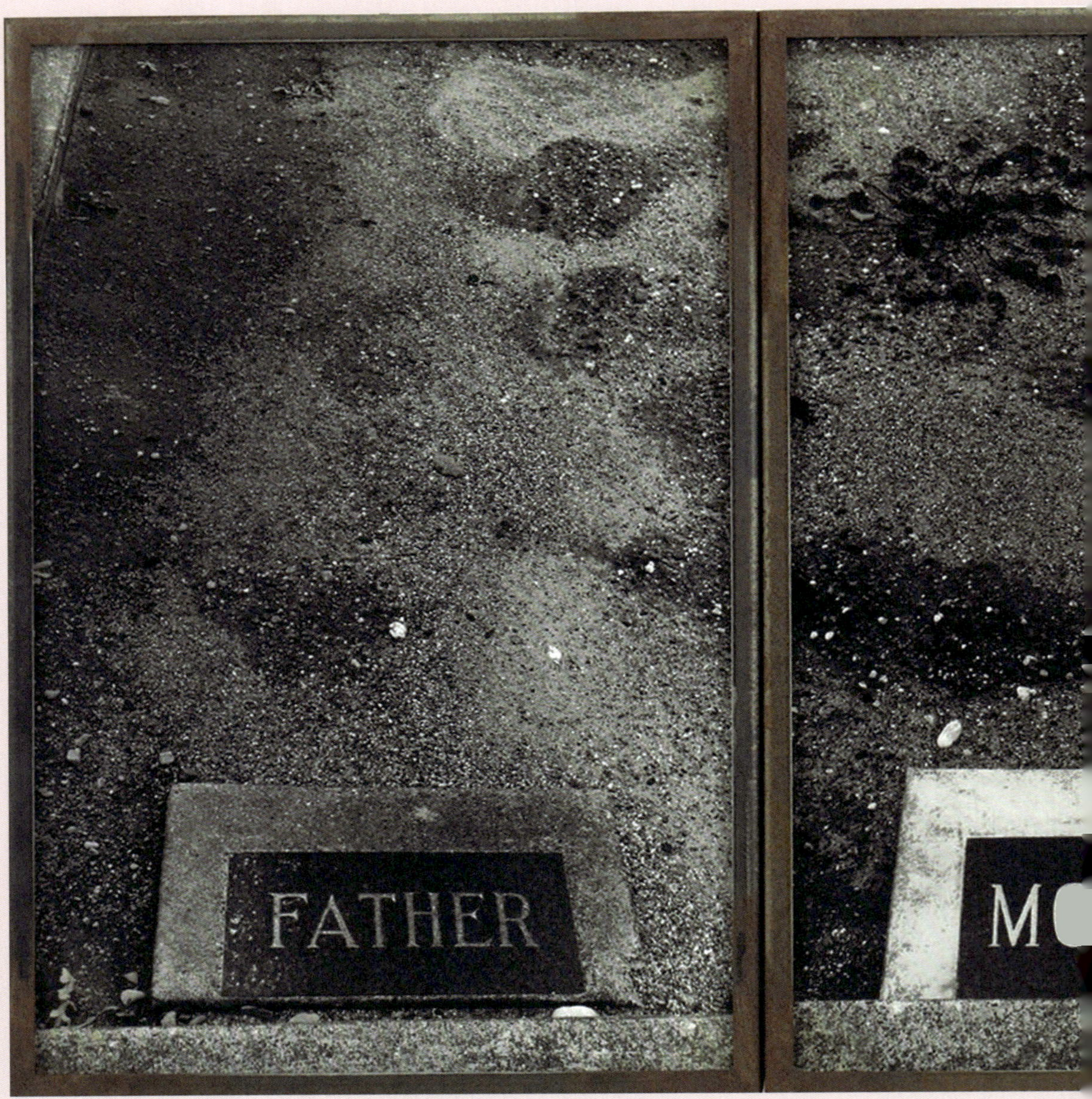

Father, Mother, Son, 1990

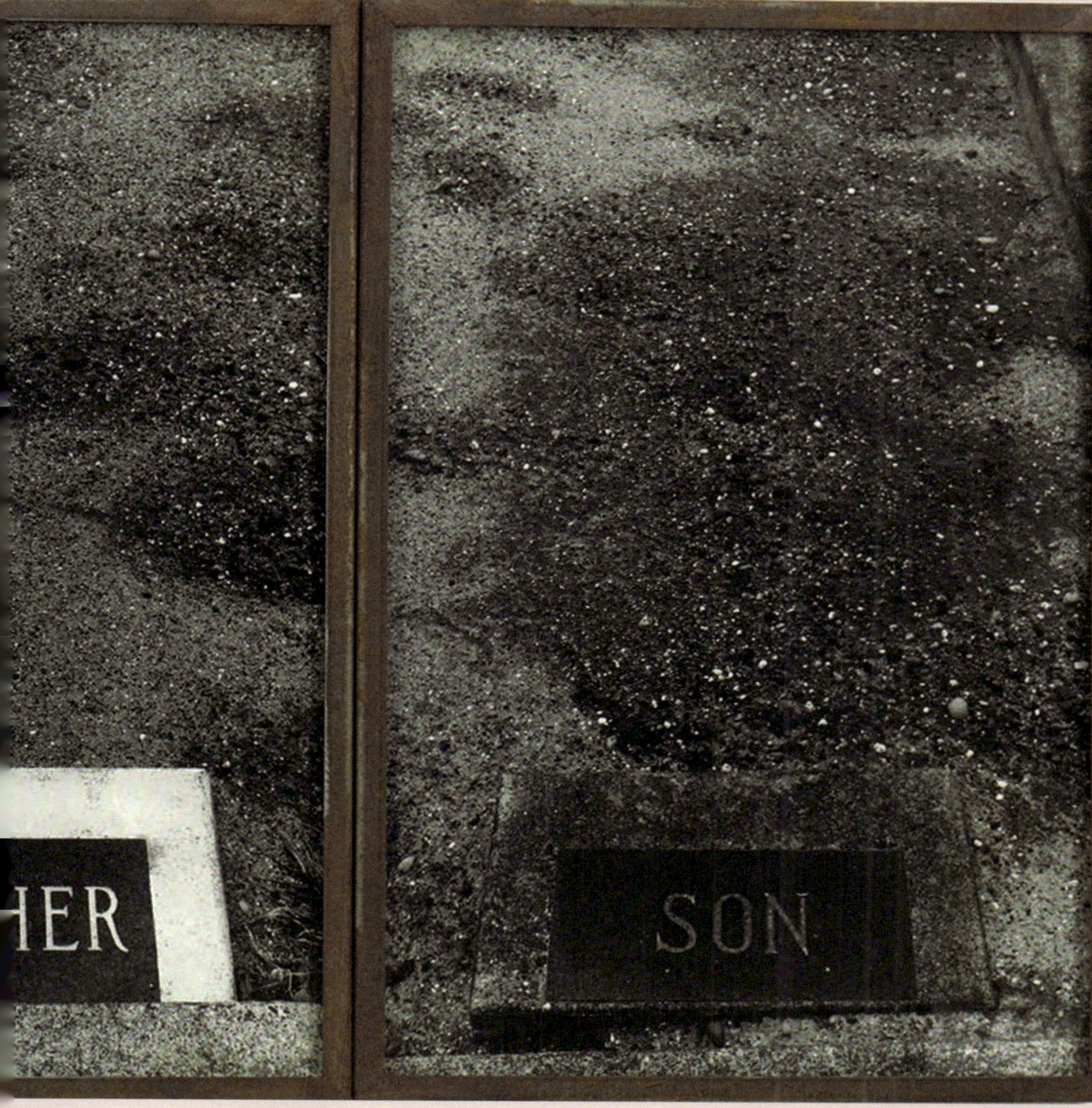
HER
SON

The Photocaptionist is a photo-literary platform that promotes the concubinage between photographs and words. The platform operates both online and offline. Online Photocaptionist offers an a-periodic cabinet of photo-literary compositions and curiosities. Offline it curates exhibitions, lectures, columns, books and events on the relationship between photography, fictions and words. Photographs and words mingle in the eyes and minds of the reader to produce a parallel third dimension that only exists in the fluid back-and-forth of looking at the images and reading the text.

For the third instalment Photocaptionist invites visual-poet Letizia Lopreiato to respond to the visual universe of Laia Abril.

Poems: Letizia Lopreiato

Images: Laia Abril
Courtesy of the artists and Les Filles du Calvaire

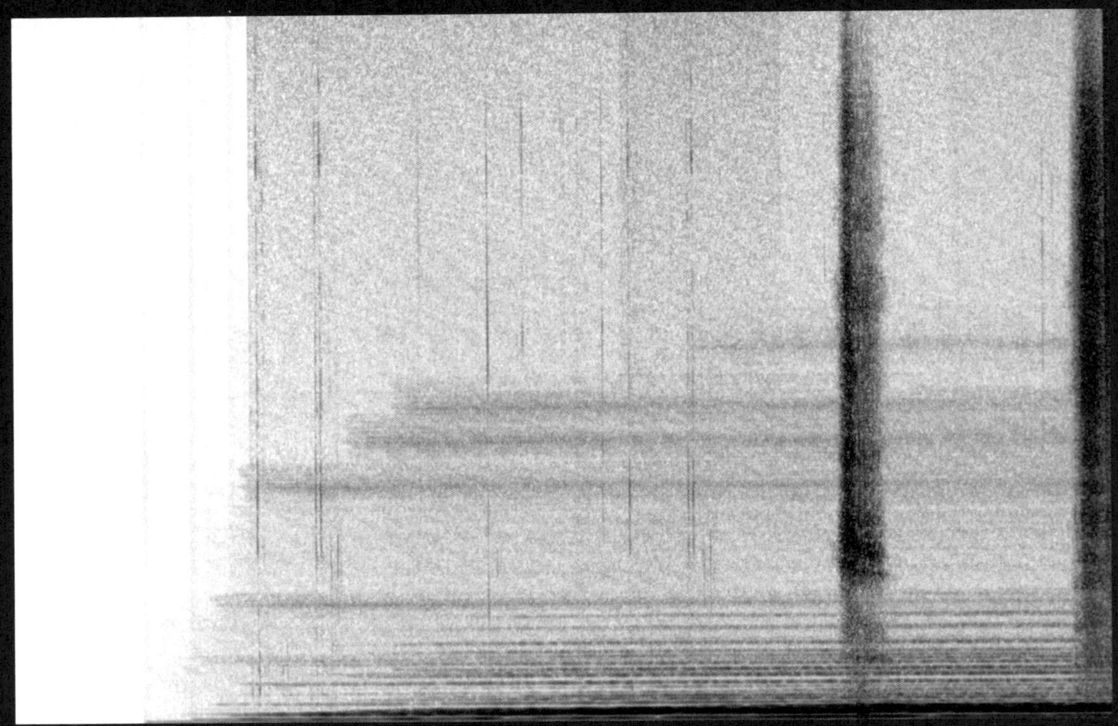

On Healing: Silent Song, 2022
© Laia Abril, courtesy Les Filles du Calvaire

I listened to those rooms as if they were silent
Corridors of a time never lived
Of a horizon
Whispered in the ear of
The Impossible

Made real

Tangible frequency
Imperceptible absence

I learnt how to love within the space of a birdsong
Turning torment into elegance
Into movement

My eyes
Now resonance cases

Made sky
Made sea
Made waves

The swirl of my breath
The sound to hold on to

And finally it was peace
It was Light.

In the Theatre of "Silence" and "Light"
Act 1 – 5 May 2022

Letizia Lopreiato is a multilingual visual poet and installation artist based in the UK and Ireland. She writes and performs her poetry in English, Italian and Spanish. The artist's work has been published and extensively exhibited internationally. Through the application of 35mm photography, Super 8 moving image and her multilingual poetry and spoken word, Letizia Lopreiato's documentary art practice focuses on fostering engagement thanks to the creation of text-, image- and sound-based installations. Her multimedia work is devoted to holding space for empathy while serving as a catalyst for a change in conversation about social inclusion. Letizia's "living installations" allow her to develop art environments that are informed by her interaction with the audience.

Of scars in the shadow I sing the song
Invisible marks
Clinging to the darkness of those voids

Standing still

I drew with burning hands

That enchanting wind
Carefully laid
By the shore of a dream

Our destinies
As crystals … Of sand

Humility

To separate the signal
From the noise.

I escape the sound

To read the music
Written

In the sky of my mind

They placed us all in a casket

The ones whose ear could not see
The ones whose eyes could not hear

And yet our heart was crying
To the sound of those notes

Chained

To the boundaries of “Time”

“Wind” will you teach us once again
How to speak out loud?

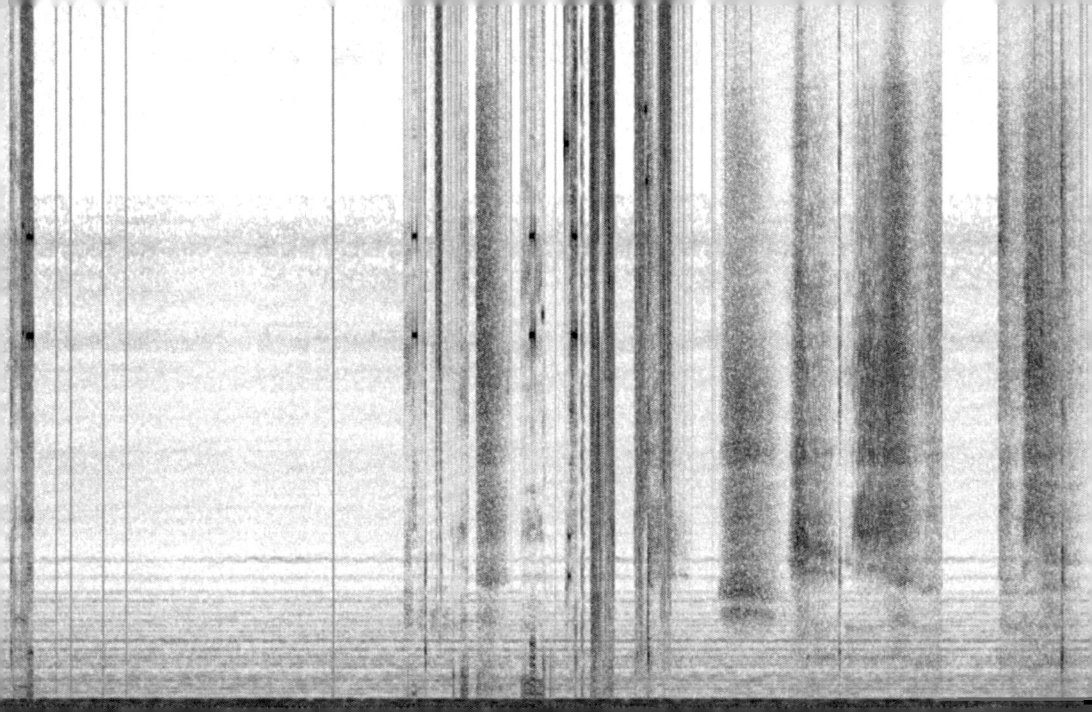

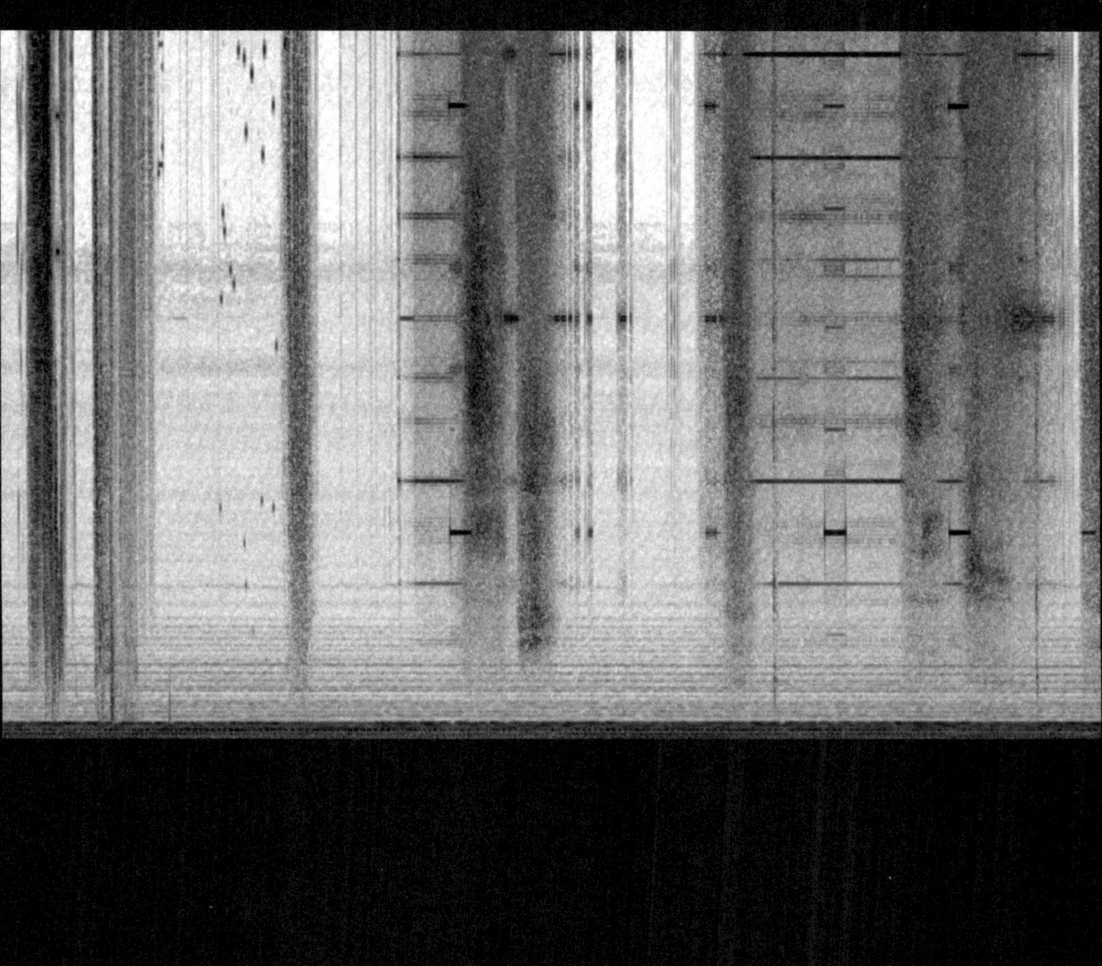

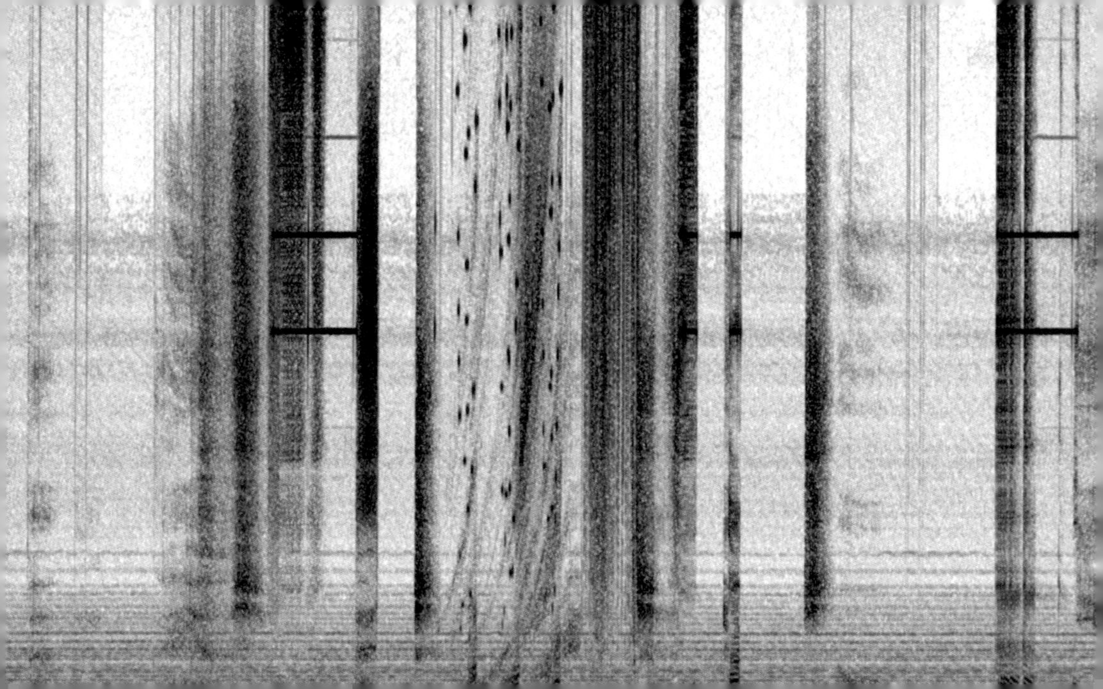

I walked
Into the forest ruled by "Silence"

A path painted by Light and Shadow

I breathe the dust of memories
Listening
to the present …

And it was there
In the "Land of Mirrors"
That "Courage" found me

"Strength" took me by the hand
And whispering to my ear she said:
-"Light" is waiting for you-
…
The walls became trees

I touched their branches

A trail appeared
…
I was home.

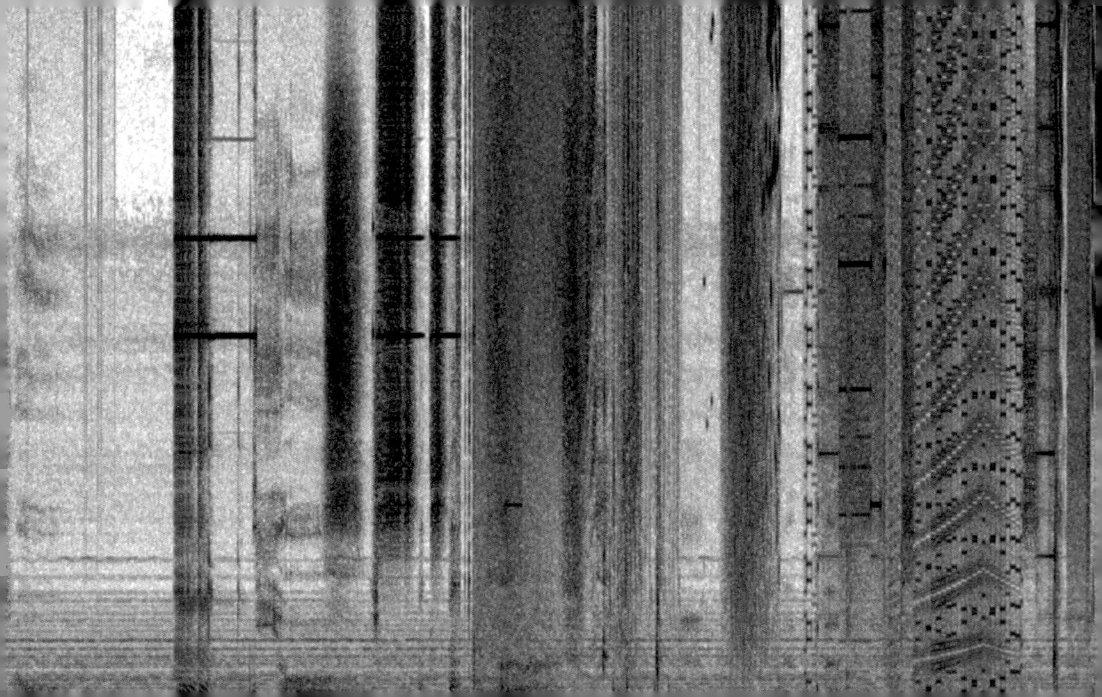

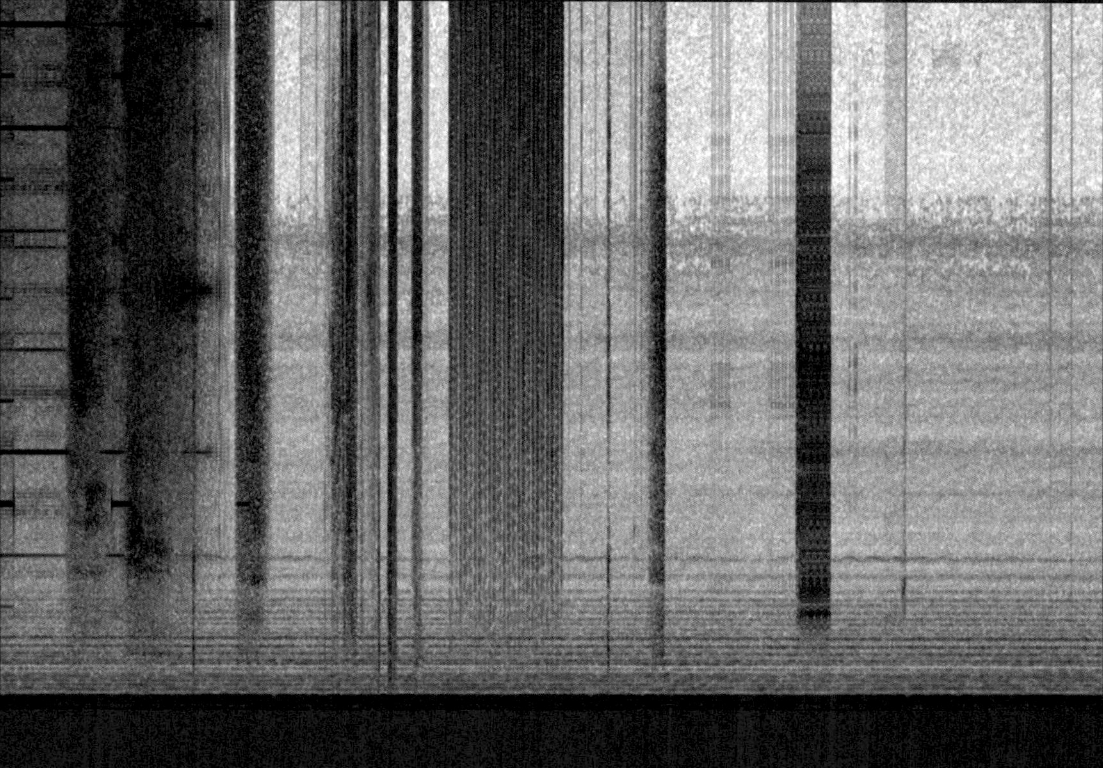

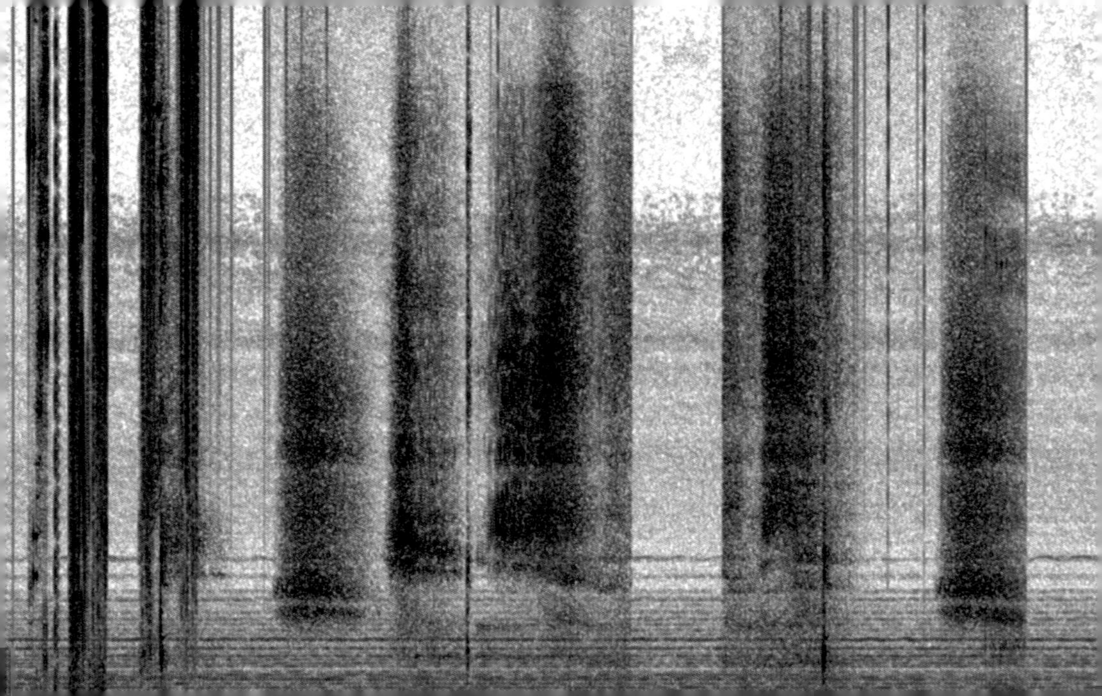

Every year, *The Eyes* offers its readers a cross-cutting vision on a contemporary social subject. This engaged editorial approach exists thanks to the support of loyal partners who are also close to the artists of today. This section is devoted to the programmes they carry out and the projects they support.

Contents

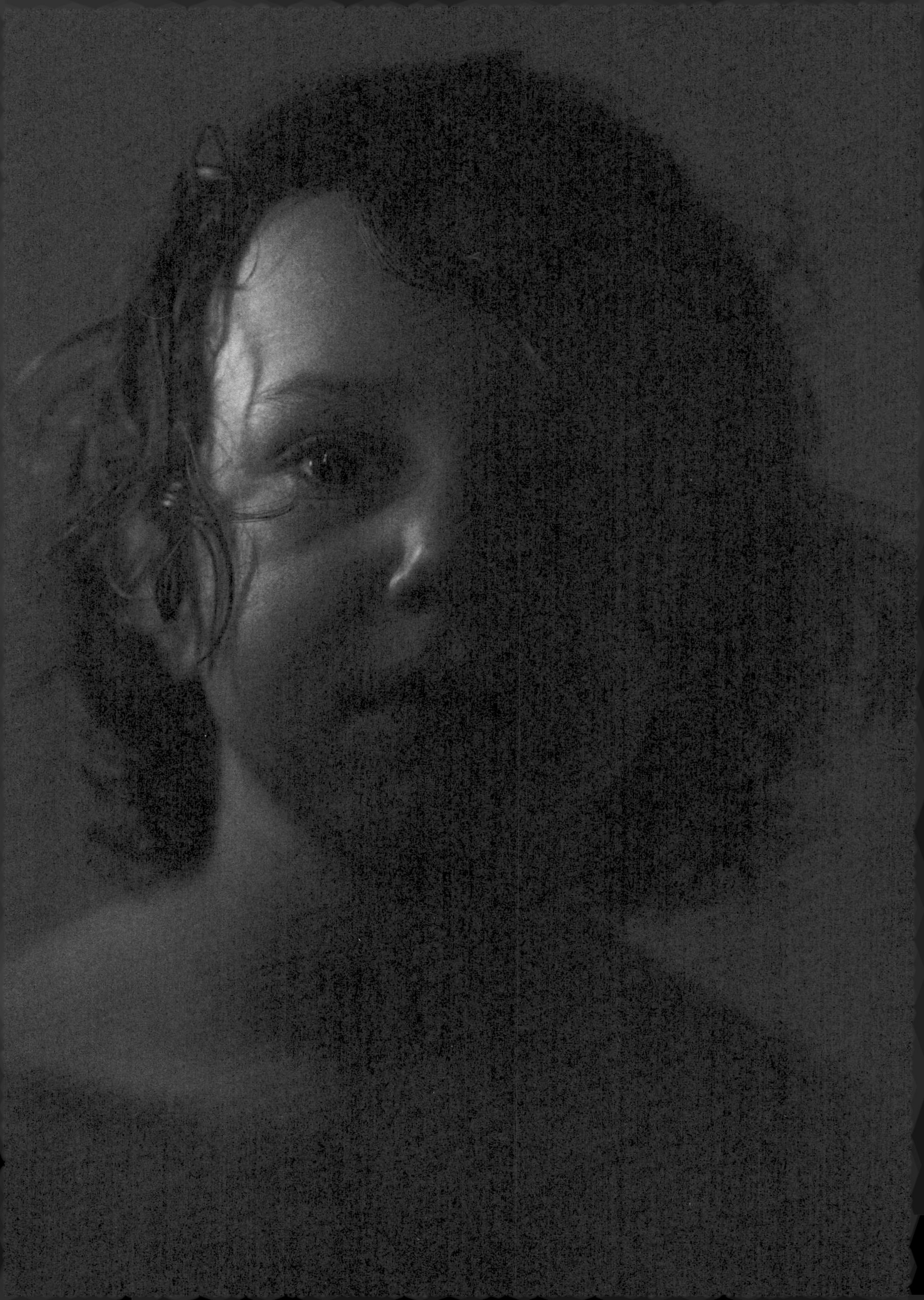

A TROUBLEMAKER IN RESIDENCE

After transhumanism, eco-anxiety is now taking Matthieu Gafsou around the world from China to Ireland, via France and the United States. The Swiss artist photographs landscapes, still lifes and portraits that are both fascinating and disturbing. His series *Vivants*, selected by the Curiosa section of Paris Photo, is a novel approach that combines images, music, poetry and personal narrative to open our eyes to climate change and the extinction of species: "A rhetoric of collapse. That's how my project started," reveals this emerging talent in the preface of his book *Vivants*. Part documentary, part visual arts, this allegorical realism in the form of a photographic essay aims to reconcile art and social science. Twilight scenes of nature, birds caught in nets and bloody rivers (artificially coloured by the author) contrast with snapshots of his children and their innocent rural games. This conflicting expression, both angry and sentimental, won the Ruinart Prize, awarded by the prestigious champagne house to an artist in the Curiosa section.

Matthieu Gafsou, the 2022 winner, was given carte blanche to explore the centuries-old wine region of Champagne, renowned for its hedonistic drink. To hell with paradise! At Paris Photo, this troublemaker-in-residence is compelling, with images of the Arcadian landscape that has been contaminated by hydrocarbons, synonymous with pollution. "Beautiful nature is sacred; it was separated from the urban landscape. But the environment is affected everywhere, and the Champagne region is also suffering," argues Matthieu Gafsou. The artist has adopted the allegorical process he used for his *Vivants* series: the pigmented prints of these landscapes, which have been stripped of their commonplace vines, have been corroded by a layer of petroleum, then cleaned, scanned and retouched on screen. In the end, the altered, surrealistic colours produce a toxic atmosphere. "This uncontrollable oil process suggests contamination but also makes the images more graphic. I like this ambivalence, which shows that things are not as beautiful as they seem," the artist explains.

In Champagne, affected by an unprecedented summer heatwave, his work is focused on the theme of heat and water. Here is a playful, enigmatic scene of holidaymakers playing on a dry beach, as if the sea had one day retreated. It becomes absurd, with shots of cranes parked along a parched field or a paltry, puddle-sized pool of water, insufficient to cool the overheated city. Is this an ecological manifesto? "I have always denied playing a role in socially engaged photography, but I am evolving," admits this father, who is concerned about the future. "Can an image, a chorus of voices, have an effect? I remain pessimistic, because change is difficult for us, and the liberal system still does not take a good look at itself. It is time to brace ourselves for a world that will be completely different."

Images:
© Matthieu Gafsou, courtesy Gallery C
Fils II, 2022
Pétrole I, 2022
Pétrole III, 2021
Cette constante brûlure de l'air # 2, 2022
Cette constante brûlure de l'air # 1, 2022

Text:
Gisèle Tavernier

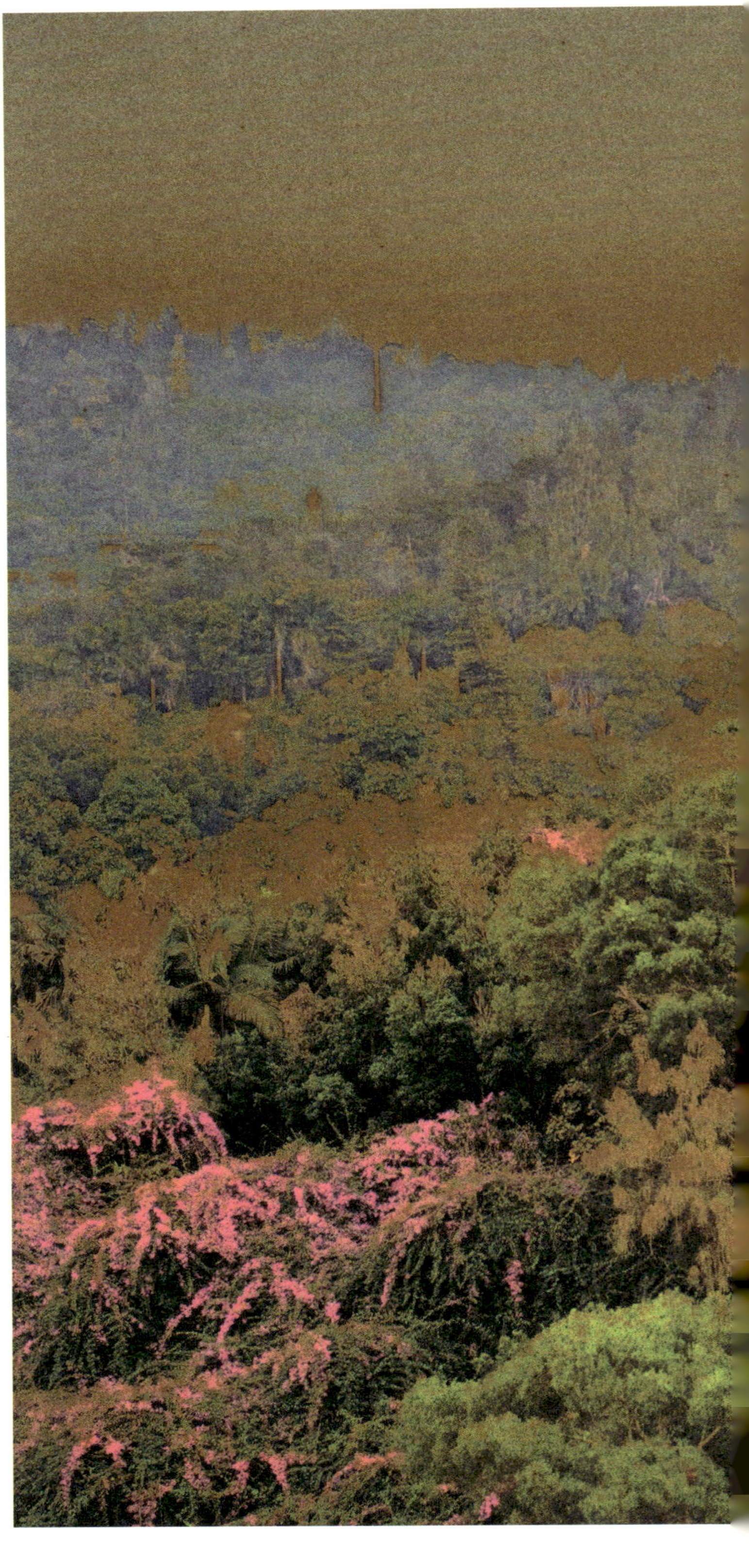

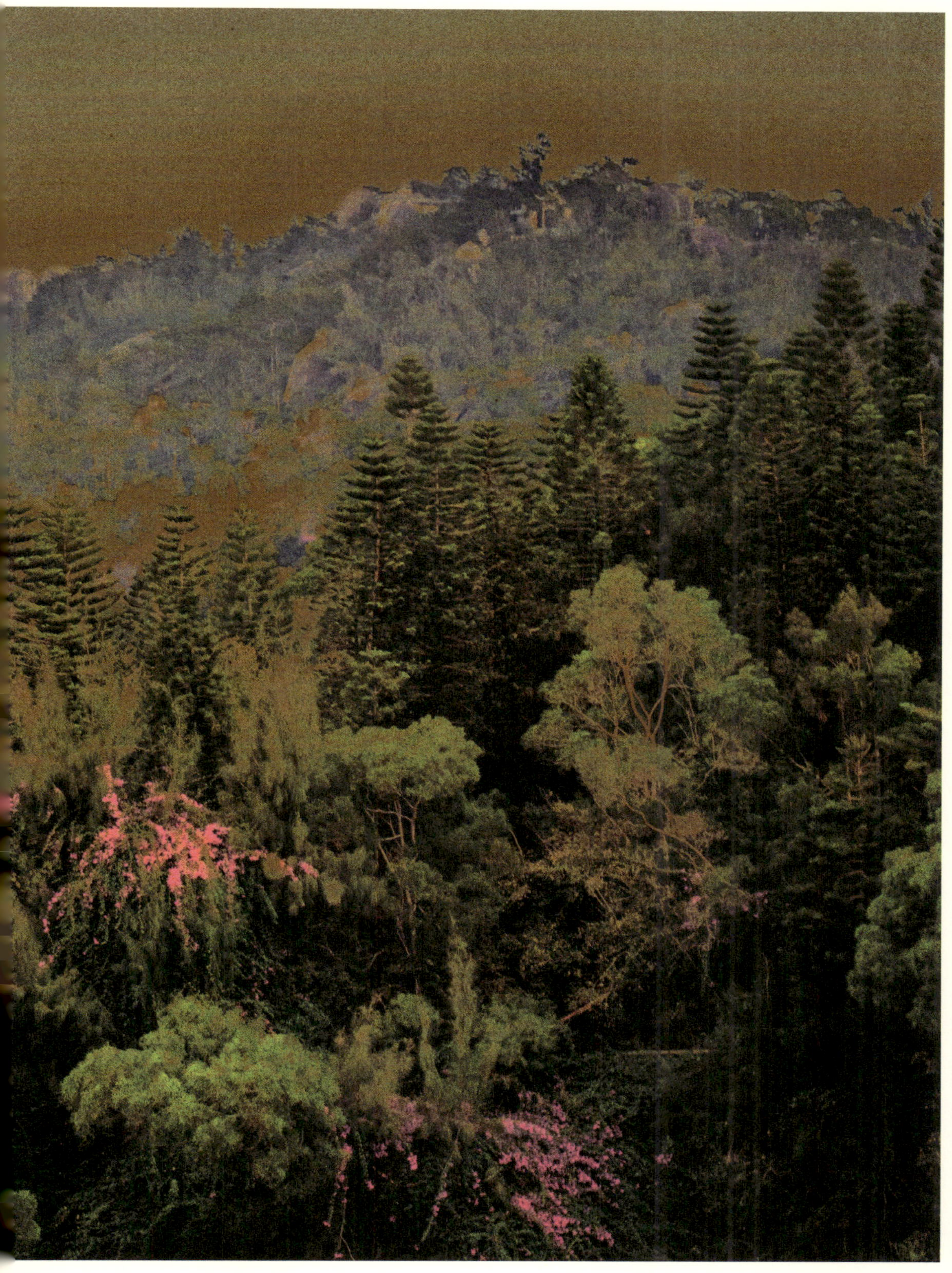

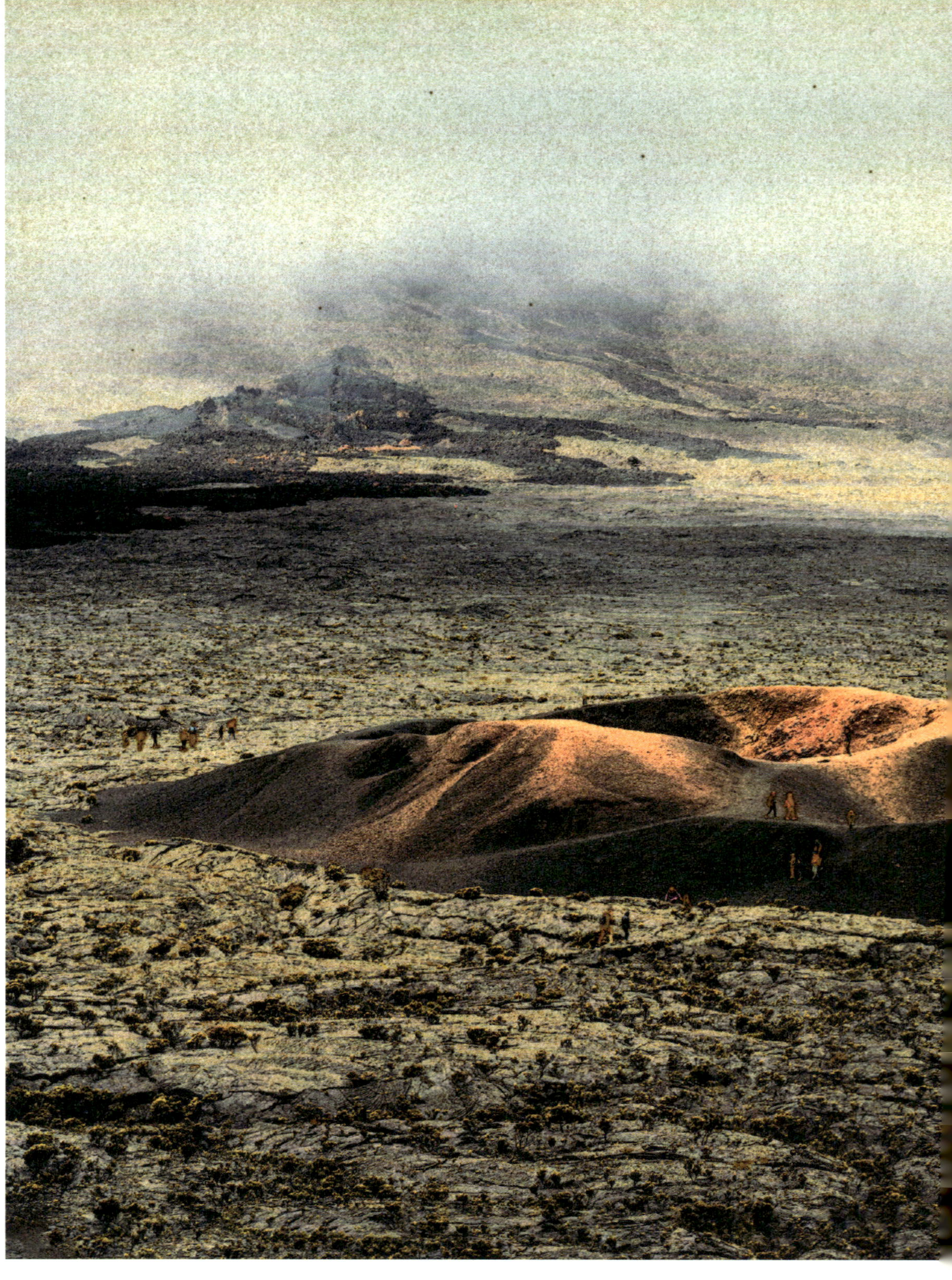

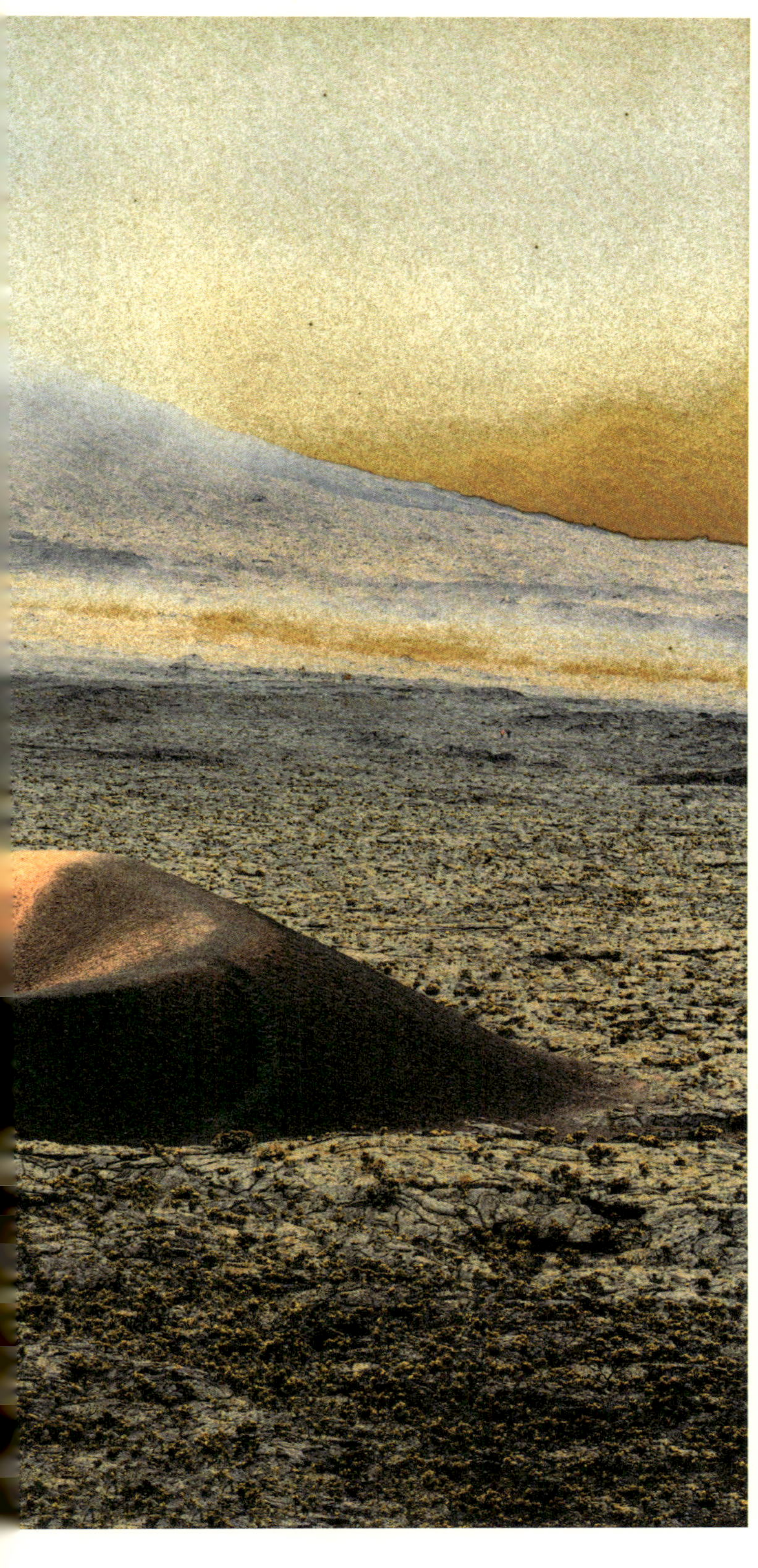

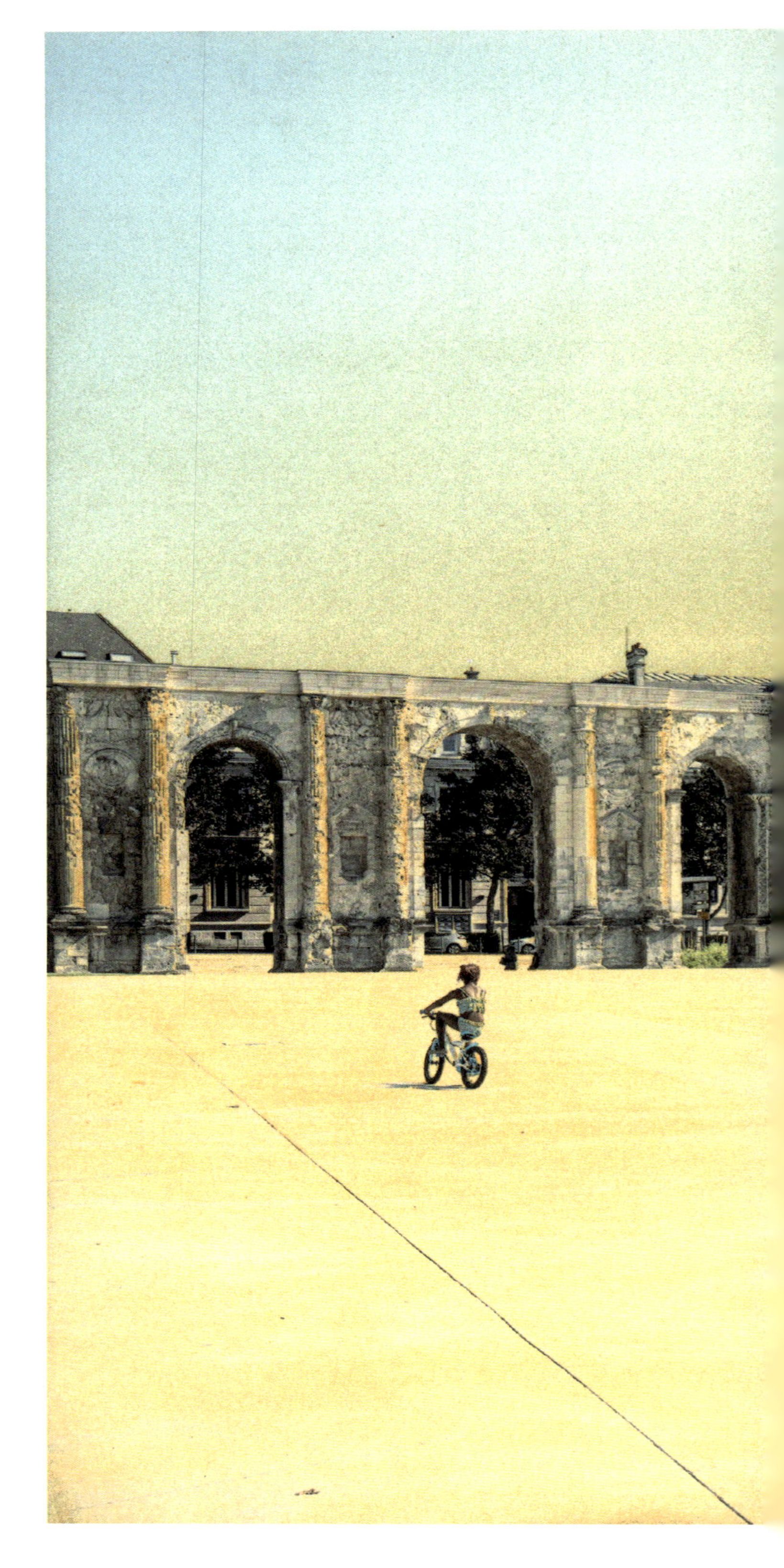

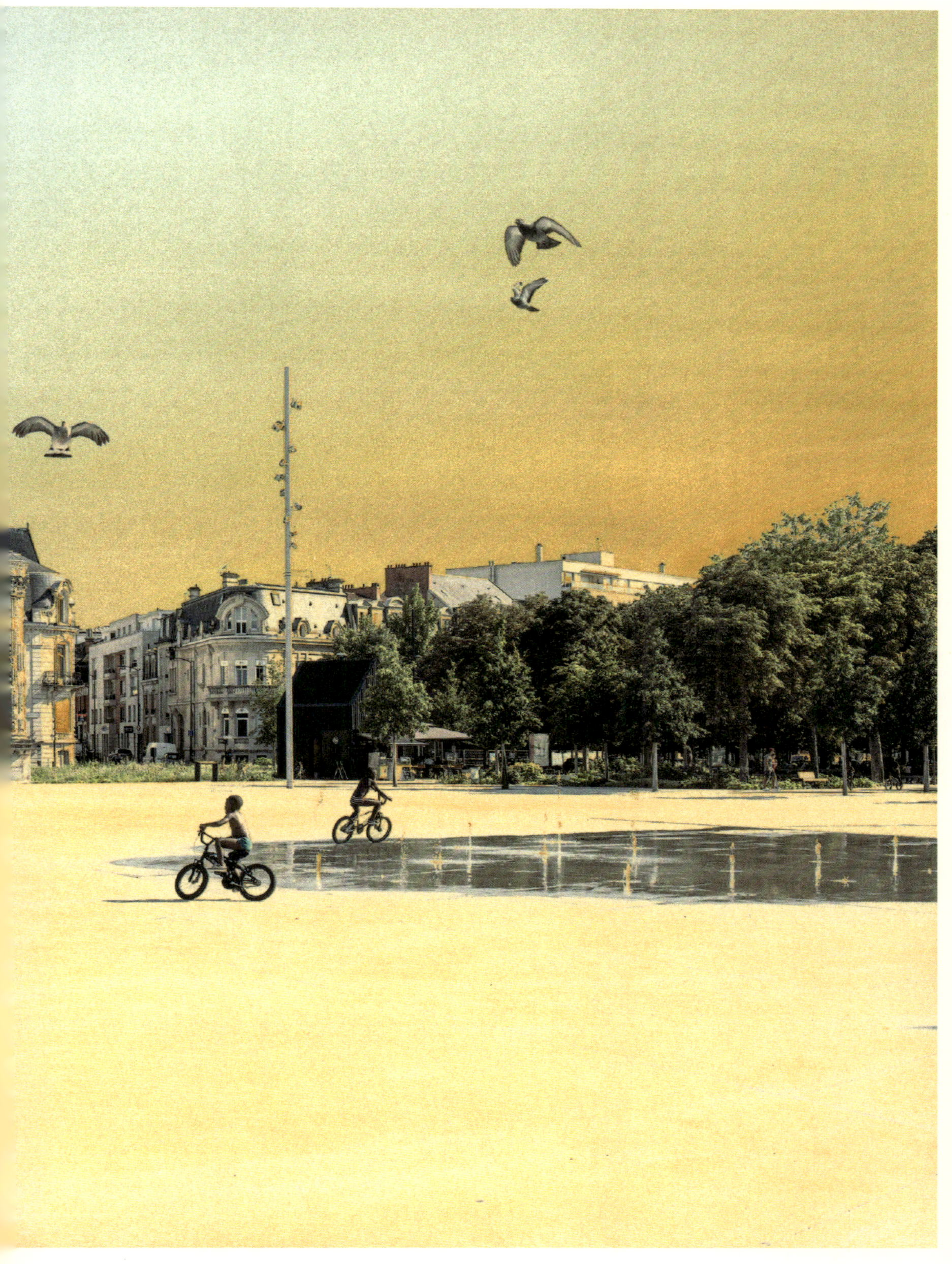

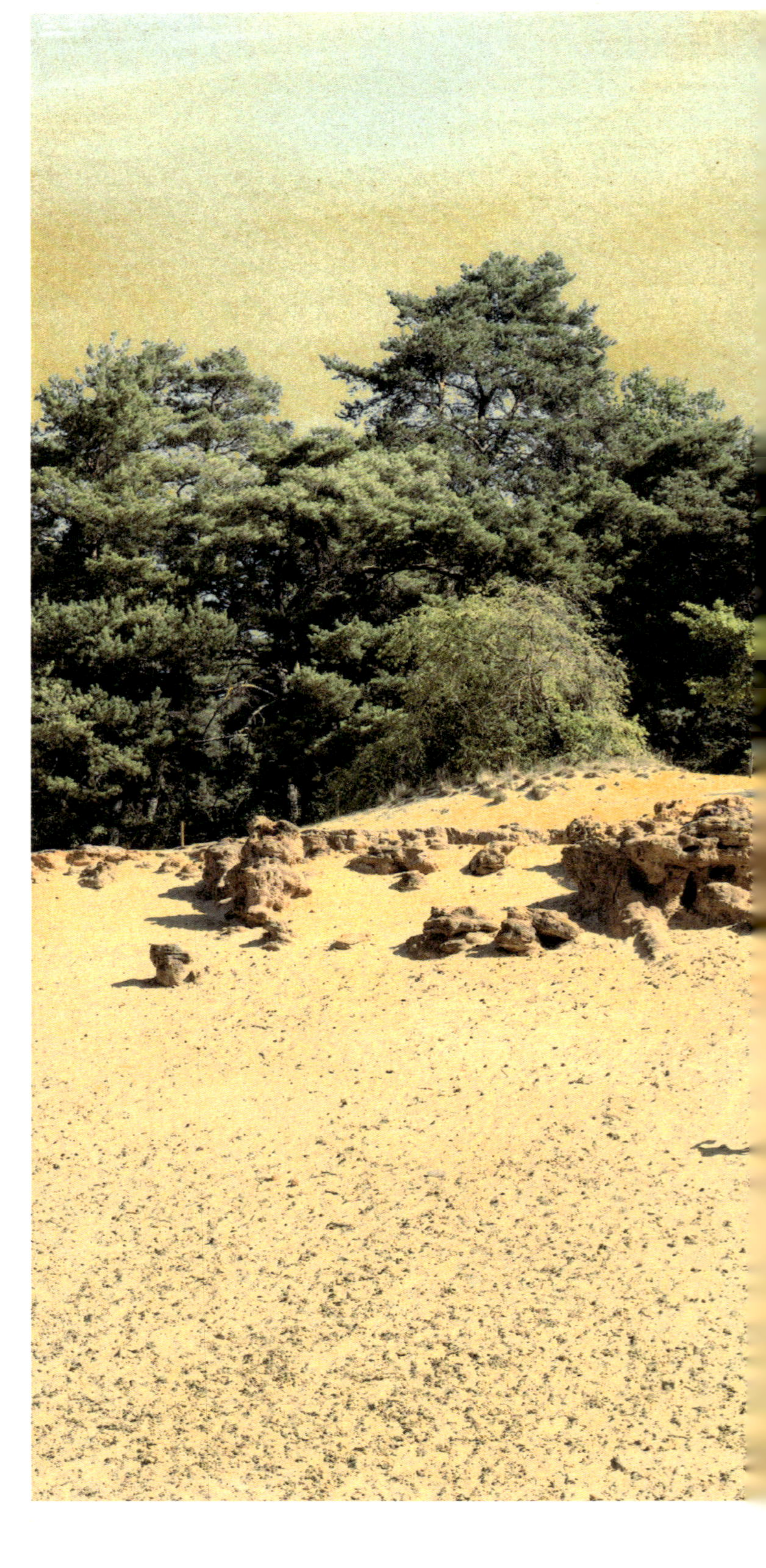

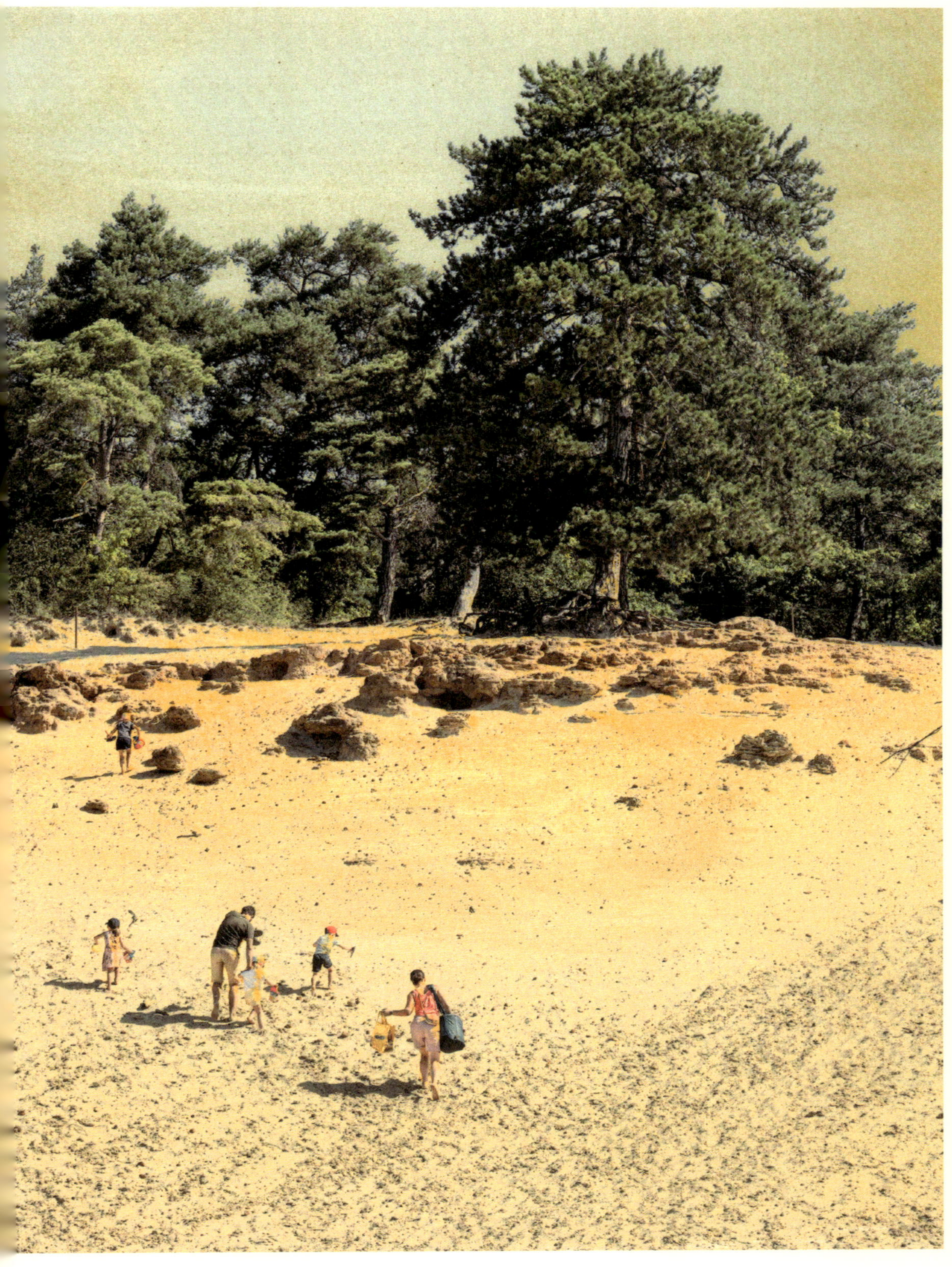

SUBURBAN HAUNTOLOGY

The complex futuristic installation *Suburban Hauntology* is both innovative and bewildering. The ghostly images of the Étoiles – habitats emblematic of 1970s utopian architecture – are combined with the expanding universe of "big data". This visual magma, exhibited at the international photography festival the Rencontres d'Arles (July– September 2022), then at the Paris Photo fair (November 2022), is the work of the artist Arash Hanaei and the curator Morad Montazami. The two protagonists are winners of the BMW ART MAKERS, the first sponsorship programme to support the emerging creation and experimentation of the image in all its forms by associating an artist-curator duo.

In this experimental jumble, the augmented reality of the metaverse, the internet of the future, merges with still and moving images made of architectural elements and portraits reworked with 3D morphing software. "This combination of deformed faces and borrowings from the aesthetics of video games could be defined as 'big data paintings'. At any given moment, pop-up images produce a permanent shift in focus," analyses Morad Montazami. In fact, the 3.0 installation navigates between digital drawings, a hologram of the Étoiles d'Ivry-sur-Seine (a group of extraordinary buildings designed by the architect Jean Renaudie) and video performances exploring in virtual mode the design, more ideological than utopian, of these buildings of the past. "The city of the future was prefigured, because the Étoiles and the metaverse, two complex spaces, appear as two dimensions of the same landscape," explains Arash Hanaei.

A speculative installation, *Suburban Hauntology* examines these parallel worlds. A virtual chess game, staged in a black box reminiscent of Samuel Beckett's Theatre of the Absurd, pits the avatars of Mark Zuckerberg, representative of ultra-capitalism extended to the metaverse, against the theoretician Mark Fisher, a radical critic of this economic system deemed to have no alternative. This game of chess without action or end is interspersed with repetitive ideological slogans. "This game, which inspires no hope, reflects views that are torn between utopia and dystopia," says Arash Hanaei. Elsewhere, the antagonistic political forces of the 21st century are embodied in a topical metaphorical sequence: the inordinately long negotiating table where presidents Putin and Macron discussed the war in Ukraine is transformed into a flaming table tennis table, while on a large screen a sprawling virtual network of undersea communication cables appears.

For Morad Montazami, these representations, halfway between reality and augmented reality taken from science fiction, "situate the installation in the geopolitical relationship of power between great forces that the metaverse generates". The key question of the future is indeed there. Who will control "big data" 2,000 leagues under the sea?

Images:
Courtesy Arash Hanaei/BMW ART MAKERS
I Begin To See, 2022
Untitled, 2022
Mark F et Mark Z. Avatars, 2022/Diasec Print, 135 x 200 cm.
Hashtag Flagged, 2022/ Diasec Print

Text:
Gisèle Tavernier

Artist Arash Hanaei and curator Morad Montazami are the winners of BMW ART MAKERS, BMW's new sponsorship programme for the visual arts and contemporary image.

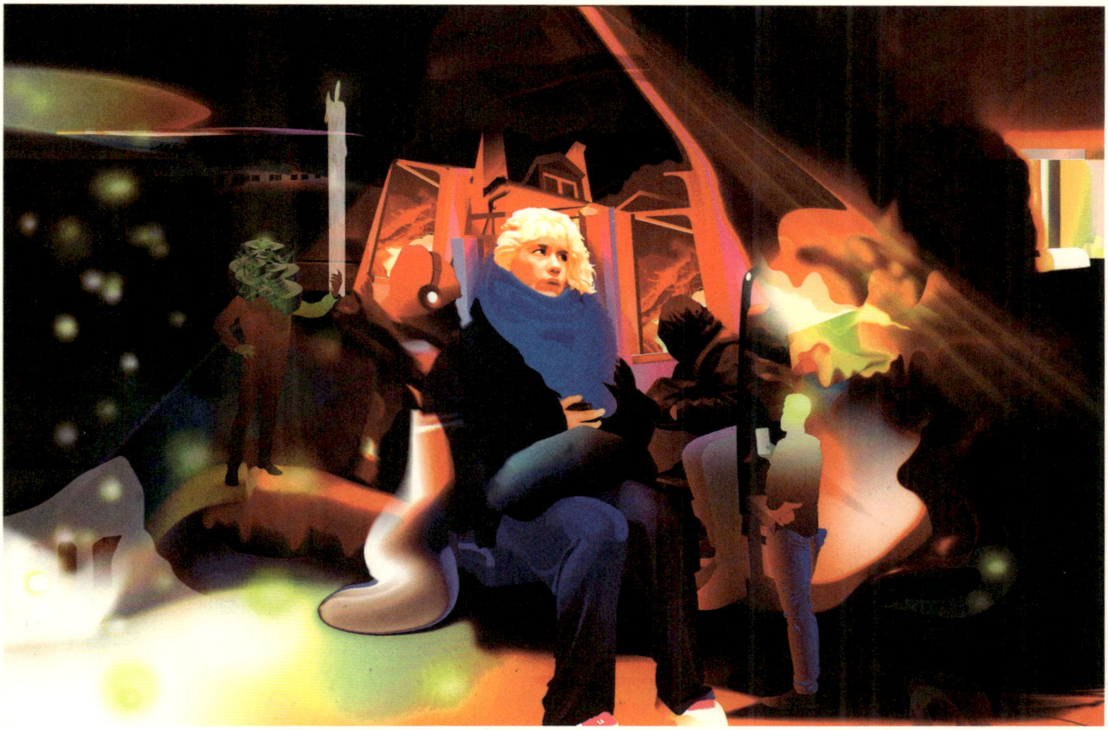

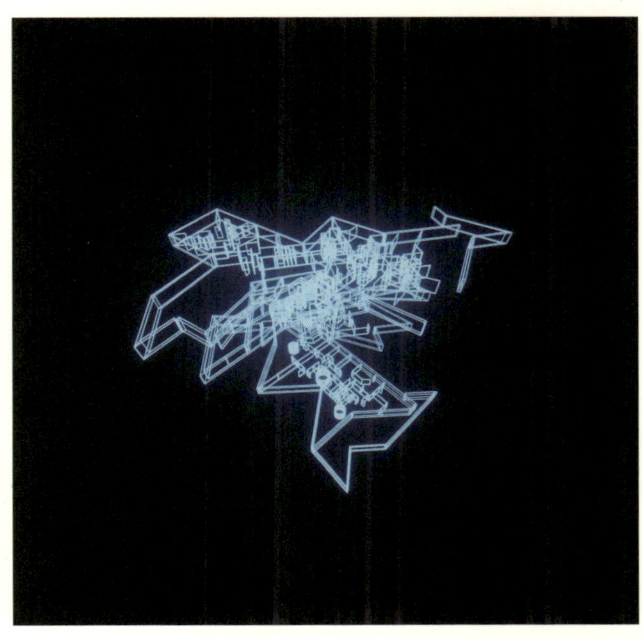

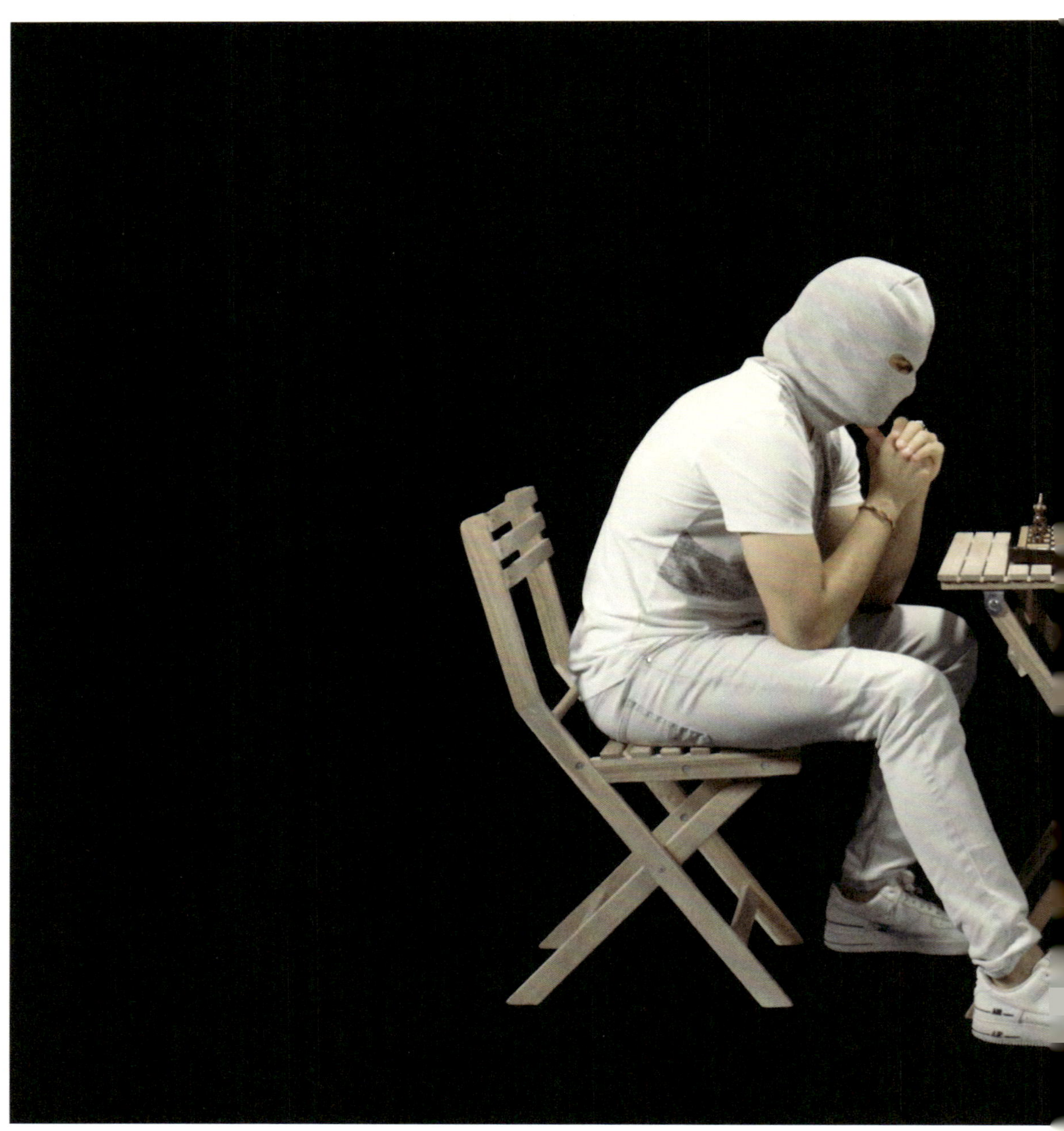

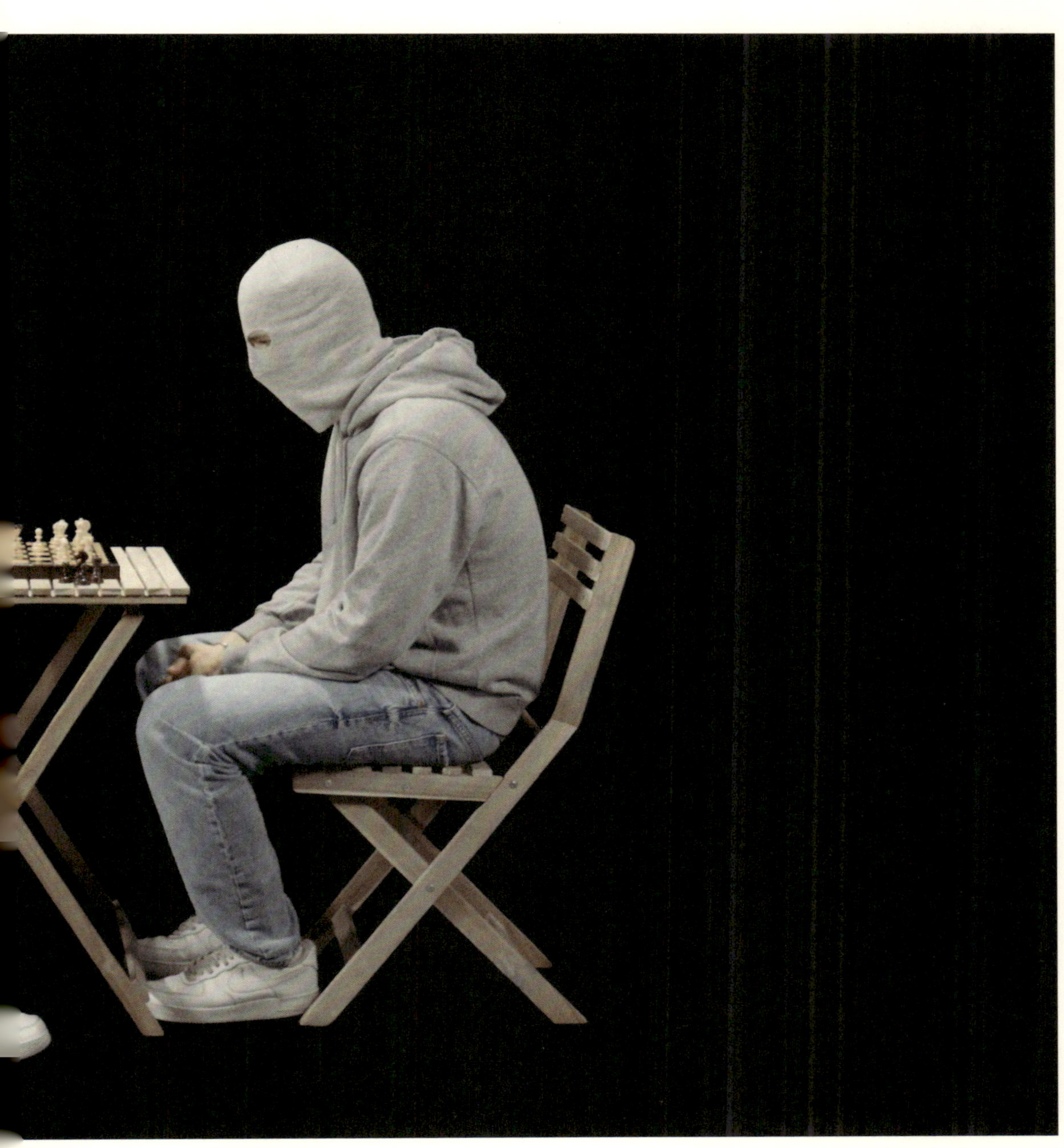

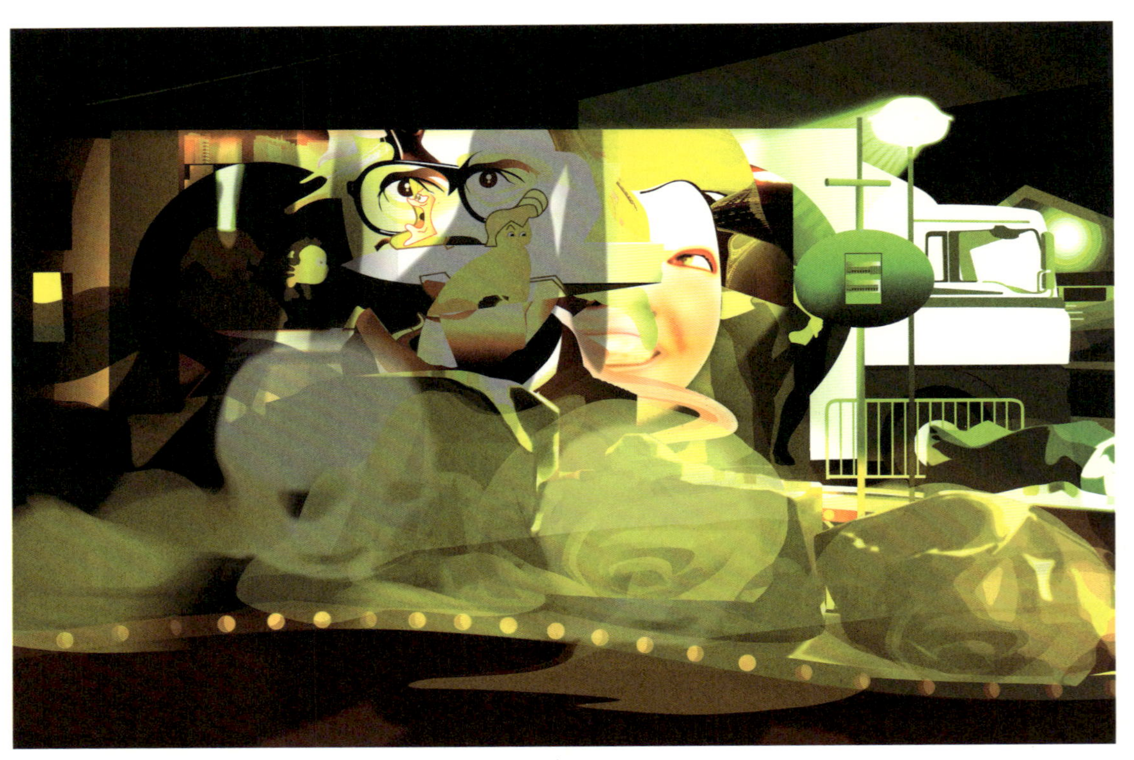

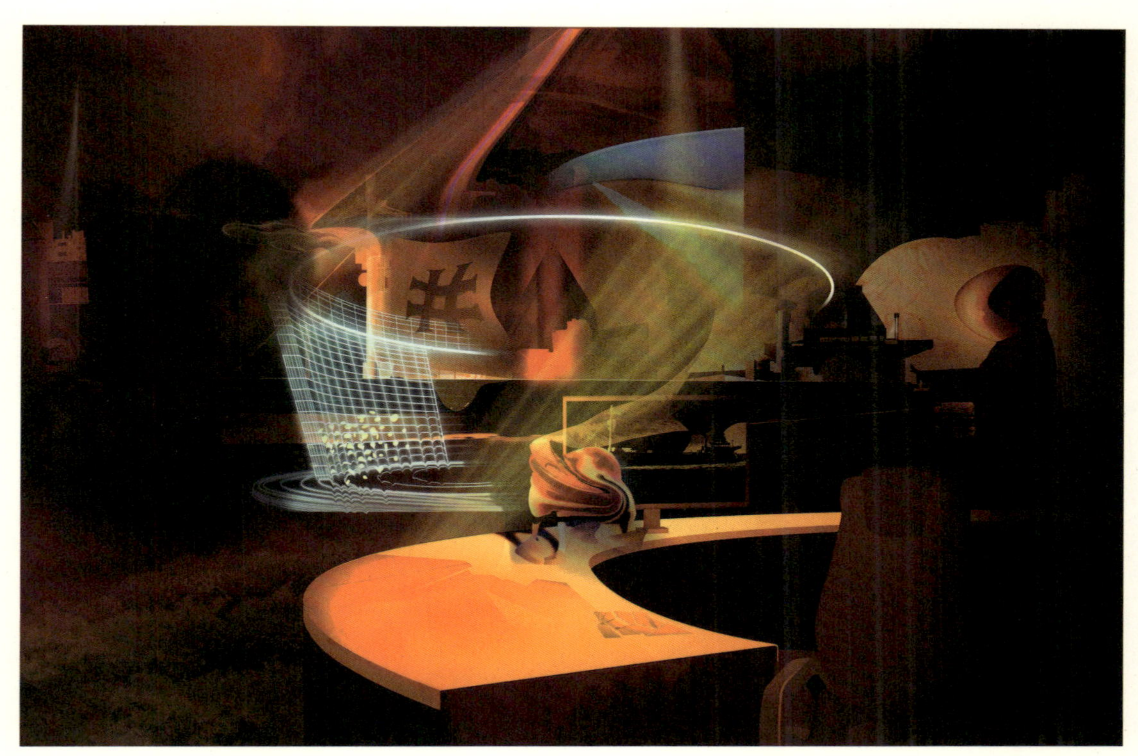

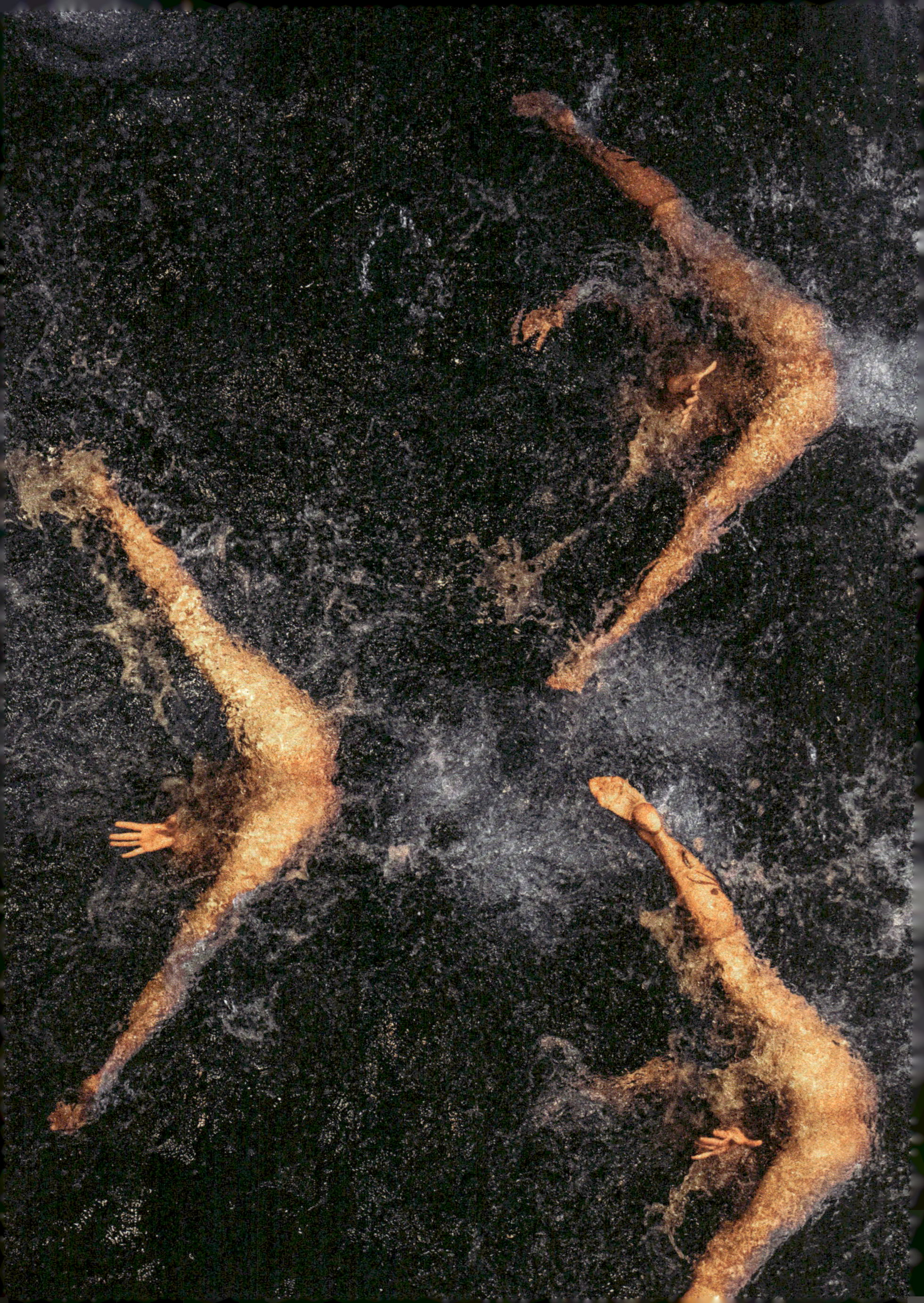

SURPRISES AT EVERY LEVEL

Images:
Las Vegas, Jeff Burton, Louis Vuitton Éditions Fashion Eye

O, Cirque du Soleil, Bellagio
O, Cirque du Soleil, Bellagio
Le soleil de Las Vegas
Interprète dans Absinthe, Caesars Palace
Chelsea Pool, the Cosmopolitan
UFC 264 poids welter, T-Mobile Arena, Stephen "Wonderboy" Thompson vs. Gilbert Burns

Text:
Sophie Bernard

This autumn, Louis Vuitton's Fashion Eye collection touches down in Las Vegas for a new edition by Jeff Burton. Since 2016, the fashion house has given carte blanche to a contemporary photographer or offered an immersion into the archival treasures of historical figures such as Adolphe de Meyer, Cecil Beaton, Saul Leiter and Helmut Newton. An intriguing tour of the world takes shape, book after book, visiting a city, a region or a country. With some 30 titles, the collection focuses on the diversity of photographic styles and destinations. The latest titles, published in June, bear witness to this: *Kilamba* (Angola) by Laura Bonnefous and *Lagos* (Nigeria) by Daniel Obasi, and this November *Buenos Aires* by the duo Sofia & Mauro and Las Vegas by Jeff Burton.

Las Vegas is a dream machine with its wealth of casinos, luxury hotels, Eiffel Tower, Strip and various shows. There are few cities like Las Vegas with so many nicknames – Sin City, City Without Clocks – and descriptions. At one time the capital of prostitution, today it is the capital of tourism and marriage, and of course gambling. Paradoxically, this city of pleasure was founded by the Mormons in 1855. Located in the middle of the desert and sparkling with thousands of lights, it is quite unique. Jeff Burton is also a paradox and a unique character in his own way. He began his career as a photographer on gay pornographic film sets after growing up in Texas, in a conservative and traditional America. He attended Christian University in Fort Worth, then returned to his native California where he attained a master's degree from the California Institute of the Arts in Valencia. A personal series of film sets, often ordinary interiors, emerged from his initial professional experience, chronicling and documenting the American culture of the late 1990s.

Jeff Burton repeats this sidestep when he photographs Las Vegas, by rejecting the obvious, in other words to focus his carte blanche on the gambling halls that are the very foundation of the city's identity. Although he avoids the casinos, he does not exclude the notion of gambling in the broadest sense of the term, relying on optical effects, illusions and other mirages, other words that perfectly

define Las Vegas. “It’s hard not to get caught up in the fabric of the city. [...] This city offers surprises at every level,” he explains in an interview with Patrick Rémy, to be found at the end of the book.
To highlight the changing and mythical character of Las Vegas, the American also uses a wide palette of saturated colours combined with various effects such as blurring, and alternating styles from realism to trompe-l’oeil to abstraction. The effect is painterly, in the style of Saul Leiter, whom Jeff Burton readily mentions among his influences. Like Leiter, he creates atmospheres rather than scenes, be it when he photographs the shows at Grant Philipo's Las Vegas Showgirl Museum, the performances at Caesars Palace, the Cirque du Soleil shows at the Bellagio or the Ultimate Fighting Championship (UFC) combats at the T-Mobile Arena. Most of the time, he opts for close-ups that make the scenes captured on the spot look unreal, depicting faces distorted by effort and treating bodies like statues. When he photographs the city itself, he shoots general views and tackles it like a set. The mundane becomes extraordinary through his lens: the Bellagio’s fountains are transformed into a strange spaceship, the Cosmopolitan’s pool looks like a miniature architectural structure and the bathers like dolls, and the sun captured in a green sky becomes an abstract painting. Like the city of Las Vegas itself, it is difficult to distinguish between reality and fiction. Welcome to the world of Jeff Burton.

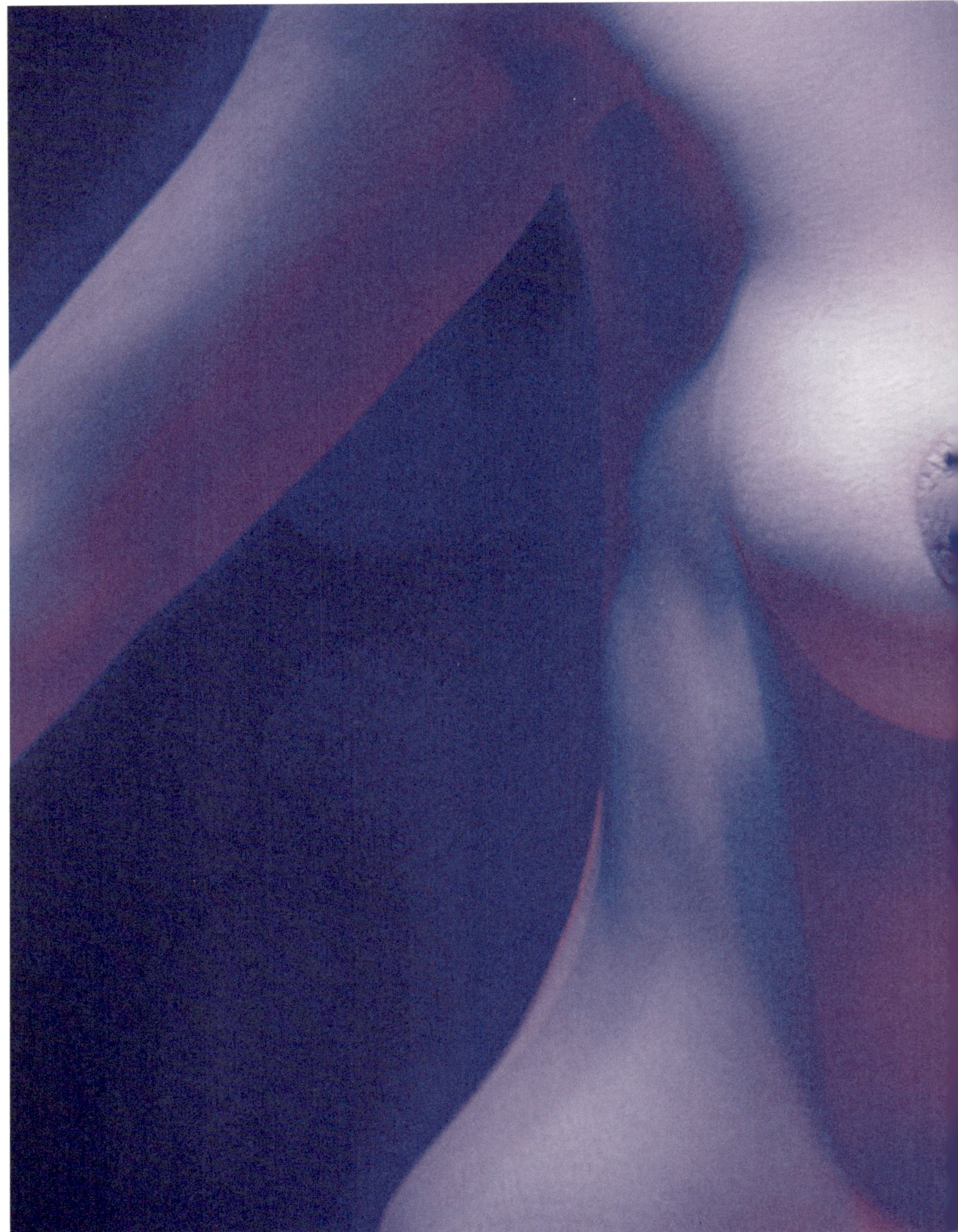

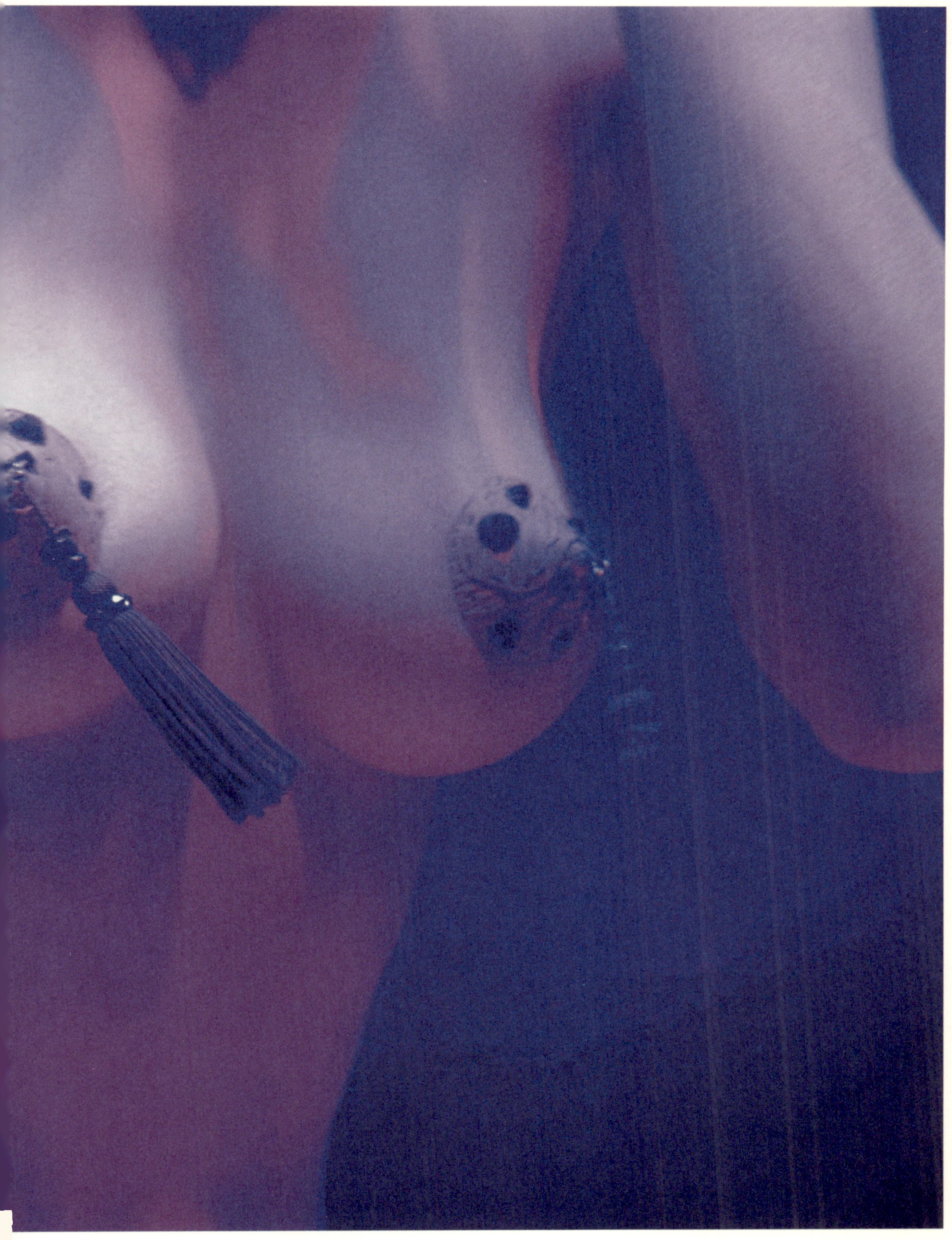

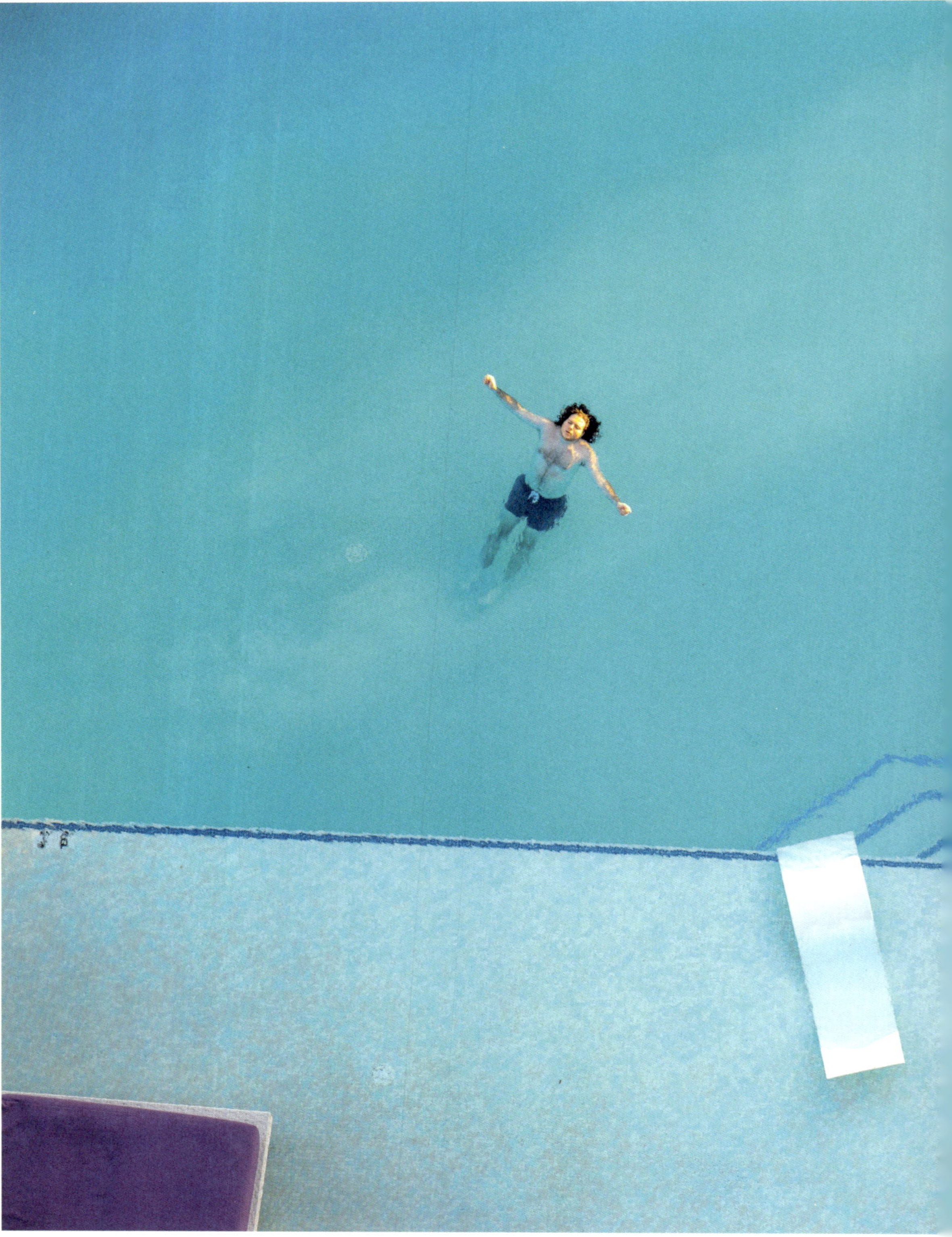

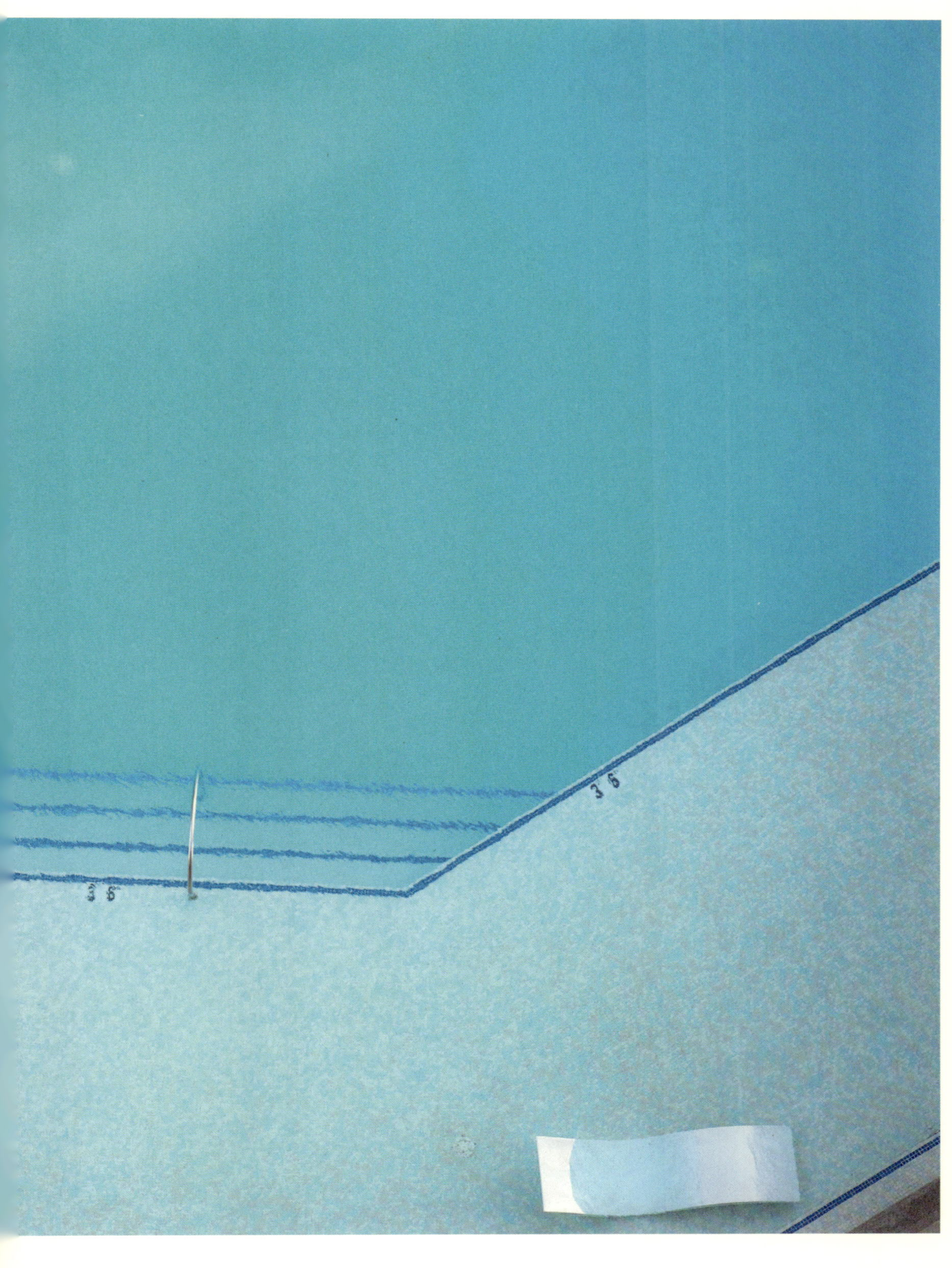

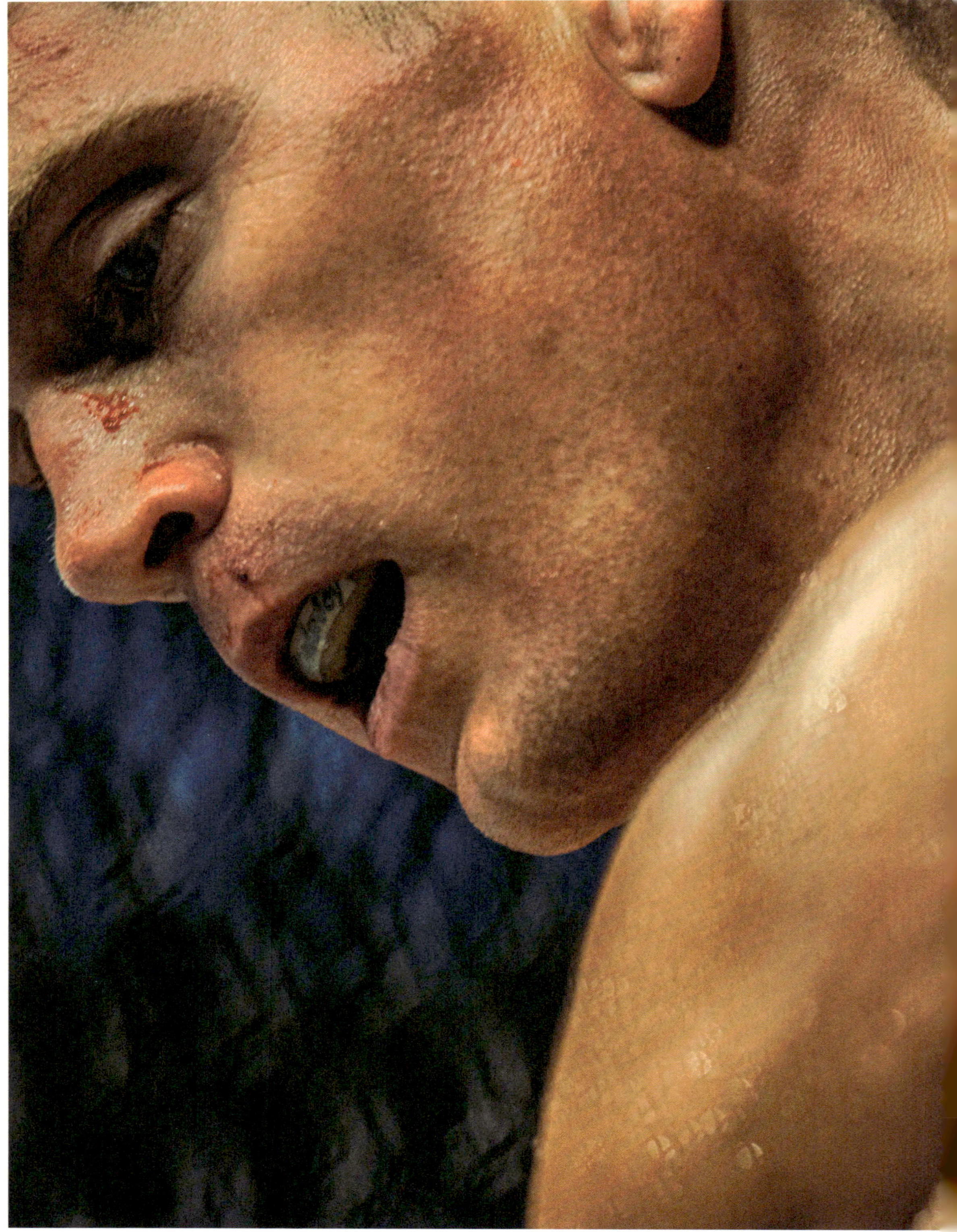

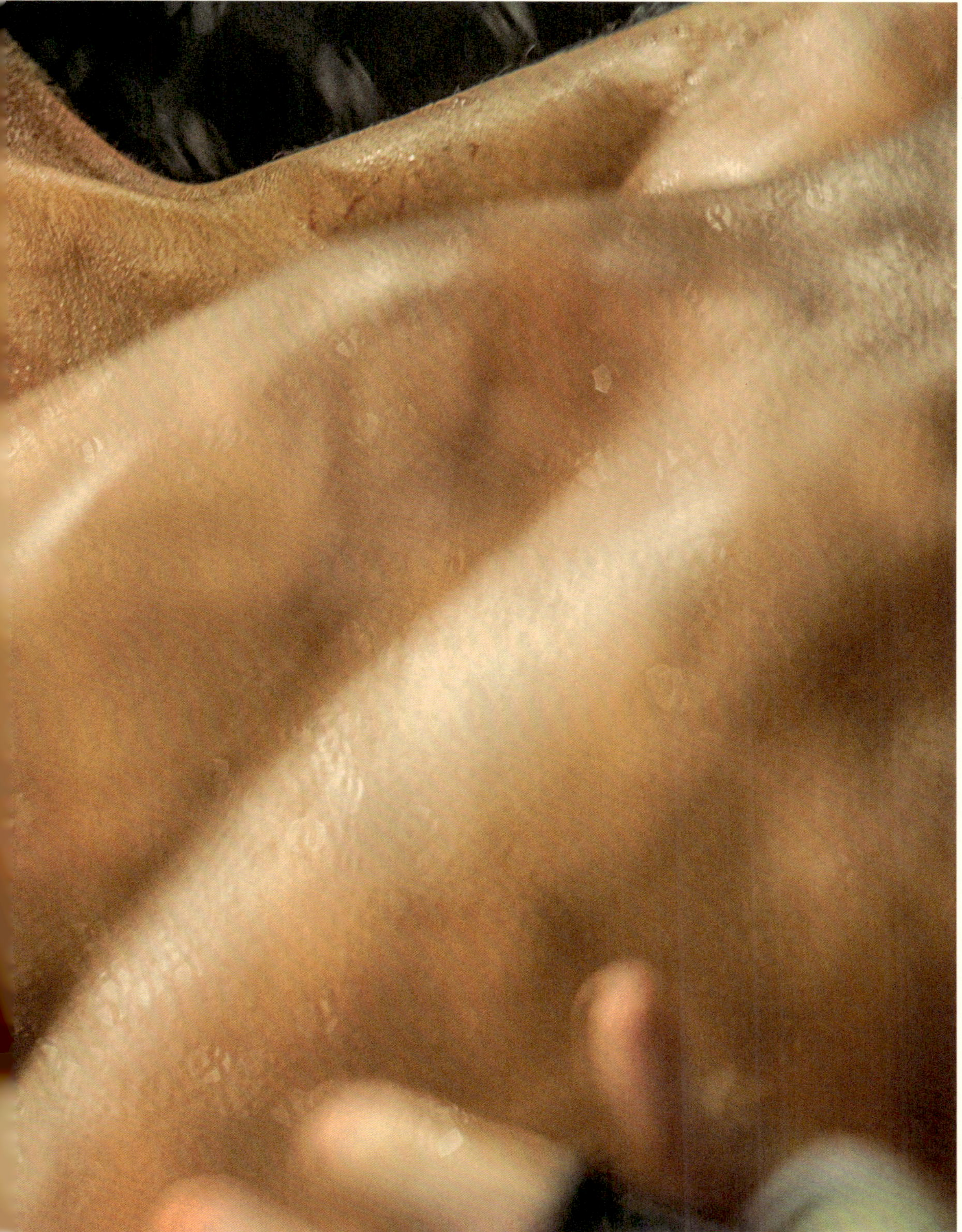

SUPPORTING

IMAGE CREATORS

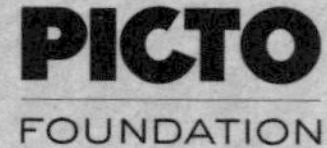

THE INTERNATIONAL MEETING PLACE FOR PHOTOGRAPHY

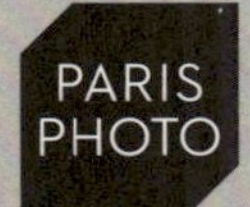

A PATRON COMMITTED TO

CONTEMPORARY PHOTOGRAPHY

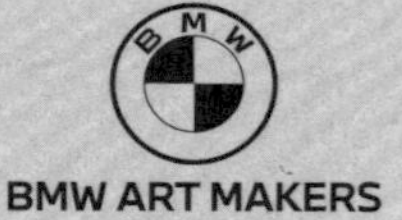